Implementing Service and Support Management Processes

A PRATICAL GUIDE

Leading IT Service & Support

Pulished by:
Van Haren
PUBLISHING

Colophon

Title:	Implementing Service and Support Management Processes: A Practical Guide
Version, date:	English edition, v1.0, March 2005
Editors:	Carrie Higday-Kalmanowitz and E. Sandra Simpson

Authors and Subject Matter Experts: Pat Albright
Mark Bradley
Chris Broome
David Chiu
Paula 'Tess' DePalma
Michael Devaney
Troy DuMoulin
Mark Ellis
Malcolm Fry
Jayne Groll
Brian Johnson
Char LaBounty
Vernon Lloyd
Ron Muns
Greg Oxton
Peter Pace
Glen Purdy
David Pultorak
Julie Quackenbush
Michelle Ross-McMillan
Faye Rukstales
Aale Roos
Cheryl Simpson
Pam Suekawa-Reynolds
Dr Frederick Van Bennekom

Quality Review Team: Pat Albright, Brenda Iniguez, Scott Koon, Robert Last, Eppo Lupes, Dick Szymanski and Phil Verghis.

Publisher:	Van Haren Publishing (info@vanharen.net)
ISBN:	90-77212-43-4
Print:	First print, first edition, March 2005. Printed in the Netherlands for Van Haren Publishing
Design & Layout:	DTPresto Design & Layout, Zeewolde-NL

Contents

Preface

Ron Muns, CEO and founder of HDI

HDI, the world's largest association of IT Service and Support professionals, is pleased to bring you the first comprehensive process guide for IT or technical Support Center organizations serving internal 'end-users' and/or and external customers. It is based upon ITIL®, but it takes the ITIL framework to a more practical level in order to assist you implement best practices specifically geared to a Support Center environment. This is the process guidance you have been waiting for! In addition to the ITIL processes covered in the *Service Support* and *Service Delivery* books, we have included several additional processes of importance to support organizations as well as a Balanced Scorecard Service Model developed by HDI.

HDI's scope and focus evolve as our member organizations change. We are no longer the Help Desk Institute, but merely HDI. Our focus recognizes the enlargement of the role and increasing professionalism of IT and the Support Organization. According to the HDI 2004 Practices Survey, 39% of all Support Organizations refer to themselves as 'Help Desk' although many other names and titles exist. The term 'IT Support Organization (or Center)' is used in this book as a generic reference to the IT Organization that represents the first point of contact for end-users (customers) (internal and external) customers. Such contact comes from phone calls, email, self help, self diagnostic tools, fax, and more. These role of the typical support organizations generally include second level support, desk side support, incident management, and involvement in most ITIL defined processes. The typical HDI member IT Support Organization performs all of the activities defined by ITIL within the "help desk," service desk, and more.

Support organization processes can be developed from the guidance presented in this book. While this book focuses on the IT Support Organization, it is vital to realize that all of IT must use common terminology and integrated processes. IT must play as an integrated team. IT must support the overall organization's strategies in a business-like fashion. This can only happen if IT is 100% committed to using common terminology and integrated practices. For IT to be a team, everyone must learn recognized IT organizational processes and the many individual and team roles within IT.

HDI has long been recognized for our conferences, open industry certification standards for individuals and Support Organizations, training curriculum, member deliverables, and opportunities for networking with peers. Now, you have asked for guidance on processes. This book is our answer to your request. If your IT organization is going to implement ITIL, you'll find this book to be extremely helpful. If your entire IT organization has not embraced ITIL, it will still provide you with important guidance for process improvement. It is not enough to know which processes need to be in place - you need to know *how* to implement, optimize and maintain those processes in your own organization. This book provides prescriptive guidance for any IT Support Organization to use - regardless of size, and whether or not internal or external customers are served. Although this book was written with Support Center managers, directors, and VPs in mind, anyone interested in best practices for the Support Organization will find this book invaluable in planning and in daily operations.

Everyone involved with the creation of this book - authors, subject matter experts, quality reviewers and the development team - is at the top of their field and extremely respected within the support industry. In addition, you'll recognize many names as ITIL experts. HDI's goal was to bring together the best of the best in ITIL and in the IT service and support industry, and we're confident that we've met our objectives.

Special thanks to all the volunteers responsible for this book - HDI appreciates all the valuable time and knowledge you have donated to make this book possible. Your passion for the industry is humbling.

Please feel free to forward me any comments you may have about this book to support@thinkhdi.com. Your feedback will be helpful to HDI in future versions of this book.

Ron Muns

Introduction

By E. Sandra Simpson

This book is the result of many discussions with a wide variety of Support Center practitioners and experts who wanted to have a process guidebook that was directed specifically at the Support Center (supporting internal 'end-user' employees or external customers). HDI assembled a content scope team, representing both Support Center practitioners and ITIL experts, to develop the following objectives for this book:

- to provide a holistic view for setting up a Support Center and to provide a reference for Support Managers as they evolve their existing Support Center
- to provide a practical approach, including prescriptive guidance, to implementing ITIL processes and other Support Center processes not in ITIL
- to provide a focus on operational metrics for the Support Center.

The intent of this book was not to rewrite existing information in the public domain (such as the ITIL Service Support and Service Delivery books) but to provide a practical guidebook that is focused specifically on the Support Center - not the entire IT Service Management domain.

The HDI Support Center Process Guidebook is relevant to anyone involved in a Support Center environment. All levels of management for both internal and external Support Centers can use this practical guide to implement, manage and optimize all relevant Support Center processes. Business managers will find the book helpful in understanding and establishing best practice Support Center services.

Each chapter of this book was written by a different author and reviewed by a number of subject matter experts (SMEs). While this approach has provided the best perspectives in the industry, each chapter is written in a slightly different style. As a result, readers may see differences in the use of terminology. We have attempted to normalize the language, but it is not an easy task, so please forgive us where we fail. A minor example relates to an age old argument over who is served: customers, users, or end-users? The ITIL preferred term is end-user for the individuals who contact the support organization for support or service. The ITIL preferred definition for the individual who leads the organizational units in which the end-user works is customer. In ITIL terminology the customer is the person who negotiates service levels and to whom the Support Center (Service Desk) report performance. You will find some inconsistency in the use of these terms, but we do not believe this will diminish the value of the book.

The term 'Support Center' goes by many names in different organizations, but no two organizations are exactly alike. While we are trying to promote the ITIL terminology for processes, we see an issue with the ITIL use of the terms Help Desk and Service Desk. ITIL has specific definitions for Help Desk and Service Desk, which often do not align with many real world Support Centers. This can cause confusion and misunderstanding.

Footnote:
In 2004, HDI changed its name from Help Desk Institute to HDI, largely because of the confusion created by the limited role that the UK Office of Government Commerce (OGC) has given to the term. Our membership has always had a much broader role and has always had primary or secondary responsibility for most ITIL processes. HDI is the leading association for IT Service and Support professionals and the function above for the Support Center represent the primary roles and responsibilities of our member organizations.

Authors and Subject Matter Experts

An international range of Support Center practitioner authors and subject matter experts provided guidance in this book. The material was developed and written by:

Pat Albright	IT Support Consultants, Inc.
Mark Bradley	JP Morgan Chase
Chris Broome	The Diagonal Group
David Chiu	BMO Financial Group
Mike Devaney	Independent Consultant
Paula 'Tess' DePalma	Nemours
Troy DuMoulin	Pink Elephant Inc.
Mark Ellis	Kronos Inc.
Malcolm Frye	Executive Remedy Partner
Jayne Groll	ITSM Academy, Inc.
Brian Johnson	Computer Associates
Char LaBounty	Char LaBounty & Associates
Vernon Lloyd	FoxIT
Greg Oxton	Consortium for Service Innovation
Peter Pace	United Airlines
David Pultorak	Fox IT
Glen Purdy	Fujitsu Consulting
Julie Quackenbush	Nationwide
Aale Roos	Quint Wellington Redwood Oy
Michelle Ross-McMillan	Nationwide
Faye Rukstales	BMC
Cheryl Simpson	BMO Financial Group
Pam Suekawa-Reynolds	Remedy Corporation
Dr. Frederick Van Bennekom	Great Brook Consulting

Quality Review Team

HDI wishes to express their appreciation to Pat Albright of IT Support Pros, Inc. and to Brenda Iniguez of Pink Elephant for the considerable time and effort they contributed to complete a full quality review of the book content.

Thank you also to following people who shared quality review comments for specific sections of the book: Scott Koon, Robert Last, Eppo Lupes, Dick Szymanski and Phil Verghis.

Content Scope Team

HDI would also like to thank those people whose guidance on the Content Scope team for this book helped ensure that this book would be relevant to its target audience. The Content Scope team was comprised of the following individuals:

Judy Benda	PCHowTo, Inc.
Malcolm Fry	Remedy Executive Partner
Carrie Higday-Kalmanowitz	HDI
Brian Johnson	Computer Associates

Scott Koon	Mayo Clinic
Dawn Mular	Sun Microsystems
Ron Muns	HDI
David Pultorak	Fox IT
Marta Scolaro	Johnson Diversey
E. Sandra Simpson	SITA INC

The content of this book was coordinated and managed by Carrie Higday-Kalmanowitz and E. Sandra Simpson.

The Best Practice Framework for the Support Center Guide

The IT Infrastructure Library (ITIL)

ITIL is the most widely accepted approach to IT service management in the world. ITIL provides a comprehensive and consistent set of best practices for IT service management, promoting a quality approach to achieving business effectiveness and efficiency in the use of information systems. (Introduction, ITIL Service Support, Office of Government Commerce, 2000)

HDI Support for ITIL

HDI supports the best practice guidance found within ITIL as it applies to the processes within the Support Center and IT at large.

HDI Support for other Support Center Processes

HDI recognizes that alongside the relevant processes found in ITIL, there are several other processes that are also relevant to the Support Center. These have been included as part of the disciplines covered in this book.

Key processes for the Support Center

They key Support Center processes identified for discussion in this book include several ITIL processes, as well as other processes determined to be important for relevant for Support Center best practices:
• Base structure processes for the Support Center
• Financial/Operational Management

Shared ITIL /Support Center processes
• Financial Management
• Configuration Management
• Change Management
• Release Management
• Incident Management
• Problem Management
• Service Level Management
• Capacity Management
• Availability Management
• IT Service Continuity Management

Additional Support Center processes
- Operational Management
- Knowledge Management
- Workforce Management
- Customer Satisfaction Measurement

Processes defined

Financial/Operational Management
Financial Management for the Support Center is a subset of Financial Management for IT as defined by ITIL. Operational Management focuses on the Support Center's Balanced Scorecard of Customer Satisfaction Goals, Employee Satisfaction Goals, Costs/Productivity Goals and Organizational Maturity.

Knowledge Management
Knowledge Management is not currently recognized as an ITIL process. Knowledge Management in the Support Center refers to the practice of managing, building, and re-using information in context.

Configuration Management
Configuration Management is the process that enables the Support Center to quickly isolate, diagnose, and restore service by ensuring up-to-date information about supported components of the IT infrastructure.

Change Management
The Change Management process manages all changes that affect services provided by the Support Center.

Release Management
Release Management manages the release of all approved changes.

Incident Management
Incident Management is the process that manages incidents that are reported to the Support Center and focuses on returning the user to an operational state as quickly as possible.

Problem Management
Problem Management manages the process of determining and removing problems that are the underlying causes of incidents that are reported to the Support Center.

Service Level Management
Service Level Management is the process used to form agreements with customers for Support Center services as well as negotiate operational agreements and underpinning contracts with suppliers to the Support Center to support customer agreements.

Capacity Management
Capacity Management ensures that the IT infrastructure has the capacity to provide the

services required to support the business, to ensure that service availability and agreed service levels can be obtained.

Workforce Management
Workforce Management ensures that there are enough support center staff available to support the required capacity.

Availability Management
Availability Management ensures that the services provided by the Support Center are available when requested by customers and to the level previously agreed via Service Level Management.

IT Service Continuity Management
IT Service Continuity Management ensures that the probability of a disruption in service is reduced and in the event of a potential or actual degradation of service availability that steps are taken to ensure service continuity to customers.

Customer Satisfaction Measurement
Customer Satisfaction Measurement processes ensure that customers are satisfied with the services and level of service provided to them and assists in identifying areas for improvement.

Getting started with process implementation
Some support organizations may be in a position to implement all processes, while other organizations may be implementing processes in stages. Whatever the situation, consider the following when developing project plans.

Management commitment
No process improvement initiative can be successful without Senior Management commitment. Some process improvement progress can be made at the line management level working in isolation without executive support. However, to be truly successful Support Center process improvement initiatives need full senior management support. In addition, a corporate or organizational culture that supports process change also needs to be in place if you expect all practitioners and stakeholders in the process to adapt and use the process in a consistent way.

End-user (customer) and service provider support for process change
To ensure process improvement success it is also important to market the need and benefits of process change to both end-users and service providers of the process. Where applicable, the implementation of Service Level Management can assist with obtaining agreement on the services that will be provided by the support organization, together with the required underpinning contracts and operational agreements necessary to deliver these to Support Center customers and end users.

Understanding of process change as a team activity
Support Center processes are interrelated to all of IT. Everyone in IT must buy in and support common terminology and process. It will be important for the entire organization to support process change and related continuous improvement activities. The Support Center can accomplish some process improvement as an "island" but real change will only occur when

you consider process improvement to be a team activity that includes all of IT.

Recommended reading and education
Readers of this book are also urged to read the official ITIL process books:

* Service Support, Office of Government Commerce, 2000, ISBN 0 11 330015 8
* Service Delivery, Office of Government Commerce, 2001, ISBN 0 11 330017 4

ITIL Certification is also strongly recommended for those who wish to implement the ITIL related processes.

Other recommended reading:
* Service and Support Handbook, HDI
* Running an Effective Help Desk, Barbara Czegel, 1998, ISBN 0 471 24816 9

Chapter 1:
Financial and Operational Management

1.1 Overview

1.1.1 Description

Effective financial and operational management of a Support Center focuses on costs, customer satisfaction, employee satisfaction and organizational maturity. When integrated in a Balanced Scorecard Service Model, these four elements form a high-level goal set with supporting key performance indicators (KPIs), also known as key business indicators or operational metrics. This is a powerful model that enables the Support Center Manager to look at past performance and trends, together with optimized forecasting of future costs, operational performance and service levels based on workload for the projected base of customers, whether internal or external. This process will even allow for almost total automation of future budgets down to the line item level.

The model will also provide a basis for effective measurement of return on investment (ROI) for new productivity technologies, workflow redesigns, outsourcing or business process re-engineering within the Support Center.

This chapter does not review basic budgeting and accounting concepts. The approaches presented in this chapter support the ITIL Financial Management framework; however, they go beyond ITIL to address the specifics of the internal and/or external Support Center environment. The chapter provides guidelines for both financial and operational management of the Support Center.

1.1.2 Metrics - using the Balanced Scorecard Service Model

The goal of the Balanced Scorecard Service Model for the Support Center is to balance service goals and supporting key metrics that may at times conflict with one another. For example, if you are 100% committed to customer satisfaction, your costs may get out of line or your employee morale may suffer. The framework, outlined in Figure 1.1, identifies the key categories for measuring the success of support.

What is a Balanced Scorecard?

A new approach to strategic management was developed in the early 1990s by Drs. Robert Kaplan (Harvard Business School) and David Norton. They named this system the 'Balanced Scorecard'. Recognizing some of the weaknesses and vagueness of previous management approaches, the Balanced Scorecard approach provides a clear prescription as to what organizations should measure in order to 'balance' the financial perspective.
The Balanced Scorecard is a management system (not only a measurement system) that enables organizations to clarify their vision and strategy and translate them into action. It provides feedback around both the internal business processes and external outcomes in order to continuously improve strategic performance and results. When fully deployed, the Balanced Scorecard transforms strategic planning from an academic exercise into the nerve center of an enterprise. *Source: The Balanced Scorecard Institute*

Customer Satisfaction Goals Supporting KPIs	Employee Satisfaction Goals Supporting KPIs
Costs/Productivity Goals Supporting KPIs	Organizational Maturity Goals Supporting KPIs

Figure 1.1 The Support Center Balanced Scorecard Service Model

The key to a successful Support Center Balanced Scorecard Service Model is to maintain continued balanced improvement in all four quadrants over time.

Customer Satisfaction Goals
Customer satisfaction is generally measured via customer surveys. To minimize bias, an external firm should ideally conduct these surveys. External survey firms may also offer comparative industry data or provide additional analytics on survey results.

The primary customer satisfaction survey is transaction based, which involves using an abbreviated set of questions based on closed incidents (phone, email or Web). These surveys are usually focused on a limited number of questions specific to an incident during a given period, and specifically target the person who generated the original incident. Standard sample questions might include:
• Please rate the accuracy of the solution provided.
• Please rate the timeliness of the solution provided.
• Please rate our initial responsiveness to your incident.
• Please rate the professionalism of the Support Engineer who answered your incident.
• Please rate your overall experience for this incident.

These questions may be rated on a numeric scale (e.g. 1 to 5) or a simple word scale (e.g. positive, neutral or negative). Most Support Centers using a transactional type survey will monitor this process to ensure they do not over survey the same customers (e.g. not surveying the same customer more than once every six months).

The second type of survey is a loyalty survey, which is usually targeted at the decision-maker for external facing customer Support Centers. This survey is generally written (hardcopy or online) and is focused on the customer decision-maker's perception of the value of the service received. These surveys generally target the broader customer base, whether or not they used the Support Center's services during the period being measured. Most Support Centers do not want to undertake this type of survey more than once a year per customer. These surveys are generally more detailed and designed to reveal specific perceptions that decision makers may have about your services to their operations.

A Support Center's overall customer satisfaction rating may be based on both types of surveys for a given period. The formula used should be biased towards the transactional survey, as this is a true measure of the operation's current level of customer satisfaction. For example, overall customer satisfaction scoring may be based on 70% transactional and 30% loyalty. Using a 5-point scale for both in this example, with 1 being low, if the average transaction survey score was 4.4 and the average loyalty survey was 3.9, then the overall customer satisfaction score for this period would be 4.25 [{.70 * 4.4} + {.30 * 3.9}].

While the overall survey scores are important for both types of surveys, the true value is found in the individual response verbatim from each survey. Priorities can be established by assimilating the verbatim feedback into specific categories, based on the type of feedback received. Support Center Managers can easily identify which issues they need to address first, as well as which areas need less attention at a given point in time.

Overall customer satisfaction is one of the primary drivers in contract renewal rates for externally facing Support Centers. This has a direct impact on contract revenue streams, which in turn drive the funding levels for most Support Centers. Internal Support Center operations are also being challenged more and more for generic application support (i.e. general off-the-shelf applications) as more and more functional segments of organizations look to lower internal chargeback costs and improve service levels through outsourcers both on and off shore.

Further information regarding the customer satisfaction process can be found in the Customer Satisfaction Measurement chapter in this book.

Employee Satisfaction Goals

In any service business, the people who deliver that service are the essential product. Despite this, many service organizations, including both internal and external Support Centers, do not properly manage and maintain their employees' general job satisfaction. This can affect customer satisfaction as well as the cost of operations.

The average time to fully train a new employee in customer support ranges from a few months to a year or more, depending on the complexity of the services and/or products supported. This does not include 'fill time' - the time from the when a replacement requisition is cut until the position is filled. Over the last ten years, fill time has averaged about 60 days. The 'fill rate' average, however, can spike significantly when labor markets get tight.

Worse still, most customer support organizations fail to capture the knowledge of people leaving the organization. Yet there are systems that can effectively do this, beyond the traditional knowledge base systems. In most cases, this knowledge of an organization's products and customers is lost when these employees leave. While some level of turnover can be healthy for an organization, excessive turnover can have a significant negative impact on the operation. It is important to remember that labor costs are generally between 60% and 70% of the total cost of any customer support operation.

Most effective employee satisfaction survey processes go beyond just asking questions. Verbatim feedback from employees should be given significant attention. By categorizing this feedback (especially for low scoring areas that have a high importance quotient) issues requiring immediate attention can be identified. A cross-section of the operation should evaluate and determine what action needs to be taken to address high priority issues. This cross-section should include rank and file support engineers, management and staff personnel. Some organizations also include a representative from HR on this team. As with the customer survey, this process should be geared toward taking action and not just generating a periodic 'number.'

An employee survey should be conducted twice a year with each employee, ideally about six months apart. Regular surveys will allow comparison of results and will identify improvement and/or dissatisfaction over time.

Finally, organizations that manage employee satisfaction effectively do not always have the highest pay scales for their area. Pay rates are often ranked as the third or fourth most important issue on employee surveys. Generally, communication and training will be more of an issue. Well-managed Customer Support Centers that can integrate employee needs into an effective service delivery model will become a target employer of future employees.

Costs/Productivity Goals
It is time for the industry to come together and agree on definitions and methods for developing cost metrics; this is the only way that benchmark comparisons can have any value. Standard costing (and operational) metrics will allow support organizations to understand their cost structures and operational efficiencies in comparison to other organizations or within the organization itself. It will help you understand and answer questions, such as:
- are we spending too little on support infrastructure and too much on labor?
- are our costs for eSupport too high?
- how much could we save by moving our end-users from phone support to self-help?
- are our costs high because we have excessive overhead allocations?
- when can we expect to get a return from the introduction of new support tools?
- we provide Level 1, Level 2 and Level 3 support and thus our cost per incident is higher than that of our competitors. Does management understand that our competitors' support costs only include Level 1 support? Or, does management understand that a competitor's support organization only provides log and route support?

At the heart of costing and costing metrics is the need to develop comparisons that include common definitions, common volumes, common costs and common methodologies. At a minimum, this needs to be done within the support organization itself for comparative purposes over time.

Financial analysis on the support organization is based on calculating costs in terms of cost per unit of work and per service delivered (e.g. per incident). The most important unit is the cost per incident, which should be computed separately by channel received (phone, self-help, chat, email, self-healing, etc.). This analysis may be further broken down by products or services offered. For high volume Customer Service Centers, such as financial institutions providing informational services (e.g. bank balances, resolving billing issues, etc.), the vast majority of their incidents are handled in one call. Their key cost indicator would probably be cost per call with the volume metric coming from the Automated Call Distributor system (ACD).

Support Centers provide their services to internal IT users or external customer-focused operations. They may provide support for software applications and/or hardware support and/or network support. These incidents are generally more complex, with a longer average call duration, and frequently will not be resolved on the first contact and/or may require follow-up to ensure closure. This type of environment should be costed out at the incident level versus the call level. One reason for this is that any service goal will drive the behavior of the organization, either directly or indirectly. It is extremely important to select goals that will drive the desired behavior of the service delivery organization. Reward systems should be based on performance against goals and not performance against supporting KPIs.

If a Support Center Manager is being measured on the group's cost per call, then the cost per call can be lowered simply by increasing the number of calls coming into the Support Center. Lowering the service level is an easy way to do this. While this strategy may well lower the cost per call, it will also lower overall customer satisfaction or employee satisfaction if this is accomplished by understaffing. It is important to remember that reward system measures for individual performance, whether managers or individual contributors, will drive behaviors in the organization. The Balanced Scorecard Service Model approach is intended to recognize the multiple priorities that we must seek to balance.

The Balanced Scorecard Service Model design must select the right goals; it must also link these goals to ensure that the operation maintains a balanced performance as part of a continuous improvement process. In the cost per unit of work example, it does little good to continually reduce the cost per incident (regardless of how it is accomplished) if the customer satisfaction rating and/or employee satisfaction rating also continues to decline.

Other cost per unit measures could also include cost per user for internally-facing Support Centers and cost per contract for externally-facing Support Centers. Both of these may be further broken down by product or services offered. Generally, better results are achieved using basic measures that can easily be understood by all levels of the organization. The average cost per user calculation would be calculated by dividing total cost for the period by the average number of users supported for the same period. Similarly, in calculating the average cost per contract, divide total costs by the average number of contracts for the same period. Calculating total costs, as well as average contracts and average number of users supported, will be discussed later in this chapter.

Organizational Maturity Goals

Of the four quadrants, Organizational Maturity is the most strategic and subjective. It is focused on the organizational structure, ability to change, quickness, responsiveness and strategic positioning of support within the larger organization. Organizational maturity enables customer and employee satisfaction with optimal cost structure. Elements to track that indicate organizational maturity include:

- visible executive support of the Support Center
- time to fill knowledge gaps - when new errors are identified, how long does it take to document the problem and the solution? How long does it take for this information to be available to the support analysts and end users (customers)?
- time to employee proficiency - how long does it take for new employees to be productive?
- time to new product proficiency - how long does it take for the support organization to be proficient on new products?
- flexibility of cost to changes in workload - how quickly can the support organization change the cost structure (up or down) as work varies?
- diversity - has the organization embraced the values of racial and cultural diversity within support? If the organization has global team members, are they aware of cultural and local issues that vary the definition of best practice?
- work elimination through problem management and change management - tracking of cost savings resulting from identification and elimination known errors
- formalization of IT processes - tracking indicators that the support organization has integrated all support processes with those of other IT functional areas

Over time most forward thinking organizations will continue to evolve, driven by competition, new products or services, new service delivery technologies or continuous improvement in process or workflow design. All world class organizations are constantly challenging themselves to find ways to continuously improve their operational efficiency through organizational optimization. For example, moving toward a generalist Level 1 environment allows for an expanded career development for the analyst; it also enables increased flexibility for the organization and more effective resource management. Product or service specialization will generally begin at Level 2 and above.

Other concepts might include 'Follow the Sun' or 'Virtual Support'. The support organization could be dispersed, operating from anywhere to anywhere in the world, using a common connected technology infrastructure (with supporting processes and workflows) and servicing customers at any time.

More mature organizations may also be capable of assisted 'self-assessment' as well as 'self direction'. Organizational and operational goal sets will need to be clearly defined and balanced by the proper level of organizational oversight to ensure that operational goals are met and the overall health of that segment of the operation continues to be maintained or improved over time.

1.1.3 Costing methodology structure

Figure 1.2 below shows the major categories of costs to consider. You could consider these as high level cost groupings. Each organization will have different departments, organizational structure and accounts. Regardless of your organizational structure, you should be able to convert your costs to the following general structure. The objective of the major and minor costing structures is to provide a framework that will allow support organizations to do benchmark cost comparisons. Following the chart is a list of the minor costing elements within each category.

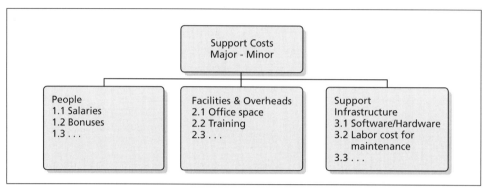

Figure 1.2 Major and minor support costing structure

People - direct labor for support personnel to include: (generally 60% to 70% of total operational costs)
- Salaries
- Bonuses
- Vacations/Benefits
- Estimated increases
- Overtime
- Contractors

Overhead allocations and facilities (percentages will vary from organization to organization)

- Office space (lease or depreciation), parking, common areas, backup facilities, and maintenance
- Training, travel and entertainment, and recruitment
- Common technology charges (lease, depreciation, maintenance) for telephones, PBX, general desktop software (not support specific), and network connectivity.
- Business Continuity/Disaster Recovery (standby facility charges)
- Professional fees/services that are general in nature
- Voice and data monthly fees/allocations

Support infrastructure (percentages will vary from organization to organization)

- Software and hardware leases, licenses and maintenance costs for tools unique to the support organization. These include (but are not limited to) ticketing systems, knowledge systems, ACD systems, chat, monitoring/remote control tools, self healing/self help tools, workforce planning/labor management, asset management, software distribution, password reset, computer telephony integration and special reporting and analysis systems.
- Labor cost for maintaining the support infrastructure
- Depreciation (hardware and applications)

The major categories of costs are also useful for comparisons. If an organization proportionally has a high per person cost and their overall cost per incidents is high, then they may not be spending enough on support technologies or it may have poorly designed workflows, processes or service delivery organizational structures. If an organization has high overhead allocations, this might explain why their cost metrics are higher than those of their peers. These metrics are useful when looked at in relationship to others or trended over time within the organization itself.

Each of the costing categories/elements should be allocated to the activities performed by the support organization. Some of the costs will be allocated based upon:
- headcounts - preferably either total headcount or more ideally Fulltime Technical Equivalents (FTEs); alternatively, total headcount
- time allocations (where staff members perform multiple activities)
- volume of work
- allocations for certain cost specific to the type of work performed, for example, cost for chat software would be allocated to cost per incident handled via chat.

Some of the costs may need further analysis and grouping before being allocated to the activities performed by the support organization, such as costs for maintaining the call ticketing system.

The key to costing is to identify what drives the cost. This method of costing is often referred to as Activity Based Costing or ABC costing.

Missing and misallocated costs
To determine the total costs of a Support Center operation, the Support Center Manager should identify the total costs as if the Support Center were a stand-alone, independent operation. When you review the items to include in each costing activity, you may determine that certain support costs are incurred in other departments. For comparisons you must add these costs to your calculations. Similarly you may have reported on costs in the Support Center's budget that apply wholly or partially to other functions. These should be removed before you begin the allocation process.

Service organizations perform many discrete activities. Each of these activities is part of the workflow process that determines the organization's outcomes. These activities may be associated with one cost metric or several. For example, the total cost per incident will include call activities, eSupport activities, Level 2/3 and more. People often perform multiple tasks, so their costs must be allocated based on the time they spend on various activities. For example, some individuals will spend part of the day handling incidents reported via the phone and other portions of their time will be spent responding to email or chat sessions.

Every organization is different and the methods by which they deliver support will vary. There will be 'company-unique' activities within support. While company-unique activities are not comparable, these activity costs can be identified and the drivers or measures can be identified to allow you to allocate these costs to standard costing metrics.

Cost allocation for support activities
Below is an example of some of the support organization activities that you may have. Once you know the total costs and the measures to use for allocation purposes, you will be able to begin the allocation process. Support activities for which you will need to determine costs will include:
- call handling
- email response
- supporting infrastructure tools
- knowledge building and maintenance
- escalation management
- Problem Management
- incident research

Level 2/3 staff support -it is impossible to obtain relevant comparisons for Level 2 versus Level 3, so these costs are grouped together:

- desk side support
- specific product(s) supported or incremental service (e.g. remote installations, remote upgrades, remote consulting, etc.)

1.1.4 Allocation from costing elements to activities

Figure 1.3 Allocation from costing elements to activities

'Activity Based Costing' or the ABC Method allows you to take costs from financial cost categories/elements and group them into the activities performed within the support organization. Once you have allocated all cost elements to the activities within the Support Center, you are ready to summarize cost into cost units. These units (metrics) are the units of measure that you will use to track how you are doing over time or for comparison to peers.
Costing performance metrics

Phone metrics:
- cost per incident - total cost for support incidents received by phone divided by the number of incidents resolved via the phone.
- Level 1 Resolution Rate - total incidents received by phone and resolved by Level 1, divided by total incidents handled by Level 1.
- Level 1 Escalated Rate - total incidents escalated by Level 1 to Level 2/3 divided by total incidents handled by Level 1.
- Level 2/3 Support Resolution Rate - total incidents resolved by Level 2/3 divided by total incidents handled by Level 2/3.
- cost per call - this is the total cost for handling end user (customer) calls regardless of the reason for the call to include call to report new incidents or from an end-user (customer) to check on the status of an open incident.
- first call resolution rate - the percent of all phone incidents that are solved on the first call. This could include the Level 1 analyst involving others in the resolution process.
- percent of total support staff handling incidents reported by phone
- average speed of answer (also referred to as ASA)
- average talk time
- dispatch/routing - cost per incident received by phone that is logged and routed with little or no attempt to resolve.

Self-help metrics:
- cost per self-help incident - this is the total cost of building and maintaining self-help technologies and knowledge divided by the number of incidents resolved by the end user (customer) using self-help technologies.
- self-help resolution rate - this is the percentage of end users (customers) that resolve their incident on their own divided by the total number that attempt before they exit the self-help system.

Self-healing metrics:
- cost per incident diagnosed - total costs (people, support infrastructure, and overhead) associated with building, deployment, and support of self-diagnostic tools divided by the number of incidents diagnosed.
- cost per incident healed - total costs (people, support infrastructure, and overhead) associated with building, deployment, and support of self-healing tools divided by the number of incidents that are resolved (healed) without the need for human intervention plus the cost per incident diagnosed. Cost for diagnostics and healing can be difficult to separate. As all incidents healed were also diagnosed, the diagnostic costs must be included as well.

Email metrics:
- cost per incident reported via email - this is the total cost of the Level 1 support staff for handling email divided by the total number of incidents reported via email. This will include all communications to/from the end user (customer) as well as communications to/from Level 2/3 support staff.
- email first contact resolution rate - the percentage of all email incidents reported that are resolved in one response.

Remote control or co-browsing metrics:
- cost per remote control session - total cost for the remote control or co-browsing activity divided by the number of sessions.
- remote control resolution rate - the percentage of all remote control sessions that end in the customer's incident being resolved.

Chat metrics:
- cost per incident reported via chat - the total cost for the chat service divided by the number of incidents reported via chat.
- chat session resolution rate - the percent of all chat sessions that end in the end user (customer) incident being resolved.

Employee metrics:
- cost per FTE - when calculating the fully loaded costs per FTE, the total costs (including all overhead costs) are divided by the number of FTEs. FTEs are direct labor headcounts, annualized, that deliver services directly to customers. The more indirect or supporting headcount in the operation, the higher the costs per FTE. The ideal ratio of direct to total headcount (of the Support Center) should be between 88% and 92% of direct headcount.
- utilization rate - a utilization rate enables the Support Center Manager to calculate how many full time employees (FTEs) are needed to staff the operation. Generally, an acid utilization rate is used to determine FTE counts. An acid utilization rate looks at total direct hours divided by hours paid for the same period, without backing out the hours paid for all non-available time (e.g. vacation, sick time, holiday, training, meetings, etc.). Experience shows an industry average of between 55% and 60%. Refer to the Capacity and Workforce Planning chapter for further information.
- other metrics: from time to time additional channels are identified in which incidents are reported where peer comparisons could be useful. If you have other channels by which you receive incidents, you should track these costs and volumes separately. This will make your other metrics comparable to those of your peers in the industry. For example, you may have a walk-up desk. You should exclude these cost from the calculations above, otherwise your metrics will not be comparable to an organization without a walk-up desk.

Incident metrics (overall or summary metrics):
- cost per incident Level 1 - total costs incurred at Level 1 divided by the total number of incidents reported. This would include all channels to include your company-unique channels (e.g. walk-ups) and incidents resolved via self-diagnostic/self healing technologies.
- cost per incident Level 2/3 - total costs for support beyond Level 1 divided by the number of incidents escalated.
- Cost per incident desk side support - this is the total costs for providing desk side assistance divided by the number of desk side visits.

1.2 Implementation

An initial Balanced Scorecard Service Model can be developed very quickly, using the KPI document in the annex of this chapter. The initial model should be simple, using specific goals selected by executive management for each of the four quantifiable quadrants with KPIs for each goal selected by the Support Center management team. If you identify the major KPIs for each quadrant of the Balanced Scorecard, you will quickly be able to see the health and performance of the Support Center. A four-by-four model is quite common; it is easy to explain and will provide an effective scorecard for the organization.

Annex A1.1 provides a listing of each of the KPIs for each of Balanced Scorecard Service Model quadrants. This KPI listing includes a definition for each KPI, as well as a likely source of the information. The intent is to simplify the process by allowing Support Center Managers, with or without their staff, to develop an initial Balanced Scorecard Service Model for their operation. It should be noted that no model is truly static and it should change over time as the business changes. The important thing to remember is to maintain a documented model and to track progress over time.

Balanced Scorecards generally have high level measures for overall performance evaluations and more detailed measures for groups or individuals within the organization. We recommend that a Support Center start by utilizing a basic spreadsheet application (e.g. Excel, Lotus 123, etc.) to lay out the initial model. Figures 1.4 - 1.8 provide a simple overview of how that might look. Depending upon the audience, the metrics to be presented will change.

Key Metrics Report

Customer Satisfaction	Industry Average	Internal Target	Jan	Feb	Mar	Apr	May	Jun	Jul	Aug	Sep	Oct	Nov	Dec	YTD	Q1FY98	Q2FY98	Q3FY98	Q4FY98
Customer Sat. Rating		9	8.8	8.8	8.8	8.9	8.9	8.9	9	9	9	9.1	9.1	9.1	8.957967	8.8	8.9	9	9.1
ASA		0	10	10	10	10	10	10	10	10	10	10	10	10	10	10	10	10	10
Abandon Call %	16.7%		16.7%	16.7%	16.7%	14.3%	14.3%	14.3%	11.4%	11.4%	8.7%	8.7%	10.0%	10.0%	12.5%	16.7%	14.3%	10.4%	9.5%
SRs Closed/Initial Contact	80.0%		60.0%	67.2%	72.3%	68.6%	66.7%	65.8%	64.1%	63.7%	60.1%	57.9%	59.4%	52.6%	62.9%	66.5%	67.3%	63.2%	56.6%
% SRs Reopened	2.0%		2.2%	3.4%	2.1%	3.4%	2.7%	2.9%	3.5%	2.5%	0.9%	1.5%	1.5%	1.9%	2.3%	2.5%	3.0%	2.3%	1.6%
% SRs Escalated	12.0%		15.2%	14.1%	16.2%	13.3%	13.7%	15.8%	15.3%	14.7%	15.0%	18.4%	14.8%	19.1%	15.6%	15.2%	14.2%	15.0%	17.4%
Average Response Time (Min)			60	62	60	50	50	50	48	46	43	43	40	40	49	61	50	45	41
Average SR Resolution Time (Min)			18	20	20	16	16	16	15	15	14	16	13	13	16	19	16	15	14
Contract Renewal Rate	92.0%		90.0%	90.0%	90.0%	95.0%	95.0%	95.0%	96.0%	96.0%	94.0%	97.0%	97.0%	94.5%	90.0%	95.0%	96.0%	97.0%	
% Performance Against SLA	95.0%		70.0%	75.0%	80.0%	92.0%	91.0%	93.0%	92.0%	94.0%	94.0%	95.0%	96.0%	94.0%	88.8%	75.0%	92.0%	93.3%	95.0%
Productivity																			
Total Closed SRs			1000	1000	1000	1200	1200	1200	1300	1300	1400	1400	1500	1500	15000	3000	3600	4000	4400
Average Cost per SR	130		$155.00	$155.00	$157.00	$132.50	$132.50	$132.50	$128.46	$128.46	$120.71	$121.43	$113.33	$113.33	$130.47	$158.33	$132.50	$125.75	$115.91
Average Cost per Customer	85		$110.71	$108.77	$106.44	$104.26	$100.95	$98.36	$96.81	$94.08	$91.35	$87.18	$82.93	$79.07	$1,142.77	$331.40	$301.26	$282.06	$248.78
Average Customers per FTE	150		140.0	142.5	147.5	138.6	143.2	150.0	143.8	147.9	142.3	150.0	136.7	143.3	143.7	143.3	143.9	144.6	143.0
Closed SRs per FTE			100.0	100.0	100.0	109.1	109.1	109.1	108.3	108.3	107.7	107.7	100.0	100.0	104.9	100.0	109.1	108.1	102.6
Acid Utilization Rate	70.0%		61.1%	70.5%	67.7%	63.9%	63.9%	61.5%	60.6%	66.3%	62.8%	60.1%	64.0%	57.7%	63.0%	66.2%	63.1%	63.1%	60.3%
Average DL per SR (Min)			60	60.0	60.0	55.0	55.0	50.0	55.4	55.4	56.7	55.7	56.0	58.2	56.2	60.0	52.3	55.6	56.7
Average Cost per DLH			$137.90	$137.41	$138.08	$128.54	$128.54	$139.84	$124.91	$124.91	$117.61	$118.30	$110.61	$106.78	$124.83	$137.80	$132.31	$122.47	$111.90
Employee Satisfaction																			
Employee Sat. Rating	8.9		8.8	8.8	8.8	8.9	8.9	8.9	9	9	9	9.1	9.1	9.1	8.95	8.8	8.9	9	9.1
# of Turnovers (Directs)		1	0	0	0	0	1	0	0	0	0	1	0	0	2	0	1	0	1
# of Churnovers (Directs)		2	0	0	0	0	1	0	0	0	0	1	0	2	4	0	1	0	3
Avg Training Hours per FTE		45	45	48.7	48.9	41.7	50.0	40.8	40.8	39.8	34.3	38.0	23.6	36.3	5679	1426	1489	1448	1316
% Sch. Perf. Evals Comp		1	100.0%	100.0%	100.0%	100.0%	100.0%	0.0%	100.0%	100.0%	100.0%	100.0%	0.0%	0.0%	76.9%	100.0%	66.7%	100.0%	33.3%

Figure 1.4 Management summary

Ref. #	Category	Target	Jan	Feb	Mar	Apr	May	Jun	Jul	Aug	Sep	Oct	Nov	Dec	YTD	Q1FY98	Q2FY98	Q3FY98	Q4FY98
	Customer Sat. Metrics																		
	ACD Data																		
1.2.1	Calls Received		1800	1800	1800	2100	2100	2100	2200	2200	2300	2300	2500	2500	25700	5400	6300	6700	7300
1.2.2	Calls Answered		1500	1500	1500	1800	1800	1800	1950	1950	2100	2100	2250	2250	22500	4500	5400	6000	6600
1.2.4	ASA		10	10	10	10	10	10	10	10	10	10	10	10	10	10	10	10	10
1.2.6	Abandon Calls		300	300	300	300	300	300	250	250	200	200	250	250	3200	900	900	700	700
1.2.8*	Abandon Call %	5.0%	16.7%	16.7%	16.7%	14.3%	14.3%	14.3%	11.4%	11.4%	8.7%	8.7%	10.0%	10.0%	12.5%	16.7%	14.3%	10.4%	9.6%
	Call Mgt. Sys. Data																		
1.1.3*	Total Closed SRs		1000	1000	1000	1200	1200	1200	1300	1300	1400	1400	1500	1500	15000	3000	3600	4000	4400
1.2.14	SRs Closed/Initial Contact		600	672	723	823	800	801	833	854	842	810	891	789	9438	1995	2424	2529	2490
1.2.15	SRs Reopened		22	34	21	41	32	35	45	33	12	21	22	29	347	77	108	90	72
1.2.16	SRs Escalated		152	141	162	159	164	189	199	191	210	257	222	287	2333	455	512	600	766
1.2.17*	% SRs Closed/Initial	80.0%	60.0%	67.2%	72.3%	68.6%	66.7%	66.8%	64.1%	65.7%	60.1%	57.9%	59.4%	52.6%	62.9%	66.5%	67.3%	63.2%	56.6%
1.2.18*	% SRs Reopened	2.0%	2.2%	3.4%	2.1%	3.4%	2.7%	2.9%	3.5%	2.5%	0.9%	1.5%	1.5%	1.9%	2.3%	2.6%	3.0%	2.3%	1.6%
1.2.19*	% SRs Escalated	12.0%	15.2%	14.1%	16.2%	13.3%	13.7%	15.8%	15.3%	14.7%	15.0%	18.4%	14.8%	19.1%	15.6%	15.2%	14.2%	15.0%	17.4%
1.2.25	# Contracts up for Renewal		100	100	100	100	100	100	100	100	100	100	100	100	1200	300	300	300	300
1.2.26	# Contracts Renewed		90	90	90	95	95	95	96	96	96	97	97	97	1134	270	285	288	291
	Contract Renewal Rate	92.0%	90.0%	90.0%	90.0%	95.0%	95.0%	95.0%	96.0%	96.0%	96.0%	97.0%	97.0%	97.0%	94.5%	90.0%	95.0%	96.0%	97.0%
1.2.31	% Performance Against SLA	96.0%	70.0%	75.0%	75.0%	80.0%	92.0%	91.0%	93.0%	92.0%	94.0%	94.0%	95.0%	96.0%	94.0%	88.8%	75.0%	92.0%	93.3%	95.0%
1.2.43	Total Response Time (Min)		60000	62000	60000	60000	60000	60000	60000	60000	60000	60000	60000	60000	60167	60657	60000	60000	60000
1.2.28*	Average Response Time (Min)	75	60	62	60	50	50	50	46	46	43	43	40	40	49	61	50	45.0549	40.9524
1.2.42	Total SR Resolution Time (Min)		18000	19500	19500	19500	19500	19500	19500	19500	22900	19500	19500	19717	19000	19500	19500	20582
1.2.29*	Average SR Resolution Time (Min)	15	18	20	20	16	16	16	15	15	14	16	13	13	16	19	16	15	14
	Customer Survey																		
1.2.33	Accuracy of Solution		70.0%	75.0%	80.0%	82.0%	81.0%	83.0%	84.0%	88.0%	85.0%	87.0%	82.0%	81.0%	81.5%	75.0%	82.0%	85.7%	83.3%
1.2.34	Timeliness of Solution		70.0%	75.0%	80.0%	83.0%	86.0%	81.0%	88.0%	85.0%	86.0%	87.0%	81.0%	82.0%	82.0%	75.0%	83.3%	86.3%	83.3%
1.2.35	Responsiveness		75.0%	75.0%	80.0%	82.0%	83.0%	85.0%	86.0%	87.0%	89.0%	88.0%	89.0%	89.0%	84.0%	76.7%	83.3%	87.3%	88.7%
1.2.36	Rate IVR Ease of Use		60.0%	60.0%	60.0%	60.0%	60.0%	60.0%	60.0%	60.0%	60.0%	60.0%	60.0%	60.0%	60.0%	60.0%	60.0%	60.0%	60.0%
1.2.37	Rate our Status Updating		70.0%	70.0%	70.0%	70.0%	70.0%	70.0%	70.0%	70.0%	70.0%	70.0%	70.0%	70.0%	70.0%	70.0%	70.0%	70.0%	70.0%
1.2.38	Did you Attempt to Use Level 0		20.0%	20.0%	23.0%	23.0%	24.0%	23.0%	25.0%	26.0%	27.0%	26.0%	24.0%	24.0%	23.8%	21.0%	23.3%	26.0%	24.7%
1.2.39	% Customers Very Satisfied		40.0%	41.0%	47.0%	45.0%	42.0%	43.0%	44.0%	47.0%	41.0%	52.0%	54.0%	52.0%	45.7%	42.7%	43.3%	44.0%	52.7%
	Customer Sat. Goal																		
1.2.40	Completed Surveys		260	257	289	302	322	310	298	333	324	343	321	331	3690	806	934	955	995
1.2.41*	Customer Sat. Rating	9.0	8.8	8.8	8.8	8.9	8.9	8.9	9	9	9	9.1	9.1	9.1	9.0	8.8	8.9	9.0	9.1

Figure 1.5 Customer satisfaction detail summary

Ref. #	Category	Target	Jan	Feb	Mar	Apr	May	Jun	Jul	Aug	Sep	Oct	Nov	Dec	YTD	Q1FY98	Q2FY98	Q3FY98	Q4FY98
	Costs/Productivity																		
1.1.1	Ending Customers		1400	1450	1500	1550	1600	1700	1750	1800	1900	2000	2100	2200	1450	1500	1700	1900	2200
1.1.2	Average Customer		1400	1425	1475	1525	1575	1650	1725	1775	1850	1950	2050	2150	1712.5	1433.3	1583.3	1783.3	2050.0
1.1.3	Total Closed SRs		1000	1000	1000	1200	1200	1200	1300	1300	1400	1400	1500	1500	15000	3000	3600	4000	4400
1.1.4	Total Closed SR DLH		1000	1000	1000	1100	1100	1000	1200	1200	1300	1300	1400	1455	14055	3000	3290	3700	4155
1.1.5	Average SRs per Customer	1	0.7	0.7	0.7	0.8	0.8	0.7	0.8	0.7	0.8	0.7	0.7	0.7	8.8	2.1	2.3	2.2	2.1
1.1.6*	Average DL per SR (Min)	30	60.0	60.0	60.0	55.0	55.0	50.0	55.4	55.4	55.7	55.7	56.0	58.2	56.2	60.0	53.3	55.5	56.7
1.1.12	Travel DLH		5	5	5	5	5	5	5	5	5	5	5	5	60	15	15	15	15
1.1.13	Project Related DLH		98	102	111	111	111	111	111	111	111	111	111	111	1310	311	333	333	333
1.1.7	Other DLH		21	21	21	21	21	21	21	21	21	21	21	21	252	63	63	63	63
1.1.14	Total DLH		1124	1128	1137	1237	1237	1137	1337	1337	1437	1437	1537	1592	15677	3389	3611	4111	4566
1.1.16	FTEs		10	10	10	11	11	11	12	12	13	13	15	15	11.9	10.0	11.0	12.3	14.3
1.1.17	Paid Days		23	20	21	22	22	21	23	21	22	23	20	23	261	64	65	66	66
1.1.18	Non Available Time		300	330	250	220	200	250	320	275	300	330	320	321	3416	880	670	895	971
1.1.19*	Acid Utilization Rate	70.0%	61.1%	70.5%	67.7%	63.9%	63.9%	61.5%	60.6%	62.8%	60.1%	64.0%	57.7%	63.0%	66.2%	63.1%	63.1%	60.3%
1.1.20	Net Utilization Rate		73.0%	88.8%	79.5%	72.1%	71.3%	71.2%	70.8%	76.8%	72.3%	69.7%	73.9%	65.3%	73.0%	79.9%	71.5%	73.2%	69.2%
1.1.22*	Closed SRs per FTE	125	100.0	100.0	100.0	109.1	109.1	109.1	108.3	108.3	107.7	107.7	100.0	100.0	104.94	100.0	109.09	108.12	102.56
1.1.21*	Average Customers per FTE	150	140.0	142.5	147.5	138.6	143.2	150.0	143.8	147.9	142.3	150.0	136.7	143.3	143.3	143.3	143.9	144.6	143.0
1.1.24*	Total Costs (K$)	$100.0	$155.0	$155.0	$157.0	$159.0	$159.0	$159.0	$167.0	$167.0	$169.0	$170.0	$170.0	$170.0	1957.0	475.000	477.00	503.00	510.00
1.1.23	Cost per FTE (K$)		$15.5	$15.5	$15.7	$14.5	$14.5	$14.5	$13.9	$13.9	$13.0	$13.1	$11.3	$11.3	$164.2	$47.5	$43.4	$40.8	$35.6
	Cost Averages																		
1.1.38*	Average Cost per Customer	$85.00	$110.71	$108.77	$106.44	$104.26	$100.95	$96.36	$96.81	$94.08	$91.35	$87.18	$82.93	$79.07	$1,142.77	$331.40	$301.26	$282.06	$248.78
1.1.39*	Average Cost per SR	$130.00	$155.00	$155.00	$157.00	$132.50	$132.50	$132.50	$128.46	$128.46	$120.71	$121.43	$113.33	$113.33	$130.47	$158.33	$132.50	$125.75	$115.91
1.1.15*	Average Cost per DLH	$50.00	$137.90	$137.41	$138.08	$128.54	$128.54	$139.84	$124.91	$124.91	$117.61	$118.30	$110.61	$106.78	$124.83	137.80	132.31	122.47	111.90

Figure 1.6 Costs/productivity detail summary

Ref. #	Category	Target	Jan	Feb	Mar	Apr	May	Jun	Jul	Aug	Sep	Oct	Nov	Dec	YTD	Q1FY98	Q2FY98	Q3FY98	Q4FY98
	Employee Metrics																		
1.3.15	Total Direct HC	12	10	10	10	12	10	12	12	12	14	12	18	12	10	10	12	14	12
1.4.1	# of Turnovers (Directs)	1		1		1		1		1		1		1	0	2	0	1	0	1
1.4.2	# of Churnovers (Directs)	2			1			1			1			2	4	0	1	0	1
1.4.10	Total Training Hours		450	487	489	500	500	489	490	478	480	456	425	435	5679	1426	1489	1448	1316
1.4.17*	Avg Training Hours per FTE		45	48.7	48.9	41.7	50.0	40.8	40.8	39.8	34.3	38.0	23.6	36.3	40.7	46.9	44.1	38.3	32.6
1.4.14	Total Perf. Eval Sch		2	1	1	1	1	1	1	1	1	1	1	1	13	4	3	3	3
1.4.15	Total Perf. Eval Comp		2	1	1	1	1	0	1	1	1	1	1	0	10	4	2	3	1
1.4.16*	% Sch. Perf. Evals Comp	100.0%	100.0%	100.0%	100.0%	100.0%	100.0%	0.0%	100.0%	100.0%	100.0%	100.0%	0.0%	0.0%	76.9%	100.0%	66.7%	100.0%	33.3%
	Employee Survey																		
1.4.23	Adequate Tools & Info?		88.0%	87.0%	86.0%	85.0%	84.0%	83.0%	82.0%	81.0%	82.0%	83.0%	84.0%	85.0%	84.2%	87.5%	84.0%	81.7%	84.0%
1.4.24	Clearly Understand Goals?		89.0%	88.0%	87.0%	86.0%	85.0%	84.0%	83.0%	82.0%	81.0%	80.0%	81.0%	82.0%	84.0%	86.5%	85.0%	82.0%	81.0%
1.4.25	Recommend ABC Company?		80.0%	81.0%	82.0%	83.0%	84.0%	85.0%	86.0%	87.0%	88.0%	89.0%	90.0%	89.0%	85.3%	80.5%	84.0%	87.0%	89.3%
1.4.26	Compensation		80.0%	80.0%	80.0%	80.0%	80.0%	80.0%	80.0%	80.0%	80.0%	80.0%	80.0%	80.0%	80.0%	80.0%	80.0%	80.0%	80.0%
1.4.27	Job Recognition		81.0%	81.0%	81.0%	81.0%	81.0%	81.0%	81.0%	81.0%	81.0%	81.0%	81.0%	81.0%	81.0%	81.0%	81.0%	81.0%	81.0%
	Employee Sat. Goal																		
1.4.28	# Employee Surveys		5	5	5	5	5	5	5	5	5	5	5	5	60	15	15	15	15
1.4.29	Employee Sat. Rating	8.9	8.8	8.8	8.8	8.9	8.9	8.9	9	9	9	9.1	9.1	9.1	9.0	8.8	8.9	9.0	9.1

Figure 1.7 Employee satisfaction detail summary

Category	Jan	Feb	Mar	Apr	May	Jun	Jul	Aug	Sep	Oct	Nov	Dec	YTD	Q1FY97	Q2FY97	Q3FY97	Q4FY97
Ending Headcounts																	
Indirect HC																	
Managers	1	1	1	1	1	1	1	1	1	1	1	1 NA		1	1	1	1
Supervisors	1	1	1	1	1	1	1	1	1	1	1	1 NA		1	1	1	1
Administrators	1	1	1	1	1	1	1	1	1	1	1	1 NA		1	1	1	1
Contractors	0	0	0	0	0	0	0	0	0	0	0	0					
Total Indirect HC	3	3	3	3	3	3	3	3	3	3	3	3 NA		3	3	3	3
Total Indirect Budget HC	7	7	7	7	7	7	7	7	7	7	7	7 NA		7	7	7	7
Total Over/Under Budget	-4	-4	-4	-4	-4	-4	-4	-4	-4	-4	-4	-4 NA		-4	-4	-4	-4
Direct HC																	
Support Techs	5	5	5	7	5	7	7	7	9	7	10	8 NA		5	7	9	8
SMEs	3	3	3	3	3	3	3	3	3	3	3	3 NA		3	3	3	3
Product Specialist	1	1	1	1	1	1	1	1	1	1	1	1 NA		1	1	1	1
Contractors	1	1	1	1	1	1	1	1	1	1	4	0 NA		1	1	1	0
Total Direct HC	10	10	10	12	10	12	12	12	14	12	18	12 NA		10	12	14	12
Total Direct Budget HC	11	11	11	12	12	12	12	13	14	14	15	15 NA		11	12	14	15
Total Over/Under Budget	-1	-1	-1	0	-2	0	0	-1	0	-2	3	-3 NA		-1	0	0	-3
Total Ending Headcount	13	13	13	15	13	15	15	15	17	15	21	15 NA		13	15	17	15
Total Budget Headcount	18	18	18	19	19	19	19	20	21	21	22	22 NA		18	19	21	22
Total Over/Under Budget	-5	-5	-5	-4	-6	-4	-4	-5	-4	-6	-1	-7 NA		-5	-4	-4	-7
Summary																	
Direct/Total HC Ratio	76.9%	76.9%	76.9%	80.0%	76.9%	80.0%	80.0%	80.0%	82.4%	80.0%	85.7%	80.0%	79.6%	76.9%	80.0%	82.4%	80.0%
Directs/Mgr Ratio	10.0	10.0	10.0	12.0	10.0	12.0	12.0	12.0	14.0	12.0	18.0	12.0	12.0	10.0	12.0	14.0	12.0
Directs/Supervisor Ratio	10.0	10.0	10.0	12.0	10.0	12.0	12.0	12.0	14.0	12.0	18.0	12.0	12.0	11.0	12.0	14.0	15.0
FTEs	10	10	10	11	11	11	12	12	13	13	15	15	11.9	10.0	11.0	12.3	14.3
Total DLH	1124	1128	1137	1237	1237	1137	1337	1337	1437	1437	1537	1592	15677	3389	3611	4111	4566
Paid Days	23	20	21	22	22	21	23	23	21	22	23	261		64	65	66	66
Non Available Time	300	330	250	220	200	250	320	275	300	330	320	321	320	880	670	895	971
Acid Utilization Rate	61.1%	70.5%	67.7%	63.9%	63.9%	61.5%	60.6%	66.3%	62.8%	60.1%	64.0%	57.7%	63.0%	66.2%	63.1%	63.1%	60.3%
Net Utilization Rate	73.0%	88.8%	79.5%	72.1%	71.3%	71.2%	70.8%	76.8%	72.3%	69.7%	73.9%	65.3%	63.8%	79.9%	71.5%	73.2%	69.2%

Figure 1.8 Headcount detail summary

The initial design should be kept simple. It provides time for all staff to assimilate a better understanding of the model and how certain actions or results will drive other numbers. For example, average direct labor hours (DLH) per closed service request is, in a way, a 'contra KPI.' Most managers will focus on some form of utilization rate, such as an acid utilization rate (measured in the appendix as total DLH for the period divided by paid hours). The industry average for acid utilization rate is between 55% and 60%. However, if the acid utilization rate increases during a certain period but both the support engineer headcount and workload (measured as total closed service requests) stays constant, then there may be an issue with:

- product quality (e.g. a new product release)
- a significant increase in off time (e.g. vacation, sick, holiday, training, etc.)
- new staff coming up to speed as a result of turnovers, etc.

This highlights an important point about the Balance Scorecard Service Model. It does an excellent job of pointing out current or future potential problems with the business; however, it rarely identifies the cause. Finding the root cause will often require more in-depth analysis. It is very likely to require more discussion with the Support Center management team, its engineers and, most importantly, its customers.

A simple design will also allow time to establish a more automated way to gather the data. Most Support Center operations will use a basic spreadsheet application (e.g. Excel, Lotus 123, etc.) to lay out the initial model. The model itself is broken down into a segment for each of the quadrants of the Balanced Scorecard Service Model, plus a headcount segment and a general summary management segment, which will summarize the high level KPIs against each of the goals on a single sheet.

In the model, the goals are highlighted in yellow. Blue designates a calculation and/or an automated feed from another sheet in the workbook. Black denotes specific input fields. The individual sheets themselves are broken down to show industry average (if known) and a targeted result for individual goals and metrics. Results are looked at monthly, quarterly, and year to date for each metric and goal. Generally, the longer the period of time, the less fluctuation in the results and the smoother the curve of any trend line. Some models will use 15 months and five quarters to allow for a comparative to the previous year's month or quarter results.

1.3 Ongoing operations

When considering ongoing operations of the Balanced Scorecard Service Model, it is important to keep in mind that the Support Center Manager is responsible for the day-to-day knowledge and operations. This means that the focus of metrics for the Support Center Manager will be at a more detailed level. As management levels increase, the amount of detail presented takes on less significance as the 'big picture' becomes more important. Figure 1.9 illustrates management level focus for metrics.

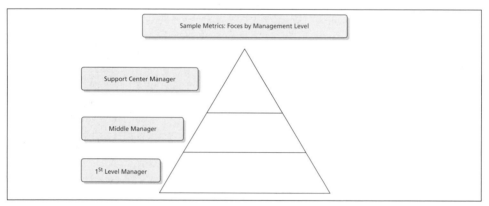

Figure 1.9 Sample metrics: focus by management level

As noted in the Implementation phase, as the organization evolves and learns how to use the Balanced Scorecard Service Model, the model will evolve into an even more powerful tool to manage the overall Support Center operation. This model can be used to manage current operational effectiveness; importantly, it can also use other forecast data to project and optimize future operations.

1.3.1 Advanced application of the Balanced Scorecard Service Model

The Balanced Scorecard Service Model outlined in figures 1.4 - 1.8 can also be broken down by products as well as by organizational support location. For example, as outlined in figure 1.10, it is possible to look at the model for a given site location by Product A or Product B in say Latin America and compare their performance with another location for the same product. Performance can be compared by site and by product; performance can also be consolidated for all sites by product. This capability will identify 'best of breed' within an organization relative to performance, which allows the organization to learn and implement its own internal best practices across the broader support organization.

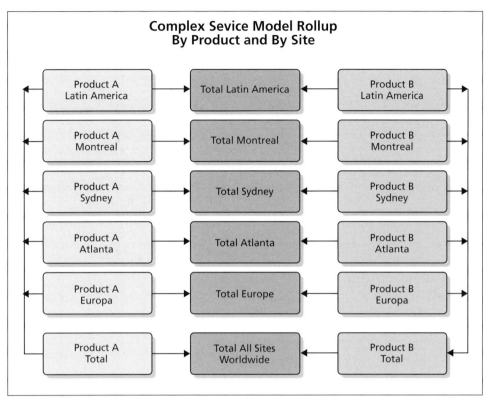

**Complex Sevice Model Rollup
By Product and By Site**

Product A Latin America	Total Latin America	Product B Latin America
Product A Montreal	Total Montreal	Product B Montreal
Product A Sydney	Total Sydney	Product B Sydney
Product A Atlanta	Total Atlanta	Product B Atlanta
Product A Europa	Total Europe	Product B Europa
Product A Total	Total All Sites Worldwide	Product B Total

Figure 1.10 Performance comparisons by product and by site

1.3.2 Using the Balanced Scorecard Service Model to measure ROI

Another major feature of the Balanced Score Card Service Model is that it allows support managers to build and use effective ROI models. These models can be used to show productivity gains generated (or not) through revised workflow processes, as well as for the justification of new productivity tools. For example, this could include 'knowledge aggregation' technologies, Web-based remote control tools, remote proactive 'phone home' technologies, voice recognition technologies etc.

Most support managers fail to take the second step in the ROI process, which involves proving the projected ROI after the fact. What this means is actually reporting back to senior management in the capital approval process if ROI objectives are reached. Besides validating the original ROI assumptions, this strategy automatically increases the prospects for approval of future projects if results are communicated back to the senior management who approved the investment.

The Balanced Scorecard Service Model can be used to demonstrate that these investments will increase productivity by:
• lowering either the number of incidents per contract or customer (or user for internal Support Centers)
• lessening the DLH per incident (as well as the elapsed time)
• improving closed incidents on initial contact rates etc.

The Balanced Scorecard Service Model can also show improvements in customer satisfaction, through hard survey score results or 'soft' results via customer survey interviews.

On occasion, in place of actually purchasing a technology solution, Support Center Managers may elect to use an applications software provider (ASP) or lease hardware. Regardless of how technology solutions are purchased, the Balanced Scorecard Service Model design provides a viable and measurable ROI model that is directly applicable to each Support Center environment.

1.3.3 Support Engineer Report Cards

The Balanced Scorecard Service Model can be broken down by site and product; it can also be modified and driven all the way down to the individual contributor. Figure 1.11 illustrates a sample Support Analyst Report Card. In this example, the report card is broken down into three major segments based on workload, customer satisfaction and non-direct time. The workload segment looks, by month, at:

• the number of incidents opened and closed
• bug escalations (called product advice reports or PARs in this sample)
• direct labor hours, hours available (paid hours less vacation, sick time, holiday, or training), paid hours and utilization rates [both acid (DLH/paid hours) and net DLH/hours available].

Figure 1.11 also looks at the number of transactional surveys that were completed based on incidents closed by this particular support engineer and further looks at incidents by individual question. Figure 1.11 is an Excel spreadsheet; however, there are a number of excellent Web-based business intelligence (BI) tools on the market that would allow full drill-down into each line of the Support Analyst Report Card. For example, it is easy to look at individual customer surveys and comments by support engineer from the individual report cards.

The final segment of this example looks at the indirect time breakdown by month.
This report card ties back to the Balanced Scorecard Service Model, thus driving the goals of the Balanced Scorecard Service Model all the way through the organization to the individual support engineer. It also provides managers with a very effective and objective tool for individual support engineer performance reviews.

Month	Cases		Backlog		Direct Labor	Hours		Utilization Rates		Surveys						
	Created	Closed	Nonpar	Par		Available	Paid	ACID	NET	Number	Timelines	Solution	Communication	Courtesy	Overall	Avg Score
January	138	72	11	0	77,54	136	160	48,5%	57,0%	0						
February	163	81	20	0	113,42	156	160	70,9%	72,7%	5	4,400	4,800	4,800	5,000	4,800	4,760
March	162	90	10	0	138,27	144	200	69,1%	96,0%	2	4,500	4,500	4,500	4,500	4,500	4,500
April	137	69	15	0	104,09	152	160	65,1%	68,5%	1	4,000	5,000	4,000	4,000	4,000	4,200
May	132	72	10	0	86,09	152	160	53,8%	56,6%	1	4,000	4,000	4,000	4,000	4,000	4,000
June	147	71	14	0	98,06	156	200	49,0%	62,9%	0						
July	105	49	6	0	154,46	136	160	96,5%	113,6%	0						
August	117	56	8	0	85,42	140	160	53,4%	61,0%	5	4,800	5,000	4,600	4,800	4,750	4,792
September																
October																
November																
December																
Average	137,63	70,00	11,75	0,00	107,17	146,5	170	63,0%	73,2%	1,8	4,500	4,786	4,571	4,714	4,625	4,640
YTD - Sum	1101,00	560,00			857,35	1172	1360			14						
Grp FTE Avg / mo	64,6	26,0	5,0	0,0	51,5	141,1	169,3	30,4%	36,5%	0,5	4,438	4,400	4,188	4,738	4,200	4,390
Grp Avg / mo	242	98	18,625	0	193	529	635	30,4%	36,5%	2	4,438	4,400	4,188	4,738	4,200	4,390
Grp Tot / yr	1939	780			1546	4232	5080			16						
Site Avg / mo	8261	8887	1215	294	11102	17793	21103	52,6%	62,4%	211	4,270	4,320	4,411	4,610	4,336	4,407
Site Tot / yr	66090	71096			88817	142346	168820			1687						

	Train	Sick	Vac	Comp	Per	Float	Hol	Other
January	0	0	16	0	0	0	8	0
February	0	4	0	0	0	0	0	0
March	32	16	0	0	0	8	0	0
April	0	0	0	0	0	8	0	0
May	0	8	0	0	0	0	0	0
June	12	0	8	8	8	0	8	0
July	0	0	16	0	0	0	8	0
August	0	8	12	0	0	0	0	0
September								
October								
November								
December								

Figure 1.11 Report Card Sample

1.4 Sustaining the process

The last step in the process involves periodic Support Center-driven operational reviews. Ideally, these should be performed quarterly. Monthly reviews at the summary level are too frequent and yearly reviews come too late to effect necessary changes to meet organizational goals.

Items covered in this operational review should include:
- the previous quarter's operational performance
- trend lines for goals and supporting major KPIs
- projections for future Balanced Scorecard Service Model Goals
- issues or concerns that may impact future performance
- product road map and/or new service offerings
- general overview of the business by senior corporate management
- review of past quarterly action items and new action items for the current period review
- awards and recognition for performance or contribution to the success of the operation

Another objective of the Balanced Scorecard Service Model is to set long-term performance targets for the Balanced Scorecard Service Model Goals. These performance targets should be aggressive but still be attainable by the organization.

Figure 1.12 provides a pictorial example of setting up long-term goals and then using the quarterly operational review process to monitor performance against those goals.

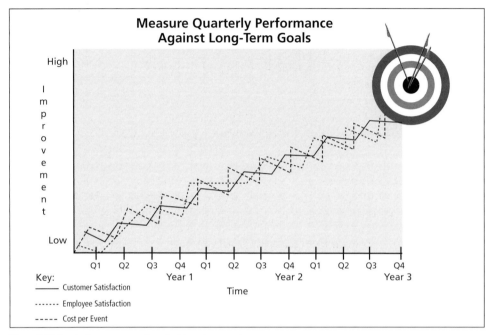

Figure 1.12 Quarterly measurement against long-term goals

The quarterly operational review process is iterative in nature. It may involve a local site or first-level manager review given to mid-level managers and the Support Center Manager. Second-level Support Center Managers may then do a formal review to the senior services managers with the Support Center Manager. This process is extremely effective in educating senior services managers at the vice president level and higher in the organization, and provides the Support Center or IT department with an even stronger link to senior corporate management. Figure 1.13 gives a simple overview of what this might look like.

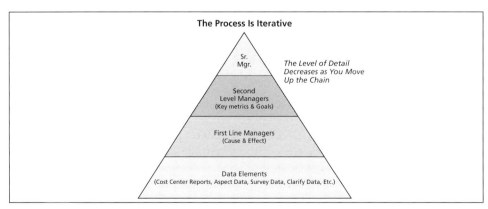

Figure 1.13 Operational review process

Operational reviews may include the following:
- first and second-level support managers, as well as the Support Center directors and above
- IT service delivery managers or business analysts who directly support the Support Center service delivery technology infrastructure (e.g. knowledgebases, CRM systems, voice and data networks etc.)
- HR managers for the Support Center
- educational services managers who directly support the Support Center
- product planning representatives
- product engineering representatives
- financial managers who directly support the Support Center
- the executive vice president of services (and occasionally Management Committee level executives).

The executive vice president of services should always start the meeting with a review of the past quarter's performance from an overall services perspective, then discuss the up-coming quarter or other significant events that are being planned at a corporate level.

Other representatives from the supporting staff organizations (e.g. HR, product planning, etc.) should be asked to give periodic presentations at the quarterly operations review when they have relevant, significant information that could or would affect the overall Support Center's current or future operations.

1.5 Summary

The key to the successful financial/operational management of Support Center operation deals with establishing a goal-based Balanced Scorecard Service Model. The goals established in this Balanced Scorecard Service Model should be agreed to by the Support Center Manager with the executive vice president of services for the organization. These goals should be linked directly to specific corporate-level goals. The Balanced Scorecard Service Model goals themselves, while separate, should be treated and managed as a whole. Long-range performance targets should be established for each goal and reported against as part of a formal quarterly operational review process. The objective is to have continuous, balanced improvement in all service goals.

While KPIs are important, managers should use them as a tool to help them understand where they may have an opportunity to improve the existing organization by pointing out potential issues. KPIs are management tools and not necessarily objectives. Reward systems need to be based on the goals of the Balanced Scorecard Service Model, and not the KPIs, to ensure that proper behavior is driven throughout the organization.

In setting up a Balanced Scorecard Service Model, establish goals first. Choose only those goal-related KPIs that will have the highest value initially, which should help keep the initial Balanced Scorecard Service Model simple. As a better understanding of the potential of the Balanced Scorecard Service Model is achieved, add more KPIs as necessary. When starting out, keep Balanced Scorecards simple. The level of detail included will increase as you move to lower levels of the organization.

Report cards should be used to drive the Balanced Scorecard Service Model concepts through to the individual contributor level to ensure end-to-end organizational alignment throughout the organization, whether it is a simple single Support Center or an international grouping of multiple Support Centers. A Balanced Scorecard approach ensures that goals are balanced and aligned with the real world of multiple priorities.

In a mature design, the Balanced Scorecard Service Model can be further broken down by organizational structure and by product structure. At the product level, the model becomes even more effective. It is generally easier to project the impact of future sales by product, making the workload as well as the number of FTEs and required skill sets easier to forecast. The impact of product quality is also more easily demonstrated when the model is broken down to the product level. The impact of a bad release can now be objectively presented back the engineering organization or vendor.

Overall, the effective design, evolution and proper management of the Support Center Balanced Scorecard Service Model process are the most important steps toward the development of a world-class Support Center operation. This is true of operations ranging from a simple internal IT Support Center to a larger multi-customer Support Center organization.

Annex A1.1 Balanced Scorecard quadrants

This annex provides details of the four quadrants of the Balanced Scorecard - Customer Satisfaction, Employee Satisfaction, Costs/Productivity Goals and Organizational Maturity.

A1.1.1 Customer Satisfaction Quadrant - Goals and Key Performance Indicators

This table is only a guideline. Users should feel free to redefine any definitions or sources listed above. However, they should maintain and distribute a documented copy to all users of this information.

Balanced Scorecard Service Model Area	KPI or Goal Name	Definition	Potential Source
Customer Satisfaction	Total Calls Received	Total Calls Received by the ACD.	ACD
Customer Satisfaction	Total Calls Answered	Total Calls Answered.	ACD
Customer Satisfaction	Customer Satisfaction Rating	This is usually the 'Overall' rating question on a customer survey. The actual calculation of the period score should be done via weighted average.	Customer Survey System
Customer Satisfaction	Completed Surveys	These would be the total completed surveys for the period.	Customer Survey System
Customer Satisfaction	Average Speed of Answer (ASA)	ASA is the time from the first ring to the time the customer speaks to a live agent. Includes time customer spent on IVR.	ACD
Customer Satisfaction	Abandon Calls	Calculated by taking 'Total Calls Received' and subtracting 'Total Calls Answered.'	Calculation (or ACD Rpt)
Customer Satisfaction	Abandon Call %	Calculated by dividing 'Total Calls Abandon' by Total Calls Received."	Calculation
Customer Satisfaction	Incidents Closed/Initial Contact	Total incidents closed on initial contact with a support rep.	Call Management & Tracking System (CMTS). Examples include Clarify, Heat, Remedy

Customer Satisfaction	Incidents Reopened	Total Closed Incidents reopened during that period.	CMTS
Customer Satisfaction	Incidents Escalated	Total incidents escalated for that period.	CMTS
Customer Satisfaction	% Incidents Closed/Initial	Calculated by dividing 'Total Incidents Closed on Initial Contact' by 'Total Closed Incidents' for that same period.	Calculation
Customer Satisfaction	% Incidents Reopened	Calculated by dividing 'Total Incidents Reopened' by 'Total Closed Incidents."	Calculation
Customer Satisfaction	% Incidents Escalated	Calculated by dividing 'Total Incidents Escalated' by 'Total Closed Incidents' for the same period.	Calculation
Customer Satisfaction	Total Response Time	Total time from the time a call is left in a CMTS queue until the support person makes initial contact with the customer.	CMTS
Customer Satisfaction	Average Response Time	"Total Response Time' divided by 'Total Closed Incident' for that period.	CMTS
Customer Satisfaction	Total Incident Elapsed Time	Total elapsed time (based on a 7x24 hour wall clock) from when the Incident was opened until it was closed.	CMTS
Customer Satisfaction	Average Incident Resolution / Elapsed Time (Min)	Calculated by dividing 'Total Resolution/Elapsed Time' by 'Total Closed Incidents' for a specific period.	CMTS
Customer Satisfaction	# Contracts Up for Renewal	Total number of contracts that will be expiring or up for renewal this period.	CMTS or Contract Mgt System
Customer Satisfaction	# Contracts Renewed	Total number of contracts renewed this period.	CMTS or Contract Mgt System
Customer Satisfaction	Contract Renewal %	Calculated by dividing 'Total Contracts Renewed' by 'Total Contracts' up for Renewal.	Calculation

Customer Satisfaction	% Performance Against SLA	This is measured as a percent of performance against SLA goals. This will be a unique measure to each group based on their specific SLA goals (e.g.. response times, resolution times, etc.).	CMTS or Contract Mgt System
Customer Satisfaction	Self-service utilization	Customer (user) use of self-service tools	Since most customers / user will not tell you if they were able to provide their own self server one of the better alternatives is to measure over time the average number of Direct Labor type events per user or contract. As self service increases the average number of events per user or contract will decrease.
Customer Satisfaction	Time to customer (user) proficiency of new technology	Amount of time necessary for average customer or user to become familiar with and able to use newly introduced technologies.	This could be a set time after the completion of the installation of this application and customer training. It could also be measured as the point where a new customer or user's average volume of incidents equals that for other customers using the same technology. In the later case the CMTS would be the primary system used to evaluate this measure.

A1.1.2 Employee Satisfaction Quadrant – Goals and Key Performance Indicators

This table is only a guideline. Users should feel free to redefine any definitions or sources listed above. However, they should maintain and distribute a documented copy to all users of this information.

Employee Satisfaction	Total Direct Headcount	Total Direct Headcount (Direct = Technical/Service Delivery).	HR Systems
Employee Satisfaction	Employee Satisfaction Rating	Employee satisfaction rating based on employee (period) survey score.	Employee Survey Process
Employee Satisfaction	# Turnovers (Directs)	Number of (technical) direct turnovers (Techs leaving the company).	HR Systems
Employee Satisfaction	# of Turnovers (Directs)	Number of direct people leaving the group but not the company.	HR Systems
Employee Satisfaction	Training Hours	Total formal classroom, Computer-Based Training (CBT), On the Job (OJT) training or other informal training time expended during the reporting period.	HR/ Time Tracking system or potentially CMTS
Employee Satisfaction	Average Training Hours per FTE	Calculated by dividing Total training hours by Total FTEs	Calculation
Employee Satisfaction	Total Performance Evaluations Scheduled	Total number of Performance Evaluations scheduled for a given period.	HR Systems
Employee Satisfaction	Total Performance Evaluations Completed	Total number of Performance Evaluations completed in a given period.	HR Systems
Employee Satisfaction	% Scheduled Performance Evaluations Completed	Percent of total Performance Evaluations competed in a given period divided by Total Performance Evaluations scheduled for that same period.	Calculation
Employee Satisfaction	# Employee Surveys	Total employee satisfaction surveys during the period.	Employee Survey Process
Employee Satisfaction	Time to employee proficiency	Time from actual start date to the point where an employee is capable of performing basic support functions	Employee Evaluation / Training Plans

Employee Satisfaction	Knowledge contribution	Total knowledge articles or content produced over a given period of time. This could be based on specific individual targets noted in employee job description. This measure is usually limited to Support Center employees classified as direct.	Knowledge or other select content based reporting systems

A1.1.3 Costs/Productivity Goals and Key Performance Indicators

This table is only a guideline. Users should feel free to redefine any definitions or sources listed above. However, they should maintain and distribute a documented copy to all users of this information

Costs/ Productivity	Ending Customers	The total ending customer (user) counts at the end of a given period.	CMTS
Costs/ Productivity	Average Customers	This is average of the past period ending customer count and the current period ending customer count.	Calculated
Costs/ Productivity	Total Incidents closed.	The total closed incidents for the current period.	CMTS
Costs/ Productivity	Average Cost per incident	Calculated by dividing 'Total Costs' by 'Total Incidents Closed' for the same period.	Calculation
Costs/ Productivity	Total Closed Incident Direct Labor Hours (DLH)	The Direct Labor Hours (time) logged against incidents closed during the period.	CMTS
Costs/ Productivity	Average incidents per Customer	Calculated by dividing the 'Total closed Incidents' by 'Average Customers' for the same period.	Calculation
Costs/ Productivity	Average Cost per Customer	Calculated by dividing 'Total Costs' by 'Average Customers' for the same period.	Calculation
Costs/ Productivity	Average Customers per FTE	Calculated by dividing the 'Average Customers' by 'FTEs' for the same period.	Calculation
Costs/ Productivity	Closed Incidents per FTE	Calculated by dividing the 'Total Closed Incidents' by the total 'FTEs' for the same period.	Calculation

Costs/ Productivity	FTEs	Headcount expressed in Full Time Equivalent (FTE) providing support. (Reserved for Full Time Technical Equivalents. Calculated by averaging the ending Technical headcount over two consecutive periods.)	HR System
Costs/ Productivity	Travel DLH	Travel time for Direct Personnel	HR/ Time Tracking system or potentially CMTS
Costs/ Productivity	Project-Related DLH	Special Project time for Direct Personnel	HR/ Time Tracking system or potentially CMTS
Costs/ Productivity	Total DLH	This field is calculated by adding all DLH associated with remote telephone support, desk side and onsite support and project related support.	Calculated
Costs/ Productivity	Utilization Rate (ACID)	Calculated by multiplying the 'FTEs' for the period by the paid days for the same period times 8 (hours) and dividing that figure into the 'Total DLH' for the period.	Calculation
Costs/ Productivity	Average DL per Incident (Min)	Calculated by dividing the total completed incident direct labor by total completed incidents for the same period. Expressed in minutes.	Calculation
Costs/ Productivity	Cost per Average DLH	Calculated by dividing the 'Total Costs' by the 'Total DLH' for the same period.	Calculated
Costs/ Productivity	Paid Days	This field is the actual paid days for a given period and it does include holidays.	HR/ Time Tracking system or potentially CMTS
Costs/ Productivity	Non Available Time	This is all time related to Holidays, Vacation, Sick Time, Disability Leave and Training.	HR/ Time Tracking system or potentially CMTS

Costs/ Productivity	Utilization Rate (Net)	This is calculated exactly the same as Acid Utilization Rate however all Non- Available time is subtracted from (the period's) Paid Days.	Calculation
Costs/ Productivity	Total Costs (These costs are for the reporting group / product team only)	Total costs of running the operation. This is a fully burden cost as reporting on a department budget, cost report. This figure should include at least the first level overhead allocation for the indirect groups (i.e. management cost centers) directly associated with the line support organization.	Financial Systems (i.e. Cost Center Reports and/or Allocation reports)
Costs/ Productivity	Cost per FTE	Calculated by dividing the 'Total costs' by 'FTEs' for the same period.	Financial Systems (i.e. Cost Center Reports and/or Allocation reports)
Costs/ Productivity	Revenue generated per employee	Total Contract or other revenue generated by Support Center divided by total Support Center employees (direct + indirect)	Calculation
Costs/ Productivity	Percent of budget	Total actual costs divided by budgeted actual costs for the same period. Express as a percentage.	Calculation

A1.1.4 Organizational Maturity and Key Performance Indicators

This table is only a guideline. Users should feel free to redefine any definitions or sources listed above. However, they should maintain and distribute a documented copy to all users of this information.

Organizational Maturity	Executive support of the Support Center	Overall backing and patronage of the Support Center by executive management	Executive use of the Support Center and outward promotion to remainder of organization by executive management
Organizational Maturity	Time to fill knowledge gaps	Time to identify and document problems and solutions; time for knowledge to be available for use by Support Center staff.	Average time from rough knowledge content creation to final edited and published content
Organizational Maturity	Time to new product Proficiency	Length of time it takes for the Support Center to be proficient on new products.	This could be measured by the average DLH per incident. During initial release the average DLH per incident will be high initially but should stabilize as the ship volumes increase and the technical support engineers gain familiarity with the new product. During this period additional feedback to the development group from support should enable development to make additional modifications that will help to stabilize the new product itself and further lower DLH per incident.
Organizational Maturity	Flexibility of costs to changes in workload	Ability of the Support Center to change the cost structure (up or down) as work varies.	Business contracts, SLAs, operational budgets, etc.

Organizational Maturity	Diversity	The value of diversity within and throughout the support organization and localization considerations.	HR Systems, internal Affirmative Action Plans, etc.
Organizational Maturity	Work elimination through Problem Management and Change Management	Tracking the cost savings resulting from identification and elimination of known errors.	Root Cause Analysis programs
Organizational Maturity	Formalization of IT processes	Tracking indicators that the support organization has integrated all support processes with processes of other IT functional areas	Support Center procedural documentation and the integration of IT/IS into the formal Support Center operational review process

Bibliography

Anton, Jon. *CallCenter Management By the Numbers,* West Lafayette, IN: Purdue University Press, 1997

Ellis, Mark W. *Using Service Goals and Metrics to Improve Help Desk Performance,* Help Desk Institute, 1997, 2003.

Harvard Business School, *Implementing the Balanced Scorecard,* Cambridge, MA, 1996

Niven, Paul R., *Balanced Scorecard Step-by-Step.*, New York: John Wiley & Sons, 2002

Chapter 2:
Knowledge Management

2.1 Overview

2.1.1 Description

Knowledge Management has been described as many things, from managing ignorance to managing intellectual property. It is a set of guiding principles related to managing information (building and maintaining information for re-use) with the underlying tenet of information in context.

Without context, information has little value. All knowledge is shaped by context and people rely on education and experience to make sense of it. The sense they make of it (or put another way, the depth of understanding) differs from person to person, depending on their education and experience. Communities of end-users with a specific interest or requirement are a key element in creation and dissemination of knowledge; though they are not the reason for a knowledge environment, they do provide focus and energy.

Much of the content of this chapter is based upon the work of the Consortium for Service Innovation. The Consortium has studied Knowledge Management for over a decade. HDI has worked with the Consortium to build standards and courseware to assist organizations implement successful Knowledge Management strategies. The Consortium's methodology for Knowledge Management is Knowledge Centered Support (KCS^{SM}). The objective of the KCS methodology is the collection, categorization, ongoing administration, dissemination and use/re-use of knowledge in the incident resolution process.

2.1.2 Why Knowledge Management is an executive issue

Understanding the flow of knowledge and information is key to success. Systems can mine gargantuan databases to establish patterns and distil information that a human could never find in several lifetimes. However, even the most advanced artificial intelligence is no substitute for what has been described as 'the human glue' that provides context and allows inferences to be accurately - or inaccurately - made.

Libraries are the old-fashioned knowledge repositories. However the principles of managing that repository are as valid today as it was 100 years ago. Who better to understand the need to organize, index and maintain massive databases than librarians? Long-term productivity depends on both investment and growth of knowledge assets. Connecting information flows, identifying and eradicating duplication of effort, streamlining data collection and distribution…all these things are crucial to managing an efficient and productive organization. All of these elements are enabled by managing information, knowledge, as an asset.

Corporate culture determines the success of any Knowledge Management initiative - executive attention is necessary. At the most basic level, there are three facets of Knowledge Management that executives must address - culture, process and technology.

Culture

Culture is led from the top. If Knowledge Management is a priority, then the board and CIO must demonstrate commitment through investment and interest in the success of Knowledge Management initiatives. If there is a culture of 'us and them', then 'silo-working' becomes normal and entrenched; Knowledge Management initiatives will fail. The executive must encourage and recognize those who participate in the usage of knowledge, creation of knowledge and maintenance of knowledge.

Process

For Knowledge Management to be successful, the organization must adopt repeatable processes. This requires standards for building the knowledge structure; these will be presented later in this chapter. Everyone's roles in the knowledge process must also be clarified.

Technology

Knowledge Management tools - regardless of the platform or tool chosen - are critical to the success of Knowledge Management initiatives. But initiatives that are technologically focused will probably fail. Focus on culture and process issues first, and then look for the right technology. The technology selected must work within the organization's platform requirements, meet the needs of its end-users, provide quality monitoring and workflow processes appropriate to its needs, and most importantly will allow for knowledge to be built at 'the speed of conversation'. Knowledge Management tools should be tightly integrated with Incident Management tools to allow for knowledge capture during the resolution process.

The Support Center will also need to consider the risks inherent in failing to address Knowledge Management. Knowledge Management, or the failure to address Knowledge Management, will affect how the organization does business in terms of being efficient and agile.

The Chief Knowledge Officer at HP, Craig Samuel, was quoted in the Financial Times as saying that support of effective knowledge sharing was not a technology issue. Work processes, in his estimation, account for 20% of problems, with 70% being cultural issues. The conclusion is that only 10% of effective knowledge sharing is attributed to technology challenges.

2.1.3 Relationship to other processes

Knowledge Management primarily affects end-users. Within the Support Center and IT organization, it is Incident Management, Problem Management and Change Management that are most strongly related to (and with) Knowledge Management processes.

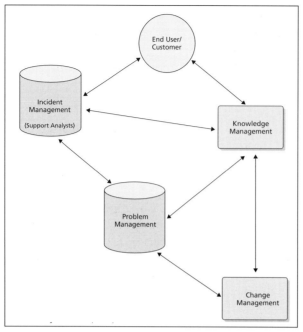

Figure 2.1 Relationship to other processes

2.2 Implementation

The goal of Knowledge Management is to simplify the process of capturing the incident descriptions and associated contextual information the first time information is gathered. Another goal of Knowledge Management is to resolve incidents in such a way that information can be easily re-used and referenced in the future. With these factors in mind, Knowledge Management will greatly enhance the productivity of the Support Center.

There are six key processes/concepts required for a successful Knowledge Management strategy. These are outlined below.

2.2.1 Capture context and incident descriptions in the workflow

Capture the context and incident description as the incident is being resolved. Capturing the customer's context (i.e., operating systems, hardware, and product) along with the user or customer's question or the incident definition is critical to the ability to find the solution in the future. If the customer's experience is not captured at the moment it is expressed, it will be lost. Solutions that are created after the fact (i.e. second or third level support) will be captured in the technical analyst's context, not the end-users/customer's context, thus reducing the chance of finding the solution in the future.

When the analyst receives an incident that they do not immediately know how to resolve, the knowledgebase should be referenced early in the process. The knowledgebase can provide information and answers to situations - or similar situations - that may have been previously addressed and/or resolved.

2.2.2 Structure knowledge for re-use

It is important to capture the contextual information along with the incident description. Words and phrases in the solution should contain complete thoughts, although they need not be complete sentences. It is important to distinguish between the incident or problem description, the environment and the resolution.

2.2.3 Searching becomes creating

If searching for a solution in the knowledgebase that is not found, save the vocabulary used in the search. The description of an issue is valuable even if it does not yet have a resolution. The resolution should be added when it is found. As analysts interact with the knowledgebase, the structured words and phrases are preserved. This is called a 'framed solution', which preserves the context of the incident in the requestor's terms. A framed solution in the knowledgebase can then be submitted to the appropriate people for resolution through the Problem Management process. When the resolution is determined it is simply added to the framed solution and finished. The process of framing and finishing solutions draws people into using the knowledgebase as the basis for incident solving, which in turn ensures that the collective experience of the organization is being captured and applied in the process of solving problems.

2.2.4 Just-in-time solution quality

If the analyst determines that a solution is good enough to deliver to a customer, that solution should be immediately available to the analyst's peers. If another analyst finds that solution, the analyst can review its appropriateness for the particular situation. The analyst may then modify or update the solution to ensure that it is appropriate for his/her specific situation. Knowledge is most valuable when it is first needed - it should be made available as soon as possible. The quality of knowledge will improve with re-use and maintenance.

2.2.5 Increase knowledge access

Limits must be assigned so that not everyone who accesses the knowledgebase system will be able to see everything or have updating capability. The organizations that have been successful with Knowledge Management link analyst rights and privileges to their demonstrated knowledge competency. Knowledge competency management is part of the performance assessment processes.

Expanding access to knowledge involves migrating access to content to new audiences based on demand and/or an analyst's judgement, and the random sampling and scoring of solutions in the knowledgebase. Generally, when a solution is first created it is only visible to a small audience. For example, if a Level 2 analyst creates a solution, that solution is immediately visible and searchable by other Level 2 analysts. If the solution is re-used by a peer and reviewed for correctness, it could then be flagged as a candidate to be made available to the Level 1 analyst. Through knowledge use, review and availability, solutions are constantly migrated closer and closer to the customer, based on demand.

2.2.6 Performance assessment programs

The organization must facilitate and encourage participation in the processes of knowledge creation and use; it must also recognize and reward those who create value. Most organizations find that they must shift performance assessment practices from individual and activity focused measurements to team and value-creation measurements. For example, knowledge may be created and added to the database, but it may not be correct, useful or searchable. The focus should be on the results of additions to the knowledgebase. Reward those who build and maintain knowledge that is re-used and rated useful by those who access it.

2.3 The role of the Support Center in Knowledge Centered Support

Knowledge Centered Support cannot be implemented and maintained without contribution from the overall Support Center organization; key roles have been identified in Figure 2.2 below.

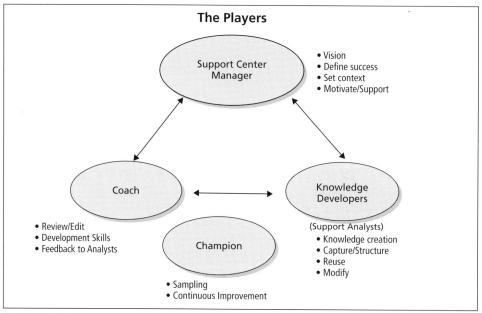

Figure 2.2 Key roles

2.3.1 Key roles

Support Center Manager
The Support Center must lead the effort by clarifying the vision and goals, as well as defining what success looks like. They need to direct their team in deciding how the work should be done (workflow) and the standards for creating findable and usable solutions (content standard).

Knowledge Developers
KCS I (front line support analyst) - basic user of the knowledgebase, familiar with searching techniques, the basic concepts of Knowledge Centered Support (KCS), and able to frame questions/solutions. All initial framing work done by a KCS I will be reviewed by the KCS Coach before release for others to view.

KCS II (more experienced front line support analyst) - has sufficient experience in creating and modifying knowledge to enable the coach to review only part of his/her work before making the knowledge available to others. The proportion of review decreases as the analyst become more experienced and as the knowledge created improves.

KCS Coach

This role is likely to be a senior or lead analyst. In larger organizations this may be a dedicated position. The KCS coach reviews 100% of the work done by a KCS I and only part of the work done by a KCS II analyst.

KCS Champion

This role is responsible for monitoring and sampling of the knowledgebase. The KCS Champion looks after the health of the knowledgebase and usually focuses on a collection or domain of content. This role requires technical expertise in the domain and profound understanding of KCS processes. The KCS Champion has responsibility for recognizing those who contribute well to the knowledgebase and those who need further training. The KCS Champion is the quality monitor for knowledge. This may be a dedicated position in a large organization or it might be part of the responsibility for a support manager, supervisor or team leader.

The KCS Champion should involve the entire organization from time to time in a continuous improvement process for Knowledge Management. The results of organizational involvement efforts lead to process improvements, creation of internal knowledge standards and development of reward and recognition programs.

2.3.2 Helpful hints for implementation, ongoing operations and optimization of Knowledge Management

- Aim for cultural acceptance - the organization needs to fully recognize knowledge and information as a key asset to be managed, fully exploited, and capable of generating significant returns.
- Reject the 'knowledge is power' theory. Sharing knowledge empowers everyone in the support organization to act as ambassadors.
- Collect and store information only once whenever possible. Use it often.
- Recognize that information assets under control in a Knowledge Management environment contribute to regulatory compliance as well as to organizational efficiency.
- Store information so that it can be linked, processed, properly maintained and presented to different audiences.
- Recognize the need to manage knowledge and its availability within the constraints of commercially sensitive information.
- Make use of appropriate infrastructure, tools and processes to support knowledge and information management initiatives.
- Make continuous improvements where necessary to avoid stagnation.
- KCS is not something we do in addition to solving problems; it becomes the way we solve problems.
- KCS is a team activity and the organization must achieve a balance between individual measures and team measures.

2.4 Measurement and reporting

Recommended reports for Knowledge Management are as follows.
Leading indicators (activities) should be tracked as trends. Do not put goals or objectives on activities; experience has shown that this will corrupt the knowledge base. Leading indicators include:

- analyst usage of knowledgebase - how many times the system is used in comparison to the number of incidents handled
- knowledge use/reuse - knowledge used to solve incidents reported by analyst(s) responsible for building or modifying the knowledge
- authoring - new solutions/pieces of knowledge added to the knowledgebase. Metrics should be broken down by analyst, by team and by knowledge category
- use of system/per call - to show the number of times analysts and end-users access the database
- knowledge re-use - use of specific solutions or knowledge by analysts and end-users
- amount of knowledge/number of solutions - size of knowledgebase and the number of items of content in the knowledgebase
- solutions per analyst/team – number and quantity of information added to the database per analyst and per team

Outcomes (results or goals - team objectives):

- quality control - knowledge rating scores by end-users and customers
- customer satisfaction - qualitative and quantitative surveys of end-users and the analysts who write and review knowledge
- time to publish/complete quality control process - length of time between the close of incident and time to access by end-users
- overall percentage of problems resolved by knowledgebase
- average handling time - benchmarked before implementation and then periodically measured as use and acceptance increases (a word of caution here: if you are delivering knowledge to the end user for self-help the average handle time will go up in the support center)
- customer satisfaction - satisfaction rates for all audiences (analysts and end-users) - that access and use the knowledgebase.
- customer success on the web – the percentage of times the customer goes to the web first and the percentage of time the customer finds what they are looking for.

Bibliography
Knowledge Centered Support Operational Model (v. 5.0)
Consortium for Service Innovation, White Paper 2003

Knowledge Centered Support Brief (v. 3.0)
Consortium for Service Innovation, White Paper 2003

Total Knowledge Management, Michael Charney
Kamoon Enterprise Expertise Management, White Paper, May 2002

Chapter 3:
Configuration Management

3.1 Overview

3.1.1 Description

The goal of Configuration Management is to maintain control of the IT infrastructure. Configuration Management ensures that only authorized IT assets are used; detailed information about these assets is kept up-to-date in the Configuration Management Database (CMDB) to support the effectiveness of other IT Service Management processes. From the Support Center perspective, the information stored in the CMDB provides invaluable information to enable the Support Center staff to:

- quickly isolate, diagnose and restore incidents
- assess the impact of a failed infrastructure component to the end-users' community
- provide information at their fingertips to quickly address end-user's queries
- enable planning and execution of service requests.

The term *Configuration Management* is often mistakenly used, interchangeably, with Asset Management and Inventory Management. Although these three processes may share the same repository or have common overlapping information, they are distinct processes with different scope and objectives.

Configuration Management is concerned with the identification, definition and ongoing verification of the accuracy of IT assets, their relationships to each other and to the IT systems and services. Inventory Management provides limited information to manage change and aid in problem isolation for a particular IT asset. Configuration Management combined with Inventory Management provides a wealth of information to support the management of all IT Service Management processes. The scope of IT assets under the control of Configuration Management is often a subset of Inventory Management.

Inventory Management deals with the identification and tracking of IT assets for the purpose of knowing its location, quantity, owner and key physical characteristics such as device configuration (for hardware devices) or version number (for software or documentation).

Asset Management is focused on the financial aspects of an IT asset. Information related to cost, depreciation, ownership, lease and contract management are some of the key characteristics of an IT asset that are managed by this process. In terms of scope, the Asset Management process may not track every asset under the control of the Inventory Management process. For example, the Asset Management process may manage only IT assets that are above a certain financial value.

3.1.2 Key definitions

Configuration Item (CI) is an IT asset that is under the management of the Configuration Management process. *A CI can be a physical IT asset or a logical representation of an IT asset.* For example, a physical CI is typically hardware (i.e. server, network devices, disk array), software (i.e. third party package or in-house developed application), document (i.e. technical document, contract, license) or a database instance. Examples of a logical CI can be an IT service, a system or a grouping of physical CIs such as a server cluster or virtual machine.

Attributes are specific information about a CI that provides more detail of its identity, configuration or other special characteristics. For example, serial number, model number, number of CPU, amount of memory and IP address are just some of the attributes of a server. Relationships are the associations or connections between two or more CIs. They provide information on how the CIs are related to or dependent upon each other. Attributes of a relationship may define whether the association is a parent-child type or a peer-to-peer type. An example of a relationship is 'Runs On', which is used to associate a software CI with a hardware CI. Another example is the use of a relationship 'Connected To' , which is used to associate a hardware CI with another hardware CI. For more examples of CI relationships, refer to the illustration in Annex A3.5.

Configuration Management Database (CMDB) is the repository that stores all the CIs, their attributes and their relationships. A CMDB can comprise one or more physical databases.

3.1.3 Relationships to other processes

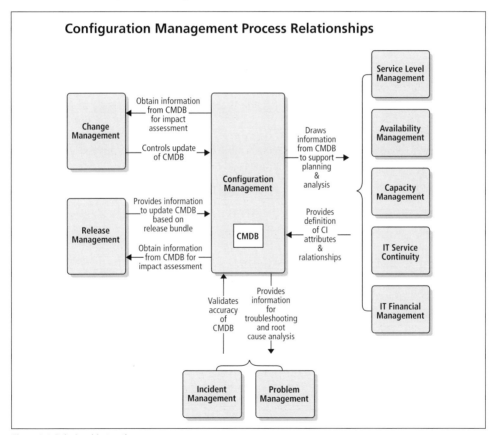

Figure 3.1 Relationship to other processes

3.1.4 Key inputs and outputs to the process

Source/ Destination	INPUT TO Configuration Management		OUTPUT FROM Configuration Management	
	Importance	Description	Importance	Description
Incident Management	High	• Validates CI information	High	• Provides CI attributes and dependency information for impact analysis of failed CI and for aiding incident recovery. • Provides end-users' profile information and hardware and software used by them. • Provides historic information related to CI such as recent changes, repairs etc.
Problem Management	Medium	• Validates CI information	High	• Provides historic information related to CI incidents, changes, known errors etc. • Provides CI dependency information between CIs for root cause analysis.
Change Management	High	• Validates CI information • Controls updates to CMDB	High	• Provides CI dependency information to assess potential impact of change. • Provides CI baseline information to aid 'fallback' of failed changes. • Provides historic information related to CI such as recent changes, repairs etc.
Release Management	High	• Triggers updates to CMDB for CI status, CI attributes and relationships. • Triggers creation of new configuration baseline in CMDB. • Triggers creation of new CIs and all associated attributes and dependencies in CMDB.	High	• Provides CI attributes and dependency information for impact analysis to prepare for testing and release rollout. • Provides historical information related to CI incidents, problems and known errors for bug fixes.

Service Level Management	High	• Triggers creation of Service CIs and their relationships between system CIs and the customers who use them. • Triggers creation of CI attributes to be used for Service Catalogue creation. • Stores SLA documents.	High	• Provides information to aid SLA creation by identifying critical CIs that are used for measurement of Service Level. • Provides information related to incidents, problems and changes for Service Performance reviews and Service Delivery reports.
Capacity Management	Medium	• Stores capacity plans. • Triggers creation of CI attributes (i.e. threshold, weighting factors and coefficients for mathematical formulae) to be used for modeling and forecasting capacity growth.	Medium	• Provides CI dependency information for end-to-end planning, analysis and monitoring of capacity utilization and performance of services and systems.
Availability Management	Medium	• Triggers creation of CI attributes (i.e. weighting factors and coefficients for mathematical formulae) to be used for calculation of service and system availability.	Medium	• CI baseline information and CI relationships to aid recovery of service and systems in the event of a disaster. • Provides information on reliability and maintainability of CIs based on incidents and changes.
Financial Management	Medium	• Aligns service CIs definition in CMDB with that of customer billing information.	Medium	• Provides end-users' profile information and services used by them for billing and charge back.
IT Service Continuity Management	Medium	• Stores IT service continuity plans and test results from Service Recovery simulations.	Medium	• Identifies CIs critical to IT Service continuity and provides information on CI dependency and CI configuration.

3.1.5 Possible problems and issues

Scope is too wide
The scope of the CI to be managed is too wide; significant resources are required to populate and maintain the CMDB.

Mitigation:
- Start small, phase in gradually. Criteria to select which services and systems to start the CMDB population can, for example, be dependent on any one of the following factors: criticality of the services and systems to the organization, amount of accurate inventory already at hand, most significant 'pain points', largest cost savings attainable.
- Integrate with auto discovery tools to obtain base inventory.
- Ensure the level of details captured in the definition of CI attributes and the relationships between CIs provides maximum control and benefits needed but at the same time minimizing the effort required to maintain them.

Wrong level of detail
The level of detail of CI attributes and relationships types is too little or too much to be useful to support groups.

Mitigation:
- Be realistic and clear on the goals for Configuration Management. Based on the goals, derive the requirements that will be used to design the CI object model. Since the object model is the source of reference when populating and updating the CMDB, it should encompass all the CI types, CI class, relationships and CI attributes, with appropriate level of details to meet the objectives of the established goals.
- Involve the support groups in the requirements gathering and development phases of the CI object model design. They are the subject matter experts for their respective technology domains (i.e. network, servers, application, database, etc).

'Bottleneck' perception
The Configuration Management group is seen as a bottleneck.

Mitigation:
- A central and dedicated group to update and maintain the CMDB should facilitate better quality of data and ensure a higher degree of process compliance. However, too much centralization leads can lead to a bottleneck if the group is not resourced properly. Conversely, if the update of the CMDB is distributed to each functional group the quality of data and process compliance may not be up to standard. The decision to centralize or decentralize depends on the volume of CMDB updates and the ability of the central group to know what changes are made in the environment. One approach that combines the best of both worlds is to distribute the updates of the CI to the individual support groups, but have a central group to oversee the governance of the CMDB updates. This central group can be responsible for audits and validation of the CMDB to ensure compliance by the rest of the support groups.

Burden of audit
Audit of the CMDB is too time consuming and resource intensive.

Mitigation:
• Employ the use of auto discovery tools to validate what has changed in the IT infrastructure against what is entered or updated in the CMDB.
• Audit of the CMDB can be approached in one of two ways:
• perform audits with smaller sample size but more frequently
• conduct audits with larger sample size but less frequently.

Inability to track changes
Changes to the CMDB cannot be tracked.

Mitigation:
• Ensure the IT service management tool that houses the CMDB repository has the capabilities to capture audit trails of CI updates. Most tools can track the creation and deletion of CIs but few have the capability to track specific changes made to the CI attributes. Modify existing tool or look for tools that have the additional functionality.
• Ensure the tool has the capability to provide role based security so that appropriate detail of access level can be defined for different job functions.

Responsibilities unclear
Configuration Management responsibilities are not clearly defined and understood.

Mitigation:
• When designing the Configuration Management process flow, ensure the process activities are defined in sufficient detail to enable delineation of responsibilities between various organizational groups or individuals.
• Use ARCI matrix (Accountable; Responsible; Consult; Inform) to map each process activity to individuals or group. Refer to Annex A3.6 for ARCI template and example.
• Provide ongoing training to all staff including management. Training should incorporate various forums and media. For example, a training program may start with formal classroom sessions, then follow with on-the-job coaching by Subject Matter Experts (SMEs) for several weeks after the initial rollout. After the 'settling' period, certain aspects of the tools or process activities may still be unclear or incorrectly used. To remedy these problematic areas, 'lunch and learn' sessions, newsletters or smaller training classes may be incorporated to target the individuals who still require further education.
• It is also possible that the process may require adjustments or corrections to address areas of confusion. Avoid the temptation to change the newly deployed process until after the 'settling' period. This period may take three to six months depending on the size of the organization.

Information not being exploited
Support staff do not exploit the information captured in the CMDB to support other Service Management processes.

Mitigation:
- Provide training, both formal and informal, to ensure that support staff understand the data model of the CI relationships, the types of attributes captured for each type of CI class and CI type and the capabilities of the service management tool.
- Ensure the service management tool has capabilities to quickly extract the required information and present them in a relevant format. For example, it is easier to understand the relationships between CIs when presented in a graphical format than in a text report.
- Change the mindset of the staff from reactive management of the IT infrastructure to a service based proactive one.

3.1.6 Quality issues
CI information is not up to date
CI information in CMDB does not reflect real configuration; CIs are missing or out of date.

Mitigation:
- Change Management, Release Management and Asset Management processes need to be in place and closely integrated with the Configuration Management process. Process activities that trigger an update to the CMDB must be clearly identified with established accountability and responsibilities.
- Increase audits to validate changes. Use discovery tools to compare CI configuration and relationships in the real world to that of the CMDB.

Inconsistent CI entries
CI entries are not consistent or partially filled.

Mitigation:
- Enforce standardization via tool functions - pick list, mandatory fields.
- Establish naming convention policies and ensure that these policies have management support.
- Determine if further education is required.

3.1.7 Security issues
Unauthorized access
Unauthorized access or updates are made to the CMDB.

Mitigation:
- CMDB data needs to be carefully classified to allow proper segregation of duties. For example, CIs managed or supported by one group may be restricted to READ ONLY for another support group. Some CIs may contain confidential information that may only be viewed by authorized personnel. Establish policies to define what is to be entered into the CMDB, who should have authorization to access the data and what level of access is permitted.
- Ensure the Service Management Tool that stores the CMDB has the functionality to control the access and updates of CIs at the appropriate security level required.

Changes cannot be traced
Changes made to the CMDB are not traceable.

Mitigation:
- Determine what data element of the CI is to be audited, then ensure the Configuration Management tool has the capability to record audit trails at the level of detail required.
- Ensure data backup policies are established and that the CMDB is backed up on a regular basis to enable recovery of deleted CIs to trace their history.

Sensitive data
Sensitive data is not protected.

Mitigation:
- Establish policies to define what type of sensitive data should not be recorded in the CMDB. For data that is deemed to be confidential, ensure that a proper level of control is defined and implemented in the Configuration Management tool.

3.2 Implementation

3.2.1 The implementation process

There are three major streams of activities involved in the implementation of Configuration Management: process design; tool selection, design and implementation; and configuration structure design and CMDB population. Throughout the implementation process, it is crucial that a robust communication plan is maintained to keep the organization informed, motivated and engaged. Figure 3.2 shows the major grouping of activities necessary for implementation. Although most of the activities between the three streams can be performed independently or in parallel to each other, there are some activities that cannot be done until one or more activities from another stream have been completed. For example, gathering of tool requirements cannot be completed until high-level process design and the configuration structure model and its attributes are defined.

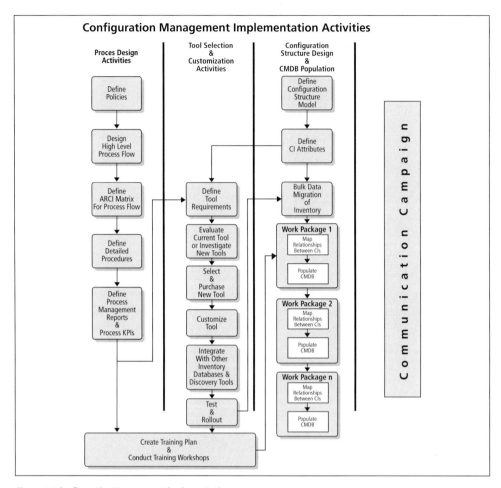

Figure 3.2 Configuration Management implementation process

3.2.2 Support Center Manager's role

Responsibilities and activities

The Support Center Manager plays a key role in the implementation of the Configuration Management. Since he/she is the link between the Configuration Management project team, the Support Center staff and the end-user community, this individual will be liaising between the three parties throughout the implementation phase to ensure the needs of all parties are addressed in a timely and effective manner:

- providing information on current process by detailing what works well and what does not
- providing input into the design of the new policy, process, ARCI matrix and the procedures, from Support Center perspective, and reviewing them for sign-off
- providing input to the tool requirements, from Support Center perspective, and sign off the requirements document
- providing input to the design of the configuration structure model and the attributes of CIs that are managed by the Support Center

- working with the project team to develop a Configuration Management plan that describes the services, systems and CIs that will be populated in the CMDB for work package 1, 2, 3 and so on
- communicating to the customers and Support Center staff the goals and benefits of Configuration Management, together with the project milestones; keeping them up to date with the progress of the project
- explaining to the customers and Support Center staff the differences they will encounter when they interact with the Support Center once the project is rolled out
- jointly developing a training plan with the project team to ensure Support Center staff are well trained in the new process, the configuration structure model and the use of the tool
- jointly deciding with the project team the rollout date, ensuring minimal impact to the end-user community and the Support Center staff
- jointly working with the project team to estimate resource requirements in terms of staff, hardware and software costs for the implementation and ongoing support of Configuration Management
- coordinating between the project team and the Support Center Manager's staff to gather hardware and software inventory managed by the Support Center; establishing relevant relationships between them for CMDB population
- coordinating between the project team and end-users to gather information about end-user profiles for CMDB population.

Deliverables
- Before the start of the project, providing any policies, process or procedures currently in use by the Service Center to manage the inventory and configuration of the services and systems they support
- Business and technical requirements for the development of the new policies, process, procedures and the Configuration Management tool, respectively
- List of inventories managed by the Service Center before start of project
- List of inventories to be managed for the implementation of the project and ongoing operations
- List of end-users and their profiles along with their hardware, software and license usage
- Requirements for training of Support Center staff for the use of the new process and tool

Requirements for management reporting and KPIs
For budget planning: requirements for extra staff for the project and for ongoing support, cost of new hardware and software licenses for the use of Configuration Management tools

Competencies
- Achievement orientation
- Influence and impact
- Team leadership
- Negotiation skills
- Listening and communication skills
- Customer service orientation
- Information seeking
- Organizational awareness

Key performance indicators (KPIs)
One of the key success factors for implementing any new process is that the implementation is conducted as a formal project, following best practice project management methodology. Many of the key performance indicators for implementation are based on the following milestones:
- sign-off for project charter and project timeline
- sign-off for new policies, process and procedures
- sign-off for business requirements document for Configuration Management tool
- sign-off for test cases and test results for tool testing
- sign-off for implementation and rollout plan
- sign-off for implementation.

3.2.3 Support Center Function's role
Responsibilities and activities
The role of the Support Center is to assist the Support Center Manager to obtain his/her deliverables. Some information will rely on the Support Center's staff experiences while others will rely on data obtained from historical management information and KPI reports produced by the Support Center. For example, CIs will need to be prioritized for population in the CMDB. Criteria could be based on systems that historically took too long to fix due to unavailability of CI configuration or due to improper identification of CIs; the Service Desk might have reports that show the trends in resolution time by CI type.

Deliverables
In addition to the deliverables provided by the Service Support Manager, the following additional deliverables should be provided by the Support Center staff:
- reports that classify incidents by CI class and CI type
- reports of incidents caused by wrongly made changes
- undocumented information or knowledge about various CI relationships accumulated by Support Center's staff over time as they learn from their troubleshooting experiences

Competencies required
- Achievement orientation
- Teamwork skills
- Listening and communication skills
- Customer service orientation
- Information seeking
- Analytical thinking
- Technical knowledge
- Technical documentation skills
- Multi-task thinking and execution skills

KPIs
Percentage completion of the deliverables as described in the Support Center Manager section.

3.2.4 Other key roles and functions in the implementation process

Executive sponsor - responsible for providing organizational leadership, guidance, advocacy and financial funding for the Configuration Management project.

Project manager - accountable for timely completion and budget spending of the Configuration Management project. He/she is responsible for developing project plans and managing all activities for the Configuration Management project and related communication and awareness campaigns.

Configuration Management process owner - accountable for the design and development of the Configuration Management process. Through leadership and influencing skills, he/she ensures that a unified process is developed across the entire organization by being an advocate and champion of the Configuration Management process.

Data model architect - responsible for defining the object model that shows the entity relationship diagram(s) of all possible CIs and their relationships to each other.

Business analyst - responsible for gathering and documenting all business and functional requirements for the customization of the Configuration Management tool. He/she will also be responsible for developing and documenting the test plans and test cases for the tool.

Technical specialist(s) for Configuration Management tool - responsible for the customization of the Configuration Management tool, based on business and functional requirement documents, through programming or tool setup and administration. In addition, bulk data loading activities to prepare CI inventory data from various sources for import into the Configuration Management tool will require technical expertise.

Process advisor/consultant - as subject matter expert on the ITIL framework, this role provides advice on process engineering methodology and best practices on Configuration Management. Facilitates meetings during design sessions for policies, process and procedures.

Configuration Manager - participates in design sessions for policy, process and procedures; assists data model architect in defining CIs and their relationships; also defines CI attributes for the CIs supported by his/her group. Collection of CI inventory for initial bulk data load to populate the CMDB will also be part of the responsibility of the Configuration Manager. For a small organization, one Configuration Manager may represent several technology support groups (i.e. UNIX Systems Administrators, Database Administrator, Desktop Support Analyst, Network Support Analyst, etc). For a large organization, each group may have their own Configuration Manager.

Process analyst - responsible for documenting all policies, process, procedures, process management reports and KPIs based on input from design sessions and from consultation with process advisor/consultant and Technology Support Group Representatives.

3.2.5 Planning for implementation
Steps to take
- Secure the executive management sponsor. The role of the executive sponsor is to ensure that adequate funding is available for the project and to provide leadership and support for this initiative. The executive may lead the project steering committee or appoint one of his/her senior managers.
- Form core project team. The core team should include a project manager, the Configuration Management process owner and process managers representing key functional or organizational groups.
- Define project scope, goals and objectives.
- Establish a communication plan to keep the organization informed throughout the project and also prepare them for the rollout.
- Perform 'as-is' assessment of current process, tools and CI information already captured in the organization. Depending on the availability of internal resources to perform this assessment, it may be necessary to hire external consultants to perform the assessment so as not to take the core team away from their existing responsibilities.
- Develop implementation approach and Configuration Management plans. Priorities and details of the deliverables and resource requirements can be established, based on the analysis of the 'as-is' assessment report. Very often, due to the large number of CIs involved, a phased approached will be adopted to implement this process. Several options and considerations for phasing the population of the CMDB are listed in the section 'Necessary Information and Data' below.

Groups to contact
- Service Desk
- Problem Management Group
- Change Management Group
- Release Management Group
- Availability Management Group
- Technical Support groups such as Network Management, Server Administration, Database Management, Desktop Support, etc.
- Application Development group
- Service Level Management individuals or groups such as Account or Relationship Manager

Necessary resources and relationships
As shown in Figure 3.2, the implementation of Configuration Management encompasses three streams of activities:
- Process Design
- Configuration Management tool selection and customization
- Configuration Structure modeling and CMDB population.

During the process design phase, a design team consisting of the Configuration Management process owner, Configuration Managers, process advisor/consultant and process analyst will be working together. They develop the policies, high-level process flow, detailed procedures, process management metrics and KPI report requirements.

The effort and resources required to customize the Configuration Management tool depend on whether the tool is already in use or if a completely new tool is to be purchased. At a minimum, a core team consisting of process advisor, business analyst and technical specialist for the tool is required to gather tool requirements, develop and customize and test the tool. Input from various Configuration Managers and a data model architect will be required during the requirements gathering phase of the tool.

The design of the Configuration Structure and the definition of the CI and relationship will be done primarily by the data model architect, with input from the Configuration Managers and process advisor.

Initial population of the CMDB can be achieved by performing bulk data load, provided that a standard format and interfaces have been developed and designed by the technical specialist. These enable the Configuration Management tool to accept data from various sources such as spreadsheets, databases or system discovery tools.

Necessary information and data

Most information and data necessary for the implementation of Configuration Management can be identified during the 'as-is' assessment. The data gathered will provide valuable information to determine the approach, scope and resource requirements for implementation. The assessment template should be completed by each of the above groups listed in the 'Groups to Contact' section. Refer to Annexes A3.3 and A3.4 for examples of 'as-is' assessment templates.

List of inventories and repositories (i.e. hardware, shrink wrap software, in-house developed applications, documentation, end-user list, databases, etc) maintained by various support groups. In addition to inventories of various CI types, the attributes captured for each CI type need to be gathered. This information will be used to gauge how complete and accurate the inventories are compared to what is actually deployed. It will also provide insight into which groupings of assets are better managed and how the attributes for each CI types are currently being used.

Policies, process and procedures currently in use for Inventory Management, Asset Management, Change Management and Release Management. This information will be used to establish integration points with the new Configuration Management process and determine new policies.

Systems architecture diagrams and technical documentation of systems that will be managed under the new Configuration Management process. This information will be used to define the relationships between CIs in the future CMDB.

In addition to the technical assessments, there will need to be an assessment of the skill sets within the organization in the areas of process design, data modeling and specific knowledge related to Configuration Management. Based on the information gathered, it may be necessary to hire external consultants to conduct training or even to be involved with the project team.

As mentioned earlier, the population of the CIs and their relationships into the CMDB will usually be phased in over time. The larger the organization, the longer the data gathering and population period will be. A number of criteria can be used to aid in the prioritization of CIs and their associations for CMDB population. The criteria could be based on criticality of the systems/services to the business, outsourcing or insourcing projects, systems/services causing the most difficulties to support due to lack of CI information, projects that require CI information such as technology refreshment, total cost of ownership etc. Depending on the chosen criteria, historical statistics and management information captured by the Service Desk, Incident Management, Change Management, Problem Management, Release Management and Availability Management processes can provide further data for decision making.

Measurements that should be in place
Completeness and approval of Project Charter, which defines such aspects as project scope, goals, funding and resource requirements.

The accuracy and completeness of the 'as-is' assessment templates to be filled by various support groups.

Completeness and details of project plan.

3.2.6 Implementing key process activities: hints and tips
What to implement first
Before attempting to implement any of the Configuration Management activities, the organization must ensure that the Change Management process has been implemented and operated at a mature level. Without a well-established Change Management process, the integrity of the CMDB cannot be maintained.

If inventories of CIs are absent, start the population of the CMDB with inventory of CIs and their attributes. CIs that are in data centers should be targeted first since these are usually better managed than those that are dispersed in end-user areas (i.e. Desktop CIs).

Things that always work
Keep design team small but conduct periodic 'walk throughs' with larger groups. A small design team will reach consensus faster, while conducting 'walk through' with larger audiences will ensure the rest of the organization does not feel alienated.

Set up a project team and apply project management methodology to ensure that dedicated resources and time are allocated. Risk of failure or prolonged implementation is high without these in place.

Ensure training is provided to the people who will be involved with the Configuration Management process. Training courses should be tailored to the various roles of the Configuration Management process to ensure the right level of detail is provided to the right people. For example, a Configuration Coordinator will receive different training from a person who is at the Service Desk. Training should be given as close to the rollout date as possible. Ensure an adequate coaching period is formally established immediately after rollout date to 'handhold' people.

Little things that deliver big returns

Senior management should communicate the vision and goals of Configuration Management to the rest of the organization at the onset of the project. One or more senior managers should also be part of the project steering committee team that meets on a regular basis to provide leadership, guidance and support to the project team throughout the life of the project.

A communication strategy should be developed to provide periodic updates to the rest of the organization throughout the life of the project. This will ease the acceptance of the new process and tool(s) when they are implemented.

Information about the dependencies between CIs may not be documented completely, nor reside in one source. The information might be in people's head across multiple groups and in various technical documents. An interview approach will need to be adopted. Recording of the CI relationships is more effective when captured on paper first, in their entirety, before capturing them in the CMDB.

When implementing a new CMDB, existing data stored on various repositories will probably be imported into the new CMDB. The data migration process and data conversion tool need to be carefully planned, designed and tested in great details. Do not underestimate the effort required to perform these activities.

The data migration process may require data preparation or 'cleanup'. If the time required to perform this activity is more than a few days, a strategy should be developed to track the changes made to the infrastructure while the data in the repository is frozen from any changes during this data 'cleanup' period.

The initial phase of the CMDB population might only focus on a subset of the CIs. However, when defining the Configuration Structure object model, consideration should be given to include all the CIs in the entire IT infrastructure.

The concept of establishing relationships between CIs will be new to most people. A 'Quick Reference Guide' booklet detailing all possible CI associations will facilitate better conformance to the defined standards.

Little things that always get forgotten

Provide training for the project team at the initial onset of the project to ensure all team members understand the basics of Configuration Management and process design methodology.

Archival strategy for CMDB data is usually forgotten or only considered when disk space for CMDB database is close to reaching maximum capacity. The archival of CMDB data should be carefully planned during the design of the CMDB.

3.2.7 Key process activities

As shown in Figure 3.2, the implementation activities consist of three streams of activities: process design, tool selection and implementation, and configuration structure design and CMDB population. A brief description of each set of activities is provided below.

Process design activities

Define policies: the policy document should include: scope of coverage of the CMDB; CI creation, update, disposal and status accounting policy; frequency of audits; and naming conventions for CIs.

Design high level process flow: all major process activities for CI identification, creation, updates and disposal should be detailed in a high level process flow. Activities for planning, audit and validation should also be included along with integration points with other processes such as change and release management.

Define ARCI matrix for process flow: once all the activities in the high level process flow are defined, the people or organization group(s) who are Accountable (A), Responsible (R), Consulted (C) and Informed (I) in the execution of these activities should be detailed in the ARCI matrix.

Define detailed procedures: the detailed procedure provides more specific information regarding how and when the activities (as defined in the high level flow and the ARCI matrix) are to be executed. Note: the procedure may contain information about process activities specific to tool functionality, but it is not meant to be work instructions or tool end-user guide.

Define process management reports and process KPIs: requirements and definition of all process reports and Key Performance Indicators necessary to monitor and manage the process are defined. The title and purpose of the reports, distribution audience and publication frequency are documented here.

Tool selection activities

Define tool requirements: when considering a new tool or customizing the existing tools, consider the following key tool requirements: alignment of the tool functionalities to perform key functions of Configuration Management as defined by ITIL; integration with other Service Management tools that capture information for Incident, Problem, Change and Release Management; capability to interface with system discovery tools or software delivery/installation tools; security and audit features; and scalability to accommodate growth in CI and in end-user groups.

Evaluate current tool or investigate new tools: too often organizations may be reluctant to make an objective investigation of new tools if there is already one in-house. Although some savings can be gained in the short term to keep the existing tool, the long term cost or lost opportunity associated with choosing to stay with an inadequate tool could be quite substantial.

Select and purchase tool (if necessary)
Customize tool: depending on the extent and complexity of the tool customization needed to meet the stated requirements, it may be necessary to involve the tool vendor to perform the customization. The expense for this specialized resource can be substantial. When planning for the project budget at the beginning of the project, allow sufficient funding to accommodate this possibility.

Integration with other inventory database and discovery tools: some organizations may choose to perform this step after the Configuration Management project goes live. However, if the number of CIs is high and dispersed across multiple geographic regions, it is advisable to include this step as part of the project rollout. The automated discovery tools should be integrated with the CMDB. If they are not, the initial CMDB population, and then the validation and audit of CIs (once the process is in operation) in the real world compared to that of the CMDB will become too manual-intensive or unfeasible.

Test and rollout: to ensure thoroughness in testing of the tool, test cases should be documented and signed off by stakeholders. Testing should be staged in a manner consistent with the Software Development Life Cycle (SDLC), which incorporates functional, regression, system integration, end-user acceptance tests (UAT) and post deployment tests. Depending on the size of the end-user base, training and implementation of the new tool may be staged over several weeks or months so as to minimize disruption to existing operations and requirements for training facilities and trainers. After the tool is rolled out, it is important to have post implementation support from Configuration Management Subject Matter Experts (SMEs) who are readily available and accessible to address any issues or questions from the end-users of the tools.

Configuration Structure Design and CMDB population
Define configuration structure model: when designing the configuration structure model, all IT CI types and their relationships types should be included in the design even though the scope of the current Configuration Management project may be limited to a subset of the available CI types. A consistent and cohesive framework can be defined by considering all CI types at the onset of the design stage. It is important to have a well-defined set of Configuration Management goals before the definition of the model. The level of detail and granularity of the model depends largely on the goals of configuration. It is best to enlist the help of a Data Model Architect to define the configuration model.

Define CI attributes: involve a representative from each technical support group to participate in the definition of the attributes for each CI type; this will avoid defining too many attributes that will not be filled in by the various technical support groups when the CMDB is rolled out . Again, the goals of Configuration Management should be referenced when defining these attributes to ensure that the right number and right kinds of attributes are defined.

Bulk data migration of inventory: various technical support groups will be keeping track of their own inventory in spreadsheets or databases. To populate the new CMDB efficiently and effectively, import utilities will need to be developed to automate the transfer of these existing inventories. Development and testing of the data import tools usually requires definition of intermediary mapping tables which requires iterative testing due to unpredictable variation in the uniformity of data. Depending on the consistency of the data, manual 'data scrubbing' may be necessary to correct the data that cannot be imported automatically. This process activity may take a considerable amount of time; do not underestimate the effort required.

Map relationships of CI and populate CMDB: in addition to the population of the physical CI inventories into the CMDB, logical CIs representing services and systems have to be defined in the CMDB before end-to-end CI relationships can be established to model a service in the CMDB. Establishing these CI relationships requires research into the system architectural design of the system and services. In some cases, up-to-date technical documentation is available to aid this effort. However, more often than not, little or no documentation is available. For the latter cases, a discovery process, in the form of interviews involving various technical support groups, will be required to gather the information necessary to map all required relationships between CIs. The mapping exercise is best done on paper until all relationships are determined. Once the completed picture of the end-to-end CI relationships is validated, the information is ready for input into the CMDB. Depending on the complexity of the service or system and number of relationship types defined to model the configuration structure, the mapping of CI relationships for a service or system can be a time consuming effort. A prioritization scheme will need to be developed for 'bundling' services and systems into work packages in order to manage the workload and allocate the resource more effectively.

Communication campaign
Implementation of the Configuration Management process will require involvement from most technical groups of an IT department. There must be a strong and highly visible communication campaign to provide information and encourage buy-in from all level of management and staff. This is essential to ensure full cooperation and participation from these groups and also prepare the rest of the organization for process rollout. A communication plan using a range of media, formats and channels of delivery should be developed to reach different audiences at different times throughout the life of the project.

3.3 Ongoing operation

The Support Center is one of the biggest end-users of the CMDB. It should work in close collaboration with the Configuration Management group to validate and audit CMDB accuracy and exceptions found. In addition, depending on the update policies of Configuration Management, the Support Center may also be responsible for updating and maintaining the currency of certain CI types in the CMDB.

3.3.1 Support Center Manager's role
Responsibilities and activities
- Continue to provide training to ensure Service Center staff is fully versed in using the Configuration Management tool and that they have a thorough understanding of how to use and interpret the relationships mapping between CIs for troubleshooting and impact analysis.
- Ensure sufficient resource is allocated for Configuration Management activities
- Review audit reports regularly to ensure that Support Center staff is updating CI attributes and their relationships when changes are made to the IT infrastructure
- Take corrective actions to address discrepancies found in audit reports
- Review process management reports to monitor compliance of Service Center staff in following the configuration process
- Ensure staff makes maximum use of the data stored in CMDB to make informed decisions when assessing impact for incidents, problems and change to the infrastructure and for analysis of service requests implementation
- For new systems and CI types under the control of the Support Center, provide guidance and review CI definition and relationships before population in the CMDB
- Assist the Configuration Manager in the definition and update of the Configuration Management plan by providing input and review
- Participate in process review initiatives to improve process
- Provide process management and KPI reports to senior management

Deliverables
- Training plan for staff
- Action plan to address discrepancies found in audit reports
- Configuration management plan for CIs under the control Service Center group
- Recommendations for continuous process improvements

Competencies required
- Influence and impact
- Team leadership
- Negotiation skills
- Listening and communication skills
- Information seeking

KPIs
- Percentage of CI types (under the control of Support Center) successfully audited
- Percentage of CI types recorded in the CMDB
- Improvement in incident resolution time for incidents that rely on configuration data
- Improvement in completion time of service requests that rely on configuration data
- All staff fully trained in Configuration Management process

3.3.2 Support Center Function's role
Responsibilities and activities
- Update or correct the CMDB as defined by Configuration Management policies and process.
- Make regular use of historic information in the CMDB to enable effective troubleshooting and timely addressing of service requests.
- Provide daily, weekly and monthly process management and KPI reports to Support Center Manager.
- Validate CMDB information about end-users and their associated CIs as part of the activities of recording end-user service calls.
- Perform a periodic 'bulk' audit of CMDB accuracy.

Deliverables
- Reports showing historic incidents related to CIs
- Listing of end-users and their associated CIs
- Reports showing compliance of CI updates
- Reports of CI updates performed by Support Center staff

Competencies required
- Attention to detail
- Customer service orientation
- Information seeking
- Achievement orientation

KPIs
Same as Support Center Manager's.

3.4 Optimization

3.4.1 The optimization process
According to ITIL, a process is operating at 'Optimized (CMM Level 5)' level when:
- the process enables alignment of business strategies and goals with that of IT
- the process is fully integrated into the culture of the organization
- the process is proactive and pre-emptive
- continuous improvement activities are established and operating as part of the process
- tools are designed to integrate with people, processes and technologies.

The process diagram in Figure 3.3 provides a high level view of the activities involved in the optimization process.

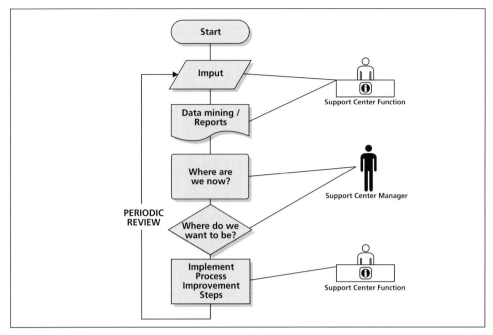

Figure 3.3 Optimization process

3.4.2 Support Center Manager's role
Responsibilities and activities
- Evaluate recommendations for process improvement from staff. Work with the Configuration Management process owner to make improvements.
- Evaluate recommendations for Configuration Management tools enhancement. Work with the technical specialist and Configuration Management process owner to make improvements.
- Identify opportunities to expand the use of the CMDB for capturing new CI attributes and relationships that could create value for the organization.
- Use information from the CMDB to support strategic planning (e.g. financial forecasting, technology refresh, new IT service development).
- Use information from the CMDB for service improvement initiatives (e.g. reduce cost related to the support of a troublesome application).
- Continue to champion the Configuration Management process and use of the tool to Support Center staff to embed a 'process-centric' mindset in the organization's culture.

Deliverables
- Continuous improvement plans
- New business and functional requirements for tool enhancements
- Reports to justify technology enhancement or new technology investments
- IT strategy plan that aligns with and supports the business plan

Competencies required
- Innovative thinking
- Strategic thinking
- Leadership
- Influence and impact
- Analytical thinking

KPIs
- Reduction in operating budget for the same number of IT services supported
- Increase in customer satisfaction score as measured by customer surveys not only in the areas of service delivery and in the planning and execution of activities to support business growth and transformation
- Improvement in quality targets

3.4.3 Support Center Function's role
Responsibilities and activities
- Identify inefficiencies in the process and propose recommendations for improvement to the Support Center Manager.
- Identify opportunities to improve the functionality of the Configuration Management tools to automate tasks for CMDB updates, reporting, validation or auditing.
- Work with customers and the Support Center Manager to design and implement new CI type templates in the Configuration Management tool; collect and populate data in the CMDB.
- Create reports for the Support Center Manager to support strategic planning and service improvement initiatives for the business.

Deliverables
- Business and functional requirements for tool enhancements
- Proposals for process improvement
- Reports of various kinds drawn from the CMDB to support Support Center Manager initiatives

Competencies required
- Innovative thinking
- Results-oriented
- Technical aptitude
- Customer service orientation

KPIs
Same as Support Center Manager

3.4.4 Future impact of this process on the Support Center

The relationships between business processes, services and IT infrastructure can be visually represented by integrating appropriate business service monitoring software tools with a well-managed CMDB. This capability enables the Support Center to monitor and respond to business relevant issues that are caused by IT infrastructure incidents. The ability to view business service alerts together with traditional IT system alerts provides the Service Center with more information to manage customers' service level targets and objectives more effectively.

3.5 Measurement, costing and management reporting

3.5.1 Implementing: benefits and costs
Why implement this process and what can be gained
Accurate accounting of the hardware, software, systems and service inventory and versions coupled with the maps of the relationships between physical CIs (i.e. hardware and software) and between these physical CIs to systems and services provides the following benefits:
- faster diagnosis and troubleshooting for incident recovery and root cause analysis for problem isolation.
- more accurate and timely information for planning activities; service/system availability calculation for Availability Management, risk analysis and contingency design for IT Service Continuity Management, performance and resource utilization analysis for Capacity Management.
- financial management process provides more accurate information for client billing.
- reduced cost of unused software licenses and avoidance of legal actions by third party software vendors due to over-usage of software.
- reduction in incidents caused by releases that used incorrect configuration data.
- reduced costs through taking opportunities for economies of scale in hardware purchase or lease renewal.

The above are just some of the many benefits attainable by the implementation of the Configuration Management process.

Cost elements for implementation
- Cost of hardware and software license for new tool
- Cost of technical consultant to implement and/or customize tool
- If an accurate inventory is not available, additional resources may be required for a short term to gather the inventory information for each type of CIs and input them into the CMDB
- Cost of temporary staff to substitute for full time staff who will be part of project team
- Cost of training staff before process rollout
- External Configuration Management process consultant

Making the business case to implement
Given the high number of virus attacks and security breaches occurring in the IT industry, it only takes one unmanaged and unaccounted PC to potentially bring down the entire business.

The cost of unproductive downtime due to this type of incident to the business is enough to justify the implementation of Configuration Management.

Management reporting
- Percentage of CIs, broken down by CI type, captured in the CMDB
- Percentage of services and systems with CI relationships established in the CMDB
- Percentage of CIs, broken down by CI type, with all their attributes fully defined in the CMDB

3.5.2 Ongoing operations
Cost elements for ongoing operations
- Maintenance cost of hardware and software license for new tool
- Cost of additional Configuration Management coordinator(s) and/or manager(s) to execute the process activities
- If system discovery tools are not integrated with the CMDB, additional temporary resources may need to be obtained to conduct a manual audit of CIs in the CMDB against CIs in actual used
- Cost of updating the process and procedures, based on periodic process review cycle, and retraining of staff based on new updates

Management reporting
- Percentage of CIs recorded in the CMDB that do not meet CI definition standards (i.e. naming convention)
- Percentage of changes implemented without updates made to the CMDB
- Percentage of CIs with association made to incident, problem and change as these events occur
- Number of CIs in various status categories
- Percentage of CIs with incorrect attributes or relationships

3.5.3 Optimization: benefits and costs
Why optimize this process and what can be gained?
Optimization of this process involves the efficient and effective execution of the process activities to ensure the CMDB is accurate and that the information captured in the CMDB is used to better align business and IT.

An up-to-date and accurate CMDB with all the necessary relationships established between service, systems and IT components puts the CMDB in a better position to provide the business with valuable information. For example, it is feasible to create business metrics and a service performance dashboard, with the right software tools, with data gathered from the underlining technology that allows customers to easily examine the impact of technical issues. When customers are presented with real-time information that they can understand, the business and its IT department can better manage and minimize impact of technology incidents, quickly divert resources to avert performance issues or simply display the status and health of the business service.

Cost elements for optimization
- Cost of new tools for real-time and proactive detection and reporting of alerts from the business service perspectiv
- Cost of resources to perform continuous improvement activities
- Cost of training

Management reporting
- Percentage of services with capabilities to display business metrics and dashboard
- Customer survey scores

3.5.4 Tools

Implementation

During the implementation phase of Configuration Management, identification of CIs and population of CIs into the CMDB are two key activities to prepare the CMDB for rollout. The inventory of CIs may be collected via system discovery tools or may reside in multiple sources such as spreadsheets, databases from other applications (i.e. Client Relationships Management system, email, HR system) or directory services (i.e. Active Directory, UNIX NIS). It is essential that the Configuration Management tool has the capability to import data through one of the following means:
- interface with adaptors/translators for vendor specific systems discovery tools
- accept character delimiter file or MS EXCEL file and convert the data via end-user definable mapping tables
- application Programming Interfaces (APIs) to map dissimilar data structures between two different databases
- interface with third party data mapping products

Ongoing operations

Once the data is populated into the CMDB, the effective use and management of the data to support all other IT Service Management processes depends on the update and reporting capabilities of the Configuration Management tool. Look for the following key functionalities when selecting a Configuration Management tool:
- access and update permission of CMDB definable by role based security, group based security and individual permissions
- creation/update/deletion of CIs and related information is auditable
- close integration with Incident, Problem, Change and Release Management tools
- capability to define CI relationships (i.e. peer to peer, parent-child) with no restrictions on number of levels in the hierarchy
- capability to customize end-user definable CI relationship types and attributes
- capability to define new versions of 'to-be' CIs and their relationships that exist in production while still preserving their current product definitions. A snapshot of a group of existing CIs and their relationships can be taken to and a new version of this grouping created with alterations to certain attributes and/or relationships. This provides the capability to conduct 'what-if' scenarios analysis or prepare for a new change request with the ability to fall back to previous CI definitions
- graphical representation of CIs and their relationships showing multiple tiers and allowing interactive selection of CI icon for drill down of detailed attribute information
- allow searching of CI by attributes.

Reporting

The reports from the Configuration Management tool are unlikely to meet all reporting requirements. Even if the tool does provide capabilities to create customized reports, these functions may not be adequate to produce advanced reports. The Configuration Management tool should have the capability to interface with other more advanced third party reporting tools through the use of ODBC drivers or generic SQL programming language. It is also desirable to have a Configuration Management tool built with a third party relational Database Management System (DBMS) with the entity relationship diagram of the CMDB documented as part of the technical documentation supplied with the tool.

Annex A3.1 Sample CI Classes and CI Types

A3.1.1 Physical CI

The table below lists examples of different physical CI Classes and associated CI Types. Depending on the scope and depth of Configuration Management within the organization the list may be expanded or reduced.

CI Class	CI Type
Computer	Mainframe Midrange Server Desktop Laptop PDA
Computing Device	Monitor Printer Modem Tape Drive Disk Array
Software	Application Operating System System Management Database Management System Middleware Database
Network	Data Circuit Voice Circuit
Network Device	Multi-slot Router Stack Router Brouter Switch
Appliance	Firewall SAN Disk Storage NAS Disk Storage
Facility	HVAC (Heating, Ventilation, Air Conditioning) Cabinet Electrical Power Unit Cable Tray UPS
Document	Process/Procedure Policy Technical Contract

A3.1.2 Logical CI

The table below lists examples of different logical CI Classes and associated CI Types. Depending on the complexity of the Configuration Management structure defined by your organization, the list may be expanded or reduced. The logical CIs fulfill two purposes: grouping for Services and Systems and grouping for virtual representation of physical CIs.

The table below lists the logical CI Classes and CI Types for the purpose of grouping Services and Systems.

CI Class	CI Type
Services	Technical System
	Professional Service
System	Business
	Infrastructure
Technology	Computer
	Computing Device
	Software
	Network
	Network Device
	Appliance
Other	Document
	Facility

The table below lists the logical CI Class and CI Types for the purpose of grouping virtual representation of physical CIs.

CI Class	CI Type
Cluster	Mainframe
	Server
	Storage
	Database
	Logical Partition

Annex A3.2 Configuration Structure Model

The basic configuration structure used to model services and their related systems and components is shown below. This four tier hierarchy model consists of logical CIs in the top three tiers while the physical CIs are represented in the fourth tier.

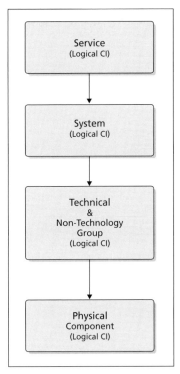

Figure 3.4 Configuration Structure Model

A3.2.1 Example Configuration Structure

The diagram below illustrates the use of logical and physical CI Classes and CI Types, as defined in Annex A3.1, to model the configuration structure for an email service. To simplify the illustration, not all the CIs for the email service are included in the diagram. This example shows the email service comprising of two different systems, Lotus Notes and MS Exchange. The MS Exchange system is modelled in more detail to include servers (e.g. msxapp01, msxapp02, mxsdbs01), software (e.g. MS Exchange, the Exchange database msxdbase01) and related documents and software licenses.

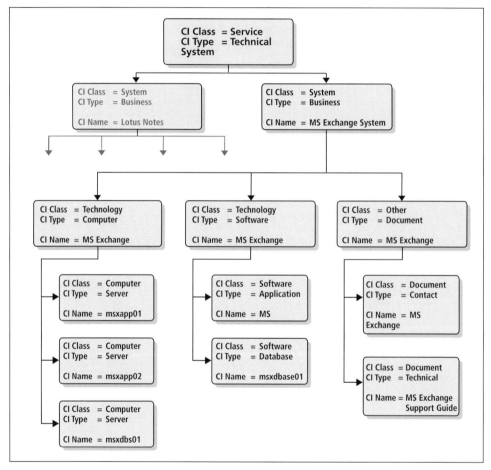

Figure 3.5 Example Configuration Structure

Annex A3.3 'As Is' Process Discovery Template

For each support group that manages acquisition, move/change and disposal of CIs, provide the following template to help them to gather the data necessary to assess the processes for managing their CIs.

Support Group Name : _____

I. Acquisition Process

1. Is this process documented?

   • Yes, provide the softcopy/hardcopy.

   • No

2. Is this process formalized within your group?

   • Yes, proceed to answer question 3, 4, 5, 6, 7

   • No, proceed to answer next process

3. Who is the owner of this process?

4. What percentage of the time does your group follow the formalized process?

   • Greater than 90% of the time

   • Between 90% to 70%

   • Between 70% to 50%

   • Less than 50%

5. Does this process update the CMDB?

   • No

   • Yes, Attributes only

   • Yes, Attributes and Relationships

6. List the CI Types governed by this process:

7. List the CI Types not governed by this process:

II. Move/Change Process

1. Is this process documented?

   • Yes, provide the softcopy/hardcopy.

   • No

2. Is this process formalized within your group?

   • Yes, proceed to answer question 3, 4, 5, 6

   • No, proceed to answer next process

3. Who is the owner of this process?

4. What percentage of the time does your group follow the formalized process?

   • Greater than 90% of the time

   • Between 90% to 70%

   • Between 70% to 50%

   • Less than 50%

5. Does this process update the CMDB?

   • No

   • Yes, Attributes only

   • Yes, Attributes and Relationships

6. List the CI Types governed by this process:

7. List the CI Types not governed by this process:

III. Disposal Process

1. Is this process documented?

   • Yes, provide the softcopy/hardcopy.

   • No

2. Is this process formalized within your group?

   • Yes, proceed to answer question 3, 4, 5, 6, 7

   • No

3. Who is the owner of this process?

4. What percentage of the time does your group follow the formalized process?

   • Greater than 90% of the time

   • Between 90% to 70%

   • Between 70% to 50%

   • Less than 50%

5. Does this process update the CMDB?

   • No

   • Yes, Attributes only

   • Yes, Attributes and Relationships

6. List the CI Types governed by this process:

7. List the CI Types not governed by this process:

Annex A3.4 'As Is' CI Inventory Assessment Template

Complete the template below for each CI Class and its associated CI Types. Refer to Annex A3.1 for lists of CI Class and CI Type.

	CI Type: a	CI Type: b	CI Type: c	CI Type: d	CI Type: e	CI Type: f
CI Class : _____						
Approximately how many CIs are in production?						
List the location where the CIs are installed. *(location a)* *(location b)* *(location c)* *(location d)* *(location e)* All of the above						
Is this CI type governed by a formalized move/add/change/dispose process? (Y/N)						
Is this CI type recorded in a repository (i.e. database, spreadsheet, etc)? (Y/N) If the answer is "Y", please complete questions 5 & 6						
Provide the name and location of the repository.						
In terms of percentage, how accurate is the inventory in the repository compare to the production environment? greater than 90% between 90% to 70% between 70% to 50% less than 50%						
Is an automated discovery tool used to collect the inventory data? (Y/N)						

Annex A3.5 Sample CI Relationships Diagram

A Quick Reference Guide should be developed to illustrate various combinations of CI to CI relationships. This will help Support staff to quickly determine and understand the relationships that a CI may have with other CIs. For each CI type, define all possible relationships it can have with other CI types. The example below shows all possible relationships a server CI (located in the circle) can have with other CI types, including another redundant server for contingency purposes. Notice the association is not only limited to physical CIs; relationship to logical CIs (e.g. System xyz) is also shown.

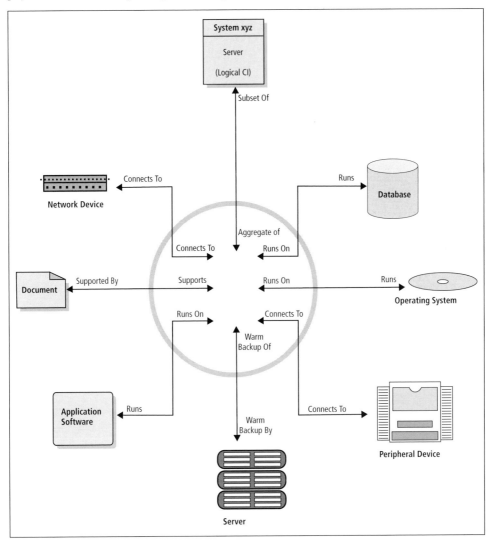

Figure 3.6 Sample CI Relationship Diagram

Annex A3.6 ARCI Matrix Template

To use the ARCI Matrix template, list all the process activities (as shown in the High Level Process flow diagram) in the first column of the Matrix. Then list all possible functional groups (e.g. Service Desk, Desktop Support, Server Support, Network Support, etc) that may be involved with the process activities. For each process activity, place one or more of the following letters in the column of the functional group if the group is engaged with the process :

A - Accountable for the process
R - Responsible to execute the process activity
C - Consulted for more information before the process activity is executed
I - Informed, either before or after the process activity is executed
(Note: 'A' only appears under the Process Owner column because the Process Owner has full accountability for the process.)

Process Activity	Process Owner	Functional Group : a	Functional Group : b	Functional Group : c	Functional Group : d	Functional Group : e
Process Activity 1	A					
Process Activity 2	A					
Process Activity 3	A					
Process Activity 4	A					
Process Activity 5	A					
Process Activity 6	A					
Process Activity 7	A					
Process Activity 8	A					
Process Activity 9	A					
Process Activity 10	A					
Process Activity 11	A					

A3.6.1 Example ARCI Matrix

#	Actions	Configuration Manager	Configuration Coordinator	Tool Administrator	Production Support Group Managers	PS Groups / Client FLS	Service Desk	Change Management Group	Senior Management
A	Procurement (Acquisition)								
B	SC&D Management								
C	Incident Management								
D	Problem Management								
E	Capacity Management								
F	Service Continuity Management								
1	Does template exist?	A				R	R		
2	Notify Configuration Coordinator	A	(I)			R	R		
3	Define CI/CI component/attribute structure and business model relationships	A/R	R	R/C	R/C	R/C			
4	Authorization by Configuration Manager	A/R	R	I	I	I			
5	Change Management	C	R/C	R/C				A/R	
6	Notify Configuration Coordinator	A	(I)	R					
7	Register new CI record (inventory, license information (CI status: Received)	A			R/I	I	I		
8	Determine product catagorization and attributes	A			R/I	I	I		
9	Storage required?	A			C				
10	Storage (CI Status: In inventory)	A			I	I	I		
11	High or low risk change?	A			R/C			C	
12	Process RFC				R/C			A/R	
13	Determine technical peer and service relationships	A	R		R			I	
14	Assess impact	C	R		R/C	C	C	A/R	
15	Determine technical peer and service relationships	A	R		R			I	
16	Approve change				R/(I)	(I)	(I)	A/R	
17	Coordinate, install/implement				R/(I)			A/R	
18	Notify Configuration Coordinator		(I)		R/I	I	I	A/R	
19	Verify/update all attributes and associations for new/existing CI record	A/R	R		R/C/I	R/I	R/I	R/I	
20	High or low risk change?	A			R/C			C	
21	Produce CI modification report; add to CI status report	A			R/(I)	(I)	(I)	(I)	(I)
21	Configuration Management meeting: validate record modification	A/R	R	C	R	I	I	R/I	
23	Post change review	R		I	R			A/R	I

Bibliography

Best Practice for Service Support, Various authors, The Stationery Office, 2000

Best Practice for Planning to Implement Service Management, Various authors, The Stationery Office, 2002

Gartner Consulting, *Key Ingredients of the IT Service Desk,* September 2001

Troy DuMoulin, Pink Elephant Inc., *ITIL Configuration Management - Planning and Implementation* (White Paper), 2002

Hewlett-Packard Company, *Activating Configuration Management In An IT Organization,* 2001

David Chiu & Dunlop Tsui, *Modeling the Enterprise IT Infrastructure - An IT Service Management Approach,* 2004

Chapter 4:
Change Management

4.1 Overview

4.1.1 Description

The purpose of the Change Management process is to ensure that all governed changes are effectively managed, thus reducing or eliminating disruptions to business services (Incidents) resulting from change. In addition, the Change Management process functions as an enabler for effectively and efficiently delivering IT changes to meet the needs of the business. There must be a considered approach to assessment of risk and business continuity, resource requirements and costs. This considered approach is essential to maintain a proper balance between the need for change against the impact of the change. It is particularly important that Change Management processes have high visibility and open channels of communication in order to promote smooth transitions when changes take place. The main components of Change Management are described below.

Change Control

The goal of Change Control is to ensure that all changes are controlled, including the submission, analysis, decision-making, approval, implementation and post implementation of the change. It is important to understand that Change Management is a process, and Change Control is a procedure. Each change needs good Change Control, but the Change Management process oversees all of the changes. It is possible to have good Change Control and still have failures - because there is no Change Management. For instance, different IT teams have good control over their own independent changes, but there is no communication between the teams. The result could be one change having a detrimental effect on the other change. Standardized procedures are required to ensure the consistent delivery of quality changes.

Change Management simultaneously manages the lifecycle and status of many controlled changes, because Change Control is a component of Change Management.

Release Management

Release Management is the process for controlling all software Configuration Items within the organization. It is costly and ineffective to have multiple copies of the same software and it is illegal to have unlicensed software. Proper management is required for internally developed software development and for the installation and support of all the organization's internal and external software products.

Effective software control and distribution (SC&D) involves the creation of a Definitive Software Library (DSL), into which the master copies of all software are stored. It is from here that control and release are managed. The DSL consists of a physical store and a logical store. The physical store is where the master copies of all software media are stored. This tends to be software that has been provided from an external source. The logical store is the index of all software and releases, versions, etc. highlighting where the physical media can be located. The logical store may also be used for the storage of software developed within the organization.

SC&D procedures include the management of the software Configuration Items and their distribution and implementation into a production environment. This will involve the definition of a release program suitable for the organization, the definition of how version control will be implemented and the procedures surrounding how software will be built, released, and audited.

Configuration Management Database (CMDB)
It is essential to have a complete CMDB in place in order to properly manage changes to the infrastructure. An incomplete repository will allow change management mistakes to occur because of missing or faulty knowledge. A Configuration Item (CI) is a component of the IT infrastructure and is subject to Change Control. This includes hardware, software, documentation, and agreements including Service Level Agreements (SLAs), Underpinning Contracts (UCs) and Operational Level Agreements (OLAs) - see Chapter 8 for more information about these agreements. This information held may be in a variety of formats - textual, diagrammatic, photographic, etc., but is essentially a data map of the physical reality of the IT infrastructure. A CMDB contains details about the attributes and history of each CI and details of the important relationships between CIs.

Choosing the level to which an organization details the CMDB is a frequent dilemma for IT departments. The level must be appropriate to manage changes in the organization, but some selection criteria include:
- information that relates multiple CIs
- information in the path from common problems and incidents to End User services
- information that illustrates relationships so that impact can be understood
- information that is not recoverable from system management tools in a simple way if the CI is operating partially or not operating at all
- information that is recommended by the organization's Operations and Support experts.

4.1.2 Relationships to other processes
Change Management is one of the five Service Support processes identified in ITIL. The Change Management process can be deployed independently of other processes, but is far more effective when deployed in conjunction with other processes. Key relationships exist between the Change Management process and the Release Management, the Project Management process and the Configuration Management processes.

The Change Management process integrates with these and other support processes:
- Incident Management; Problem Management; Change Management; Release Management; Configuration Management; Knowledge Management
- Project Management; Change Management; Release Management; Configuration Management; Knowledge Management
(See Annex A4.1 for how these support processes work together.)

In addition, the Change Management process interfaces with those of ITIL Service Delivery, such as Service Level Management and Availability Management.

Before a planned change is authorized, it must be reviewed and authorized by:
- Capacity Management
- Availability Management
- Service Continuity Management
- Service Level Management
- Financial Management.

The ITIL framework is non-vendor and non-tool/platform specific; however there are alternatives. ISO9000, COBIT, eTOM, Balanced Scorecards, Six Sigma and the Capability Maturity Model (CMM-I) all offer guidance and quality frameworks for effective IT Management.

CMM is a framework established to guide software developers through the challenges of creating solutions that are truly aligned with business requirements. Process maturity can be improved by means of techniques in the Capability Maturity Model that identify the current state of software development processes and how to achieve maturity improvements.

ITIL is a framework that has been developed to guide IT managers through the challenges of managing their IT infrastructure. Total Quality Management techniques (e.g. ISO 9001) show process improvements in efficiencies (e.g. costs) and effectiveness (e.g. process throughput). The ISO9000 and ITIL combination is in fact a very powerful one. The primary difference between the two is that while ISO9000 requires structured processes to be in place, ITIL actually defines those structured processes for the IT environment. Both ISO and ITIL methodologies are in a state of continual update and improvement, and both endeavor to reflect the current nature of business environments throughout the world.

These frameworks are very often complementary, rather than mutually exclusive. There may be wider organizational quality initiatives into which Change Management must fit, and aspects of ITIL can be an integral part when combined with other frameworks.

4.1.3 Service Desk integration
Integration with the Service Desk function is necessary as modifications to staffing capacity (Workforce Management), support documents, and processes may be required as a result of changes.

(See Annex A4.2, A4.3 and A4.4 for how the Support/Service Desk, Incident Management and Problem Management work together with Change Management.)

4.1.4 Key inputs and outputs to the process

Description	Source	Importance
INPUTS		
Business requirements	Business	High
Capacity review	Capacity Management	Medium
Availability review	Availability Management	Medium
Service Continuity review	Service Continuity Mgmt	High
Service Level Agreement	Service Level Mgt	High
Architecture Plan	Architecture Mgmt	Medium

Service Support Requirements	Service Desk	High
Security requirements	Information Security	High
Release Plan	Release Management	Medium
Resource requirements	Workforce Management	Medium
OUTPUTS		
Forward Schedule of Change	Change Management	Medium
Change Authorization/Approval	Change Management	High
Configuration Item Updates	Configuration Management	High
User/Customer acceptance	Business	High

4.1.5 Possible problems and issues

As with the initiation of all new processes, there will be numerous barriers, problems and issues. Below are some key areas of concern.

Possible problems

Lack of management support: senior management needs to fully support the deployment of the change management process. Without such support, change initiators will circumvent the process and continue with business as usual. This will diminish the effectiveness of the process and inhibit the achievement of success.

Lack of process definition: in order to achieve success, it must first be defined. It is essential to establish a mission/purpose statement for the Change Management Process. Once the purpose is clearly articulated, it can be communicated throughout the organization. *(See Sample Purpose with Mission Statement in Annex A4.6)*

Lack of process buy-in: process acceptance requires communicating the process and its purpose throughout the organization. Process stakeholders generally view process as being bureaucratic and inefficient. It is critical that stakeholders' needs are incorporated into the process. If there is no perceived or real value in the process, acceptance will not be gained.

Lack of information: there must be information about the business service and the supporting IT infrastructure to be able to make an effective assessment about the impact and risk associated with a change. This information should be available in a CMDB, but typically organizations have this information stored informally or formally in various pockets. Because the configuration information is often distributed and not centralized, or access to the information is not centralized, the impact and risk associated with changes is very difficult to predict.

Absence of process integration: Change Management as a stand-alone process can have a profound impact on the availability and integrity of business services, but a far greater impact will be felt once other processes are initiated and integrated as well.

Lack of process automation: once the Change Management process is designed and implemented, it should be automated to increase process efficiency. The extent of automation will depend on the volume of change activity in the organization. A tool should aggregate the requests and changes so that they can be handled as a single group. Other functions can help logging sequencing, staging, tracking and correlating the information. Automating the change lifecycle brings the process, the activities that area generated by the process and the data that is changed by the process all together in one place.

Lack of resources (funding/staffing): key to execution is the availability and assignment of qualified resources, whether through headcount or full time equivalents (FTE). Even with senior management support, buy-in from all stakeholders, CMDB information, good process definition, integration and automation, an understaffed resource pool will not be successful in delivering quality Change Management.

Absence of organization guidance: a key part of managing changes in IT is to have a Change Advisory Board (CAB). It is an integral part of a defined Change Management process, and is designed to balance the need for change with the need to minimize inherent risks. The CAB is responsible for oversight of all changes in the production environment. The CAB is tasked with reviewing and prioritizing requested changes, monitoring the change process and providing managerial feedback. It coordinates requests from management, customers, end-users and IT. The changes may involve hardware, software, configuration settings, patches, etc. Both customers and project/release managers should be members of the CAB. A decision made solely by IT may fail to recognize the concerns of other groups such as Accounting. A CAB provides the multiple perspectives necessary to ensure proper decision-making.

Lack of customer involvement and end-user acceptance: the customer should be actively involved in the change lifecycle. This will ensure customer testing and acceptance before a change. After changes have been implemented, customers need to validate that all of their requirements are being met and formally accept the change.

Quality issues
Ineffective/immature release/project management: the success of the change management process is reliant on the effectiveness of the Quality Assurance process incorporated in the Release/Project Management process. The likelihood for change success diminishes if ineffective test plans, use cases, scripts, and implementation plans do not exist. This will result in end-users encountering problems and initiating calls to service and support. Since a goal of the Change Management process is to minimize service calls and service disruptions, Quality Assurance for releases and projects is of critical importance.

Lack of CMDB information: quality will be adversely affected if the CMDB is inaccurate or has missing information, which will result in poor decision-making about proposed changes. Quality will be adversely affected if the CI level is not adequately detailed in the CMDB or fails to identify dependencies and relationships. The CMDB should have three levels of known or discovered information - physical, configuration and relationship.

Lack of integration with Service Delivery processes: it is not practicable to implement all aspects of ITIL Service Support at one time (Big Bang). This means that not all the required process inputs will be available when the Change Management process is initiated. There will be information quality issues where key process input areas are absent. It is difficult, if not impossible, to assess the impact of a change on business service availability, capacity and continuity if supporting processes do not exist. This increases the likelihood of problems resulting from the deployment of production changes and increases the likelihood of not meeting the service level expectations of the customer in regard to capacity, availability and service continuity. Representatives from IT Service Level Management, Capacity Management, Availability Management and Service Continuity Management should be included in the CAB. These representatives would be made aware of the impact of changes on the user community, as data is collected over time, as the remainder of the processes are deployed and as these processes mature.

Security issues
Lack of inclusion in planning: information security is a critical function of the IT organization. It is essential to include information security in the authorization of all changes. This ensures that security is accounted for in the development of the change. A representative from the Information Security Group should be included in the CAB.

4.2 Implementation

The Change Manager (who may be the Support Center Manager) is responsible for the implementation of the Change Management process. The organization has acknowledged that control over IT changes is necessary to minimize the likelihood of disruption, and that good change management can provide substantial value. While there will be some change errors at this stage since not all other IT processes and supporting infrastructure are in place, steps can begin to implement the basics for proper change management.

4.2.1 The implementation process
Education:
• knowledge of the Change Management process is a key to the success of process implementation. There must be a clear understanding of the goals of Change Management and the key process that it integrates with. This knowledge can be gained through reading, attending industry meetings, or through formal training. If implementing ITIL, it is recommended that the Change Manager attains ITIL Foundation Level Certification as well as practitioner level certification in Change Management.

Define process purpose/mission:
• create a mission and purpose statement to articulate clearly the desired results of implementing the process.
(See Sample Mission/Purpose Statement in Annex A4.6)

Ensure the support of senior management:
• it is critical to communicate the process purpose to senior management and ensure their buy-in.

Create a Change Management policy:
• clearly define the scope of the process and the guidelines for planning and implementation of a change.
(See Sample Change Management Policy in Annex A4.7)

Process definition:
• when knowledge of the Change Management process has been obtained, process definition can begin.

Procedure definition:
• after the process flow is documented and agreed to, Change Control procedures and support documents can be developed for the phases of the Change Management Lifecycle. These will include work instructions, forms, checklists, and communication goals.
(See Change Management Lifecycle Diagram and Key Checkpoints in Annex A4.8)

Establish process scope:
• determine the scope of governance for the Change Management Process. This will ensure that stakeholders know when they expected to follow the process.

Ensure an accurate and up-to-date CMDB exists:
• an accurate and complete CMDB that is integrated into the change process and the Service Desk tool provides the CI information, relationships to services and thereby enables impact assessment for changes.

Gain buy-in:
• again, validate buy-in from senior management. In addition, seek feedback from key process stakeholders to ensure that their needs are considered and that they are included in the planning process.

Implementation planning:
• there must be formal project planning to deliver the successful implementation of the process, with a project manager assigned to oversee the implementation.

Determine the budget:
• after the initial planning is complete; establish a budget for implementing the process. This should include the implementation costs and the on-going support costs. If necessary, forecast the Return on Investment (ROI) and establish metrics for performance against plan (this role should be filled by a project management professional).

Seek budget approval:
• present the business case to senior management to gain approval for the initiative.

Communicate:
• communicate the implementation plan and the purpose of the process to key stakeholders. Again, seek their feedback to ensure that their needs are incorporated in the process and that you have their ongoing support.

Implementation:
• the rollout of the Change Management process should be phased so that modifications to the process can be made as needed before rollout across the organization (this mitigates risk and increases the likelihood for success). Organizations should consider phasing by

application, by geographic location or by line of business. Select an area that is already working well in manual mode. This indicates that its current processes are well understood; it will be easier to monitor the transition to new ways of working and identify anomalies.

4.2.2 Support Center Manager's role
Responsibilities and activities
The Support Center Manager should actively partner with the Change Manager during the implementation phase and establish regular communications for joint success. In many organizations it is unwanted changes that most affect the quality of Support Center services; thus this partnership is the single best opportunity for the Support Manager to remove existing errors in the support environment and best support the business. The Support Center Manager role in the Change Management implementation process is to assure insight into the support environment by providing the Change Manager with post-change incident statistics, outage and problem information. The Support Center Manager participates in the Change Advisory Board.

4.2.3 Change Manager's role
(Change Manager may also be the Support Center Manager)
Responsibilities and activities
When changes to the IT environment are made, all too often the unpredictable results of those changes are failure or degradation of critical business services. The culprit of business service failures - some estimates are as high as 80% - is typically traced back to unmanaged changes and configurations in the IT environment. The Change Manager must have the authority and accountability to create an effective change management function.

The Change Manager is responsible for defining, validating, and maintaining the change process, as well as overall monitoring, measuring, reporting and operations:
* chairing the CAB
* raising and recording changes *(See Sample Change Status Report Used in CAB Meeting in Annex A4.9)*
* assessing impact, cost, benefit and risk of proposed changes
* developing business justifications for change and obtaining approval
* managing and coordinating change implementation
* monitoring and reporting on the change implementations
* responsible for final decision and disposition of changes
* responsible for defining metrics.

4.2.4 Support Center Function's role
The Support Center function does not play a role in the implementation of the Change Management process. There is process integration after the rollout of the process, however. Support Center staff should be trained in the Change Management process. To be successful, all members of the Support Center must know which business processes they support, who their customers are and the expected end result. This establishes the foundation needed for a clear set of objectives and common understanding of the scope and depth of the team's involvement and responsibilities in post change activities. The Support Center function provides service delivery through established channels (which may be multiple service

channels: telephone, email, web interface) and is responsible for:
- contact ownership (first, second and third level) of all tickets related to changes
- logging, prioritization, tracking, and correlation of tickets associated with changes
- participation in the CAB.

Deliverables
- Business needs are understood
- Objectives, goals and deliverables are clearly defined
- Change processes are defined and documented
- Change management process is communicated, implemented, and accepted by all stakeholders

Competencies required
- Leadership
- Initiative
- Analytical skills
- Process expertise
- Interpersonal and communication skills

KPIs
- Process acceptance
- Timely implementation
- Desired results (compared to baseline)

4.2.5 Other key roles and functions in the implementation process

Process implementation sponsor - as with all process implementations, there must be a sponsor to represent the project and to help to remove barriers as the implementation progresses. This person must have credibility in the organization and possess the authority to make decisions.

Project manager - this role is responsible for assisting in initiating the project, establishing a project plan, executing, controlling and closing the project. The project manager is also responsible for providing status updates at all key milestones.

Human Resources - a representative from HR is valuable to assist in the creation of job descriptions, to aid in establishing compensation packages and to ensure role alignment within the organization. They may also play a significant role in identifying internal candidates for newly created roles.

Training - an internal training team can provide support for selecting the appropriate ITIL training provider and for handling the logistics for the training.

Purchasing - with the guidance of the purchasing department, they may be able to negotiate special training rates with the vendors.

Applications Development - experts from the internal applications development teams can provide assistance in selecting Change Management process software. In addition, the internal operations/hardware support team can help with hardware requirements associated with the software packages under consideration. It is important to discuss all software products being considered with the other Service Support and delivery groups to ensure that product integration between processes is easily facilitated. Ideally, the call tracking tool should accommodate the change component.

Business Support Liaison (or Business Systems Manager) - the function of this role is to represent the line of business to the Change Manager. This person clearly understand the needs of the business, and all future planned initiatives, and helps in communicating and translating technical terms into business terms for the line of business.

4.2.6 Planning for implementation
Steps to take
1. Gain process and product expertise
   - attend training and/or ITIL foundation training classes level training (if required)
   - refer to the Change Management Chapter in ITIL Service Support
   - survey customers on expectations/deliverables from CM process (what is in it for them?) *(See Sample Stakeholder Goals in Annex A4.10)*
   - survey other support groups to understand their needs and expectations
   - create project charter and gain approval from customer and sponsor
   - create project plan and determine resources required and timelines
   - gain support for plan
   - assemble project team and hold start-up meeting
   - identify implementation risks
   - determine implementation success criteria.

2. Establish communication plan

3. Groups to contact (involve)
   - business service customers/owners
   - IT support groups (service desk, Configuration Management, release management and problem management)
   - project management
   - senior IT managers
   - IT service delivery groups (Availability Management, Capacity Management, IT Service Continuity Management, and Financial Management).

Necessary resources and relationships
Potential change initiators:
- Application Development
- Storage Management
- Hardware Management
- Network Management
- Information Security
- databases
- facilities
- Project Management group
- Release Management group
- Problem Management group
- Incident Management group
- Configuration Management group
- Service Level Management group
- Capacity Management
- Availability Management
- IT Service Continuity Management
- Financial Management

Necessary information and data
Pre implementation process assessment (baseline)
- Process scope
- Volume of changes
- Nature of changes (classification) *(See Sample Change Classification Options in Annex A4.11)*
- Risk classification *(See Sample Risk Classification in Annex A4.12)*
- Application portfolio
- Critical system identification
- CMDB including relationships
- SLA and OLA information
- Change windows *(See Sample Maintenance Window in Annex A4.13)*
- Freeze windows

Measurements that should be in place
- Progress to plan
- The project cost - earned value analysis (the physical work accomplished plus the authorized budget for the work, compared to the amount of the work planned)

Resource commitment and automation guidelines
The implementation of a functional Change Management process requires full-time effort from the following resources, and may involve considerably more resources for very large organizations:
- Implementation Leader (Change Manager) - responsible for gaining organization acceptance and leading the implementation team; ITIL training if needed
- Project Manager - works closely with the implementation leader to manage the delivery of the process implementation

- Process Specialist - develops process documentation consistent with the agreed to processes and procedures
- Process Support Specialist - responsible for support tool implementation and reporting and metrics development.

Automating the change process varies widely in time and cost depending on the size of the organization (end-user community), and the scope of governance (volume of changes). There are a number of tools that assist with Change Management. These are priced and targeted to the needs and size of the organization - small, medium or enterprise level.

The needs of the organization must be identified before selecting a tool; they drive the required Change Management capabilities. Tools to automate Change Management vary in functionality, adaptability, scalability and price. An appropriate match for your organization can be made by balancing costs and required functionality. However, it cannot be overstated that an adequate CMDB is essential as the base for decision-making for all changes. It would also be most advantageous if the call/ticket tracking tool automatically interfaces with the Change Management function. Some differences in tools will include:

- level of asset and financial management that supports full asset life cycle process, including discovery (physical, configuration and relationship)
- ability to support the ITIL framework for Change Management, and intersect with other core processes (Incident, Problem, Configuration Management and CMDB)
- integration with network and systems management products
- multi-platform support
- multi-language support
- built-in approval process and full audit capability.

Small organizations need an attractively priced product that is feature-rich, very easy to install and requires almost no maintenance. These organizations generally have about 500 or fewer employees, and perhaps three to eight analysts, but no more than fifteen concurrent analysts and administrators. ITIL processes can be applied in all sizes of organizations. The principles - or framework - are still the same. Small organizations should consider support for the core processes of Incident, Problem, Change and Configuration Management - and can manage their change environment according to accepted best practice.

Medium sized organizations range from 500 to 2,500 employees and may not be based in a single geographic location. This makes it more difficult to manage the IT infrastructure and requires remote administration. Medium sized organizations may outsource some commoditized activities. In addition to basic time-based performance tracking to help meet service levels, medium sized organizations need asset inventory and tracking to identify, record, control, modify and remove IT assets. Their needs include support for the core processes of Incident, Problem, Change, and Configuration Management, plus a more robust Change Control process. Change Control consolidates and supports standardized methods and procedures for efficiently handling change, minimizing the impact of change related incidents on service quality and improving the organization's operations. These organizations require a tool to track detailed asset information that is available for use by the service desk. It is not uncommon for the change management evaluation phase to take three to six months, followed by the change management implementation phase taking an additional six months to a year.

Enterprise organizations range from 2,500 employees to very complex global environments, with multiple language support and much higher scalability needs. In these organizations, maintaining service quality at committed service levels while continually changing the underlying IT infrastructure presents an enormous challenge. Needs for enterprise level organizations include automatically tracking detailed asset data that is available for use by the service desk; robust time-based, availability, threshold- and event-monitoring; Service Level Management including the ability to assess the cost of service; extensive Asset and Financial Management that supports the full asset life-cycle process and provides detailed asset information in support of other Service Management processes.

Enterprise level organizations require Change Management tools that facilitate business justification, financial and organizational impact, risk assessment, and support for the full change life cycle process. They will also require a CMDB that automatically gathers and consolidates all IT infrastructure data into one central data repository. These organizations may also apply Business Service Management (BSM) principles - focusing on a clear understanding of which business services are dependent on the IT components being changed. For enterprises, the change management evaluation and implementation may span one or two years.

Another variable that must be considered is socializing; training and communications required guaranteeing acceptance and adherence to the new Change Management processes. It is not unheard of for a new Change Management sponsor who is receiving inadequate sponsorship to stop the project, regroup and gain sufficient sponsorship before proceeding.

4.2.7 Implementing key process activities: hints and tips
What to implement first
- Evaluate the current state ('as is').
- Create mission/purpose statement - we must know where we are going! It is helpful for organizations to define their mission and their purpose, both for the end-user customer base and as a team building exercise for the IT Change group. After defining a set of statements that clearly articulate the way the Change Management function wants to relate to those it affects, publish the Mission Statement/Purpose to everyone. Post it on the wall, email it to everyone, put it on the organization's intranet. Review the mission statement/purpose periodically, especially when significant overall business changes have taken place (acquisitions, downsizing, or new directions in business objectives), and revise and reissue the statements. *(See Annex A4.6)*
- Define the 'to be' process (include emergency change process). If a current process exists, document it. Then document the desired state for the process ('to be'). *(See Sample Emergency, Non-Emergency Guidelines in Annex A4.14)*
- Establish a Change Management policy. To define the scope of the process, change the standards for submission of changes and change ownership. *(See Annex A4.7)*
- Determine the change review process. Establish information standards. What information is required to assess a proposed change? What logistical information is required?

- Create Change Request Submission Process and forms - these forms are vehicles for submitting proposed changes, and documenting change deliverables. A standard should be established to ensure consistency in the information being submitted. *(See Sample Change Request Form in Annex A.4.15 and Sample Change Deliverables Checklist in Annex A.4.16)*
- Define the change approval process. What are the criteria for approving a change? These will vary, depending on the types of change that are being managed. *(See Sample Standard Change Request Approval Criteria for CAB Form in Annex A4.17)*
- Define the post implementation review process. How do we measure success? Standards for success must be understood so that opportunities for improvement can be identified and so that there is a method for verifying success.
- Create and communicate a Forward Schedule of Change and a Change Calendar. Creating a change schedule is a vital part of operational communication. This Forward Change Schedule provides a way for all groups to see and plan their other activities in the calendar year, as well as for monitoring successful changes. All support groups should share this information, and it should be readily available - such as on the intranet. *(See Sample Forward Schedule of Change Form in Annex A4.18)*
- Automate the process, sub-processes, and procedures.

Little things that always work
- Start with a controlled scope of governance with a group that accepts the new change process.
- Keep the process simple (no automation) so that small wins can be achieved and so that the process can be modified quickly to accommodate the needs of the stakeholders. It is better to achieve a smaller success than to take on too much and fail.
- Communicate progress and success of process - this should be ongoing throughout the implementation.
- Do not be afraid to admit when the process is not working - be honest! Be flexible, versatile and adaptable.
- Ensure that there is a purpose for each step in the process. If you do not know why you are doing something, ask why. If there is not a good reason, challenge the necessity of the task. This is ongoing.
- Include process stakeholders in the improvement process. The Change Manager is the process owner, but it is important to pay attention to what customers, end-users and stakeholders have to say. They are the reason for implementing the process in the first place.

Little things that deliver big returns
- Have a defined process purpose that is understood and accepted. Ensuring that the process implementation team and all key stakeholders agree to the purpose of the implementation is of utmost importance. There should be no doubt as to why the initiative is being pursued.
- Listen to the process stakeholders. Part of effective communication is listening. Listen to your stakeholders, as they are a valuable source of information and a necessary ally if success is to be achieved. Do not implement and deploy the process without active participation by stakeholder groups. The project manager must engage all stakeholders.
- Share success. Share the success of the process implementation throughout the organization. Include even the most remotely associated resources with success. The more success is shared, the more organizational acceptance and compliance will be gained.

- Challenge the status quo. You will hear many times over that someone has tried an initiative similar to yours, only to fail. You must insist that your implementation team let the failures of the past go. They should learn from past experience but should not see it as an indicator of future results.
- Provide training. Whether on tools, processes, technical or soft skills, training brings great value and is often underused as a success factor. Training, like documentation, is viewed as 'nice to have' rather than essential. Often projects are implemented without having individuals adequately trained to support them post-launch.
- Automate. Automation of your defined and successful process, sub-processes, procedures and performance management reports will make a big difference to effectiveness.

Little things that always get forgotten
- Documentation updates: documentation is often left until the process is ready to be implemented, because it is not viewed as being part of the project. It is, however, critical to the success of the project as it provides a means of communicating and supporting the process in a consistent way.
- Document control: an index of the policies should be in a controlled location, complete with adequate document control, including when and by whom they were approved, reviewed and last issued.
- Process/solution/tool training: tool training, especially combined with process training can greatly enhance compliance with the change process. It combines the 'how' with the 'what' and reinforces the learning retention so often lost when time separates the two activities.
- Continual communication: without effective communication, no one will know the process exists and their need to comply with the process. Communicate to your stakeholders at all key stages of the implementation. Establish a communication plan as part of the overall project plan and maintain communication throughout the project. Build excitement and continual momentum for the process implementation!
- Celebrate success: celebrate your small successes. As hurdles are overcome and milestones achieved, celebrate. These do not have to be big, formal celebrations. Sometimes an email recognizing the event or verbal congratulations is all that is required.
- Recognition/achievement: since projects are often viewed as being complete once they are released to production, recognition is often overlooked. Frequently project managers and other resources are quickly allocated to other initiatives. This does not provide the opportunity for celebration. This is a critical step as it officially brings closure to the project implementation and provides an opportunity for all project team members to share in the project team's success.

4.2.8 Key process activities
Step-by-step prescriptive implementation guidance for each activity
Create a Change Management Process Lifecycle *(See Annex A4. 8)*

Develop Change Request Intake Procedure
- Establish change governance
- Determine change information required
- Change submission form (automated v. manual)
- A manual process should be established and managed first. When the process is fine tuned,

consider automating the process to improve efficiency. All newly submitted change should have a status of 'New'.

Change Request Review Procedure
- Changes with a status of 'New' should be reviewed by the Change Management group.
- Establish Change Classification - (remember change state classification will vary in different organizations - the following are sample organization status classifications).
- Information review for completeness - review the Change Request. If incomplete information is provided, refuse the request and advise the submitter.
- Information accuracy review - if inaccurate data is received (proposed date, incorrect asset or device, etc., refuse the request and advise the submitter.
- Change Acceptance - upon review of the proposed change, if information is complete and accurate, the change manager accepts the change. The status of the change should indicate that it is 'Awaiting CAB Review'.

Change Review (CAB) - Authorization
- Risk assessment - assess risk of change based on established assessment criteria *(See Annex A4.12)*
- Impact assessment - change impact assessment should be reviewed based on the potential disruption to service caused by the change
- Change conflict assessment - determine if the proposed change conflicts with a previously scheduled change or a planned business activity (marketing campaign, financial planning cycle, other activity).
- Capacity assessment - gain input from the capacity management group to assure that the proposed change will not have a negative impact on the current services and that the infrastructure can support the proposed change.
- Availability assessment - discuss the potential impact of the proposed change on system availability. Include the Availability Management group in the change review process.
- Security assessment - include the Corporate Security team in the review process. Ensure that the change complies with the security policy. Update Change Status to 'Awaiting QA approval'.

Change Approval
- QA testing approved - in conjunction with Release Management, ensure that the change has been tested and certified by the Quality Assurance Group. Update change status to "Awaiting Documentation Acceptance."
- Documentation updated/accepted - support and infrastructure documentation must be available and accepted; once accepted, change status to "Awaiting user acceptance."
- User acceptance received - gain approval for the change from the user community- update change status to 'Awaiting deployment plan approval.'
- Deployment and back-out plans created and tested - review and validate the proposed deployment and back-out plans. Change status to 'Awaiting Implementation'
- Change approval communicated - depending on the magnitude of the proposed change and the degree in which the resulting new implementation impacts utilization, both the end user and Support Desk staff may need to be trained. For example, if an organization is changing from one email system to another, it may require an extensive training program - end user,

administrative and support personnel - in addition to a communications program to help ease the transition and guarantee successful change.

Change Deployment
• Change implemented
• Change tested
• QA
• Users
• Change accepted
• Deployment communicated (completed) - change status to 'Completed'

Post Implementation Review
• Review problems encountered
• Identify opportunities for improvement
• Desired results achieved (customer acceptance)
• Change Closed - update status to 'Closed'
• Advise the configuration management group of the successful change

Documentation Updates (Configuration Management)
• CMDB
• DSL
• DHS
• Support Process/Procedures
• Architecture

Close Change

4.2.9 Methods and techniques

Asking questions, brainstorming and performing knowledge transfers and 'lessons learned' exercises from other implementations are good ways to uncover information and gain group acceptance. Other techniques include:
• Delphi technique (subjective analysis, particularly appropriate when a decision has to be made in a political or emotional environment, or when there are strong factions with opposing preferences, or when the scale of the decision to be made is very large)
• Ishakawa diagramming (a facilitation technique graphically displaying a detailed list of causes related to a problem or conditions, for the purpose of discovering root causes and not just the symptoms)
• Force field analysis (weighing the pros and cons of a change - analyzing in balance sheet format with driving forces on the left, and restraining forces listed on the right).

*Audits for effectiveness**

Process effectiveness must be monitored, reviewed, and improved on a continuous basis:
• number of changes completed per period/per platform
• number of successful changes completed versus total (percentage successful completion)
• number and ratio of emergency changes per period
• number of incidents caused by a change compared to number of outages caused by a change

- number of changes requiring backout
- number of changes requiring a partial backout
- on-time delivery rate of changes
- number of changes implemented without approval
- percentage of changes rejected due to incomplete/inaccurate data
- time lag between a workaround being developed and deployment of the workaround.

(*Also refer to CobiT)

4.3 Ongoing operation

4.3.1 The ongoing process

The Change Manager is responsible for the ongoing operation of all changes, and must have the authority and accountability to influence the overall effectiveness of the change management function. This role's level in the organization is related to the degree of dependence of the business on its IT capability. For example, if the loss of IT service has a major revenue impact, then the Change Manager position should be more senior and thus able to affect more control. Ongoing Change Management operations support the business by providing control and oversight of normal and urgent changes. Change Management must be applied by fully understanding the impact of changes from the end user's perspective, and the change's ultimate impact on the organization's ability to function, to thrive and to compete.

ITIL best practices allow Change Management processes to be executed in fully manual, partially automated or completely automated ways. However, if much of the Change process is not automated, risks increase dramatically. The IT infrastructure potentially touches every part of the modern organization, and Change Management involves many people in different parts of the organization. The demands of manually keeping records of exactly where in the process each change stands are burdensome; the probability of human inattention, communication failure, or error is high. Software automation can assist greatly by drawing against a more complete and accurate CMDB, making sure changes are aligned to business needs.

4.3.2 Support Center Manager's role
Responsibilities and activities
The role of the Support Center Manager in the ongoing operations of Change Management is to continuously monitor the impact of changes on the services offered to the organization, including the level to which SLAs are being met or breached.

4.3.3 Change Manager's role (may also be the Support Center manager)
Responsibilities and activities
The Change Manger is responsible for maintaining and improving the change process, as well as overall monitoring, measuring, reporting and operations:
- chairing the CAB
- raising and recording changes
- assessing impact, cost, benefit and risk of proposed changes
- developing business justifications for change and obtaining approval
- managing and coordinating change implementation

- monitoring and reporting on the change implementations
- responsible for final decision and disposition of changes
- responsible for defining metrics.

4.3.4 Support Center Function's role
Responsibilities and activities
- Incident Management tracking new incidents related to changes
- Incident Management to provide insight for errors and associated incidents related to changes
- Changes performed without approval tracked

Deliverables
- Change processes are monitored and measured
- Change Calendar available
- Forward Schedule of changes
- Change Management process is communicated and accepted by all stakeholders

Competencies required
Commitment to quality services
- Customer relationship skills
- People management skills
- Process improvement skills (best practices)

KPIs
Reduced number of incidents and outages caused by an approved change
Reduced number of changes performed without CM approval
Improved change approval success rate
Compliance with maintenance and freeze windows

4.3.5 Other key roles and functions in the ongoing operation process
- CAB
- CAB chairperson
- Release Manager
- Configuration Manager
- Process owner
- Change builder
- Change tester
- Purchasing manager - responsible for obtaining pricing, negotiation and purchasing required for changes
- Accounting/Financial manager - responsible for assessing the cost feasibility related to changes

4.3.6 Steps and tips for maintaining this process
- Continue to involve all stakeholders
- Communicate success and opportunities for improvement at stakeholder staff meetings
- Schedule internal process reviews

- Standard/pre-approved change list
- CAB membership list
- Audit your organization's change management effectiveness *
- Change Request Completeness
- Change success rates by type
- Individual and Group success rates

(*Refer to COBIT)

4.4 Optimization

4.4.1 The optimization process

Change organizations that are functioning operational well will want to optimize their delivery. Excessive control hampers being responsive to business needs, but many IT departments overvalue control. Competitive businesses seek quick responses, but may underestimate the risk involved with changing interdependent IT components. Finding the right balance of control and change is the key. Combining the disciplines of Change and Configuration Management in an integrated approach can provide the opportunity to control the IT environment, yet still provide the agility required by the business.

Interdependencies among IT components are complex and changes to the IT production environment are the primary cause of system failures. IT departments that make changes in one area can break functionality in another area, causing system failures that affect the very business operations they are supposed to support. Be mindful that it is changes made by the IT department - not hardware failures, or even disasters - that are the leading reason for IT business disruption. Using a Business Service Management approach, where all IT elements are associated with the business processes they support, along with fully understanding the business needs and timelines, provides the best guidance about the appropriate timing and potential impact of changes.

Organizations can optimize to be simultaneously responsive and controlled by bringing together the processes, activities and data - then integrating and automating change lifecycle management and desired state management. When all the activities are truly process-aware and if all the data is able to be interchanged across the activities, then the combined power of all those tools become a single optimized solution. Combining process, activity and data can achieve leverage of all the existing investments that have been made in change and configuration management. In addition to these efficiencies, fewer resources are required in the IT environment.

4.4.2 Support Center Manager's role
Responsibilities and activities
Much of the Support Center Manager's role is to inform when interacting with the Change Management in the Implementation phase, and to constantly monitor in the Operational phase. In the Optimization phase, the Support Manager should be able to proactively intervene when changes could cause or are already causing drops in services, or when costs to provide agreed services are increasing.

An optimized Support Center should have an established recognition/reward system for analysts that uncover flaws and problems in the organization's infrastructure, rather than a culture that encourages 'heroes' who solve problems independently of approved processes and controls.

An optimized Support Center values repeatable processes and controls over massive automated changes that may result in widespread damaging results in a very short time. It should be particularly watchful and vocal when this type of change is proposed and/or scheduled. An optimized Support Center also has a robust support tool in place to capture, relate and track all contacts and provide agreed upon services. It has adequate budget for a training program that includes process, tool, technical and soft skills.

4.4.3 Change Manager's role
Responsibilities and activities
The Change Manager is responsible for assessing and improving the change process, as well as overall monitoring, measuring, reporting on process delivery:
- chairing the CAB
- raising and recording changes
- assessing impact, cost, benefit and risk of proposed changes
- developing business justifications for change and obtaining approval
- managing and coordinating change implementation
- monitoring and reporting on the change implementations
- responsible for final decision and disposition of changes
- responsible for refining metrics and making them available
- identifying process gaps and responsible for continuous process improvement.

4.4.4 Support Center Function's role
Responsibilities and activities
An optimized Support Center can identify and flag volatile components that support vital services, and put detective controls in place to prevent unauthorized changes to flagged components. It also prevents standard configuration 'drift' by enforcing rigid adherence. It should also be able to track comprehensive service statistics such as the following.

Incident information:
- total number of incidents related to changes
- mean elapsed time to achieve resolution or workaround, by impact code
- percentage of incidents handled within agreed response time (SLA)
- average cost per incident/change
- incidents/change processed per technician
- number and percentage of incidents/change resolved without desk side visit
- percentage of incidents/changes closed by Service Desk requiring forwarding to other levels of support.

Problem information:
- number of problems and errors per change by
- status

- service
- impact
- category
- CI (asset)
- by change initiator/submitter
- user/business group
- total elapsed time on closed problems
- elapsed time to date on open problems
- mean and maximum elapsed time to close problems or confirm Known Error, measuring from problem record initiation, by impact code, and by support group (including vendors)
- temporary resolution actions
- expected resolution time for open problems.

Deliverables
- Management by fact
- Controls are visible, verifiable and regularly reported
- Culture of causality
- Organizational learning through history of successful change management
- Accurate and complete CMDB repository
- Volatile components with stable infrastructure
- Detective controls in place on infrastructure

Competencies required
- Process integration expertise
- Commitment to quality
- Posture of compliance and trusted working relationship with other IT managers
- Ability to influence business decisions

KPIs
- Number of deviations from standard configurations
- Reduced level of resources and time required as a ratio to number of changes
- Reduced number of disruptions and service availability caused by the change process
- Reduced number and percentage of emergency to non-emergency changes
- Business recognition of effective change process

4.4.5 Other key roles and functions in the optimization process
- CAB
- CAB chairman
- All IT process owners/sponsors
- IT Operations Managers
- QA Manager
- Business Support Liaison (or Business Systems Managers) for each business unit
- Senior Executive Management of organization

4.4.6 Steps and tips for optimizing the process
- Establish process performance metrics and KPIs
- Define Critical Success Factors *(See CobiT Maturity Model in Annex A4.20)*
- Monitor and measure process performance
- Quantify current cost savings including personnel productivity
- When IT systems go down, supported employee productivity is affected. Organizations reduce the time supported employees are kept from working on their core tasks. As a result, overall organizational productivity is increased. It is hard to quantify the cost of lost employee productivity; however, the value may be estimated as downtime avoided/recovered (estimate $20 per hour productivity cost per employee)
- Value = Avoided Employee Downtime * Employee Productivity Cost
- Communicate performance and current cost savings at stakeholder staff meetings and all process review meetings
- Estimate additional cost savings for the Change Process, for Support Call Volume and for Support Call Length:

Change process cost reduction
The cost of making any kind of change in IT involves process, workflow, planning and approval activities. Optimizing the planning and implementation can be estimated. Industry analysts estimate an average change process cost of $150 per change with a possible 30% cost reduction opportunity.

Value = Annual # Changes * Cost per Change * Reduction factor (the key variable is the number of annual changes in the organization)

Support call volume cost reduction
System failures resulting from poorly managed changes cause a call to the support desk. Up to 80% of (IT) outages are self-inflicted. Optimized Change Management can reduce that volume by up to 35%. Gartner estimates that this is 20% of your total call volume. Figure $12 per call.

Value = Annual Call Volume * Cost Per Call * Volume reduction factor (the key variable is the annual call volume of the organization)

Support call length reduction
By limiting and standardizing the supported configurations, organizations can reduce complexity and decrease support call length. Gartner estimates that if a support call lasts 17 minutes, 9 of those minutes are spent in hardware and software qualification. Optimized and controlled standard configurations can reduce those 9 minutes by up to 75%.

Value = Annual Call Volume * Cost Per Call * Length reduction factor (the key variable is the annual call volume of the organization)

Additional cost savings can be estimated for system installations and software deployment:

Installation cost reduction

Installing new IT systems is an ongoing cost. Industry averages assume a turnover every three years. Optimizing Change Management by streamlining the implementation and installation process can save as much as $20 per install:

Value = Installation # per Year * Cost Per Installation factor (the key variable is the number of installations per year in the organization)

Software deployment cost reduction

Manually deploying software patches and application upgrades is time-consuming and error prone. Optimized and automated patch collection, application packaging, and deployment can reduce costs up to 50%. Assume an average cost of headcount resource at $75,000 per year

Value = Distribution headcount * Annual Headcount * Reduction factor (the key variable is the Distribution headcount used in the organization)

Leverage change success rates, current performance and cost savings to gain acceptance and backing to further optimize Change Management.

External validation/certification

Successfully passing external programs that measure maturity for IT processes has multiple benefits, including the validation of the organization's parity or superiority of process. Process immaturities identified during these certification programs can be the basis and rationale for an optimization project. *(See CobiT Maturity Model in Annex A4.20)*

Training

Industry experts estimate a 7:1 dollar payback for training, yet it remains an underused way to optimize IT organizations. Training pays off in better utilization of all systems, process adherence, as well as support avoidance. Combining both tool and process training in close time proximity with one another can have real added value.

Marketing

According to leading analysts, up to 80% of business service failures are caused by improperly managed changes. For Change Management to move from a high-risk, unpredictable 'burdensome' image in an organization, to one that is embraced for competitive advantage requires optimized Change Management. The IT department must market its successes, much like any service organization, in order to be perceived as enablers of critical business services. All successes must be quantified, communicated and marketed internally to all stakeholders on an ongoing basis. Smart IT organizations use traditional marketing techniques and stakeholder/end user gatherings, intranet and other communications methods to market their contribution to the organization's bottom line.

4.4.7 Future impact of this process on the Support Center

Information technology (IT) professionals are under intense pressure to maintain agreed service levels for the critical IT services. This is difficult enough in a static environment, considering the complexity of today's information networks, but IT environments are not static. To maintain competitive advantage and to assure vendor-supported environments, new technologies and upgrades of existing systems must be achieved. Maintaining service quality at committed service levels while continually changing the underlying IT infrastructure presents an enormous challenge. All efforts must be made to balance the need for a change against the impact of the change on critical services to the organization. The Support Center is the best source of information on supported services and the health of those services for the Change Manager.

4.5 Measurement, costing and management reporting

4.5.1 Implementing: benefits and costs
Why implement this process and what can be gained
• Organizational visibility to changes in the infrastructure
• Management and planned control of changes
• Standardization of changes to the infrastructure
• Consistency
• Repeatability
• Minimize business service disruptions
• Provide higher level of service availability, quality, reliability and performance
• Better coordination of changes
• Reduced risk associated with change
• Better communication of changes and potential impacts
• Better communication between IT and the business
• More effective trouble-shooting and better problem resolution resulting from well
  documented and approved changes

Cost elements for implementation
The cost of implementation is primarily manpower to manage and oversee the process. The ratio of resources to number of changes varies between organizations. Typically a change management resource can manage a volume of four to eight changes per day. As a process improves in efficiency, this volume may increase.

Software products and their deployment are another significant cost. Licensing costs vary between products and deployments. In addition to the application licenses, there are options in both fixed and floating licenses for support analysts. There are also ongoing maintenance fees to have access to new versions of the software. Finally, there are levels of support for the application based on hours of service, method of access, and response/resolve rates. It is best to thoroughly understand the organization's process, needs and budget before selecting software products.

Making the business case to implement
• Justifying the cost of implementing a change management process and group in the
  organization should begin with an assessment of the current state of your IT infrastructure.
• Are there unplanned outages resulting in service disruption? If so, what are the disruptions
  costing the organization?
• If the service supports $10,000 in revenue per hour and you typically lose that service once

a week for an hour, then your annual revenue loss is $520,000!
- Gather information from the Availability Management group or Service Management group to provide a baseline of service availability. Talk to your service customers to establish an impact by business service. Determine the positive impact of implementing a Change Management process. Will it reduce outages by 50%? What are the costs associated with the new process, such as manpower and software products? Making a business case is often not a science, but an art. You need to interpret information and make predictions and assumptions.

Metrics and Key Performance Indicators
- Number of changes per month
- Number of changes backed-out per month
- Number of incidents and outages caused by a change
- Number of emergency changes
- Number of rejected changes

Management Reporting
- Forward Schedule of Change
- Changes by risk level
- Changes by platform
- Changes by line of business

(See Sample Change Activity by Month in Annex A4.21; Sample Report of Changes by Classification by Month in Annex A4.22; and Sample Report of Change by Risk by Month in Annex A4.23)

4.5.2 Ongoing operations: costs
Cost elements for ongoing operations
Cost elements for ongoing operations are concerned with needs for measuring and monitoring activities. In addition to appropriate detection and diagnostic tools, costs may be incurred for staff training and for outside third party monitoring assistance.

Metrics and KPIs
- Changes made across distributed business, technology and process boundaries
- Reduces costs by the efficient use of resources and technology
- Supports the optimization of IT investments
- Enables lean and effective support services
- Helps to ensure long term customer retention /end-user satisfaction
- Assists in the identification of business opportunities

Management reporting
- Changes per group with success rate
- Changes per platform, per application
- Changes with incidents count with minutes
- Changes per service with incidents
(See Sample Monthly Scorecard Report Changes/Group/Success % in Annex A4.24; Sample Report

Changes/Incidents/Minutes/Trend in Annex A4.25; and Sample Report Service with Change Incidents/Minutes/Commentary in Annex A4.26)

4.5.3 Optimization: benefits and costs
Why optimize this process and what can be gained
Process optimization is often desired by the process purist, but is not always a necessity for the business. Striving for a repeatable, effective process that integrates efficiently with other internal processes is the most conservative goal. However, there is increasing interest in industry specific standards like ISO-9000 and CobiT, which require the organization to strive for process optimization. More importantly, process optimization may be required to comply with government regulations such as Sarbanes-Oxley or other industry standards.

Cost elements for optimization
- Costs elements in the Optimization phase include more highly paid resources able to understand overall architecture, business needs, emerging technologies and trends, and design and execute optimization strategy. Also, a key activity for optimized change management organizations is the external validation of their change management program compared to industry standards. Costs include the fee for the validating program, the auditor and travel etc. costs. There are also costs for external auditing /certification in the internal resources from various change roles required to participate in the audit/certification process. Estimate two weeks of time per change resource identified as the lead participant and additional hours/per other change resource per major activity.
- Manpower
- Certification program/Auditor/Auditing staff
- Rigorous process measuring
- Rigorous statistical analysis
- Software and licensing - automation generally necessary for optimization in all but smallest environments

Making the business case to optimize
Studies of high performing IT organizations indicate several common areas of proficiency. They are able to illustrate a higher service levels, longer mean time between failures, lower mean time to repair, and a higher percentage of planned changes relative to unplanned work. They also have a lower ratio of server to administrator, and more timely incident resolution. Evidence of good relationships with other IT areas, business owners and executive management also indicate maturity. All of these metrics captured and presented, with supporting data from industry experts and other best-in-class companies, can be used to illustrate to the organization that the tactical processes are maturing, and that the Support Center and Change Manager are qualified to take the organization to the next level of optimization.

Possible operations improvements include:
- 25-35% reduction in unplanned downtime and service desk calls
- as much as 80% reduction in server support costs
- 2-30% reduction in desktop support costs
- improved server-to-administrator ratio from 1:18 (the industry average) to 1:100

Well functioning organizations are collecting large amount of data and can analyze that data constructively. An important step is to be sure you are collecting the right data elements that will surface all the important issues. Statistical analysis of this information will identify opportunities to avoid costs associated with poor changes, and the cascading value associated with good changes. Armed with these analyses, Change Managers can effectively articulate the value of proper Change Management.

Metrics and Key Performance Indicators
- Changes made successfully across distributed business, technology, and process boundaries
- Reduces costs by the efficient use of resources and technology
- Supports the optimization of IT investments
- Enables lean and effective support services
- Helps to ensure long term customer retention /end-user satisfaction
- Assists in the identification of business opportunities

Management reporting
Reporting, in terms of the level of detail, technical nature, frequency and presentation style should be tailored to the stakeholder. Internal operational partners should be presented with the most technical and frequent report format. There should be textual explanations to augment the factual representation.

External stakeholders should be consulted about the level of detail about their particular area they require on an ongoing basis, the frequency and the format in which they would like the information presented.

Automation of the report should be in place, as well as the ability to drill down in order to explain exceptions.

Executive stakeholders should have the ability to see individual and aggregate information, including exception and drill down capability in a visual, near real time mode.

4.5.4 Tools
Implementation
- Project management and planning software
- Project Management Body of Knowledge (PMBOK)
- Configuration Management Database software - some tools populate the CMDB extremely well and others poorly. A mismatch between the CI data and the changes on which they are made will result in poor Change Management. Access to a well-defined CMDB is a critical success factor in Change Management. Look for tools that provide a data repository in which there is information about the configurations and configuration items (CIs) in the system.Multiple configurations may exist in the CMDB at any one time - for example - discovered configuration; active configuration; desired configuration; 'golden master' configuration; etc.
- CMDB software that works in conjunction with a reconciliation engine, allowing organizations to reconcile multiple datasets; to merge datasets; and to identify differences between datasets

- The reconciliation engine should use the concepts of 'trusted sources' and 'distrusted sources' to help resolve conflicts, allowing you to store expected, new, desired and future configurations - and determine the differences between them.
- CMDB should provide for automatically gathering and consolidating all IT infrastructure data into one central data repository. It can be populated by one or many external sources - connected via an open API. These external sources may replicate only high level data; they may replicate all data or they may use the CMDB as their own database.
- Change Management software - choices include robust Change Management software that enables business justification, financial, risk assessment, and support for full change life cycle process. This software is capable of managing, coordinating, monitoring and reporting changes with complete audit trails; approval and escalation functionality, and the ability to explore and explain the impact, cost, benefit and risk of proposed changes.
- Key benefits may include seamless integration to Service Level and Availability Management in addition to the core processes of Incident, Problem, Configuration Management and Change Management. This software is geared for organizations interested in Business Service Management (BSM) capabilities to assess impact to business services organizational impact.

Ongoing operations
- Incident tracking software - capable of identifying incidents related to change so they can be easily reported on separately from other incidents
- Reporting software - report automation software helps to standardize and streamline the reporting process
- Network search tools - these tools identify all devices deployed. Some are capable of identifying software versions and hardware configurations.
- Automated auditing tools - these tools can compare your documented infrastructure to the actual infrastructure.
- Change detection tools - used to identify changes to the infrastructure and compare to the approved changes documented in the change management tool.
- System infrastructure monitors - used to monitor device availability during planned outages associated with a change
- IT Service monitors - Provide insight into service impact resulting from a change
- Self-Service tools - enabling end users to self-serve and freeing resources for proactive work
- Detection tools - to alert IT of intrusions and possible threats

Management reporting
- Reporting and publishing software - information from the above data sources is organized and published with the assistance of software.
- Process Dashboard creation

Annex Documents

Overview
Annex A4.1 - How Best Practice Processes Work Together
Annex A4.2 - Sample Change Management Process
Annex A4.3 - Sample Change Request Process - Support/Service Desk
Annex A4.4 - Sample Incident Request - Change Process
Annex A4.5 - Sample Problem Process - Change Process
Annex A4.6 - Sample Mission/Purpose Statement

Implementing, Ongoing and Optimization
Annex A4.7 - Sample Change Management Policy
Annex A4.8 - Sample Change Management Lifecycle Diagram and Key Check Points
Annex A4.9 - Sample Change Status Report Used in CAB Meeting
Annex A4.10 - Sample Stakeholder Goals
Annex A4.11 - Sample Change Classification Options
Annex A4.12 - Sample Risk Classification Options
Annex A4.13 - Sample Maintenance Window
Annex A4.14 - Sample Emergency, Non-Emergency Guidelines
Annex A4.15 - Sample Change Request Form
Annex A4.16 - Sample Change Deliverables Checklist
Annex A4.17 - Sample Standard Change Request Approval Criteria for CAB Form
Annex A4.18 - Sample Forward Schedule of Changes Form
Annex A4.19 - Sample Change States
Annex A4.20 - Excerpt of CobiT Maturity Model

Measurement, Costing and Management Reporting
Annex A4.21 - Sample Change Activity by Month
Annex A4.22 - Sample Report of Changes by Classification by Month
Annex A4.23 - Sample Report of Change by Risk by Month
Annex A4.24 - Sample Monthly Scorecard Report Changes/Group/Success %
Annex A4.25 - Sample Report Changes/Incidents/Minutes/Trend
Annex A4.26 - Sample Report Service with Change Incidents/Minutes/Commentary

Annex A4.1 How Best Practice Processes Work Together

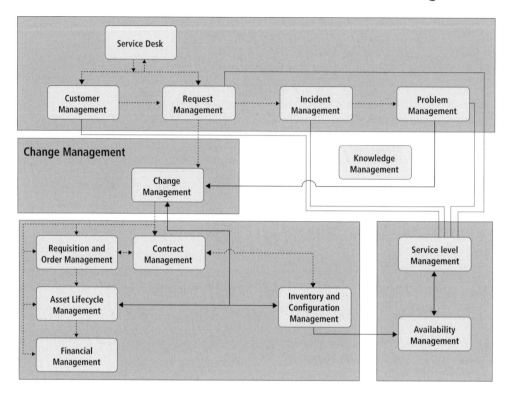

Figure 4.1 Best practice processes

Annex A4.2 Sample Change Management Processes

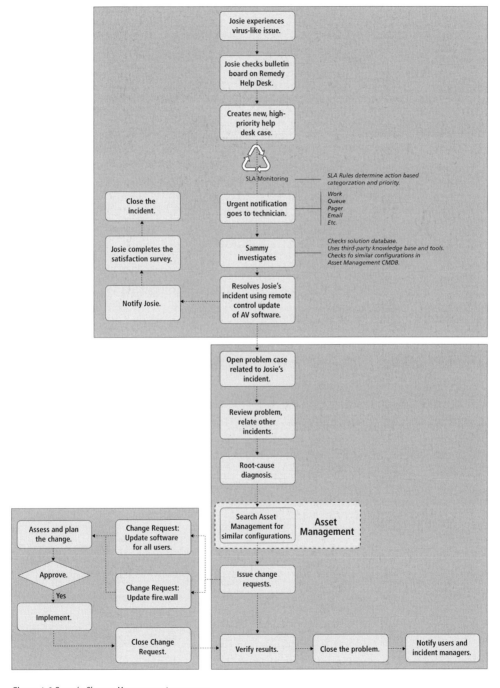

Figure 4.2 Sample Change Management processes

Annex A4.3 Sample Change Request Process - Support/Service Desk

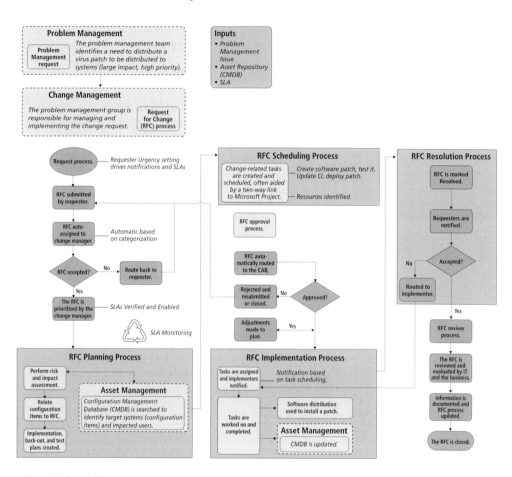

Figure 4.3 Sample Change Management process

Annex A4.4 Sample Incident Request - Change Process

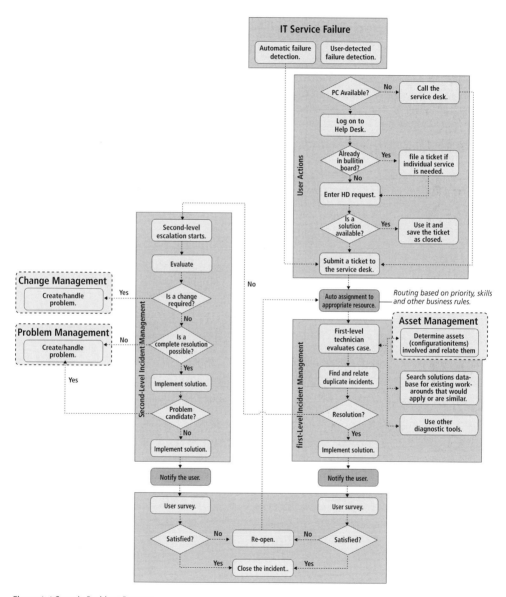

Figure 4.4 Sample Incident Request

Annex A4.5 Sample Problem Process – Change Process

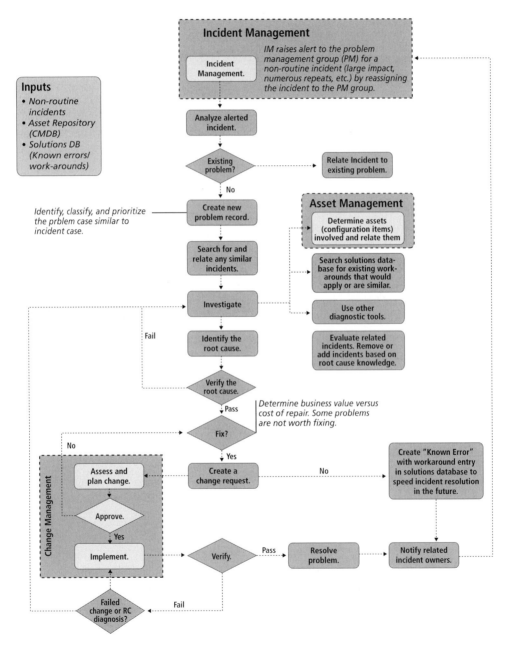

Figure 4.5 Sample Problem process

Annex A4.6 Sample Mission/Purpose Statement

To be seen as the "enablers" of technical changes to Production Environments, meeting our business objectives.

Our purpose: to ensure that changes made to Production Environments are tracked, reviewed, tested, communicated, implemented, and validated - reducing/eliminating negative impacts to the business.

Annex A4.7 Sample Change Management Policy

The following policy is for the planning and execution of all changes affecting the IT infrastructure (including buy not limited to computer, network, facilities, and environmental activities) and related business partners.

1. All changes need to follow the established Change Management Process.

2. Any change submitted for approval that involves multiple system interfaces, multiple customer groups, multiple tasks and/or multiple technical support resources must be accompanied by a detailed script. It will be the Project Manager/Requestor's responsibility to make sure scripts are reviewed and approved prior to any change being scheduled. Once the change is approved, any deviated from the pre-approved scripts will require Change Management approval.

3. Every change request must include the following:
   a. Description of activity
   b. Justification detail
   c. Potential impacts to customer and other production systems
   d. Scheduled start and end time
   e. Resources required

4. Every change request must include a proven fallback situation.

5. All changes involving outside vendors brought in to do work on our behalf required that resource be onsite to manage the activity.

6. The Change Requestor/Project Manager will be responsible for the work activity from beginning to end, including the coordination of all vendor activities.

We expect each of the above to be understood and carefully followed. Any deviation from these policies will be cause for disciplinary action up to and including termination.

Annex A4.8 Sample Change Management Lifecycle Diagram and Key Check Points

Change Management is a powerful process that helps coordinate, automate, and streamline each request for change. Each change request can be managed using the change lifecycle, which has four stages: request, plan, implement, and verify.

With an optimized approach, a change request proceeds through the request stage, is scheduled for planning, and goes through the planning phase. During implementation, the change might be applied using multiple tools and be carried out by multiple people at multiple times. You must be able to track these things from start to finish, and at every point in time have clear visibility into what was requested, who is working on it, how many sub-requests were created, how many components were affected, and so forth. This capability is called orchestrated change lifecycle management.

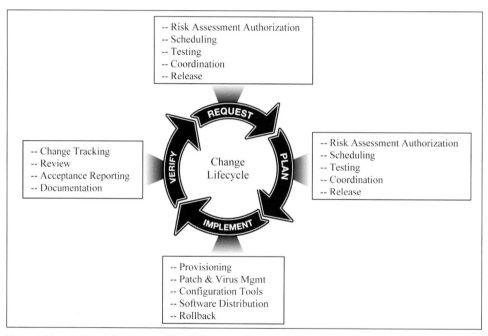

Figure 4.6 Sample Change Management lifecycle diagram and key checkpoints

Key checkpoints:
• resource availability
• date scheduled
• quality assurance approval
• user acceptance
• script created
• back-out plan created
• back-out plan approved
• service level management approval

- service desk approval
- application development approval, etc.
- training completed
- monitors installed
- support documents available
- capacity adequate
- architectural design complete
- communication

Annex A4.9 Sample Chance Status Report Used in CAB Meeting

Changes scheduled to be in production

Ticket #	Description	Platform	Requestor Name	Planned Start (date & time)	Review Status

Changes awaiting clarification

Ticket #	Description	Platform	Requestor Name	Planned Start (date & time)	Review Status

New changes to be reviewed by the CAB

Ticket #	Description	Platform	Requestor Name	Planned Start (date & time)	Review Status

Annex A4.10 Sample Stakeholder Goals

- Operations Support - Stability
  - Fewer changes to the IT infrastructure

- Service Support - Visibility
  - Advance notification of changes

- Business - Flexibility
  - Ability to respond to market demands

- CTO - Control
  - Reduce number of incidents caused by changes

Annex A4.11 Sample Change Classification Options

Option #1: based on the nature of the change
- Normal - a change that is planned as a result of a problem fix or enhancement related to a project or release
- Emergency - a change required as a fix to an incident that requires immediate resolution
- Recurrent - a change that is done on a routine/recurrent bases

Option #2: based on the criticality of the service impacted by the change
- Mission critical - service necessary to support mission critical process (business cannot function without the service)
- Business critical - service necessary to support business critical process (key business service)
- Important - service necessary for a non-critical business process
- Standard - service not core to business operation

Annex A4.12 Sample Risk Classification Options

Major   - 4
High   - 3
Medium - 2
Low   - 1
None   - 0

Criteria for establishing risk:
- Change classification as mission critical or business critical = 1; other = 0
- Change preparation fast track = 1; normal planning = 0
- Service outage required yes = 1; no = 0
- Change occurring during approved maintenance window no = 1; yes = 0

Add up the total and document the risk on the change request form. Major and high risk changes required review and approval of senior management (include in change management policy).

Annex A4.13 Sample Maintenance Window

Maintenance Windows - Examples

Wednesday-Thursday Change Window
Type of Change	Time of Change
Normal**	8:00p-6:00a
Special***	12:01a-5:00*a

Friday-Saturday Change Window
Type of Change	Time of Change
Normal	8:00p-8:00p
Special	12:01a Sat-9:00*a

*These changes will complete by designated time.
**Infrastructure changes that will not impact any production environment
***Infrastructure changes that will affect impact of any production environment and can possibly cause a site outage.

Annex A4.14 Sample Emergency/Non-Emergency Guidelines

1. Emergency situation requiring immediate action:
   (Do change first, then submit open/submit request)

   a If there is a need to reboot implement a change immediately and it cannot be deferred to a better time due to customer disservice, contact the change management on-call resource.
   b Assess risk and impact associated with change.
   c Perform the change activity.
   d Open a Change Request.
   e Upon completion of the activity, mark the Change Request "complete"
   f Change Management will review the activity during the next scheduled Change Advisory Board meeting.

2. Non-emergency changes:
   (Submit Change Request, obtain Change Management approval, then proceed with action)
   a Submit a change request.
   b After Change Management has approved the Change Request, complete the stated actions.
   c Change the SCR status from "approved" to "completed"
   d In the event of fallback, change the status to "fallen-back"
   e Change Management will review the activity during the next scheduled Change Advisory Board meeting.

Annex A4.15 Sample Change Request Form

Requester Information
Name
Email
Phone#

Change Request Details
Type of Change
Help Desk Ticket #
Requested Date to Production (month/day/year)
Business Unit Impacted
Environment Impacted
Located Impacted
Stat Time
Estimated Duration
Title of Change
Technical Description of Change

Risk Analysis
Contractual Obligation
Risks/Impact
Technical Description of Backout Plan
What is the Impact of Not Implemented?
What are the Dependencies for this Change?
Will Site Functionality be Impaired (ie. Darkpage)? If Yes, How Long?

- All change requests must be submitted 48 hours prior to CAB meeting review -

Annex A4.16 Sample Change Deliverables Checklist

Project Name:				
Application Name:				
Director:				
Manager:				
Project Manager:				
Platforms:				
Equipment:				
Target Cutover Date:				
Phase	Yes	No	N/A	Checklist Criteria
Initiation	–	–	–	Identify Change Management participant
Design	–	–	–	Change Management participates in the Technical Design Review
Develop	–	–	–	Preliminary activity – management adherence policy
(30-45 days prior to intended cutover)	–	–	–	With Change Management, determine what support training will be required.
	–	–	–	Develop cutover script and conduct interviews (including outage coordination with other associated applications) until all key stakeholders approve a Final.
				Begin development and review of necessary documentation.
	–	–	–	Complete list of deliverables.
	–	–	–	
Develop (15-30 days prior to intended cutover)	–	–	–	Provide agreed-upon training appropriate for each specific 1st and 2nd level support group. _ Complete application training overview _ Arrange logistics for training class _ Change Management invites appropriate support groups _ Develop user notification
Develop (10-14 days prior to intended cutover)	–	–	–	Deliver final documentation to Change Management.
	–	–	–	Deliver final cutover script for Change Management approval.
Closure	–	–	–	Review new system performance with Change Management

Annex A4.17 Sample Standard Change Request Approval Criteria for CAB Form

Change #
_____

Date Submitted:
_____

QA Approved?
_____

Resources Required?
_____

_____

Communication?
_____

_____

Dependencies?
_____

_____

Backout Plan?
_____

_____

Scheduled Date:
_____

_____

CAB Approval?
_____

Additional Info:
_____

_____

Annex A4.18 Sample Forward Schedule of Changes Form

Scheduled Date	Change Number	Title	Platform	Customer Impact	Start Time	Duration	Status

Annex A4.19 Sample Change States

Change states are unique to the business being governed by Change Management. There is no right or wrong. Determine what is necessary to successfully deliver changes to your governed environment. Some examples of various states include:
- New
- Awaiting CAB review
- Awaiting scheduled date
- Awaiting CAB authorization
- Awaiting quality assurance approval
- Awaiting user acceptance
- Awaiting resource assignment
- Awaiting deployment script acceptance
- Awaiting implementation
- Complete
- Fallback
- Modified
- Closed

Annex A4.20 Excerpt of CobiT Maturity Model

Maturity Model Levels

Control over the IT process "Manage Changes" has the business goal of minimizing the likelihood of disruption, unauthorized alterations and errors.

0 - Non-existent - There is no defined Change Management process and changes can be made with virtually no control. There is no awareness that change can be disruptive for both IT and business operations, and no awareness of the benefits of good Change Management.

1 - Initial/Ad Hoc - It is recognized that changes should be managed and controlled, but there is no consistent process to follow. Practices vary and it is likely that unauthorized changes will take place. There is poor or non-existent documentation of change and configuration documentation is incomplete and unreliable. Errors are likely to occur together with interruptions to the production environment caused by poor Change Management.

2 - Repeatable but Intuitive - There is an informal Change Management process in place and most changes follow this approach; however, it is unstructured, rudimentary and prone to error. Configuration documentation accuracy is inconsistent and only limited planning and impact assessment takes place prior to a change. There is considerable inefficiency and rework.

3 - Defined Process - There is a defined formal change management process in place, including categorization, prioritization, emergency procedures, change authorization and release management, but compliance is not enforced. The defined process is not always seen as suitable or practical and as a result, workarounds take place and processes are

bypassed. Errors are likely to occur and unauthorized changes will occasionally occur. The analysis of the impact of IT changes on business operations is becoming formalized, to support planned rollouts of new applications and technologies.

4 - Managed and Measurable - The change management process is well developed and consistently followed for all changes and management is confident that there are no exceptions. The process is efficient and effective, but relies on considerable manual procedures and controls to ensure that quality is achieved. All changes are subject to thorough planning and impact assessment to minimize the likelihood of post-production problems. An approval process for changes is in place. Change Management documentation is current and correct, with changes formally tracked. Configuration documentation is generally accurate. IT Change Management planning and implementation is becoming more integrated with changes in the business process to ensure that training, organizational changes and business continuity issues are addressed. There is increased coordination between IT Change Management and business process re-design.

5 - Optimized - The Change Management process is regularly reviewed and updated to keep in line with best practices. Configuration information is computer-based and provides version control. Software distribution is automated and remote monitoring capabilities are available. Configuration and release management and tracking of changes is sophisticated and includes tools to detect unauthorized and unlicensed software. IT Change Management is integrated with business Change Management to ensure that IT is an enabler in increasing productivity and creating new business opportunities for the organization.

Source: CobiT Maturity Model, Management Guidelines, A16, Page 59.

Annex A4.21 Sample Change Activity by Month

Sample Change Request (SCR) for YTD 2003

Change Count	% of Total	Category	Emergency Count	% of Total	Fallback Count	% of Total
4559	65%	ON PLAN	233	3%	30	0.4%
2154	31%	PRODUCTION FIX	1426	20%	13	0.2%
303	4%	NOT ON PROJECT PLAN	62	1%	27	0.4%
7016	100%	Totals	1721	25%	70	1.0%

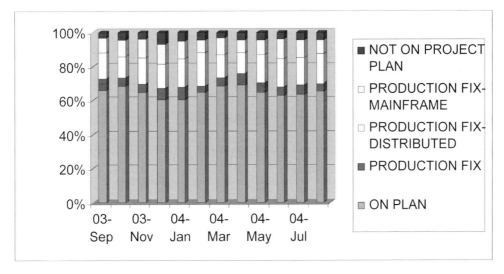

Figure 4.7 Sample Change Activity by month

Annex A4.22 Sample Report of Changes by Classification by Month

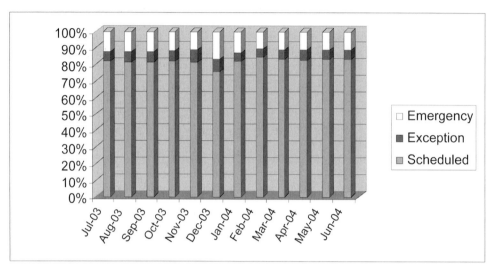

Figure 4.8 Sample Report of Changes by classification by month

	Scheduled	Exception	Emergency
Monthly Averages:	3857 Changes	287 Changes	564 Changes
	82%	6%	12%

Annex A4.23 Sample Report of Changes by Risk by Month

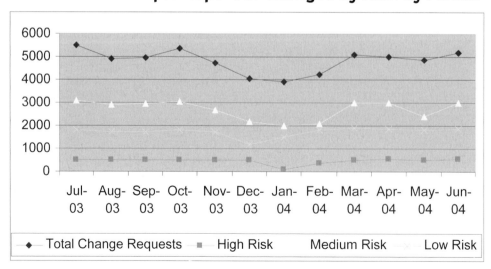

Figure 4.9 Sample Report of Changes by Risk by month

Annex A4.24 Sample Monthly Scorecard Report Changes/ Group/Success %

MONTHLY SCORECARD

Corporate	Technology Group	Successful Install	Scheduling	Process Exceptions	Total Unauthorized	Overall
-Division	Name	% Grade	% Grade	% Grade	Count Grade	Grade

Annex A4.25 Sample Report Changes/Incidents/ Minutes/Trend

Service Description	Last Month Count	This Month Count	Movement Count (+ or -)
- Incidents			
- Outages			
- Incident Minutes			
- Outage Minutes			
Change Description			
- Planned Changes			
- Emergency Change			
- Genuine Emergency			
- Unplanned Emergency			
- Changes Causing Incidents			
Customer Relationship	Last Month Grade	This Month Grade	Six-Month Trend Grade
- Administrative			
- Sales			
- Marketing			
- R&D			
- Executive Branch			

Annex A4.26 Sample Report Service with Change Incidents/Minutes/Commentary

RECOMMENDATIONS/ACTIONS:

TOP 10 EVENTS	DATE	INCIDENT MINUTES	OUTAGE MINUTES
MAJOR OUTAGES			
Service Name			
FOLLOW-UP STATUS	Description	Progress	Date
- Project			

Changes Causing Major Incidents	Incident Minutes
Description/Date	
Technology Group Involved in Major Incidents	
- Group Name	

COMMENTARY:

Overall, (month) was a (rating) month. Outage count is (up/down), and Outage minutes are (up/down), representing Change Management progress

Bibliography

The Goals of ITIL and Service Support Metrics, Malcolm Fry, 2004

The Visual Ops Handbook Starting ITIL in Four Practical Steps, Information technology Process Institute; Kevin Behr, Gene Kim and George Spafford; June 2004

Chapter 5:
Release Management

5.1 Overview

5.1.1 Description

A release is defined as a significant change to the IT infrastructure in the form of new configuration items or planned upgrades to existing configuration items. The Release Management process ensures that all technical and business aspects of a change to the infrastructure are considered equally. No other infrastructure change has as much potential risk for the business and impact on the Support Center as a release.

Too often, sudden call volume spikes surprise Support Centers. Spikes often result from an unexpected release of new or upgraded hardware, software or operating systems. Ensuring the Support Center is prepared for the release is one of the many benefits of the Release Management process. A successful release has many dependencies such as development, quality assurance and testing as well as on the quality of the Support Center's compliance with the defined procedures. The Release Management process also strives to offset the potential risk of a major release by defining the criteria, training and acceptance policies that must be met before Change Management is authorized to approve the implementation of the release. Release Management cannot completely eliminate service interruptions, including incidents. A well-planned, tested and executed release will equip the Support Center, as well as the Problem and Incident Management processes with the training, knowledge, tools and escalation paths necessary to minimize business impact. A well-planned and executed release will have little impact on service desk call volume.

To enable the Support Center to "Stop Being A Victim"[1] of unexpected releases, untrained support staff and unexpected call spikes, a Support Center representative should be assigned to (and actively participate in) each release team. This will enable the Support Center to play an important role in successful Release Management. As a proactive participant and voice of the customer, the Support Center can propose requirements for the release to minimize any adverse impacts on the customer. The Support Center will also know precisely when a release is going live. This will ensure that they are not caught off-guard when calls about a new release are received by Support Center staff.

5.1.2 Relationships to other processes

The Release Management process has a close relationship with pre-production environments such as Development and Quality Assurance. The majority of the process execution actually takes place outside the production environment. This IT Service Management process is one of the few to bridge the gap from the live production environment to the development environment.

The primary relationships of the Release Management process are other service support processes - specifically, Change, Incident, Problem and Configuration Management. Release Management will also take into consideration Availability, Capacity, Service Level Management, IT Service Continuity Management and Security Management. However, the Release Management requirement will be addressed early in the business requirements stage.

---

1 Stop Being a Victim! Char LaBounty, © 2000, Help Desk Institute

Change Management

Changes to the production environment may be initiated through business requirements. This may be new technology that is being introduced or regulatory requirements. Changes may also be initiated through Problem Management. Changes of this nature may be proactive maintenance (such as security patches) or reactive (such as bug fixes), in order to correct an error in the infrastructure.

By viewing the service support processes through W. Edwards Deming's cycle for continuous improvement, the 'Plan-Do-Check-Act' process improvement cycle, Change Management fulfills the activity of 'plan' by planning the scheduling and implementation. Change Management also ensures that backout scenarios and implementation support are fully documented. They obtain all approvals of the release. Release Management plays a critical role by handling all the 'do' activities including build/buy considerations, design, build, testing, documenting, training and installation.

Incident Management checks the process by managing the resolution of any resulting issues. Problem Management acts on the analysis and trends, through problem and error control activities that result in new actions, or changes to be implemented. All these processes are linked together through the Configuration Item(s) they refer to. These configuration item records are located in the Configuration Management Database (CMDB).

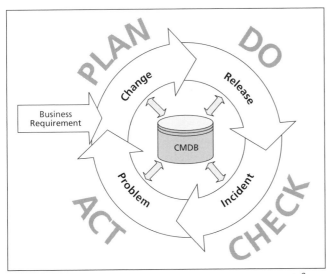

Figure 5.1. Relationship of IT Service Support processes and Deming Cycle [2]

[2] *Adapted from IT Service Management, an Introduction, © May 2002, itSMF International*

5.1.3 Key inputs and outputs to the process

Source/ Destination	INPUT TO Release Management		OUTPUT FROM Release Management	
	Importance	Description	Importance	Description
Configuration Management	Low	Describes the current environment	High	Additions to the CMDB to correspond with each item added to the Definitive Software Library, and Definitive Hardware Store, licensing and documentation
Change Management	High	A Request for Change is the input into the Release Management Process, scheduling of the release by the CAB	Low	Release Management is represented on the CAB
Incident Management	Low	Incidents as a result of the release	High	Training of staff involved in incident management (including the Support Center)
Problem Management	High	Problems as a result of a release, Known Errors to be corrected	Medium	Problems and known errors identified before production
Service Level Management	High	Service Improvement Plan, requirements for new services	High	Updates to Service Level Agreements for the provisioning of the release
Capacity Management	Medium	Available capacity	Medium	Actual requirements that may affect capacity
Availability Management	High	Impact of release on availability, availa bility requirement targets	Medium	Impact to availability during the release implementation
Financial Management	Medium	Budgeting for Release Management Process, budgeting for the release, cost benefit analysis	Low	Validate budgeted vs. actual costs for the release
IT Service Continuity Management	Medium	Requirements and disaster recover plan, risk reduction measures for the release	Medium	Releases that may affect Service Continuity in case of a disaster, identification of risk exposure of release
IT Security	High	System and Data Security policy as it relates to the release	Low	Effects of new release on security, security access as required
Project Management	High	Requirements including business and technology	Medium	Status updates

5.1.4 Possible problems and issues

Possible problems
Lack of Release Management process: it is not unusual for Release Management and Change Management to be combined into a single process, usually Change Management. If there is no delineation between the two processes, the Support Center can still ensure that its requirements are met by applying its requirements to the Change Management process. At a minimum, engage with the Change Advisory Board (CAB) and ensure that the Support Center is kept informed about the Forward Schedule of Change (FSC).

If project management or a project manager is involved in a release, be represented on the release team. The Support Center requirements should be provided at the outset. Review the project charter and provide feedback. Ensure the Support Center's requirements are included as a deliverable in the project plan. Attend the project status meetings and be aware of any date and scope changes that may affect the Support Center's ability to meet the needs of the business immediately following the release.

Authority of Support Center Manager: the Support Center Manager must be empowered with the authority to define requirements for the release. Equally important is the Support Center Manager's authority to halt a release from being implemented where there is a strong reason to do so.

In some circumstances, the Manager may provide a delegate, perhaps a team leader as the representative, for a release or at the Change Management CAB. The delegate must also have the authority to speak on behalf of the Support Center and the Support Center Manager. Complementary process: Release Management is viewed as an infrastructure process. However, because the majority of the process activities take place in pre-production, it is not unusual for the Release Manager to appear to be hampering development. This is especially true if the development team has its own best practice approach. An example of this may be the Software Engineering Institute's Capability Maturity Model (SEI/CMM). Some of the requirements of Release Management overlap with SEI/CMM. Ideally, any difference in terminology should not be an issue. As Release Management is implemented take advantage of existing process steps and repositories, regardless of the terms used to identify them.

Release Management ensures that quality enters the production environment: the Release Management process ensures that quality releases are implemented in the production environment. If any area (Design, Building, Testing, Training and Communication, Implementation) does not ensure that all release criteria have been met, the release process will suffer. Sign-off should take place at the end of each phase. Random audits may be necessary to ensure that the release criteria sign-offs are being met rigorously. Requirements of the Support Center should not be taken lightly. The Support Center must be involved in the sign-off process.

Quality issues

Completeness of information: the deliverables of the release that directly affect the Support Center must be complete. This includes quality documentation and complete and accurate escalation lists. If these are not complete, the Support Center Manager may determine that there is just cause to exercise their right at the change management CAB meeting to reject the change.

Issues should not be held back until the CAB meeting. Whenever possible, they should be raised with the release manager so that they can be addressed in good time.

Training: the Support Center should receive formal training on any new release or major upgrade. This training may be developed in-house or provided by a third party in advance of the release. On-the-job training that occurs once the release has been implemented may cause unnecessary delays and frustration for the customer. If adequate training has not taken place, the Support Center Manager should address the issues as soon as possible. As a last resort, the Support Center manager may feel that there is just cause to delay the release and choose to exercise their right at the CAB to reject the change.

Access to systems for account creation and password resets: it may be expected that the Support Center will provide access to the new system/software once implemented. The Support Center should be trained, granted access and provided with procedures and printed or online access authorization forms.

Compliance with security policies: IT Security is an important consideration. The Release process must ensure that established security policies established are incorporated in all phases of the Release. This will minimize any adverse security issues. In some organizations, an IT Security representative is assigned to a release project to ensure compliance with security policy.

5.2 Implementation

5.2.1 The implementation process

The following section outlines the activities required to design and implement the Release
Management process as it directly relates to the Support Center. It is expected that the
Support Center will be a participant in the Release Management process design.

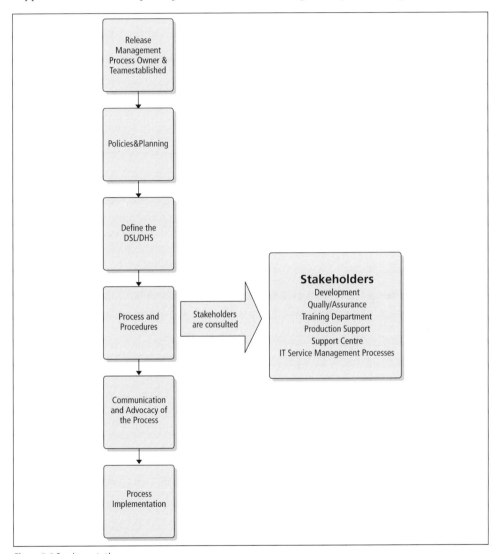

Figure 5.2 Implementation process

Figure 5.2 shows the process steps required to implement a Release Management process. The
input from stakeholders may occur throughout the process design stages, but will be most
prominent during the development of the process and procedures. It is at this stage where
stakeholders will determine the release criteria they require to participate in a successful release.

Release Management process owner and team
Ideally, the stakeholders of the release should make up the process implementation team.
A stakeholder is a group or role with an interest in the activities of the release as it affects
them. In some cases, such as very large releases, the stakeholder team may be structured as a
small core team with an extended team reporting to it. When this occurs, there should be
ongoing communication and consultation with all the stakeholders. The Support Center is a
stakeholder in each release.

5.2.2 Policy and planning
In this stage, the Release Management process owner and team will establish the policies that
will govern the Release Management process.
Planning will include considerations for facilities and equipment necessary for staging, testing
and user acceptance testing of releases.

Define the DSL/DHS
The Definitive Software Library (DSL) and Definitive Hardware Store (DHS) are defined.
Where these already exist, they are documented and refined where necessary.

A DSL contains the master copy of all production software. Software to be installed will be
obtained directly from the DSL. Its purpose is to ensure that only the most recent, tested
and authorized software is moved to production. Software is moved from development into
the DSL. All software installed on test machines and in production is taken from the DSL.
The Support Center will use the DSL for installation and repair of software such as desktop
application. It is not unusual to have more than one DSL. In-house developed software may
be stored in a shared networked location; commercial software or shrink-wrapped software
may be stored and managed from a cabinet.

The Release Manager will co-ordinate the creation of a Definitive Hardware Store (DHS).
The Definitive Hardware Store (DHS) is a location where spare parts are kept. It contains
only authorized hardware configuration items. It may include keyboards, mice, hard drives,
CD-ROMs, monitors or even entire workstations or servers. The items chosen for inclusion in
the DSL may depend on historical data, if available, for the items that most often fail. The
support group accesses the DHS when a failed part replacement is required to restore service.
It is controlled by release and change management. Inventories are recorded in the
Configuration Management Database (CMDB).

Process and procedures
The process and procedures stage will require input from various areas including the IT
architecture group, development, quality assurance, the Support Center, training and
production support. In addition the IT Service Management processes play key roles.

Communication and advocacy
Creating a process and implementing it requires effective communication and advocacy. The
process owner and the stakeholders can all assist with this by promoting the benefits of the
process.

Process implementation
Once the process is implemented, it is up to each participant to ensure his or her responsibilities are being met. KPIs and reporting are especially important at the early stages of process implementation. It is here that the greatest resistance to new processes will be felt.

5.2.3 Support Center Manager's role
Responsibilities and activities
The Support Center Manager is responsible for ensuring that all the Support Center requirements are provided to the Release Manager. These requirements will ensure that the Support Center is prepared for release implementations. Being prepared is the first step in providing quality service to the customer.
(See Sample Requirements Document.)

In addition, the Support Center Manager is the advocate of the business. The Support Center manager may deal with the business when there is a higher than usual call volume at the Support Center or when a rollout has not gone according to plan. Understanding the needs of the business is an important aspect of the Support Center manager's role. As the Support Center manager makes him/herself aware of all new releases as well as understanding the business, he/she is able to provide feedback on such items of concern as conflicting rollout or month-end requirements that will affect business productivity.
(See Business Considerations in the annex.)

Deliverables
- Requirements checklist *(see Annex)*
- Communicate to Support Center team
- Formal request to Release Management for reporting and management information requirements
- Business considerations *(see Annex Business impact analysis of Release Plan)* - month end, holiday, end-users informed, educated etc, planning in conjunction with the activities of the business or with IT activities: business considerations or IT considerations
- Policy for Standard Requests

Competencies
- Organization communication
- Advocacy for the Release Management process and its benefits
- Understanding of the business
- Training requirements of the Support Center Function
- Negotiation skills as requirements sign-off may be met with resistance

Key performance indicators (KPIs)
- Active participation in the process design
- Release Management's acceptance of the requirement provided by the Support Center
- Sign-off of process design, roles and responsibilities

5.2.4 Support Center Function's role
Responsibilities and activities
The Support Center Function should provide Release Management with a list of issues that the Support Center typically experiences with releases. Among all the requirements that the release team receives, the issues of the Support Center may seem insignificant; special attention may be required to ensure that the issues are dealt with appropriately.

The Support Center Function supports the Support Center Manager by providing/supporting the Manager with the requirements and needs of the team. Historically, having dealt with several implementations, the Support Center Function can relate first hand to the manager the challenges faced with each release.

Deliverables
• Review the Requirements List drafted by the Support Center Manager
• Identify areas of concern as they relate to historical releases
• Provide updates to the Requirements List as necessary

Competencies required
• Sound understanding of the policies and procedures of the Support Center
• Ability to pinpoint areas of issues with releases
• Ability to prioritize importance of issues raised
• Ability to translate needs into concrete deliverables

KPIs
• Number of incidents
• Comparison between this release and last major release
• Average talk time
• Average resolution time
• Technical questions, end-user training issues
• Overtime required to support issues

5.2.5 Planning for implementation
Steps to take
• Obtain buy-in from executive management. Before undertaking any major initiative, it is essential to have buy-in from executive management. They must be supportive of the new process and the benefits it will bring to the business and to IT. They will provide the funding for the initiative and will take a leadership role, providing guidance. If a steering committee is being considered for the design of the process, they will be members of the committee.
• Establish the team. The main members of the team will include the Project Manager, process owner, Process Manager, process design analysts and documentation specialists. There will also be representatives from various areas in the organization (stakeholders) including Development, Quality Assurance, Testing, Production Implementation and Technical Support Groups. Additional resources can be introduced to the team as required. This includes the gathering of specific requirements from other IT Service Management processes, such as Service Level Management, Problem Management etc. There would also

be sign-offs by stakeholders in the process who are not represented in the main team.

- Define the project scope, goals and objectives. This will assist the project team to focus on the implementation task.
- Provide comprehensive documentation. Document the policies, roles and responsibilities and the process and procedures.
- Promote and communicate the process. Promotion and communication of the process and the benefits to key stakeholders will assist with breaking down barriers and resistance, as is common with any new process implementation. Promote the benefits of release management to the areas that will be affected by the new process.
- Develop necessary repositories (DHS, DSL), quality assurance, user acceptance testing, staging areas, laboratories and procurement strategies.
  (See Planning for implementation requirements in the Annex.)

Groups to contact

Many groups are involved in the release management process. This is a list of typical groups that will interface with the planning stage of Release Management.

- Development
- Technical Support Groups
- Change Management
- Service Level Management
- Availability Management
- Quality Assurance
- Support Center

Necessary resources and relationships

The following relationships will be required for Release Management.

- Development - to incorporate requirements as they relate to the design and development of releases
- Quality Assurance - for testing of releases
- Problem Management - access to the Problem and Known Error Database
- Configuration Management - access to the Configuration Management Database
- Security Management - to provide necessary security requirements for releases
- Support Center - first level support
- Technical Support Groups - ongoing support

Necessary information and data

- Definitive Software Library (DSL) - established. It will be used to re-install software if an installation become corrupted. The DSL will also be used in ongoing installations (future requests, post initial implementation) of software by the Support Center.
- Definitive Hardware Store (DSL) - established. It will be used for spare parts inventory.
- Configuration Management Database (CMDB)- used to verify the correct hardware or software version that is currently in place. The CMDB will also provide the Support Center with information that will aid in determining impact analysis of an incident.
- Problems and Known Errors - along with release notes, this information will assist the Support Center in quick diagnosis and provide a workaround for previously identified issues.

- Documentation - including installation and back out procedures, configuration details and other documentation that may be available.

List of stakeholders:
- Support Center - they will support the release
- Technical Support Groups - they will receive the escalations
- Change Management - the gatekeeper, ensuring that all the deliverables are complete before the release is implemented
- executive sponsors - they are funding the release
- Development - designs the release
- Quality Assurance - ensures the release meets quality standards before installation.

Requirements checklist - each stakeholder will provide their requirements checklist, as well as processes that interface with Release Management The Support Center's own requirements checklist can be referenced to ensure all requirement and deliverables have been provided. A continuous review and update will ensure the Support Center's ongoing requirements are met.

Measurements that should be in place
- Roles and responsibilities assigned and understood
- Distribution of the process and procedures
- Documented work instructions and tasks to accompany the process and procedures

5.2.6 Implementing key process activities: hints and tips
What to implement first
- Definitive Software Library and Definitive Hardware
- Quality Assurance group
- Testing, staging laboratory
- Communication Plan

Things that always work
Training - train all necessary personnel on the process and procedures before the implementation date. For the Support Center, relying on peer training at implementation time may not be feasible. If the release has caused an influx of calls to the Support Center, all necessary personnel will be required. On-the-job training at this time will frustrate the customer (who is without service) and cause undue stress for Support Center staff. Formal comprehensive training on the features and the functionality of the impending release is critical. The Support Center Manager is responsible for facilitating the delivery of pre-release training of the highest possible caliber.

User Acceptance testing (UAT) -the Support Center should be involved in User Acceptance Testing. This acts not only as a training aid; it also allows the Support Center to become aware of issues that they may encounter at implementation. In addition, testing laboratories provide the Support Center staff with a training environment as well as error re-creation.

Pilot - if a pilot release is taking place, it will be beneficial to involve a few key members of the Support Center. This will allow them to experience the new hardware or software at first hand and understand the types of questions that customers will be calling about.

Documentation - insist on sign-off of the documentation before implementation. It should be delivered in enough time for the team to review and ask questions. Consider the Support Center's work schedule and their available time to review materials over the course of a given day.

Specialized support tools - specific tool requirements to support the release must be in place before implementation. In addition, training requirements on the tools must also be completed.

Little things that deliver big returns

What are the top 10 questions/calls to expect? These are the questions that are expected to result in 80% of the expected calls. Have the answers documented and distributed to the Support Center Function before implementation. This is a deliverable from the implementation team and should be included in the requirements document.

Escalation List - the Support Center needs to know who to contact if they cannot resolve the incident. Is second level support handled by the release team and for what period of time (as may be the case with large rollouts)? Are the usual support groups aware of the escalation requirements?

Service Management Tool - updates to the Service Management Tool should be completed before each implementation. This may require updates to the categorization section for record logging, as well as inclusion of the names and details (location, phone number email address, Cost Center) of new customers who will be calling the Support Center as a result of the release implementation. This can dramatically cut down on the call logging time as the main detail record for the caller is available. It will also reduce any customer frustration, as they do not have to spend time dictating their details to be entered into the Service Management Tool.

Support Center staff must log all calls, regardless of how insignificant they may seem. Logging all calls is essential for the Support Manager to justify budgeting for and hiring of additional staff. The metrics must reflect the reality of the staff being overloaded. Insist on this - as it truly does deliver big returns.

Little things that always get forgotten

Problems and Known Errors database accessible by the Support Center: the implementation groups may fail to make available the problems and Known Errors - or Problem Management may fail to update the database in time for the implementation. This database contains valuable information including troubleshooting symptoms that may help diagnose incidents that are received from the customer The database will contain workarounds to help mitigate adverse effects by getting the customer up and running sooner.

Communication to the end-users about each release: something is about to change for the end-users. The release team may be planning for everything to go off without a hitch, so they downplay the potential impact of the release. If no communication is delivered to the end-users and issues arise, this will be perceived negatively.

Communication to management: ensure that management is aware of major releases. Nobody wants senior management to be given no advance warning, then have to deal with a customer who is complaining about a release and the adverse impact it has had on their business. Make sure the executive is aware of all major releases. Be sure to inform them of any minor releases that may affect the customer in some way. A line of business manager may bypass the Support Center and complain directly to management when something goes wrong. Be sure to make management aware of issues and the resolution or expected resolution time. If a customer does make direct contact with them, management will be familiar with the issue and be able to respond with confidence.

5.2.7 Key process activities
Step-by-step prescriptive implementation guidance for each activity
The key activities that the Support Center is responsible for are included in the Requirements Checklist *(see Annex Requirements Checklist)*.

It is essential that the requirements provided by the Support Center are returned in sufficient time to take action on any specific requirements.

Training for the Support Center - ensure all required personnel are trained before implementation. On-the-job training during the implementation of the release will cause unnecessary stress on the Support Center Function and frustration for the customer in reporting the incident. Be sure to account for schedule training around vacations, shifts etc.

Documentation - provide comprehensive documentation for install/de-install, support etc. The Support Center should review all documentation to ensure it covers all aspects of support. In some circumstances, it will be necessary to create scripts as well as work and task instructions for releases. This will take time; plan accordingly.

Service Management Tool updates - addition of names, addresses etc. of new customers will help to speed up call logging. Updates to other aspects of the Service Management Tool as required should take place before the implementation date. This may include additions to the classification/categorization of systems, services, hardware etc.

Management information reports - Service Level Management will require reports to support the agreements for service. Special report generation should be planned for as early as possible. The Support Center can assist the Release Management Team by providing frequent reports regarding incidents that arise during the implementation. When implementations span several days, weeks or months, these reports can be used to mitigate reoccurring incidents.

Staffing requirements - it is essential that staffing requirements are considered. The implementation may be expected to generate call volumes greater than the capacity available with the current staff and the volume is expected to be maintained for an extended period of time. If so, additional full time or part time staff should be considered. Additional staff means training, training material, instructors and probably opposition to the associated costs. Bear these factors in mind and plan early for the implementation of these tasks. The alternative would be longer wait times and higher volumes of abandoned calls, which often results in lower customer satisfaction and service.

Hardware/software - if there is new hardware or software to support, the Support Center should have access to the equipment and software. The Support Center will benefit from this in two ways:
- they can see and touch what is often only described to them over the telephone
- they can replicate the issue if necessary.

Methods and techniques
Staffing requirements: understand where the Support Center's time is being spent. There will be a requirement for additional staff to support the ongoing maintenance of the new implementation as well as justification for the additional resource. To this end, it is essential that the Support Center staff log all incidents, service requests and all other requests in the Service Management Tool. The Service Management Tool provides the data that will demonstrate the volume of work being done in the Support Center. If less significant calls - or short calls - are allowed to go unrecorded, it may be even more difficult to justify the need for additional staff. Consider automating quick call logging. Resources such as the HDI Practices Survey may help to justify the need for additional staff.

Training: many Support Centers will be faced with the challenge of maintaining current service levels while attempting to train all their staff.

Types of training for consideration:
- 'train the trainer'
- classroom
- Release Notes
- training documentation
- 'lunch and learn'
- Web based training
- project implementation team temporary assignment.

Awareness campaign: conduct an awareness campaign about the Release Management process. This should include the policies, process and procedures together with contact information and feedback sessions.

5.2.8 Audits for effectiveness
Minimize adverse impact to the business
With any new process implementation, it is essential to monitor and audit the process for effectiveness. Overall, Release Management is tasked with delivering quality release implementations. The direct result of this effort will be the number of incidents (specifically related to this implementation) logged in the Service Management Tool. The Support Center can validate this through management information.

Because organizations vary in size and implementations vary from organization to organization, it is impossible to be specific about the number of incidents per release to determine if a release was effective. An analysis of incidents, time to resolve and whether they were resolved at first level support or second level support or beyond can help to determine if the release process was effective in minimizing any adverse impact on the business.
(See Audit for effectiveness in the annex.)

5.3 Ongoing operation

5.3.1 The ongoing process

Establishment of the policies, processes, procedures and initial requirements must be in place before the initial implementation. These same policies, processes etc. should be followed for all subsequent releases.

Once the initial rollout/implementation is complete, the Support Center will receive service requests for additional installations. It will interface with Configuration Management, the Definitive Software Library, the Definitive Hardware Store and Change Management. By following basic installation instructions, the Support Center can carry out routine software installations itself, or send support personnel to complete an installation.

Figure 5.4 shows the stages within an initial rollout, including the interface of information (Configuration Item Registration and updates), source code control (Definitive Software Library) and hardware inventory (Definitive Hardware Store) with each step in a release. The Ongoing Installations section shows the steps that will be followed by the Support Center after the initial rollout.

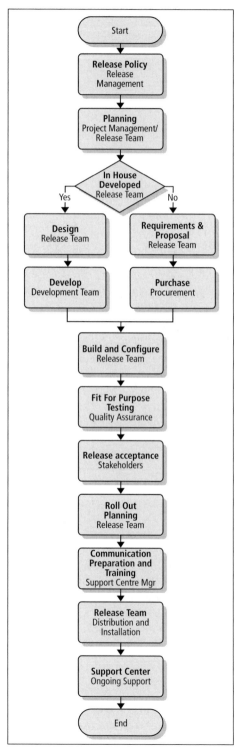

Figure 5.3 The ongoing operation of Release Management

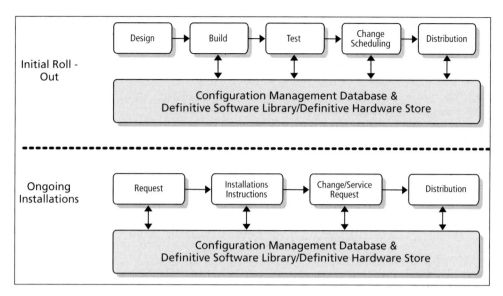

Figure 5.4 Initial Release rollout and the Support Center's role in the ongoing operation

5.3.2 Support Center Manager's role
Responsibilities and activities
- Monitor activities; liaise with the business and interface with senior management in the event of a high volume of calls.
- Institute 'on the fly' procedures to mitigate any issues from releases (e.g. extra staff - borrowed perhaps from other areas; front-end telephone message).

(See Ongoing Release Management process/Support Center Manager checklist in the Annex.)

Deliverables
- Updates to requirements as needs change
- Feedback to release management on call volumes, issues
- Participation in Project Implementation Review meetings
- Provides estimate for the cost of supporting the new service

Competencies required
- Team management skills
- Technical understanding of the environment
- Communication with other managers
- Budget and costing knowledge
- Authority to institute staffing changes in extreme situations (bring in temporary staff from external vendors, or internal areas outside the Support Center)

KPIs
- All Support Center requirements have been met.
- All staff adequately trained.
- Average talk time for 'issue' calls not to exceed level expected.
- Release Metrics for successful implementation

5.3.3 Support Center Function's role

Responsibilities and activities

The Support Center Function is required to:
- actively participate in training and user acceptance testing
- comply with policy and procedures set out by the release management team
- have access to Definitive Software Library
- have access to Configuration Management Database
- have access to problem and Known Errors data
- be equipped with support tools.

(See Ongoing Release Management/Support Center Function Checklist in the Annex.)

Deliverables
- Incident capture
- Successful restoration of service following incidents caused by a release
- Effective use of support tools (including Definitive Software Store, Configuration Management Database and Problem and Known Error Database)

Competencies required
- Ability to follow process
- Ability to multitask
- Quick learner
- Communication skills (both written and verbal)
- Ability to deal with customers in a friendly, supportive and helpful manner
- Basic Troubleshooting skills
- Ability provide the customer with friendly and understandable instructions based on technical documentation

KPIs
- Average talk time
- Quality Assurance verification of telephone calls (monitored or recorded)
- Recorded details of incidents complete and accurate
- Appropriate procedures for escalation
- All calls and requests to the Support Center are logged (recorded)

Steps and tips for maintaining this process
- Management Information Reports
- Active involvement in all releases, including participation in User Acceptance Testing and pilot implementations
- Active involvement in Change Management Change Advisory Board

5.4 Optimization

5.4.1 The optimization process

Inputs into the optimization of the Release Management and the analysis of the information will help to build the steps required for optimization. Figure 5.5 shows the optimization of Release Management from the Support Center's perspective. The Support Center Function provides the inputs and reports that the manager will review. Based on the information, the Support Center Manager analyzes the current state and determines the next stage for the Support Center within the Release Management process. The Support Center Function then executes the necessary steps towards improvement. Periodic review should occur at regular intervals and additional reviews as required.

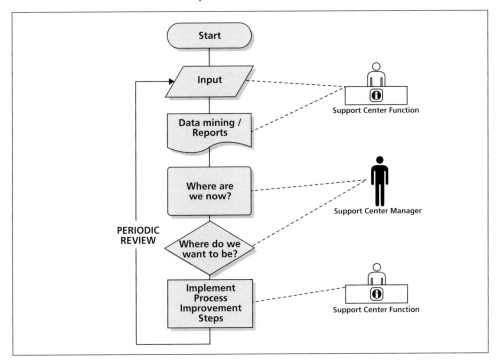

Figure 5.5 Optimization process

Below is a list of areas to investigate for optimization opportunities. The process must be operational for a period of time in order to evaluate its true impact on the environment. Consider the following guidelines and adjust them according to your circumstances. The process should be in operation for three to six months or produce four to five significant releases.

- Process and procedures
- Sign-offs
- Definitive Software Library

- Definitive Hardware Store
- Configuration Management Database
- Incident Data
- Change Management Reports

It is important to note that optimization does not need to take place area by area, such as 'all process and procedures' or 'all release criteria'. Consider looking at the most significant opportunity. This may be the optimization that will make the largest impact, provide the greatest waste saving or reduce the most cost. Continue through the cycle by optimizing the next largest obstacle and so on. Your process will never be more efficient than the largest bottleneck. *(See Annex Opportunities for optimization.)*

5.4.2 Support Center Manager's role
Responsibilities and activities
- Review management information of previous releases
- Compare outcomes of post-implementation releases to pre-implementation releases
- Review call volume trends compared to staffing level
- Updating and maintaining the requirements document
- Determine the greatest area for improvement
- Identify areas of improvement and prioritize
- Build action plan to initiate improvement
- Continuous improvement cycle of 'Plan-Do-Check-Act' must be repeated on a regular basis
(See Optimization requirements for the Support Center Manager in the Annex.)

Deliverables
- Review and update the Requirements Document as required and provide to Release Management
- Prepare and distribute management information to Release Management, support areas, and other interested parties regarding rollout statistics (include charts/graphs as required)
- Project plan to train staff for next major rollout
- Budgeting for staffing levels are at required levels
- Tools are sufficient and well authored
- Provide feedback to Release Management and/or project team
- Identify weak links - determine action to remedy

Competencies required
- Strategic positioning of the Support Center
- Analysis of trend metrics
- Ability to assimilate information and create strategic plan for improvement
- Authority to make it happen

KPIs
- Measure management information
- Productivity gains
- Incident Reduction

- Talk Time Reduction
- Average time to Resolution Reduction
- First Contact Resolution Increase

5.4.3 Support Center Function's role
Responsibilities and activities
In the optimization of the process, the Support Center Function is responsible for implementing process improvement initiatives as defined by the Manager. The Support Center Function will identify potential gaps in the process to the Manager and provide suggestions to improve the current situation.

Deliverables
- Identify potential process and procedure gaps.
- Implement and adhere to process and procedure updates.

Competencies required
- Ability to recognize and articulate improvement suggestions
- Ability to accept and adjust to updated processes, procedures, and work instructions on an ongoing basis.

KPIs
- Support Center Function implements and follows updates to process, procedures, work instructions effectively and efficiently

5.4.4 Steps and tips for optimizing this process
Accept feedback from those using the process. Feedback provided will assist in improving the process, reducing resistance and maintaining commitment to the process execution. The Support Center may identify repetitive and time-consuming tasks that might appear to be minor. These irritations could be causing a significant amount of stress to both customers and staff. Find ways to automate and simplify what is being done. Macros, templates and short-cut keys in the Service Management Tool can all assist with the optimization of the Release Management process.

Management Information will play a key role in determining what to optimize. There are two reference lists in the Annex. One provides a scale to measure the effectiveness of the implementation, and rate the elements with higher impact. The other provides hints as to where to begin looking for the cause of an issue. *(See Annex Audits for effectiveness.)*

The most obvious but often avoided step in optimization is the initiation of actions to improve the current situation. Prioritize the areas where the biggest benefits will be realized. Continue to manage the optimization process cycle by continuing to look for opportunities.

5.4.5 Future impact of this process on the Support Center
A well planned release takes into consideration all the best practice of Release Management including development, quality assurance, training and documentation. It includes the Support Center and all the Support Center requirements as early in the release process as

possible. It will have little impact on call volumes and talk times. Since the requirements of the Support Center will be included in the release criteria, training (Support Center and end user), awareness and communication will have all taken place before each release. This in itself should help to reduce the adverse impact that Releases can have on the Support Center.

There should be evidence of a decline in the call volumes caused by releases over a period of time. Consider extracting information that will show trends from the Service Management Tool.

A positive effect of this process on the Support Center would be reduced stress levels for its staff, because:
- new services are no longer a surprise and the Support Center Function is prepared to deal with issues that arise from releases in a timely, efficient and effective way
- there are fewer complaints from both external and internal customers
- call spikes are lower
- the Support Center is prepared, which enables it to answer questions and provide support.

One of the biggest impacts of the process is a satisfied customer. Not only will they see fewer implications and downtime from a release, their experience with the Support Center will be enhanced. The Support Center will:
- experience shorter queue wait times (due to a reduced influx of calls, emails and chat sessions)
- be better prepared to solve the incident at the first level - translating into quicker resolution for the customer and lower overall support costs.

Overall, IT will be seen favorably, as IT is usually seen as a reflection of the Support Center's ability to deal effectively with incidents and the customer. The Support Center and IT will benefit from higher satisfaction survey ratings from the business to IT (if applicable).

5.5 Measurement, costing and management reporting

5.5.1 Implementing: benefits and costs
Why implement this process and what can be gained
Proper release planning can deliver significant cost savings over 'rush to market' implementations. While the build and implementation cycle will be longer and incur some upfront costs, a quality release will offset the costs by mitigating the risk of business disruptions and high incident volumes.

Release Management can result in the following cost savings:
- lower support costs through lower call volume (average $32/call) [3]
- lower costs per call through faster resolutions
- fewer incidents means less business interruptions
- less cost in redundant work, fixing, and backouts
- lower support costs by supporting only authorized software releases
- lower licensing costs through control, compliance and recycling.

3 Source: HDI 2004 Practices Survey

Cost elements for implementation

Some of the cost elements associated with Release Management may already be in place in some IT organizations:

- development environment (including tools, servers)
- testing environment that replicates - or at least simulates the production environment
- version control tools
- Definitive Software Library
- Definitive Hardware Store
- Configuration Management Database (CMDB)
- technical writing resources.

The softer costs of Release Management are incurred through potentially longer build and implementation cycles. This may stem from training time and CMDB population and maintenance to problem database updates for related release units and known errors. However, the lower probability of lost revenue from system downtime more than justifies any incremental costs.

In general, process improvement projects will have similar costs:

- project management and/or consultant resources
- establishment of the team
- costs of providing substitute resources as applicable.

Making the business case to implement Release Management

Maintaining a stable, sustainable and flexible technical environment is IT's charter and contribution to the business. Nothing can damage that charter more than poorly planned, poorly coordinated and poorly tested releases. The dependence on technology makes the cost of downtime just too great.

To measure the true value of Release Management, one approach would be to measure the costs of a failed release against that of a Release Management managed quality release after implementation. By benchmarking a pre and post release model, the benefits and cost savings should be clear.

Metrics and Key Performance Indicators
During the implementation phase of the Release Management Process, the Critical Success Factors (CSF) will drive the Key Performance Indicators.

CSF: Process documentation

KPI:
• Process, policies, procedures, roles and responsibilities are clearly documented

CSF: Training and awareness

KPIs:
• Support of management has been established
• Awareness of Release Management to organization
• Documentation is distributed to all involved parties and their management
• Training for all stages of the process has been completed
• All mandatory training participants have completed training

CSF: All requirements of the process have been established

KPIs:
• Development environment established
• Hardware laboratory/Definitive Hardware Store in place
• Definitive Software Library is accessible (access permissions may apply)
• Release criteria are established
• Problems and Known Errors are recorded and accessible
• Lines of communication are established (to/from Support Center)
• Integration with Change Management Process (for sign-offs) defined

5.5.2 Ongoing operations: costs
Cost elements for ongoing operations
Support for new services - the technical support groups, those who are managing new servers and services, are not the only ones who require additional staffing resources to support new services. The volume of calls and requirements of process will require the Support Center staffing to be reviewed on a regular basis.

Review the metrics for additional number of incidents and service requests received in a given time frame. Look at the trends for these numbers. As new services are added, these numbers will increase. As old services are retired, the numbers will decrease. Trend analysis will assist in determining if the overall incidents and service requests will require additional staffing.

Cost of quality assurance laboratory - servers, workstations and all software and directly connected peripherals will provide appropriate simulation for testing.

Cost of documentation - customizing documentation and creating work instructions for the Support Center on an ongoing basis will require resource. Some questions to consider include:
- how often does a Release occur?
- what type of additional documentation does the Support Center prepare?
- are scripts required for each Release?
- what is the average time to create these?

Cost for tools to manage (if not already in place) - questions to consider include:
- is hardware required?
- if the Support Center is expected to support a piece of hardware that requires human interface, do they have a demonstrator in their area to sample? Examples include: PDAs, all-in-one printers, scanners and specialized monitors.

Metrics and Key Performance Indicators
In keeping with the goal of Release Management, Metrics and Key performance Indicators (KPI) should be driven from the process' critical success factors (CSFs).

Critical Success Factors (CSFs) for Release Management [4]
CSF: Consistent and repeatable process for software and hardware rollouts

KPIs:
- All releases go through Change Management process
- Releases conform with release criteria set out
- Software is checked into the DSL
- Urgent release implementations are not a result of poor planning

CSF: Quality Software and Hardware releases

KPIs:
- Reduction in failed or backed out changes (from releases)
- Reduction in incidents from Changes
- Reduction in incident resolution times for incidents from releases

CSF: Efficient implementation timing of releases

KPIs:
- Urgent requests due to planning deficiencies are reduced
- Process is not bypassed due to urgent nature of the release (there is compliance with the minimum requirements established for this purpose)

4 Planning To Implement Service Management, The Keys to Managing IT, © Crown Copyright 2002, The Stationery Office

Management reporting
KPIs can be derived from Management Reporting. KPIs provide the target audience with a snapshot of the performance of the process. Management Reporting can provide further details about specifics of the operation of the process.

Reports:
- percentage of incidents associated to release related problems and Known Errors
- percentage of releases implemented through source files in the Definitive Software Library
- percentage of retired software that has been removed and archived from the Definitive Software Library

5.5.3 Optimization: benefits and costs
In addition to the specific optimization opportunities the Support Center can initiate within their area the Release Management process as a whole should be reviewed on a regular basis. *(See Optimization, the optimization process, previously in this chapter.)*

Why optimize this process and what can be gained
Optimization of the Release Management process can save both time and money. Once the process has been implemented and has operated over several large and small releases, it can be further evaluated for optimization benefits.

A sure way to recognize the need for optimization is through stakeholders. If they are complaining about the process, there is room for improvement. A taskforce or committee made up of the process stakeholders will provide the biggest input into the areas to optimize. These stakeholders will provide feedback on what is working well and what needs to be improved.

Some Release requirements may be important for the initial release. For a Release that is repeated verbatim every week or month, efficiencies in processing as well as streamlining criteria may be possible.

Tools and tool integrations that were not considered in the initial implementation may be identified in the optimization process.

Efficiencies may be lacking in areas of sign-offs from development through to production. Development, Quality Assurance, User Acceptance Testing and Production Environments differ to such an extent that it could hinder the requirements for a quality release.

Cost elements for optimization
If the establishment of a taskforce is used to gather requirements, consider the time of each member of the team as well as any preparatory time and post meeting time required to formalize and review the information gathered. If meeting rooms and refreshments are included in meetings, these too will need to be considered as part of the cost of optimization.

Taskforce:
- planning costs: setting the agenda, organizing the meeting, booking the room or conference bridge
- meeting time (multiplied by the number of people in attendance)
- post meeting analysis: documentation of issues, review, analysis, proposal

Tools and tool automation: it may be possible to set up and administer a Release Management process without the use of formalized tools. Manual control of a Definitive Software Library (DSL) or manual monitoring of version numbering on documentation may work in the short term. However, over a longer period of time, maintaining the manual process may become more difficult and cost prohibitive.

Request for Proposal process:
- putting together the proposal
- researching potential vendors
- reviewing returned proposals
- meeting with potential vendors
- acquisition of the tool and licensing costs, and any additional hardware (if applicable)
- consulting fees to install/customize or integrate existing tools
- training (on-site, offsite)
- ongoing support and maintenance

When optimization concerns the review and update of process and procedures, internal and external resources may be required.

Process review and update:
- team members
- documentation specialist
- project management (as required)

Making the business case to optimize Release Management
The business case to optimize Release Management should include cost justifications as well as strategic vision. Through cost justification, you should estimate:
- the amount of time and effort required to perform and execute a specific task
- the cost when the task is not performed accordingly (to the Support Center, to IT, to the business)
- the number of times this happens due to lack of automated tools
- the total cost for these types of errors (historically, in the future)

Metrics and Key Performance Indicators
When optimizing the Release Management Process, the information that will help gauge the effectiveness on the optimization can be derived from all areas of Release Management:
- percentage of releases with fewer than X incidents
- percentage of releases with completed release criteria (QA, documentation sign-offs, DSL updates etc)
- percentage of completed releases that are successfully implemented

- percentage of releases that successfully complete the process before production implementation
- percentage of release implementations without incidents
- reduction in time from start to implementation of standard releases
- reduction in time to sign-off required for documentation.

5.5.4 Tools
Implementation
Service Management Tool: the service management tool should include integration between incident, problem (including Known Errors) and Change Management.

Change Management: as the Release Management process makes use of Change Management's requirement to record and track information about releases, this tool should provide automation wherever possible. The ability to authorize a change directly within the tool provides electronic sign-off, efficiency and metrics.

Software version control: an essential aspect of Release Management is the assurance that only correct and authorized versions of software are made available in production. Consider a tool that automates the registration of software and version numbering. The tool should be used from development, Quality Assurance through to production, including the Support Center's ongoing requirements to install or re-install the software on a customer's computer.

Ongoing operations
Automation of release distributions: the ability to 'push' to the desktop or 'pull' from a server releases, updates and patches as required.

Remote control: the ability to access a computer remotely will provide the Support Center with a time saving tool.

Some benefits and features include:
- the reduction in the number of questions that the Support Center Function must pose to the customer
- ability of the Support Center Function to visually demonstrate to the end-user the know-how necessary for them to help themselves in the future
- ability to remotely install software to fix or upgrade a customer's computer.

Reporting
The use of reporting tools must not be underestimated. If the tools selected do not include reports that meet your needs, consider a third party reporting tool to allow you to extract data into formatted reports. Some reporting tools are able to read and understand a variety of databases and data formats. In addition, importing raw data into a spreadsheet will allow for data sorting and analysis.

Annex A5.1 Requirements Checklists

Sample Requirements Document: Lists possible requirements that the Support Center may offer to the Release Management Team as ongoing requirements for each new release.

X	Sample Requirements Document
	Documentation
	End User Documentation sign-off
	Technical Documentation sign-off
	Top 10 expected questions the Support Center will receive (resulting in 80% of calls)
	Escalation Lists (provided)
	Service Level Management Requirements
	Service Level Agreements in place and expectations communicated to Support Center
	Operational Level Agreements in place and communicated to all involved staff
	Underpinning Contracts in place and contact & escalation details disseminated
	Reporting requirements delivered to Support Center
	Support Center Staffing Considerations
	How many 'net new' users will be calling the Support Center
	The expected call volume for this implementation initially and ongoing
	All 'New' Clients' personal details been added to the Service Management Tool
	Support Requirements
	Installed and functioning hardware in the Support Center for familiarization and ongoing learning, testing and reference - to support the customers
	Software - installed on a comparable piece of equipment
	Configuration Management Database updated
	Definitive Software Library updated
	Problem and Known Error database updated and accessible
	Training
	All required Support Center staff have received training that is fit for purpose
	Schedule of number of Support Center Staff who can be trained at any given time
	Support Center - scheduled to participate in User Acceptance Testing
	Service Management Tool Updates
	Categorization fields/Classification of new incidents
	New customers (name, address, location) for incident registration added to tool

A5.2 Audits for effectiveness

The benefits of the Release Management process are in its ability to minimize the adverse impact of releases on the business. This can be determined through: Service Level Breaches or by sheer incident/all volumes due to the release. The following table of audit descriptions may assist with pinpointing the cause of incidents.

Audit	Details
Review Incident Records (depending on the volume, automation available and resource, this may be all records or a sampling of the records logged as a result of the Implementation	Categorize issues logged and provide feedback to appropriate area and the Release Manager. For new Releases, this task may occur very frequently (hourly or daily basis). As this specific implementation ages, the feedback may occur weekly, monthly etc. This may be repeated for each new Release.
Process Effectiveness	Was the incident a result of process breakdown? Were all steps followed in the process?
Quality of Requirements Issue?	Were any incidents a result of a requirement not being completed or delivered incomplete?
Business Impact	Did affected users know the release was being implemented? Was there any business conflict in the timing of the release?
Training Effective	Was the training provided to the Support Center effective? Were any incident resolutions delayed (see talk times) due to the Support Center function requiring additional time to read the instructions/release notes?
Problem Management & Problem and Known Error Effectiveness	Were any new problems identified after the implementation? Were any issues related to an existing problem/Known error? Was the problem & Known Error Database used as intended? Did it assist with resolution of incidents?
Configuration Management	Was the CMDB updated?
Software Errors	Did customers discover errors in the software after implementation?
Hardware Configuration Errors	Did customers discover errors in the hardware configuration after implementation?
DHS/DSL	Were new versions of software registered in the DSL? Were spare parts registered in the DHS?
Other Issues (e.g. Security)	Other issues/reports - may be categorized individually if numbers warrant.

A5.3 Release Management - Business Consideration

Quality communication between IT and the business is critical to successful release management. As the rollout plan is being developed, key business units must be consulted to determine the optimum timeframe for implementation. Several considerations may affect release - such as day of week, time of month, business projects, marketing campaigns, etc. Coordinating release implementation with business activities will reduce incidents and increase the success of the release.

The following checklist will help IT plan releases according to the needs of the business.
Release Management - Business Consideration Checklist
Release name: _____ Planned Release Date: _____
Business units impacted: _____

Business Impact	Business Unit 1	Business Unit 2	Business Unit 3
Impact on release dates			
Best day of week			
Worst day of week			
Best day(s) of month			
Worst day(s) of month			
Best time of year			
Worst time of year			
Impact on business activities			
Dates of departmental events (campaigns, projects deadlines, end of month accounting)			
Impact on hours of operation Regular operations Extended hours of operation Weekend hours of operation			
Blackout dates			
Comments			

A5.4 Planning for Implementation Requirements List

Listed in the following table are responsibilities of the Release Manager and Support Center Manager in the planning stage of Release Management.

Planning For Implementation	
Release Manager:	Support Center Manager:
Buy-In (Support) from Senior Management	
Establish Release Management Team Stakeholders required.	Support Center Manager or permanent designate (for continuity) assigned (for initial and subsequent releases
Define the project scope, goals and objectives	Support Center Manager participates
Documentation Policies Roles and Responsibilities Process Procedures	Provide input and review documentation. Assign Support Center resources to document specific Support Center procedures and work instruction.
Promotion and Communication	Distributed via standard means (this is often the Support Center's Responsibility Support Staff (2nd/3rd Level Support) Managers of the staffed areas Business
Requirements Procurement Development Quality Assurance IT Service Management Processes 2nd Level/ 3rd Level Support Support Center	Support Center Manager or Designate will provide "Support Center Requirements" check list
Coordinate the creation of policy and/or procedures around the DSL	Training, including policy and procedures for the Support Center Function
Coordinate the creation of policy and/or procedures around the DHS	Training, including policy and procedures for the Support Center Function

A5.5 Ongoing Release Management process

The following two tables outline the responsibilities of the Support Center Manager and the Support Center Function in the ongoing Release Management process.

Support Center Manager's Task List
Once the process and procedures have been implemented and the pilot Release passes through the process, the ongoing process cycle carries on. For each Release, the standard activities will still need to be completed. The following table shows the phase in the Release process and the task the Support Center Manager should be engaged in.

Phase	Task
Design	Continued participation and input on all implementation initiatives
Build	Provides consultation as required by the implementation team
Test	Assign resources to participate in User Acceptance testing. Makes Support Center resources available for pilot stage on implementations
Request For Change	Participates in the Change Advisory Board to ensure all Support Center Requirements have been signed off before implementation.
Distribution	At initial distribution, ensures call volumes are complimented with appropriate staffing levels. Adds staff to telephone queue as required (this may involve 'borrowing' staff from other areas) Considers modifying the incoming message on the phone to alert the caller that excessive call volumes are being received. Updates senior management and business as required as to the status of Release (such as high call volumes, trouble with automated distribution that will have a significant impact on the customers).

Support Center Function Checklist
The following are some Support Center Function responsibilities associated with ongoing releases.

X	Support Center Function Responsibilities and Activities in the Release Process
	Attend training
	Review problem and known error database
	Understand the escalation path
	Read the user and technical documentation
	Read and understand Policy and Procedures
	Be able to accurately log, including classification any issues reported
	Participate in User Acceptance Testing
	Participate in Pilot Testing
	Be willing to follow scripts and work/task instructions that compliment that process and procedures
	Comments:

A5.6 Steps for Maintaining the Release Management Process

Support Center Manager Checklist

For Release Management to be continuously successful, the process must define repeatable activities that produce consistent results. A checklist to ensure the process and procedures are being followed should be completed with every release. The following are examples of checklist items.

Phase	Task	Date Started	Date Completed
Scope Requirements	Received - by the Support Center Manager Reviewed - by the Support Center Manager		
Testing	User Testing Support Center Function Testing		
Training	User Training Support Center Function Training		
Documentation	Documentation Received Documentation Reviewed/Accepted Known errors published		
CMDB	Affected CIs updated and reviewed		
DSL	New versions registered Older versions retired		
Incident logging	Categories and Priorities defined Escalation paths defined		
Staffing	Peak and volumes predicted Staff schedules adjusted for rollout		
Reporting	Reporting Requirements Received Reports Developed and Tested		
Backout/Continuity	Backout plan for Continuity defined and tested		
Rollout Plan	Published to Users/Support Center Adjusted - Business Considerations Accepted (Users/Support Center)		

As assigned by the Support Center Manager, the Support Center Function must understand and complete the tasks defined in the above checklist for every release. Key Performance Indicators for the Support Center would include compliance with the Release Management activities that require Support Center participation or performance.

A5.7 Opportunities for Optimization

Revisit the list used in the Audit for Effectiveness to determine the areas for optimization. Place a value on a scale of 1-4 in the column on the right.

1 = Strongly Agree (Critical Impact)
2 = Agree (High Impact)
3 = Disagree
4 = Strongly Disagree

Audit	Details	Score
Process Effectiveness	Incidents were a result of process breakdown	
	Not all steps were followed in the process	
Quality of Requirements Issue?	Incidents were a result of requirements not being completed or delivered incomplete	
Business Impact	Customers were surprised by the Release implementation	
	The business was affected by the 'untimely' Release	
Training Effective	The training provided to the Support Center was not effective	
	Incident resolutions were delayed due to the Support Center Function requiring additional time to read the instructions/release notes?	
	There was a significant number of How-To questions	
Problem Known Management &	Problems were identified after the implementation?	
	Incidents were not related to an existing Problem/Known error	
Problem and Error Effectiveness	The Problem & Known Error Database was not used as intended	
	Problem and Known Error Database was not used to assist with incident resolution	
Configuration Management	The CMDB was not updated	
Software Errors	Errors in the software discovered by customers after implementation	
Hardware Configuration Errors	Errors in the hardware configuration discovered by customers after implementation	
DHS/DSL	New versions of software were not registered in the DSL	
	Spare parts were not registered in the DHS	
Other Issues (e.g. Security)		

The scores associated with each question may assist you in determining which to take action on first. Those that scored 1 had a more negative effect than the scores of 2.

Evaluate the Optimization Chart to determine what areas to focus on. Look at the items scoring 1s and 2s. The chart below provides some suggestions on areas for further investigation. Finally, initiate action to remedy the situation so that it does not recur.

Details	Where to begin investigative action
Incidents were a result of process breakdown. Not all steps were followed in the process	Were support groups adequately trained on the process and procedures to be followed?
Incidents were a result of a requirements not being completed or delivered incomplete	Did all requirements receive sign-off before implementation?
Customers were surprised by the release implementation. The business was affected by the 'untimely' release	Was communication to the business effective? Were considerations for the Release date taken into account?
The training provided to the Support Center was not effective. Incident resolutions were delayed due to the Support Center Function requiring additional time to read the instructions/release notes. There was a significant number of How-To questions	Did the training target the correct audience? What additional training would better prepare the Support Center? Does the Support Center staff require quiet time to read necessary documentation? Was end-user training considered?
Problems were identified after the implementation. Incidents were not related to an existing problem/Known error. The Problem and Known Error Database was not used as intended. Problem and Known Error Database was not used to assist with Incident resolution	Were QA and UAT effective? Do the Testing plans require additional detail? Is this easy to research and complete? Is there an issue with executing the Incident Management Process? Were the problems and Known Errors entered in the Problem Management Database in time for the rollout? Was the information from the Release Team provided in the correct format?
The CMDB was not updated	Review procedures in Configuration, Release and Change to determine where the process breakdown occurred.
Errors in the software discovered by customers after implementation	Were QA and UAT effective? Do the Testing plans require additional detail?
Errors in the hardware configuration discovered by customers after implementation	Were QA and UAT effective? Do the Testing plans require additional detail?
New versions of software were not registered in the DSL. Spare parts were not registered in the DHS	Review release process to determine breakdown.

A5.8 Optimization Requirements for the Support Center Manager

The following checklist may be adapted for the Support Center manager's use. It is intended to assist with optimizing the release process as it affects the Support Center.

X	Optimization requirements for the Support Center Manager
	Review management information of previous Releases Compare the outcomes of Releases that were implemented with the new process to those that were implemented before the process Has the Release had a positive effect on the Support Center? Are there any negative effects? What could be done to mitigate them?
	Review call volume trends compared to staffing levels Are staffing levels sufficient? Are additions or reductions required?
	Update and submit to release management, the requirements document Are any requirements unnecessary? Remove from list. Are new requirements required? Make additions to list
	Identify areas of improvement Is the process effective? Are the procedures useful? Are the scripts/work instructions and tasks effective? Are calls easy to log in the Service Management Tool? What can be done to speed up the logging of Incidents?
	Prioritize your findings What is the top process improvement to be implemented? What is next on the list?
	Build an action plan to initiate improvement What are the steps required to implement the improvement Who needs to buy-in to the improvements? How long will this take to complete? Action the improvement
	Monitor the improvement process, report regularly and adjust as necessary What is the key performance indicator for each improvement activity? Is the implemented improvement achieving its desired outcome?
	Comments

Bibliography

Stop Being a Victim! Char LaBounty, © 2000, Help Desk Institute

HDI 2004 Practices Survey, © 2004, HDI

Best Practices for Service Support: The Keys to Managing IT, © Crown Copyright, 2000, The Stationery Office

Planning To Implement Service Management, The Keys to Managing IT, © Crown Copyright, 2002, The Stationery Office

IT Service Management, an Introduction, © May 2002, itSMF-International

Chapter 6:
Incident Management

6.1 Overview

6.1.1 Description
An incident is any event that is not part of the standard operation of a service and which causes, or may cause, an interruption to, or a reduction in the quality of a service. Incident Management processes restore normal service operation as quickly as possible and minimize any adverse impact on business operations, thus ensuring that the best possible levels of service quality and availability are maintained. "The Support Center exists to professionally manage, coordinate and resolve incidents as quickly as possible and to ensure that no request is lost, forgotten or ignored."

6.1.2 Relationships to other processes
Processes that are directly affected by Incident Management include:
- Service Level Management (staffing issues may affect ability to meet service level agreements)
- Knowledge Management (knowledge collected may be added to the CMDB (and/or Knowledgebase)
- Problem Management (a collection of incidents may be identified as a problem, and Customer Service Management (poor or inadequate Incident Management will show up in poor customer service ratings).

Incident Management may be affected by any other process. Overall, the affect of, and on, other processes will vary widely across organizations. Some considerations include the maturity level of the IT department, the complexity of the technology being provided and supported, and the level of adoption of formal processes.

Incident Management should interface very closely with Problem Management and Change Management processes, as well as the various functions of the Support Center. If they are not properly controlled within an organization, changes to systems may introduce new incidents, so mechanisms for tracking changes are required. Most ITIL experts recommend that incident records are recorded on the same Configuration Management Database as the problem, known error and change records (or at least linked somehow) to improve interfaces between the various processes. (ITIL IT Service Management Essentials Course Workbook: 91) Figure 6.1 shows some of the possible relationships with other processes.

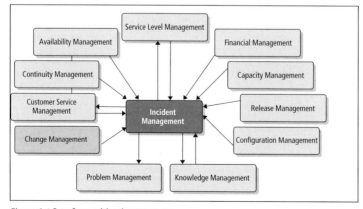

Figure 6.1 Interfaces with other processes

6.1.3 Key inputs and outputs to the process

Description	Source	Importance
Inputs		
Incident details	Support Center Network Group Computer operations Customers	High
Configuration details	Configuration Management Database (CMDB)	High
Response from incident matching against problems and Known Errors	Problem and Known Error Databases (in CMDB and/or Knowledgebase)	High
Resolution details	Incident Management Problem Management	High
Response on Requests for Change (RFC) to effect resolution for incident(s).	Change Management Problem Management	Medium
Outputs		
Resolved and closed incidents	Incident Management	High
Communication to customers	Incident Management Problem Management Customer Service Management	High
RFC for incident resolution; updated incident record (including resolution and/or workarounds)	Change Management, Problem Management Incident Management	Medium
Management Information (reports).	Incident Management Problem Management Change Management	Medium
Knowledgebase and/or CMDB	Configuration Management Knowledge Management	High

6.1.4 Possible problems and issues

Potential problems associated with implementing incident management within an organization include the following.

Issue/problem	Potential resolution
Shortage of resources needed for implementation and subsequent maintenance Lack of commitment from senior management might also result in other issues/problems (i.e. difficult to obtain buy-in from stakeholders) Issues other than lack of commitment could result in shortage of resources (e.g. poor planning)?	Constant communication with senior management as key stakeholders will keep them informed of progress while regaining their current commitment. Use of robust forecasting techniques from financial, project management and resource staffing perspectives will provide a good roadmap. Obtaining feedback from all the business units and extended team members about what will be needed to complete the work estimated in the next fiscal year will help provide the needed funding and resources to cover the work planned. These might include: additional employees, system capacity, tools, consulting services, process maintenance/maturity activities and auditing functions.
A lack of awareness or understanding among employees about what incident management is or how it applies to them.	A successful awareness campaign crafted with all stakeholders in mind can help overcome this issue. To build awareness consider 'branding' the effort through the use of targeted communication, themes, rewards and recognition programs.
Customer service levels are not defined or inadequately defined.	These should be established through the introduction of Service Level Management within your organization. Evaluating the customer's current perception of service levels is a place to start so that improvement can be measured once the service level agreements are in place.
Lack of knowledge or inadequate training for Support Center staff to resolve incidents.	Allocate funding and enlist the support of senior management to strengthen your staff training program. This alone will add credibility to the reputation of your Support Center as being knowledgeable and efficient in solving customer incidents, and increase levels of service. Provide the best training you can afford. For maximum impact and ROI, be sure to provide continuing education after Implementation training to reinforce the original training and to introduce changes.
Low customer confidence in the Support Center - perception that the Support Center is inadequate.	Identify the issues that create a poor perception of the Support Center among its customers. For instance, were negative comments provided in a customer satisfaction survey? The key is to define the perception issues and create strategies to build customer confidence in the Support Center. (For examples of potential questions to ask in a Customer Satisfaction Survey, refer to the Customer Satisfaction chapter in this book and/or the Annex Support Center- Customer Satisfaction Survey.)

	Develop a marketing campaign to promote what has been done to address customer complaints, and report to customers on how the Support Center is meeting SLAs, improving in specific areas, etc. to manage customer perceptions.
Poor integration with other processes, especially Service Level, Change and Problem Management	Define your incident process first. Then implement an automated tool to support your incident process. Do not buy a tool first and then fit the process to the tool.
Resistance to change. Staff will resist changing the way they conduct their day-to-day work activities.	Incorporate principles of organizational change (ensure everyone understands the end goal vision, gaining buy-in from staff, etc.) to help to minimize resistance. (Refer to Annex document titled Organizational Change References.)
The same problems are being resolved repeatedly rather than identifying and eliminating them from the infrastructure.	A compliant Incident Management process will record the incident details and match them against known errors and problems, so the same ones will not resurface.
Workarounds are not shared with other support staff when they are identified.	Workarounds should be entered into a knowledgebase or CMDB immediately and made available to all support staff instantaneously.
Not being kept up to date with changes and/or Releases being made in the business.	Once the Support Center is established as the single point of contact for customers, ensure that the business reports all planned changes/Releases in a timely manner. This enables the Center to be adequately prepared to respond to enquiries about those changes.
No management information available, so decisions are made on what the support representative thinks instead of what they know.	Appropriate metrics must be identified, and then information about them captured. Metrics reporting will enable the Support Center to base its decisions about training needs on reliable data rather than educated guesses. If training gaps are identified through metrics reporting, Support Center management can provide direction for future training sessions for Support Center staff. This will enable them to make use of knowledge rather than guessing at troubleshooting techniques.
Lack of agreed customer service levels.	Build relationships with all your customer bases and begin to put service levels in place that both parties agree to.
Poor software tools to support Incident Management.	Listen to the feedback from tool users and begin to document new requirements for a tool that will better support the process in place. Build the case to build or buy a better tool when economically feasible.

Quality issues

Potential quality issues associated with Incident Management within organizations may include the following.

Standardization - during all phases of Incident Management process development and implementation, the use of a technical writer to provide a consistent 'look and feel' to Incident Management materials is strongly recommended. In ongoing operations as well as working toward optimization, staff from the areas affected by Incident Management process changes should be included in identifying current process gaps and their associated process improvement initiatives.

Budgetary constraints - implementing Incident Management will cost money. A cost-benefit analysis will help to identify opportunities to improve current processes. It may be necessary to hire consultants to assist with gap analyses and/or training efforts, hire staff dedicated to Incident Management efforts or purchase new tools to help support the process. However, the potential benefits to the customer and business will outweigh the costs.

Skill shortages - certain skill sets will be needed when implementing a new process, based on the Incident Management goal state. The necessary skill sets may or may not already exist in the organization. Plans will need to be put in place to bring personnel up to speed on Incident Management frameworks and processes; training plans for new staff must be created; and initiatives started to ensure new skill sets are identified at the same time as new process improvement opportunities.

(For additional information, see Annex A6.1 Overview of the Capability Maturity Model and Annex A6.2 Questions to Guide Sustainable Change.)

Security issues

It is important to determine the security issues that might arise as a result of implementing Incident Management. These might include the following.

Security departments within the organization may not be comfortable with the Support Center handling such incidents as password resets. These may have to be handled by the central Security Department instead.

Authorization forms may be required for Support Center personnel to gain access to certain security-related products and services.

New processes may be necessary to ensure that products and services are recovered quickly, yet within secure parameters so as not to compromise IT security policies.

Physical access to computer and network equipment should be restricted to authorized personnel only.

A decision not to implement Incident Management may result in:
- no one managing and escalating incidents, which may ultimately have an adverse impact on IT service quality
- specialist support staff interruptions, making them less productive (when many issues could have been resolved by first-line Support Center personnel)
- disruption of normal work duties within departments as co-workers ask one another for help instead of contacting the Support Center
- lack of coordinated management information
- lost, incorrectly managed or badly managed incidents.

6.2 Implementation

6.2.1 Support Center Manager's role
Responsibilities and activities
An important part of the Support Center Manager's role is to define what Incident Management means to the Support Center. The Support Center Manager will also need to define how the Center's use of the process interfaces with other processes (Change Management, Problem Management, etc.), functions and/or departments. A good starting point in implementing service management is to ask the question: 'What best practice elements are already established and in operation?'

The Support Center Manager should also take part in determining how Incident Management behavior can provide data relating to other processes. As the central point of contact for customers, the Manager must ensure that information detected and classified by the Support Center will be of value to other parts of the organization.

Deliverables
The Support Center Manager should first conduct a current state assessment. The Manager should take into consideration what differentiates this Center from others. Implementing Incident Management is not a 'one size fits all' proposition; the Manager should create a 'differentiation document.' This will provide a clear understanding of the current state of the Support Center, to enable effective definition of the goal state and how to achieve it.

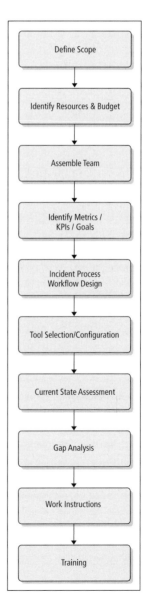

Figure 6.2 The implementation process

Consider the following questions when creating this document:
• What is the norm in Support Centers? Use existing Support Center/Service Desk research to determine how your Support Center compares with other Centers.
  What makes the Center unique? Consider the unique attributes of your Center. Are all customers in the same region? Does your Center support international customers? Are there different regulations that must be followed for different customer bases?
  How complex or diverse are the applications and systems that are being supported?
  The resulting 'differentiation document' can then be used to drive processes related to Incident Management, including (but not limited to) hours of operation and staff needs.[4]

The Support Center Manager should compare the Center to maturity models. Examples include:
• the Capability Maturity Model, which helps to apply process improvement techniques using lessons learned from previous projects
• ITIL Best Practice framework information available in the public domain. (Refer to description in Quality Issues section)

A Gap Analysis document should be created that identifies the current state of the Support Center and any gaps that exist (between the Center and other Centers and also between current state and desired goal state). This document will drive such activities as the creation of work instructions, training materials, job aids etc.

The Support Center Manager will probably need to develop a budget for implementing Incident Management. Additional information can be found in the *Measurement, Costing and Management Reporting* section at the end of this chapter.

Competencies
The Support Center Manager who is rolling out Incident Management should be a strong leader. The manager will act as, or coordinate with the Project Manager for all the activities required for a successful implementation. Communication and financial skills will both be assets before, during and after implementation.

The Support Center Manager should have a good understanding of the organization where Incident Management will be implemented. The Manager should have good interpersonal skills (and the ability to influence others), Project Management abilities and a certain level of authority within the organization. The Support Center Manager will need to create a team of people with representatives from each area or department that is being implemented. This team should socialize and communicate the changes ahead, working to build trust and acceptance. Most problems and difficulties in implementation are a result of a resistant audience that will fight the process changes internally.[6]

A Support Center Manager who is supportive and encouraging in leading the Center and organization through changes, and is able to partner closely with other departments and areas as they are implemented, will achieve more through cooperation and integration than one who does not. Specific competencies include ITIL, metrics and measurement (Six Sigma), workflow and integration points with the other processes such as understanding the Root Cause Analysis (RCA) within Problem Management.

Key Performance Indicators

With the assistance of Support Center staff, the Manager should consider measuring the following types of critical success factors to ensure the planning and strategies of Incident Management were successful:

- Gap Analysis - did the current state assessment and future goal state truly allow for an appropriate gap analysis to occur? Were any gaps identified through the course of the assessment left open?
- work instructions - were quality work instructions specific to the Support Center created and implemented as part of rollout?
- training materials - how satisfied were Support Center users with the training materials related to Incident Management created for implementation? How many gaps were identified? Have these been closed?
- knowledge transfer - use competency checks amongst Support Center staff to determine the success of knowledge transfer about the Incident Management process
- timely completion of implementation - was Incident Management implemented in the timeframe originally committed to?
- stakeholder buy-in - did all the applicable stakeholders 'buy in' to the concept and processes associated with Incident Management?

6.2.2 Support Center Function's role

Responsibilities and activities

With the direction of the Support Center Manager, the Support Center staff will implement the Incident Management process. Its primary role within the process will be to serve as the customer-facing, single point of contact for customers. It will provide guidance to customers and work toward restoration of service, monitor incident resolution and assist the Manager in providing reporting information.

Specific to Incident Management planning and implementation, the Center will provide input into:

- the Gap Analysis by helping the Manager identify where gaps exist between current state and future/goal state processes
- work instructions, as the Center staff best understand the level of detail that will be needed to ensure that everyone understands what will be required in the future
- training materials, because Center personnel can gauge what kinds of materials will (and will not) be successful
- how knowledge about the Incident Management process will be transferred to the staff.

Deliverables

Working together, the Support Center and Manager will develop a blueprint for how Incident Management will function within the Center. Because each Center is unique with a different set of needs, it is important that a significant amount of time goes into planning what is required for the organization's Incident Management rollout to be a success.

High-level deliverables to be created during implementation may include:
- Current State Assessment
- Gap Analysis
- work instructions
- job aids
- tool and core process training materials.

Competencies

As with the Support Center Manager, there is no specific set of experiences or backgrounds that must be in place to ensure a successful Incident Management process rollout to the Center. There are, however, several intangible qualities that should not be overlooked when identifying personnel to assist with Incident Management implementation planning. People who are willing to champion change, have positive 'can-do' attitudes and have a strong work ethic as team players will keep the momentum going.

In general, the Manager should consider the qualities needed in both first-line (and second-line as applicable) support staff, as well as any operations personnel who will help roll out Incident Management.

Best practice suggests that all staff involved in supporting customers should be:
- customer-focused
- articulate and methodical
- trained in interpersonal skills
- able to understand the business's objectives.

Operations experience (specifically call center / help desk experience) generally is associated with greater levels of empathy with customers' issues and results in more customer satisfaction within the Incident Management process. The abilities to adapt easily and quickly to change and to perform under pressure are necessities for both first-line support staff and operations leadership.

A search for staff with process design, development, implementation and application experience should also be considered. Technical skills are, of course, necessary for successful Incident Management. However, those technical skills must be paired with a general understanding of the systems and applications that support the business.

Key Performance Indicators

The Support Center Manager should create the vision for the Center environment when Incident Management processes have been implemented and integrated. The Support Center staff will assist the Manager in measuring the following types of critical success factors to help determine whether implementing planning and strategies used were successful:
- Gap Analysis - did the current state assessment and future goal state truly allow for an appropriate gap analysis to occur? Were any gaps identified through the course of the assessment left open?
- work instructions - were quality work instructions specific to the Support Center created and implemented as part of rollout?

- training materials - how satisfied were Support Center users with the training materials related to Incident Management? How many gaps were identified? Have they been closed? Do they understand how to perform their jobs in the new environment?
- knowledge transfer - the level of knowledge about the Incident Management process can be determined by competency checks among the Support Center staff
- timely rollout - was the Incident Management process implemented on time?

Other key roles and functions in the implementation process
In addition to the Support Center manager and analysts, some additional functional roles may be helpful in the Incident Management implementation process:
- process design consultant: a process design consultant may be used to perform gap analyses and write associated work instructions for groups to help them close any identified gaps between current and goal states

  process trainer: trainers may be employed to train areas on Incident Management processes and detailed work instructions

  class registrar: additional staff may be used to not only register people for upcoming training sessions, but also to track the people who have gone through process training, which will help ensure everyone has participated.

  technical writer: a technical writer on staff can help with all your documentation - the process handbook, assisting with meeting minutes or helping with the content and compilation of training materials.

6.2.3 Planning for implementation
Consider using the following project management strategies and documents in putting together a toolkit for Incident Management implementation: Refer to the Annexes for sample documents (where applicable).

- Meeting agenda template to be used for status meetings, start-up meetings, etc.
  (See Annex A6.3 Agenda for Implementation Meeting)

- Representative list of the personnel representing various areas *(See Annex A6.4 Project Teams)*

- Deliverables Contract defining which deliverables the sponsor will sign off
  (See Annex A6.5 Deliverables Contract)

- Incident Charter, a document explaining the implementation and why it is being done
  (See Annex A6.6 Project Charter sample)

- Incident Scope defining the areas/applications that will implement Incident Management
  (See Annex A6.6 Project Scope sample)

- Project work plan providing the dates and schedule for delivery (including milestones and key deliverables) *(See Annex A6.8 Support Center - Implementation Workplan)*

- Communication Plan showing how, when and to whom the Support Center will be communicating (as well as the vehicle(s) that will be used) *(See Annex A6.10 Steps to developing a Communications Action Plan)*

- Training Plan for who needs to attend, invitation strategy, location information, materials to be used, etc

- Current State Assessment with questions to determine the organization's current maturity

- Gap Analysis to identify any gaps between current state and ITIL/Incident Management goal state *(See Annex A6.11 Gap Analysis Questionnaire)*

- Incident Work Instructions showing a detailed, step-by-step process for conducting Incident Management within the area

Steps to take
At a high level, the following project activities should be part of the Incident Management implementation:
- Determine scope
- Identify key roles
- Address awareness
- Identify gap-related opportunities (between current and goal states)
- Identify and develop documentation (training materials, policies, work instructions, etc)
- Schedule and conduct training
- Formally implement the process

Groups to contact
- Service Level Management
- Change Management
- Problem Management
- Any other process groups in existence in your organization
- Communications Department

Before the planning stage, make every attempt to engage top management and gain their support for implementation efforts. During the planning phase, determine the key stakeholders for implementation. Every in-scope area that will be affected by the Incident Management implementation (as well as any external projects with touch points) should be included in all communication strategies.

Necessary resources and relationships
The first and foremost relationship for ensuring a successful implementation is gaining sponsorship within the organization. Without an active senior level sponsor, the initiative would go nowhere. Enroll all personnel responsible for the current Support Center function into the process of improving the strategies already in place. Then, identify a framework such as ITIL to provide guidance for the efforts.[7]

Necessary information and data
Start the implementation planning process within the Support Center by base-lining current levels of activity. The Center can explore basic transaction volumes to determine the effectiveness of the current system. This will help to establish the cost associated with the effectiveness (or ineffectiveness) of processes within the current system. A review of such data can point to obvious improvements.

Improvement areas may include time to resolve, number of tickets that can be handled 'first time final' versus escalated tickets, etc. Look at the lifecycle cost of the process, but recognize that costs may be high before process improvements are made. Costs will go up during implementation, but then reduce over time. [7]

Measurements that should be put in place
The planning phase of Implementation should include determining what will be measured with each Incident Management activity. Examples include:
• ensuring that all gaps identified during the Gap Analysis are closed as necessary
• competency checks after process training
• periodic evaluations of effectiveness compared to the baseline.

6.2.4 Implementing key process activities: hints and tips
What to implement first
• The Support Center Manager should determine the vision / mission for Incident Management within the organization. All additional activities should align with this vision / mission.

Things that always work
• Gain highly visible and vocal executive / senior management sponsorship for implementation efforts
• Partner with all stakeholder areas
• Gain commitment for resources and budget in advance to ensure coverage and growth
• Focus on culture change as necessary to ensure the goals of Incident Management are met (restoring normal service operation quickly and keeping customers satisfied)
• Consider including a relevant objective on every employee's evaluation/scorecard to ensure cooperation

Little things that deliver big returns
• Senior leadership support/sponsorship
• A detailed and well-executed communication plan
• Branding the project / ITIL efforts internally
• Use of Themes
• Conduct a session taking trainees through 'A day in the life of an incident'.
• Rewards and recognition - reward people for following new ITIL/Incident Management procedures. Little things like movie tickets or company logo items can go a long way to motivate employees. [20]
• Create a recognition program in which recognition notes are left at associates' desks as acknow-ledgement for following IT Service Management practices. Catch people doing things right. [19]

- When designing a new tool for the market, pair technical leads with each functional area manager, so that functional specifications for the tool are developed in partnership. [9]

Little things that always get forgotten
- Ask for, and listen to, suggestions from all personnel involved in following Incident Management procedures and using new or enhanced Incident Management tools.
- If a new tool is being rolled out as part of Incident Management implementation, consider building in a mechanism for real-time feedback during testing. Employees asked for feedback about particular enhancements during testing can say whether certain elements truly add value to the process tool - or not. This helps developers to process feedback more quickly and make adjustments along the way. [9]

6.2.5 Key process activities
Process rollout to the Support Center

Define scope	Together with your executive sponsor, define a clear scope of who should be included in the implementation. This should be documented in a charter and scope document.
Identify resources and budget	Depending on your budget and the resources that your sponsor can commit to the Incident Management implementation, begin to identify your core team. Then identify those team members within the departments in scope that will commit resources to the implementation efforts.
Assemble team	Bring your team together, and share with them the charter and scope to get them started. Build the team and spend time to move from 'forming and storming' stages to get to a high performing team. Learn what strengths you have in your team and make best use of those strengths as you define who will do what.
Meetings	Start-up with team Conduct weekly implementation meetings Sponsor meetings
Identify metrics/KPIs/goals	Understand what will constitute success for your Incident Management implementation. Support it with data and statistics that your business partners and customers will understand. Keep it up to date and communicate it often to show progress.
Workflow design	You should have a team of process designers who have defined the Incident Process for your organization. The document / handbook that represents your organization's Incident Management process is what you will be implementing. It includes a workflow diagram (model), policies and procedures, tool requirements, management information, roles and responsibilities and a glossary.

Tool selection/configuration	Tool requirements from the process document / handbook are an input to this activity Build or buy decision Coordinate tool needs - if implementing a tool, this is a project in its own right Select vendors if required Choose tool/software Install tool/software
Current state assessment	Identify current state Use a questionnaire to interview those who have input on the current state
Perform Gap Analysis	Compare current state to goal state (any core processes and/or work instructions) Identify tool and process gaps Document gaps Gap Analysis sign-off from stakeholders MILESTONE: Complete Change / Incident Gap Analysis
Work instructions	Create step-by-step instructions for how to perform Incident Management processes in each department or area of the organization Share generic work instructions that already exist Review work instructions Revise work instructions as needed Deliver work instructions to the team and then to the customer Work instruction sign-off from customer MILESTONE: Work instructions complete
Perform training	Identify core process training needs Prepare training materials including handouts and presentations Communicate core process training Schedule core process training Deliver core process training MILESTONE: Core process training complete
MILESTONE	Incident process rollout complete

6.2.6 Methods and techniques

Overcoming resistance to change may be the single biggest factor in implementing Incident Management. In order to overcome this challenge, consider partnering with all in-scope stakeholders to gain their buy-in to the change as well as their input for creating processes that make sense for the organization.

Ensure that process training is clear and concise, all gaps between current and goal state have been closed appropriately and that people understand what they need to do under the new Incident Management processes and why.

6.2.7 Audits for effectiveness

A wide variety or combination of audit strategies may be used to indicate the effectiveness of implementation. These include:

- competency checks to determine the level of Incident Management maturity within affected groups
- surveys of individuals to determine Incident Management competency level
- training material and presentation assessments
- risk documents created by internal auditors if gaps still exist
- an assessment of whether any additional gaps were identified during implementation
- a list of any stakeholders who did not 'buy in' to Incident Management and why.

6.3 Ongoing operation

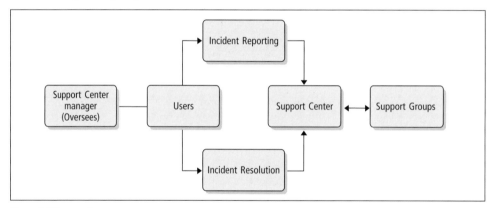

Figure 6.3 The ongoing process

6.3.1 Support Center Manager's role

Responsibilities and activities

Serving in the role of Incident Manager, the Support Center Manager is accountable for:

- driving the efficiency and effectiveness of the Incident Management process
- producing management information
- managing the work of Incident support staff (both first-and second-line, as applicable)
- controlling the closure process associated with registered incidents
- monitoring the effectiveness of Incident Management and making recommendations for improvement
- participating in the development of Incident Management systems and maintaining those systems
- ensuring that status and resolution progress checks are done on all incidents to ensure they are resolved (and within agreed Service Level targets)
- ensuring that follow-up occurs with owners/solvers of Incidents that are likely to breach agreed Service Level targets

- ensuring that any incidents moving between different specialist support groups are particularly noted (as they may be indicative of uncertainty about an issue or a dispute amongst support staff groups)
- ensuring that affected users are kept informed of progress on Incidents

Competencies required

To help facilitate the ongoing efforts required with Incident Management, the Manager should:
- be a strong champion for IT Service Management
- understand the business the Center supports and assist it in meetings its goals
- work to keep morale and productivity up with high-performing personnel in place
- ensure that training related to Incident Management and supporting customers is ongoing, so that staff are regarded as experts who can solve issues competently
- promote continuous process improvement programs and activities to ensure incident management goals are aligned with the business goals.

Key Performance Indicators

Clearly defined objectives with measurable targets must be set to assess how well Incident Management processes are performing within the realm of the Support Center. The Support Center Manager should consider requesting that Center personnel use these Key Performance Indicator targets to monitor the effectiveness and efficiency of the Incident Management process:
- total number of incidents
- percentage of incidents handled within agreed resolution and response service levels
- average cost per incident
- percentage of incidents closed 'first time final' by the Support Center
- number and/or percentage of incidents processed per Support Center analyst and/or workstation
- number and percentage of incidents resolved remotely, without the need for a site visit
- mean time before failure
- mean time to repair.

Critical Success Factors (CSFs) and Key Performance Indicators (KPIs)

The Support Center Manager is accountable for determining how often reporting associated with these key performance indicators will be run, as well as who will receive the reports.

6.3.2 Support Center Function's role

Responsibilities and activities

The Support Center owns the incident process and all associated incidents. Its role is to serve as the customer-facing point of contact for customers. The Center:
- provides advice and guidance, working toward the rapid restoration of service
- is responsible for monitoring the resolution of all registered incidents, including the closure process
- provides reporting of business-focused management information related to incident service level agreements.

Support Center responsibilities include:
- incident registration
- initial support and classification
- ownership, monitoring, tracking and communication
- resolution and recovery of incidents not assigned to second-line support
- closure of incidents.

In many instances, second-line support is also included as part of the Support Center. This area's tasks and responsibilities include:
- monitoring incident details (including any Configuration Items that are affected)
- incident investigation and diagnosis
- detection of possible problems (and assignment of them to the Problem Management team)
- resolution and recovery of assigned incidents
- creation of knowledgebase entries.

Deliverables
The Support Center owns, monitors, tracks and communicates information related to incidents. These tasks include:
- monitoring the status and progress toward resolution of all open incidents
- keeping affected users informed about progress
- escalating processes as necessary.

Competencies required
For ongoing Incident Management efforts, the same skill sets are important to ensure all support staff delivers first-class service by being:
- customer-focused
- articulate and methodical
- adept in interpersonal skills
- able to understand the business's objectives
- equipped with technical documentation skills.

Support Center personnel should have core IT skills and a desire to interact with customers at all levels. Consideration should be given to hiring staff who already possess extroverted personality traits because the IT skills can generally be taught. [10]

Key Performance Indicators
The Support Center Manager has authority for defining Key Performance Indicators that are aligned with the business goals. As previously stated, the Support Center may want to consider using metrics on the following items to determine the effectiveness and efficiency of the Incident Management process:
- total number of incidents
- percentage of incidents handled within agreed resolution and response service levels
- average cost per incident
- percentage of incidents closed 'first time final' by the Support Center
- number and/or percentage of incidents processed per Support Center analyst and/or workstation

- number and percentage of incidents resolved remotely, without the need for a visit.

With input from the Support Center Manager, also consider making this data available to users and customers, as applicable. Provide the data in a format that is user-friendly to your audience.

6.3.3 Other key roles and functions in the ongoing operation process

The Incident Group members liaise with application providers to create Operating Level Agreements and Service Level Agreements. They also manage the Support Center's knowledge base and management reporting. The group is instrumental in maintaining focus on the needs of their business customers instead of on their systems issues. [10]

A knowledge management specialist will help maintain all troubleshooting knowledge the Center uses in its day-to-day Incident Management operations. They can ensure that knowledge is easy to find, and also that its associated category makes sense, that it is adequate and accurate and that opportunities for improvement are identified.

Reporting specialists provide data specific to the Incident Management processes to allow for investigation into process improvement opportunities.

Steps and tips for maintaining this process

Evaluation of Incident Management processes is key to ensuring behavior continues to follow the new performance guidelines. Maintaining focus on the future state and measuring against that will enable the Center to stay on target. Specific examples of maintenance tips include:
- keeping Incident Management processes in line with business goals
- ensuring that new employees receive adequate process and tool training
- using Key Performance Indicators to determine potential process improvement opportunities
- gaining and using candid feedback from users about what is (and is not) working well.

6.4 Optimization

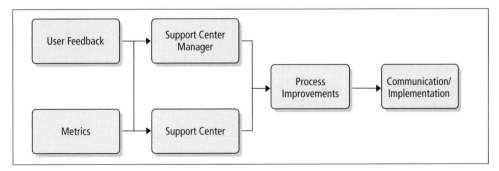

Figure 6.4 The optimization process

6.4.1 Support Center Manager's role

Responsibilities and activities

The Support Center Manager's role is to monitor Service Level Agreements that have been set as part of Incident Management. This is accomplished through the enforcement of existing processes and through continuous improvement plans created as part of the Incident Management Implementation Plans.

The Manager participates in an ongoing review of critical performance indicators set by the Support Center for supporting the IT organization. The Manager should monitor the status of such Key Performance Indicators as call volume rates, 'first time final' rates, incidents being incorrectly assigned etc. The Manager should have a high-level awareness of what is happening within the Center, but not necessarily the details related to the key performance indicators. [11]

Additionally, the Manager should continually update other functional and process managers on the effectiveness of current Incident Management processes, and determine whether there is anything other process owners (Problem and Change Management, etc) need from the Center. The goal is to both provide and receive any information that could help the entire Incident Management process run more smoothly.

Deliverables

As part of monitoring the status of Key Performance Indicators, the Support Center Manager should work with Center staff to improve staff knowledge and overall effectiveness. Deliverables associated with these efforts may include:
- gaining access to additional tools and/or applications to conduct their support successfully
- training (job aids, additional knowledge, etc) in order to facilitate a higher 'first time final' rate.

Competencies required

Ability to work with the Incident Management practitioners to gather continuous process improvement suggestions and implement them., The person leading optimization efforts should have a clear understanding of the current state processes in place, together with an idea of what the future goal state is at various stages - six months, one year, three years etc. [8]
The Manager should have a clear understanding of how people, process and technology work together, to ensure that making a positive change to one of the three does not negatively affect one (or both) of the others.

Key Performance Indicators

The ultimate goal of optimization related to Incident Management is to make the Support Center more connected with the entire business/organization. The Center should strive to achieve more integration between Incident Management and other processes.

6.4.2 Support Center Function's role

Responsibilities and activities

The Support Center should continually review Incident Management processes and procedures to determine which are still valid and which are in need of updates. Additionally, incident analysis occurring through the review of Key Performance Indicator metrics reporting should drive the creation and delivery of new reference materials, training materials, job aids, process updates, etc.

The incident reporting and review process should produce reports that enable Support Center management to make informed decisions and monitor performance (based on Service Level Agreements).

Deliverables
The ability to provide good quality management reporting information demonstrates a level of maturity within the Support Center. Metrics around such items as trends and workloads can provide management with the information they need in order to justify budgets for additional resource needs such as additional staff, tools, etc.

Competencies required
Support Center staff must have a good understanding of the role they play at the Center in Incident Management processes. They must also understand what types of optimization the Center is interested in attaining. This information, along with a thorough understanding of the business's objectives, will allow personnel to provide feedback to management about the strategies that could help to attain the optimization goals.

Key Performance Indicators
The goal of optimization related to Incident Management is to help the Support Center become more connected with the entire business/organization. The Center should strive to achieve more integration between Incident Management and other processes. Critical success factors to be monitored might include:
• comparing Support Center performance to commitments
• performance data, customer feedback and industry intelligence inputs to improve processes and interfaces
• outsourcing options considered based on requirements
• skill levels of staff
• number of staff
• maximizing physical workspace
• maximizing Support Center technology
• applying monitoring and metrics for continuous improvement.

6.4.3 Other key roles and functions in the optimization process

In addition to Support Center personnel, it is important to include as many Incident Management practitioners as possible in optimization efforts. Working as a group, this cross-functional team can bring their various viewpoints together to determine the best optimization opportunities within the organization.

Functions performed by this group may include determining the items to be addressed, producing requirements documents, prioritizing opportunities and testing solutions.

6.4.4 Tips for optimizing this process

• A good forecasting effort should define and plan for the needs ahead. What skill sets will be

required? Technical writers may be needed for expert documentation and reporting, and Six Sigma expertise for metrics and measurement efforts.
- Consider all three sides of the IT triangle: people, process and technology. Be prepared to invest in needed resources and commitments.
- Create metrics to report whether key performance indicators are being met.
- Maintain ongoing communication with customers using Incident Management. Consider their feedback about what is working well, what is not working well and what they would improve.
- Remember that there is always room for improvement.

6.4.5 Future impact of this process on the Support Center

Successful optimization strategies ultimately have the ability to improve more than Support Center productivity. Availability of applications, increased customer satisfaction etc can also be improved. Some specific impacts of optimization strategy may include:
- some metrics may be useful for proving the need to give the Support Center more responsibility for resolving incidents that have previously been passed to specialty groups that are more expensive to the organization. Providing the first-line support staff with the tools to handle additional types of incidents can demonstrate reduced costs, as well as improving customer satisfaction because customers' issues are resolved more quickly.
- additional tools to assess impact and criticality of certain types of issues will also lead to improvements between the Incident Management and Problem Management processes.

6.5 Measurement, costing and management reporting

6.5.1 Implementation: benefits and costs

Ensuring that the Support Center activities are in line with the business needs of the organization makes good business sense in any organization. The Incident Management process should contribute positively to keeping customers up and running so they can perform their duties efficiently and effectively.

Why implement this process and what can be gained

Examination of the current environment and objectives to be achieved in the goal state, once Incident Management is in place, will help determine what types of benefits could be realized as a result of implementing Incident Management. With the Support Center becoming the single point of contact, benefits might include increased customer satisfaction and revenue enhancement.

Incident Management provides consistent metrics for use in problem analysis, providing greater capability for reducing or eliminating future incidents. It can also reduce the volume of incidents escalated to groups outside the Support Center. Ultimately, customers know they can expect to receive consistent levels of service, and they tend to have a higher satisfaction rate as more of their issues are being resolved quickly, or in many cases first time final.'

Cost elements for implementation

Costs associated with implementing Incident Management may include:

- the purchase of new tool(s) as necessary to ensure success
- tool-related expenses such as knowledge base transfer, licensing fees, tool customization, professional consulting and cost to implement..)
- training staff on the Incident Management framework and the processes put in place to support it
- training on new tools (if applicable)
- creation and maintenance of a configuration database (if one does not already exist).

Making the business case to implement Incident Management
As a detailed investment proposal, the business case should provide analysis of all costs, benefits and risks associated with the proposed investment of implementing Incident Management. The investment decision is put into a strategic context. It positions the business objectives and options that will affect both the decision and the investment.

Consider following these steps to build the business case:
- Examine the current environment. Use a technique such as SWOT analysis (Strengths, Weaknesses, Opportunities and Threats) to determine the current state of the Support Center. *(See Annex A6.12 SWOT Analysis)*
- Determine objectives. Armed with results from the SWOT analysis, determine what the goal state looks like and what objectives would need to be undertaken to achieve that state.
- Identify risks. What potential risks exist with implementing Incident Management within the Center?
- Perform a cost analysis. Demonstrate how implementing Incident Management will improve efficiency, improve customer satisfaction, and ultimately result in cost reduction due to quicker incident resolution.
- Document the business case. Ensure that information related to the previous four steps is included.
- Present the business case. Provide the written business case to appropriate sponsors and stakeholders and sell the idea of what Incident Management can do for the organization.
- Implement the improvements. After obtaining buy-in from sponsors and stakeholders, take the steps necessary to implement the processes

Metrics and Key Performance Indicators
Before rolling out Incident Management, consider placing the following types of measurable targets in place for the Support Center's involvement in Incident Management implementation:
- decide and set metrics to measure the effectiveness of the Support Center
- establish a baseline before discussing formal Service Level agreements with customers
- provide a framework to collect metrics and use them to measure performance against the SLA criteria
- ensure customers are aware of what is being done with Incident Management processes and why, if there are changes occurring that are not transparent to the customer.

Management reporting
After determining the metrics to be used for measuring the Center's success and the framework that will be put in place to help meet those targets, ensure that the reporting to be produced clearly demonstrates whether targets are being met.

6.5.2 Ongoing operations

Costs

In order to keep Incident Management efforts alive in the organization, the following cost factors will probably exist:

- ongoing costs associated with Incident Management tools, including the incident-tracking tool, knowledge base, reporting tool, etc.
- training costs associated with ensuring that staff are equipped to meet customers' needs (which may include cross-training)
- licensing fees associated with keeping the tools up to date
- the need for promotions/incentives to build and maintain morale within the Center.

Metrics and Key Performance Indicators

To determine the effectiveness and efficiency of the Support Center's Incident Management processes, consider using some of the following measurable targets as key performance indicators:

- total incident volume
- incidents processed per Support Center workstation or analyst
- percentage of incidents handled within Service Level Agreements
- percentage of incidents closed by the Support Center 'first time final'

(See Annex A6.14 Incident Metrics Report)

Metrics visually demonstrate the processes in action. They also enable the Support Center to:

- evaluate the processes for further refinement or enhancement
- evaluate the usage of the processes in each area
- define the basis for continued process improvement.

The following excerpt lists several common problems symptomatic of an organization that does not produce regular, relevant and accurate management reports:

- unclear direction or focus for improvement actions
- limited ability to make qualified and quantified strategic decisions
- dissatisfaction with IT provision by the business
- poor perceived availability of IT services.

6.5.3 Optimization: benefits and costs

The ultimate goal of optimizing Incident Management processes is to better help the business reach its goals by streamlining processes. Byproducts of optimization often include higher levels of customer satisfaction and better motivated Support Center staff.

As Incident Management processes become more mature, it also allows organizations to focus on activities to interact with other processes such as Change Management and Problem Management.

Why optimize this process and what can be gained?

Optimization is synonymous with increasing efficiency and with reaching higher levels of performance maturity. More efficient and streamlined processes generally decrease costs.

Implementing processes to help the Support Center support its customers more effectively generally results in greater customer satisfaction.

Cost-effective process changes such as cross training tend to minimize boredom within the Center. When personnel believe they have the ability to make a difference, retention levels tend to be greater.

Making the business case to optimize

Using management reporting to help optimize Incident Management processes can help identify items that were missed in various stages of application development (before the time when the Support Center begins supporting a new application, release of an application etc). A rapid and sharp increase in calls is generally indicative of a larger issue. Is additional application testing necessary in the future? Are there opportunities to close gaps in the development organization? Should the customers have received additional communication about or training on application changes? The Support Center is in the unique position of helping the IT organization understand how to optimize its processes in the future to ensure that its customers are satisfied. [15]

Metrics and Key Performance Indicators

Key Performance Indicators should be linked to business goals. Look periodically at the metrics being used in ongoing operations and determine whether they still make sense. Is there a need to revise the way some information is being looked at or reported on?

A team of specialists might be assembled to conduct an analysis of high volume call categories to contribute to a better understanding of root cause and recommend process improvements. A 'Top 10' list of those categories has been created, and opportunities for reducing call volumes have begun to be identified.

Management reporting

Information used for management reporting must be accurate, reliable and communicated in a timely manner each reporting period. The types of information the Support Center should consider supplying in such reporting includes:
- historical data based on the key performance indicators that have been set, so that management can make informed decisions about what future strategies may be needed
- customer perception of the Support Center
- information related to potential action items that may help the Support Center better align its services with business and customer needs.

In very general terms, management information can be used to validate decisions, to direct the goals and targets of Support Center activities, to justify specific courses of action related to Incident Management and to assist when intervention activities related to the Support Center are necessary. (Refer to Annex for supporting documents titled Support Center Scorecard - Daily, Support Center Scorecard - Monthly, and Support Center - Customer Satisfaction Survey.)

The best way to present management information is to show charts with trending information and provide explanations where changes are above or before a threshold defined as acceptable for your organization. For instance, a goal of 95% may have an acceptable threshold of +/-1%, meaning anything between 94% and 96% is attributable to normal fluctuations but anything lower or higher than needs to be investigated and a cause determined. Such information enables management to identify where changes may be necessary, e.g. processes, staffing, hours of operation, etc. Again, all key performance indicators should be included in this reporting. Look for direct and indirect correlations between indicators. For instance, is there any correlation between 'Speed to Answer' and 'Abandon Rate?' Do customer satisfaction/perception scores rise when more calls are being resolved 'first time final'?

Use management information to validate the IT decisions that did (or did not) make sense, to direct future goals and activities and to justify specific courses of action.

Incident Management Metrics	
Metric	Definition
Ratio of Minor, Significant and Major Incidents	Comparison of volumes by severity level.
Ratio of Incidents by Owning Group	Comparison of volumes by group creating the incident ticket.
Ratio of Incidents by Responsible Group	Comparison of volumes by group in possession of the ticket when the SLA becomes measurable.
Ratio of Incidents by Customer Type	Comparison of volumes by 2-digit code derived by BCR type.
Ratio of Incidents by Disbursement Code	Comparison of volumes by cost center.
Volume of Incident by Period	Volumes for a specified period that tally Carried Over Open Items, Current Period Submitted Items, Current Period Closed Items, and End of Period Open Items.
Number of Incidents Reassigned	Volume of incidents that were changed due to an incorrect identification of cause/severity.
Number of Incomplete Incident Tickets	Number of items submitted that were incomplete.
Number of Incidents Related to Implementation of a Change	Related to root cause identification and used to identify issues with Change Process.
Elapsed Time Between Phases in Incident Management Process.	Elapsed time (hours or days) between phases in the Incident Management Process at the Business Sponsor, CAB, and Priority levels as well as compared to the SLAs (if any).
Variances Between Elapsed Times Between Measuring Points	Differences in time (hours or days) between phases in the Incident Management Process at the Business Sponsor, CAB, and Priority levels as well as compared to the SLAs (if any).

6.5.4 Tools

Tool selection

ITIL methodology suggests that any tools chosen should follow ITIL processes. Consider using these suggestions when selecting an Incident Management tool:

- seek to understand requirements for the tool by analyzing current processes, functions needed and capability requirements. Be sure to consult with different kinds of potential users for the tool who act in different capacities related to Incident Management. (Consider both functional and interface requirements.)
- keep in mind the possibility that there may be many more users of the new tool than any current tool(s) in place due to Incident Management process implementation. Consider any potential impacts to the infrastructure as a result of both a new tool and an increased volume of users
- define reporting requirements early in the process to ensure they are not an afterthought
- each documented requirement should be assigned a level of importance. (Decide what is absolutely necessary, what the organization can do without if necessary, etc.)
- analyze proposed system solutions (new tools) based on their ability to achieve he defined requirements
- if a large amount of tool customization is required, consider how customizable a tool is and what kind of effort will be required
- consider the expertise required to build/customize a tool. Is that expertise available within your organization? Is the expertise widely available on the market? Is it highly sought after, but not widely available? (Differences in external vendor/contractor prices may directly affect the bottom line of what tool is ultimately chosen.)

Testing before implementation
Clearly define testing scenarios, but allow for the flexibility to test variations of each scenario (i.e. - normal paths vs. alternate paths to achieve the same outcome).

Give identical scenarios to multiple testers. The idea behind this technique is that a distinct possibility exists for the testing of scenarios using different strategies (and some of these different strategies may uncover flaws in the system or processes).
Test the new tool from multiple perspectives (first-line, second-line, third-line/specialty group, etc). Build testing scenarios based on the perspective of all possible types of users.

Brainstorm about ways users may misuse the tool (intentionally or unintentionally) and document the results. Consider whether misuse cases require system modifications to prevent their possibility or whether a clear and concise communication plan may avoid the scenario.

Implementation
The need for a clear and detailed Training/Communication plan cannot be overstated. Ample time should be provided between development and implementation phases to allow trainer(s) to prepare training materials with screenshots of how the system will look when implemented.

All users should be provided advance notice of the upcoming tool change, and enough time should be allowed to properly educate users. (Plan a communication approach that will reach users multiple times using varying communications techniques/strategies.)

Consider a phased rollout or pilot release approach instead of an 'all-at-once' or 'big bang' implementation approach. (This is especially important if both the process and tool are being rolled out simultaneously.)

Use the pilot phase of the implementation to identify any bugs in the tool and/or process. Take steps to alleviate these issues before the main rollout.

Ongoing operations
After implementation (especially the first few weeks following implementation), many issues will be identified that require resolution. Additionally, users will begin requesting enhancements. It may be challenging to balance the needs of resolving tool issues and work on enhancement requests simultaneously. Establish a plan well in advance of this time to ensure that adequate resources (time, people, etc.) will be available to work on both efforts.

From the first phase of implementation throughout rollout to 100% capacity, ensure appropriate monitoring of hardware and software for efficiency, capacity and traffic management are in place.

Reporting
Reporting requirements should be considered with any other functional requirements at the beginning of the tool selection/analysis process. Reporting needs may direct processes and tool build vs. buy selection.

In the System Design phase, consider having a section devoted to Reporting. Make sure the design accommodates the reports that the Support Center (and other users / customers) will need and expect.
Note that a complete understanding of the kind of data to be reported in the future may not be available until after System Design is complete. As the design unfolds, so will the need for new reports. Allow for flexibility to reevaluate reporting considerations from the tool analysis phase throughout system design.
Finally, consider balancing the need for data against the effort to collect it. Assign each reporting need a level of importance, and think about how much development effort the organization is willing to spend to achieve the creation of the report.

Additional tools/resources that may be useful in supporting the Incident Management process within the Support Center include (but are not limited to):
• ACD (telephone) systems integration for automatically registering certain sets of information about users/customers (name, phone number, etc.)
• diagnostic tools, such as a natural language search 'knowledge base' of information
• tool(s) that allow for automatic logging of incidents when issues are detected on systems (as well as notification to affected parties)
• if a Configuration Management Database is in use, a tool that automatically extracts data from it (which can be useful for quickly identifying failed items and affected items)
• a 'ticker' that shows live data related to Support Center activities. This may include such information as call volume, known outages and service disruptions, average wait time for customers, the number of calls offered, calls abandoned etc.
• lowered cubicle walls to support knowledge transfer between staff. (Note that this knowledge transfer technique is not a replacement for a knowledgebase, but rather a supplement to it.)

Annexes: Checklists, Examples and Sample Documents

ANNEX INDEX

Annex A6.1 Overview of the Capability Maturity Model

The Capability Maturity Model (CMM) was developed by the Software Engineering Institute (SEI), a federally-funded research and development center operated by Carnegie Mellon University. The definitive resource is The Capability Maturity Model: Guidelines for Improving the Software Process, (Carnegie Mellon University/Software Engineering Institute), published in 1995 by Addison-Wesley. The CMM serves two major purposes: to guide process improvement efforts in a software organization, and to assist with identifying contracting organizations that are qualified to perform software work.

The five maturity levels (Initial, Repeatable, Defined, Managed, and Optimizing) represent evolutionary plateaus on the road to a high level of software process capability. Each maturity level, except the first, defines several key process areas or KPAs - groups of related software practices - all of which must be satisfied in order for an organization to attain that level (Table 1).

Each KPA has two to four goals, all of which must be achieved in order to satisfy the objectives of that KPA. In addition, each KPA describes a number of key practices that typically lead to achieving that KPA's goals. These practices are grouped into five 'common features'. The key practices of the common feature called Activities Performed define technical and managerial activities that typically lead to satisfying the KPA goals, thereby establishing a specific process capability in that key process area.

Maturity Level	Key Process Area
1: Initial	None
2: Repeatable	Requirements Management, Software Project Planning, Software Project Tracking and Oversight, Software Subcontract Management, Software Quality Assurance, Software Configuration Management
3: Defined	Organization Process Focus, Organization Process Definition, Training Program, Integrated Software Management, Software Product Engineering, Intergroup Coordination, Peer Reviews
4: Managed	Quantitative Process Management, Software Quality Management
5: Optimizing	Defect Prevention, Technology Change Management, Process Change Management

Table 1. Key Process Areas of the Capability Maturity Model.

The other four common features relate to institutionalization of the practices performed in a software organization. Institutionalization means that a practice is routinely applied across the organization, even in times of crisis. Application of that practice has been ingrained in the group's culture, and it is supported with an infrastructure of policies. Common features of institutionalizing are:

- Commitment to Perform (encompasses the presence of an organizational policy relating to the KPA and specifically assigning key responsibilities)
- Ability to Perform (includes training, resources, and other prerequisites)
- Measurement and Analysis (describes the status and quality measures that are used to control and improve the process)
- Verifying Implementation (describes steps taken to ensure that activities are performed according to established processes and procedures).
- Several common themes run through the key process areas of the CMM. As a starting point, written organizational policies state management expectations around the practice of each KPA. Status and issues are to be reviewed periodically with senior management. A recurrent expectation is that practitioners are trained to perform the activities expected of them. Most activities are to be performed according to documented procedures (in contrast to the oral history of many software cultures). Appreciating such philosophical and practical themes of the CMM is as important as remembering the nuances of each KPA.

Excerpt from Misconceptions of the Capability Maturity Model by Karl E. Wiegers, originally published in Software Development, November 1996. Found on www.processimpact.com.

A6.1.1 SEI Capability Maturity Framework

The maturity framework provided by CMM establishes a context in which:

- practices can be repeated. If you do not repeat an activity there is no reason to improve it. There are policies, procedures and practices that commit the organization to implementing and performing consistently
- best practices can be rapidly transferred across groups. Practices are defined sufficiently to allow for transfer across project boundaries, thus providing some standardization for the organization
- variations in performing best practices are reduced. Quantitative objectives are established for tasks; and measures are established, taken, and maintained to form a base-line from which an assessment is possible
- practices are continuously improved to enhance capability (optimizing).

Process Definition Criteria are the set of information that must be included in a software process description for it to be usable by the people performing the process. To establish the criteria you are asking the question: 'What software process information do I need to document?'

Process Element	Answers
Purpose	Why is a process performed?
Input	What work products are used?
Output	What work products are produced?
Role	Who (or what) performs the activities?
Activity	What is done?
Entry criteria	When (under what circumstances) can processes begin?
Exit criteria	When (under what circumstances) can processes be considered complete?
Procedure	How are activities implemented?

Other process elements are:
- reviews and audits performed
- work products that are to be managed and controlled (or placed under configuration management)
- measurements to be made
- training
- tools.

Excerpt from *A Software Process Framework for the SEI CMM* on
www.sei.cmu.edu/pub/documents/94.reports/pdfhb01.94.pdf

Annex A6.2 Questions to guide sustainable change

John Kotter, the Konosuke Matsushita Professor of Leadership at Harvard Business School, is a noted authority on leadership. He has written[2]: After conducting fourteen formal studies and more than a thousand interviews, directly observing dozens of executives in action, and compiling innumerable surveys, I am completely convinced that most organizations today lack the leadership they need…and the shortfall is often large. I'm not talking about a deficit of 10%, but of 200%, 400%, or more in positions up and down the hierarchy. Kotter's model of change management is excellent and we contend that it, like so many other useful approaches to change, leadership and organizational development, can be usefully enhanced with the introduction of more integral perspectives.

The following table conveys our understanding of Kotter's[3] change model in columns 1 and 2. We have aligned Kotter's eight stages of change with potential leadership questions to guide action based on integral theory as defined by Ken Wilber. We present four categories of questions for each stage of change designed to capture the thoughts and actions necessary to implement sustainable change.

Individual thoughts and actions are captured in Column 3 (What do I intend?) and Column 5 (What do I do?)

2 Kotter, John P. What Leaders Really Do, Harvard Business School Press, 1999

3 Cohen, Dan S. and Kotter, John P. The Heart of Change: Real Life Stories of How People Change Their Organizations, Harvard Business School Press, 2002

The implementation is tailored to the specific culture when answering the questions in Column 4 (How do we talk about this?)

The organization systems, processes, and infrastructure are incorporated into the implementation why answering the questions in Column 6 (How do we do this?)

When implementing a sustainable change, it is critical to consider the individuals leading the change, the culture in which the change takes place and the systems, processes, and infrastructure that either reinforce the status quo or support the change. For change efforts to deliver the expected value in a sustainable manner, the entire organizational system must be taken into account and the change management effort must address not only the system (as is common) but also the individual and the culture.

Change agents and coaches working with the individuals and teams charged with creating and implementing these changes will make the best use of time, money, energy and thought by using these questions as a way to guide their efforts. We do not prescribe specific actions. The questions will guide the user to create their own approach tailored to the specific change effort, the people involved and the organization.

(1) Stages of Change	(2) What Works?	(3) What do I intend?	(4) How do we talk about this?	(5) What do I do?	(6) How do we do this?
Create Sense of Urgency	Showing others the need for change with a compelling object they can actually see, touch and feel Showing people valid and dramatic evidence from outside the organization that demonstrates that change is required Looking constantly for cheap and easy ways to reduce complacency Never underestimating how much complacency, fear and anger exists, even in good organizations	Reflect on the urgency of the change. What does it mean for you personally? What will you need to change about yourself (your approach) to lead the change effort successfully? Will you lead the same way this time or will you change from what you have done in the past?	What is perceived by the employees as urgent? Do different groups of employees perceive different things as urgent? How will this change affect the individuals in the organization? How will you create a sense of urgency for different segments of the organization (by department) based on their priorities, goals, and pains?	How will I model appropriate response to the sense of urgency by my actions? What segments of the population that will change most rapidly? How will I encourage the segment that is most likely to change without ignoring others? How will I explain the impact of change in a manner consistent with culture? What stories can I use that are linked to corporate folklore to illustrate prior examples of urgency and positive outcome? How can I convey messages that use emotion (personal stories) and external sources to demonstrate urgency?	What are the influences and constraints that will affect success (legal, financial, building, staffing mix? What resources are required to succeed and how will we secure them? What measures should we track to understand employee sense of urgency? Based on the measures, once we have achieved the correct level or urgency, move to step 2, Build a guiding team

(1) Stages of Change	(2) What Works?	(3) What do I intend?	(4) How do we talk about this?	(5) What do I do?	(6) How do we do this?
Build a guiding team - 'first who, then what''	Showing enthusiasm and commitment (or helping someone do so) to help draw the right people into the group Modeling the trust and teamwork needed in the group (or helping someone to do that)] Structuring meeting formats for the guiding team so as to minimize frustration and increase trust Putting energy into raising urgency if you cannot take on the step 2 challenge and if the right people will not.	Do I believe this change is possible? Do I realize that people are affected by my belief in the success of this change?	What are the social and cultural norms that dictate who should be leading the project? Do they still fit for where we are going?	How do I communicate the criteria for 'right' people on the team? ('Right' includes character traits, innate capabilities, and skills and knowledge) Who are the best people and how do I place them in charge of the biggest opportunity (not the biggest problem)? What comments and actions will I take that demonstrated my belief that change is possible? Am I looking for opportunities to support the project as events unfold?	What trust building activities can we conduct to improve the team dynamics? How do I lead the team based on the task at hand? I may run the risk of appearing aloof and detached from the rest of the organization because I am so focused on the change project. What measures should we track to reinforce desired team behaviors?
Get the vision right	Visualize, literally, possible futures with such clarity that they can be articulated in one minute or written on one page. Legacy statements with potential emotional engagement, such as a commitment to serving people Sufficiently bold strategies focused on making bold visions real Watching for objective and subjective cues as to the tolerance for and speed of change	How do I see our organization within the larger environment? (Ranging from the company to the global environment)? What are the connections between possible business futures and my personal mission, passion, and economic goals (hedgehog principle[3])?	How does the organization see itself in the context of the larger community? What does the organization see as connections between possible futures to organizational mission, passion, and economic variables (hedgehog principle[3])?	What organizational vision and strategies will move my part of the business into a position of long-term success? What are the visions and strategies within my part of the organization (departments)? How do I translate the vision into long and short term timelines? How do I incorporate specific tangible goals into the timelines? What do I fund based on the timelines and when?	How do we cascade the shared vision of possible futures (realistic and wild card options) to all levels of the organization? How do we aggregate organizational goals that align with the overall vision? What measures help the organization measure progress toward goals?

(1)Stages of Change	(2)What Works?	(3) What do I intend?	(4) How do we talk about this?	(5) What do I do?	(6) How do we do this?
Communicate for buy-in	Keep communication simple and genuine, sufficiently but not unnecessarily complex for the task and audience at hand. Doing your homework before communicating, especially to understand what people are feeling, sensing and saying. Being aware of and, if necessary, speaking to anxieties, confusion, anger, and distrust Ridding communication channels of junk so that important messages can go through Using new technologies to help people see the vision (intranets, satellites, etc.) Bringing forward approaches that work.	What personal stories (actions and emotions) will convey my struggles in heartfelt manner and empower others to act? What do I communicate when the situation and priorities change	What is the appropriate language and message content based on the values, goals, language and culture of each audience segment (department)? What objective and subjective feedback are we receiving from these segments?	How do I show my conviction through my actions ('walk the talk')? How do I deliver messages tailored to different segments of the organization that motivate everyone to accomplish the vision? How do I convey messages that will make a strong statement using both the languages of feelings and of logic to appeal to multiple groups? How do I demonstrate humility and give credit to others? How do I communicate the vision in a manner that is hard hitting and realistic and still conveys our confidence that it is achievable? How do I communicate progress, challenges and my support? How do I communicate the facts and hope for the future?	What are the different audience segments based on function, profile, and other factors (union membership etc)? What stories will convey messages effectively? Do we have any applicable stories connected with company folklore? Of our current communication methods and vehicles, what will most effectively convey the messages? Can we combine and/or eliminate any current communications? Would communication be more effective if multiple projects were communicated in a joint vehicle to help the audience understand the linkages and impacts? How do we communicate measures and rewards for successfully accomplishing the vision (ensure clear linkage between vision and rewards)?

(1) Stages of Change	(2) What Works?	(3) What do I intend?	(4) How do we talk about this?	(5) What do I do?	(6) How do we do this?
Empower for action	Finding individuals with change experience who can bolster people's self-confidence with 'we-won-you-can-too' anecdotes. Recognition and reward systems that inspire, promote optimism, and build self-confidence. Providing feedback that can help people make better vision-related decisions. Clarity on the nature of change required.	What is my individual role and value within the organization? How can I effectively grow and empower others and support their success and the success of the organization? How can I benefit from the success of the project? Do I need to change my perspective or skills to succeed?	What is the appropriate reward system based on the organizations values, goals, and culture? What are the stories of prior organizational success? How can we connect prior successes to the current change effort? Why did we have failures in the past? How do we minimize previous barriers to success? Are we building a culture that supports the behavioral traits necessary to support ongoing change such as freedom and empowerment, where employees are free to act within limits to meet their goals? Is this first order change or adaptive change?	How will I deliver clear, concise feedback that will empower others to correct, redirect or recalibrate their behavior and feel motivated to make the necessary changes? How am I funding projects and acting to increase organizational awareness and commitment? What creative solutions can I find to increase organizational awareness? How am I following through on the pre-established consequences for behaviors that undermine our success? How can I respond to undermining conflicts as learning opportunities? How do I encourage bad news as well as good? How am I assigning work to ensure the change is accomplished?	How will the organization build a reward system aligned with the new environment and that meets multiple motivations (among people or departments)? Have we set goals and expectations (measures and behaviors) for each individual that supports the overall organization and the change effort? Have we created evaluation and feedback processes that support new behaviors? Have we created, communicated and used processes to identify those not exhibiting or supporting the new strategies and behaviors? Why is this happening? What are we doing to measure, communicate and fund 'learning organization' processes and activities without sacrificing financial security?

(1) Stages of Change	(2) What Works?	(3) What do I intend?	(4) How do we talk about this?	(5) What do I do?	(6) How do we do this?
Create short term wins	Wins that are visible to as many people as possible Wins that penetrate defenses by being unambiguous Wins that are meaningful to others - the more deeply meaningful the better Early wins that speak to powerful players whose support you need and do not yet have Wins that can be achieved cheaply and easily, even if they seem small compared with the grand vision.	What do I consider personal wins? What do I consider wins for my team? What do I consider wins for the organization? Why do we need short term wins? How do we incorporate short term wins into the project without affecting long term project success, schedule or cost?	What wins will be provide meaningful business results? What wins will provide emotionally meaningful results? What stories can we tell about the wins that will be shared with the organization in public settings such as town hall meetings? Who are the leaders within the sub-cultures who can best communicate wins?	What wins can I identify and support that solve "problems" for others or that are seeds for future shifts? How do I publicly recognize people who accomplish the wins? How does this communication reinforce my own values among the group?	Who do we need to support the change effort for it to be successful? How can our project help these key people meet their personal objectives? How will we identify short term wins in the context of the larger project objectives? How will we connect wins to vision and measures to demonstrate the impact of small steps forward? How will we measure (objectively and subjectively) and communicate the merit of wins in relation to overall goals? How will we support systematically achieving shifts from key people and the overall organization?

(1) Stages of Change	(2) What Works?	(3) What do I intend?	(4) How do we talk about this?	(5) What do I do?	(6) How do we do this?
Build momentum	Aggressively rid yourself of work that is no longer yours to do - tasks that may have been relevant in the past but not now, tasks that can be delegated to those who should be doing the work. Looking constantly for ways to keep sense of urgency heightened without over stimulating. Using new situations opportunistically to launch the next wave of change Show them - show them - show them	How do I deal with both profound progress and a need for continued change? How do I deal with unresolved issues and uncertainty as we move forward?	How is morale maintained by different departments (subcultures)? How do specific departments want to be recognized beyond public recognition?	What do I communicate that conveys both progress and continued urgency Am I 'walking the talk'? Am I living up to the standards I have set for others? Am I perceived as acting with integrity with regard to meeting my commitments?	What processes will we establish to identify work that is no longer appropriate or necessary in the changing environment? What processes will we create and staff to scan the environment of opportunities that can be leveraged to create additional momentum? Are we reviewing measures regularly and recognizing results toward the change goals?

(1) Stages of Change	(2) What Works?	(3) What do I intend?	(4) How do we talk about this?	(5) What do I do?	(6) How do we do this?
Make change stick	Continued attention until the changes have taken root Using new employee orientation to compellingly show recruiters what the organization really cares about. Using the promotions process to place people who act according to the new norms into influential and visible positions Telling vivid stories over and over about the organization, what it does and why it succeeds Making sure you have the continuity of behavior and results that help a new culture grow.	What progress have I made as a leader/person? Are my assumptions still valid? Am I still in the right role for my personal values and mission? When I think of my mental, emotional, moral and physical state, am I still the right person for the job ahead?	How will organization goals and values change based on the change effort? How do we shift our focus in support of long change effort without losing value of recent gains? How do we incorporate new language, best practice and human interest into emerging organizational stories? How do we reward the small accomplishments toward the overall organizational success?	What do I do that reinforces the value of the change? How do I continue to send my emotional engagement, the logical case and the senior management support for the new way of doing business? How do I emphasize the focus on systematic change that encourages but does not insist on personal growth?	How does the organization fund, staff and supply sufficient and appropriate infrastructure to support and reinforce new behaviors and culture? (These including promotions, orientation, rewards and recognition that meet people's natural way of doing business) Have we sufficiently updated employee orientations and other human resources and IT systems to support changes in goals and values? Have we reviewed objective and subjective measures regularly and recognized results toward the change goals? Are we reinforcing actions that positively influence the larger vision and inquiring into those that do not?

Authors: Metcalf, Maureen (2004). Metcalf Associates President and Forman, John (2004) Integral Development Associates Managing Partner.

3 See Collins, Jim "Good to Great" Harper Business 2001

Annex A6.3 Agenda for implementation

A6.3.1 Support Center/ITIL Process Implementation
Start-off for Organization

Date: Thursday, June 13, 200X
Time: 2:00 PM - 3:30 PM
Location: Address
Invitees: <list names here>
Others: <more names>
Facilitator: Name

Goal:
- To begin working on the socialization and implementation of the XYZ Support Center (process/processes) across Organization XZY
- Agenda/Objectives:
- To review implementation approach
- To discuss implementation teams and members
- To assign implementation tasks to Working Group
- Handout and review questionnaires
- Discuss socializing ITIL within the Organization areas
- Handout & review status report

Notes:
Expectations:
Commitment
Support
Gap Analysis
Work Instructions
Socialization
Requirements:
Points of discussion:

Annex A6.4 Project teams list

Functional Area 1:
Core Team contact: name
Working Team Representatives: name
Working Team Back ups: name
Implementation Committee: multiple names
Functional Area 2:
Core Team contact: name
Working Team Representatives: name
Working Team Delegees: name
Implementation Committee: multiple names

Functional Area 3:
Core Team contact: name
Working Team Representatives: name
Working Team Delegees: name
Implementation Committee: multiple names
Functional Area 4:
Core Team contact: name
Working Team Representatives: name
Working Team Delegees: name
Implementation Committee: multiple names
Functional Area 5:
Core Team contact: name
Working Team Representatives: name
Working Team Delegees: name
Implementation Committee: multiple names

Annex A6.5 Deliverables Contract

Project Name:				
IT Project Manager/Lead:		Business Project Manager/Lead:		
IT Sponsor Acceptance Signature:		Business Sponsor Acceptance Signature:		
Milestone / Deliverable	Owner IT or Business	Date Planned	Date Completed	Acceptance Form Required?

Annex A6.6 Project charter worksheet

Project Charter	project name
	Document Author
	Project Sponsor
	date

Business Need/Problem Statement
Project Goals and Objectives
Proposed Solution
Benefits

Tangible Benefits:

Description	Dollar Amount	Likelihood* (High, Medium, Low)
1.		
2.		
3.		
TOTAL		

* High - Very likely to be realized, probability is greater than 80%
  Medium - May or may not be realized, probability is 20 to 80%
  Low - Unlikely to be realized, probability is less than 20%

Intangible Benefits:

Description	Likelihood* (High, Medium, Low)
1.	
2.	
3.	

* High - Very likely to be realized, probability is greater than 80%
  Medium - May or may not be realized, probability is 20 to 80%
  Low - Unlikely to be realized, probability is less than 20%
  Major Assumptions/Constraints

Description	Assumption or Constraint	Importance* (High, Medium, Low)
1.		
2.		
3.		

* High - Critical to project success - If not valid then schedule would be delayed by over 1 month and/or budget would be exceeded by more than 25%
Medium - Would affect the project - If not valid then schedule would be delayed by up to 1 month and/or budget would be exceeded by up to 25%
Low - Minor project impact - If not valid then schedule would be delayed by less than 1 week and/or budget would be exceeded by less than 10%

Risks

Risk	Likelihood* (High, Medium, Low)	Impact# (High, Medium, Low)
1.		
2.		
3.		

* High - Very likely to affect project, probability is greater than 80%.
Medium - May or may not affect project, probability is 20 to 80%.
Low - Unlikely to affect project, probability is less than 20%
* High - Schedule delay of over 2 weeks and/or over budget by more than 10%
Medium - Schedule between 1 and 2 weeks and/or 5 to 10% over budget
Low - Schedule delay of less than 1 week and/or less than 5% over budget

Dependencie

Project	Likelihood* (High, Medium, Low)	Description of Impact
1.		
2.		

* High - Very likely to be realized, probability is greater than 80%
Medium - May or may not be realized, probability is 20 to 80%
Low - Unlikely to be realized, probability is less than 20%

Project Structure and Key Roles

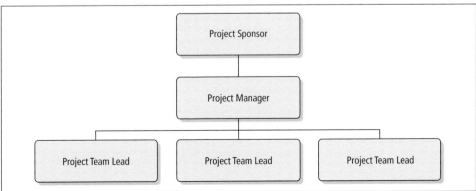

Project Charter Acceptance

Date	Role	Signature	Date Signed	Signed?

Project Charter Revision Log

Date	Description	Change ID	Author	Approved by

Annex A6.7 Project scope worksheet

Project Scope	project name
	project manager
	date

Project Description

Business Need

Project Goals

Project Objectives

Benefits

Major Assumptions

Constraints

Logical Scope
Within the Scope of the Project

Outside the Scope of the Project

Organizational Scope
External Organizations affected by the Project
Name:
Impact:
Name:
Impact:
Departments affected by the Project
Name:
Impact:
Name:
Impact:
Major Systems affected by the Project
Name:
Impact:
Name:
Impact:
Other Projects affected by the Project
Name:
Impact:
Name:
Impact:

Major Project Deliverables

Deliverable	Description

Project Scoped Acceptance

Name	Role	Signature	Date Signed	Signed?

Project Scope Revision Log

Date	Description	Change ID	Author	Approved by

Annex A6.8 ITIL/Support Center Implementation Plan

A6.8.1 Incident Management Process Workplan

1.5	Line of Business Implementation plan	START DATE	DUE DATE
1.5.0	[ITIL Support Center Implementation]		
1.5.1	Scope		
1.5.1.1	Identify IPOCs		
1.5.1.2	Identify specialty groups		
1.5.1.2.1	Identify Change Mgmt Specialty Groups		
1.5.1.2.2	Identify Incident Mgmt Specialty Groups		
1.5.1.3	Identify other affected areas		
1.5.1.3.1	Identify other areas affected by Chg process		
1.5.1.4	Identify training needs		
1.5.2	Roles		
1.5.2.1	Identify existing roles		
1.5.2.1.1.	Identify existing Chg Mgmt roles		
1.5.2.1.2	Identify existing Incident Mgmt roles		
1.5.2.2	Update roles and responsibilities		

1.5.2.2.1	Update Chg Mgmt roles & responsibilities		
1.5.2.2.2.	Update Incident roles & responsibilities		
1.5.2.3	Identify Who will fill Chg Mgmt roles		
1.5.2.3.1.	Identify Local Change Coordinators		
1.5.2.3.2.	Identify CAB Members		
1.5.2.4	Identify project team roles		
1.5.2.4.1	Identify Implementation sub-team		
1.5.2.4.2	Identify Working Team reps		
1.5.2.4.3	Identify process go-to people		
1.5.3	Awareness		
1.5.3.1	Develop awareness materials		
1.5.3.2	Conduct awareness sessions		
1.5.4	Gap		
1.5.4.1	Capture existing process information		
1.5.4.1.1	Capture existing Change Process info		
1.5.4.1.2	Capture existing Support Center Incident Process info		
1.5.4.1.3	Capture existing eComm Incident process info		
1.5.4.2	Capture existing policy information		
1.5.4.2.1	Capture existing Change Policy info		
1.5.4.2.2	Capture existing Support Center Incident Policy info		
1.5.4.2.3	Capture existing eComm Incident Policy info		
1.5.4.3	Capture existing work instructions		
1.5.4.3.1	Capture existing Chg Mgmt work instructions		
1.5.4.3.2	Capture existing Support Center Incident Mgmt work instructions		
1.5.4.3.3	Capture existing eComm Incident Mgmt work instructions		
1.5.4.4	Validate against core process		
1.5.4.4.1	Validate against core Change Process		
1.5.4.4.2	Validate against core Incident Process		
1.5.4.5	Document additional requirements		
1.5.4.5.1.	Document additional requirements		
1.5.4.5.2	Document upcoming Major Changes		
1.5.4.5.3	Document types of Standard Changes		
1.5.5	Documentation		
1.5.5.1	Identify documentation requirements		
1.5.5.2	Develop LOB/application handbook		
1.5.5.2.1	Develop LOB Incident Handbook		
1.5.5.2.2	Develop LOB Change Handbook		
1.5.6	Policies		
1.5.6.1	Identify missing policies		
1.5.6.1.1	Identify missing Change Policies		
1.5.6.1.2	Identify missing Incident Policies		
1.5.6.2	Submit additional policies for approval		
1.5.7	Work Instructions		
1.5.7.1	Capture Work Instructions		

1.5.7.1.1	Complete Chg Mgmt work instructions		
1.5.7.1.2	Complete Support Center Incident Mgmt work instructions		
1.5.7.1.3	Complete eComm Incident Mgmt work instructions		
1.5.8	Use Case Walkthroughs		
1.5.8.1	Validate design via Use Case walkthroughs		
1.5.8.1.1	Validate Change Mgmt design		
1.5.8.1.2	Validate Incident Mgmt design		
1.5.8.2	Identify Use Cases		
1.5.8.2.1	Identify Change Mgmt Use Cases		
1.5.8.2.2	Identify Incident Mgmt use cases		
1.5.9	Training		
1.5.9.1	Identify Training Audience (Process, Tool, or Both)		
1.5.9.1.1	Identify Who needs Chg Mgmt process training		
1.5.9.1.2	Identify who needs Incident Mgmt process trng		
1.5.9.1.3	Identify who needs TCM training		
1.5.9.1.4	Identify who needs TPM training		
1.5.9.1.5	Identify who needs Chg Manager detailed trng		
1.5.9.1.6	Identify who needs ITIL Essentials trng		
1.5.9.1.7	Identify who needs ITIL overview trng		
1.5.9.2	Schedule Training		
1.5.9.2.1	Schedule Chg Mgmt process training		
1.5.9.2.2	Schedule Incident Mgmt process trng		
1.5.9.2.3	Schedule Change Tool training		
1.5.9.2.4	Schedule Incident Tool training		
1.5.9.2.5	Schedule Chng Manager detailed training		
1.5.9.2.6	Schedule ITIL Essentials training		
1.5.9.2.7	Schedule ITIL overview training		
1.5.9.3	Reserve & Prepare Training facilities		
1.5.9.3.1	Reserve facilities for Chg Mgmt process trng		
1.5.9.3.2	Prep room & materials for Chg Mgmt process trng		
1.5.9.3.3	Reserve facilities for Incident Mgmt process trng		
1.5.9.3.4	Prep room & materials for Incident Mgmt process trng		
1.5.9.3.5	Reserve facilities for Change Tool training		
1.5.9.3.6	Prep room & materials for Change Tool training		
1.5.9.3.7	Reserve facilities for Incident Tool training		
1.5.9.3.8	Prep room & materials for Incident Tool trng		
1.5.3.9.9	Reserve facilities for Chg Manager detailed trng		
1.5.9.3.10	Prep room & materials for Chg Manager detailed trng		
1.5.9.3.11	Reserve facilities for ITIL Essentials training		
1.5.9.3.12	Prep room & materials for ITIL Essentials trng		
1.5.9.3.13	Reserve facilities for ITIL overview training		
	Prep room & materials for ITIL overview training		
1.5.9.4	Conduct Process Training		
1.5.9.4.1	Conduct Change Mgmt process training		
1.5.9.4.2	Conduct Incident Mgmt process training		

1.5.9.4.3	Conduct Change Manager detailed training		
1.5.9.4.4	Conduct ITIL Essentials training		
1.5.9.4.5	Conduct ITIL overview training		
1.5.9.5	Conduct Tool Training		
1.5.9.5.1	Conduct Change Tool training		
	Conduct Incident Tool training		
1.5.9.6	Training Completed		
1.5.9.7	Train Implementation subteam		
1.5.10	Implementation		
1.5.10.1	Roll out process to targeted areas		
1.5.10.2	Provide Coaching and Mentoring		
1.5.10.3	Rollout Completed		
1.5.11	Evaluation		
1.5.11.1	Review of Impelmentation		
1.5.11.1.1	Review Change Mgmt implementation		
15.11.1.2	Review Incident Mgmt implementation		
1.5.11.2	Revise Core Process		
1.5.11.2.1	Revise Change Mgmt Process		
1.5.11.2.2	Revise Incident Mgmt Process		
1.5.11.3	Revise Training		
1.5.11.3.1	Revise Change Mgmt process training		
1.5.11.3.2	Revise Incident Mgmt process training		
1.5.11.3.3	Revise Change Tool training		
1.5.11.3.4	Revise Incident Tool training		
1.5.11.3.5	Revise Change Manager detailed trng		
1.5.11.3.6	Revise ITIL overview training		
1.5.11.4	Recommend Policy Changes		
1.5.11.4.1	Recommend Change Mgmt policy changes		
1.5.11.4.2	Recommend Incident Mgmt policy changes		
1.5.11.5	Build Audit Process		
1.5.11.6	Evaluate Rollout		
1.5.11.7	Modify Process Based on Evaluation		

Annex A6.9 Steps in developing the Communication Action Plan

- Look at current vehicles
- Rate how they are doing
- What changes to current vehicles need to take place
- What gaps exist?
- Who are the chosen target audiences?
- Short term
- Long term
- What do we want to say?
- How to fill those gaps

Steps to create a specific Communication item:
- Expectations of the communication vehicle:
- What is the overall objective of the communication?
- Who is the intended audience?
- What form(s) of delivery will the communication take?
- How will it be delivered to its audience?
- What will be the basic layout (size, shape, etc.)?

Content
- What is to be said and why? Provide some detail here.
- How frequently will this be published or updated?
- When is the information given (If there are to be updates or future issues, for example, what information is given when? Provide a timeline.)

Project
- Who will lead the project?
- Who is on the team?
- Who will create what parts from the content?
- Who takes ownership for updating or for future issues, if applicable?
- What is the timeline for the project?
- If hardcopy format, how many are to be created, and when (single or multiple batches)?
- Points to stress/remember:
- Simplify (hide complexity where possible)
- Value to them - how do we show this (adds value to business and decision making)
- Educate on how the guidelines work, (changing standards in response to market)
- Tie to business strategy, local, global
- Show success story
- Flexibility will give us strength in changing marketplace, makes IT environment more responsive
- What do we need to communicate?
- High level vision - process
- More immediate level - return on investment
- What do we need from them?
- When do we need it?
- What might their objections be and how do we handle them?
- Is there anyone else that needs to be onboard prior to communicating to them?
- How do we communicate?
- Benefits to organization

Annex A6.10 Communication plan

Project Manager

Comm #	Document Location	Stakeholder(s)	Message Purpose/Content	Media Used	Frequency of Updates	Originator	Date due to approver	Target Delivery Date	Actual Delivery Date	Approvers

Stakeholder Assessment			
Stakeholder	Project involvement / interest	Influence over others	Direct control of resources

Annex A6.11 Implementation scope questionnaire for Gap Analysis

When filling out this questionnaire, please be sure to include information for all areas that you are representing for your department. Questions that ask about your "area" refer to all teams you are representing in this assignment, not just to your immediate team.

A6.11.1 General Information

Working Group representative names:
Name of delegates (if applicable):
Department name being represented:
Division names being represented within the department:
Identify what technologies/disciplines your department is directly responsible for:

- For incidents involving your area, what are the Initial Points of Contact (IPOCs) for your customers? In other words, where do your incident tickets come from?

- Support Centers - what support centers do tickets come to your area from?

- Monitoring Tools - if incident tickets for your area are created automatically, please list what tools create those tickets.

- Self-initiated - does your area currently identify incidents yourselves? If so, how and where do these tickets get logged (e.g. not logged, call the data center and they open the ticket, logged in a departmental database or spreadsheet, etc.)?

- Other - list any other ways in which incidents may be initiated with your area (e.g. calls directly from customers, monitoring tools that page you directly, etc.)

- For Incident Management, please list all Tool specialty groups that belong to your area. Identify whether these groups are used for Level 1,2 or 3 support.

Tool Specialty Group Name	Support Level

For Change Management, please list all Tool specialty groups (if different than above) that belong to your area.

Tool Specialty Group Name

List below all other areas that are (or can be) directly affected by incidents/problems from your area.

List below all other areas that are (or can be) directly affected by changes initiated and/or implemented by your area.

List below all people in your affected areas and what type of training they have.
For the Role column, use the following categories:
Support (handles incidents/problem/calls/pages, etc.) = S
Administrator (ID admin, server admin, etc.) = A
Implementer (makes changes to production) = I
Lead (project lead, project manager, etc.) = L
Management (manager, director, administrative support, etc.) = M
Other = O

Name	Manager	Role S,A,I,L,M,O

A6.11.2 Process Documentation Questionnaire

When answering these questions, please consider documentation to include paper hardcopy documents, electronic softcopy documents and files, web pages containing this information, diagrams, handbooks/user guides etc. Also, if a document does not exist but the information is 'known' by the individuals or teams doing that work, please list the names of those individuals who know that information.

General Documentation questions:
• What methods of awareness building are you using to communicate these changes to your teams and increase the acceptance of the new processes?

Change Management documentation
- Do you currently have a Change Management or Change Control Process?

- If so, please list below the locations of the documentation for this process or attach copies of the documents.

- If the process is not formally documented, please identify a list of individuals who know the process and can explain it to the implementation team.

- Are there any types of changes that currently do not follow this process because they are too frequent, low risk, or other reason? If so, please list those types of changes here.

- Do you currently have any policies regarding Change Management or Change Control that your areas use?

- Please attach the policy documents or locations, or list individuals that can describe these policies if they are not documented.

- Do you have any type of Change Management work-instructions that are used in your area or by users of your areas' services? These could be located in such places as Team guidelines, checklists, handbooks, websites, etc.

- In the new process, changes that occur frequently in high volume and have a high success rate can be considered Standard Changes. Please list below all types of changes that your areas might perform that you believe could be candidates for being declared Standard.

- Do you have any upcoming changes planned or types of changes that could be coming soon -that would be considered 'Major' changes? If so, list them below. These would be:
  - changes that would have new technologies
  - changes that are part of an executive strategic project
  - changes that would cost over $XXX
  - or changes that could have major impacts to the business

To help validate that the Change Management process will work efficiently for your areas, please list below 5-10 types of changes that we can walk through the process. These should include several types of changes in each of the following categories:
Emergency changes:

Typical frequent, recurring changes:

Non-frequent but low impact types of changes:

Changes that could have huge impact:

A6.11.3 Incident Management Documentation

Do you currently have an Incident Management, Problem Management, or other support Process?

If so, please list below the locations of the documentation for this process or attach copies of the documents.

If the process is not formally documented, please identify a list of individuals who know the process and can explain it to the implementation team.

Are there any types of incidents or problems that currently do not follow this process because they are too frequent, there is no help desk support, or other reason? If so, please list those types of incidents/problems here.

Do you currently have any policies on Incident Management or Problem Management that your areas use?

Please attach the policy documents or locations, or list individuals that can describe these policies if they are not documented.

Do you have any type of Incident or Problem Management work-instructions that are used in your area or by users of your areas' services? These could be located in such places as team guidelines, checklists, handbooks, websites, etc.

To help validate that the Incident Management process will work efficiently for your areas, please list below 5-10 types of incident or problems that we can walk through the process. These should include several types of incidents in each of the following categories:
Severity 0, major impact incidents:

Low Severity, low urgency incidents:

Incidents identified through automatic monitoring tools:

Incidents identified and reported by your team:

A6.11.4 Roles and responsibilities

When filling out this questionnaire, please be sure to include information for all areas that you are representing on the Working Team. Questions that ask about your "area" refer to all areas you are representing in this assignment, not just to your immediate team.

Who will be your go-to person(s) for Change Management questions and coaching?

Who will be your go-to person(s) for Incident Management questions and coaching?

List anyone in your area currently performing any Change Management roles or functions.

Name	Current role/function

List anyone in your area currently performing any Incident Management roles or functions.

Name	Current role/function

Who in your area will act as the Local Change Coordinators for changes initiated in your area?

Name	Types of changes they will coordinate

Identify who in your area will participate regularly on Change Advisory Boards (CABs)

Name	Role

Annex A6.12 SWOT analysis - sample questions

Strengths What are we good at? How do we help the business achieve its goals?	*Weaknesses* What do we do poorly? Where are the gaps? (People? Processes? Technology?)
Opportunities Identify new service opportunities. What is happening within the industry?	*Threats* What is happening within the business? How will technology changes affect us?

A6.13 Proposed Metrics and Priority Codes

Process	Metric	Description	Benefit	User	Tool	ITIL Recommended
Support Center	Workload Analysis	Amount of time required to resolve each incident	Staff optimization	Incident/Major Incident Manager	Capable	Yes
	Actual Time vs. SLAs	Resolution time as compared to established service average	Evaluation of service capabilities	Incident/Major Incident Manager/Users	Capable	Yes
	Escalations by Group	Volume of incidents having to be referred to specialty groups for resolution	Identifies potential problem areas where additional training or knowledge transference may be needed.	Incident/Major Incident Manager/Specialty Group	Capable	Yes
	Service Breaches	Volume of incidents not resolved within SLA causing service escalations	Identifies service failures for review regarding cause of breach and future prevention.	Incident/Major Incident Manager/Users	Capable	Yes
	Outstanding Incidents	Incidents unresolved	Reports on incidents that are still open so that they can be reviewed and evaluated and to ensure that none 'fall through the cracks'	Incident/Major Incident Manager	Capable	Yes
	Service Availability	Reports time that system was available for use	Performance indicator and touchpoint to Availibility Management	Incident/Major Incident Manager/Users/Availibility Management	Requires Research	Yes
	Incident Areas Volumes	Reports volumes by incident type to highlight problem areas	Performance indicator focused on volume by incident type.	Incident/Major Incident Manager/Users	Capable	Yes
	Incident Areas by Work Time Requirements	Ranks incident types by work time to resolve	Performance indicator with attention to time spend on incidents by type.	Incident/Major Incident Manager/Users	Requires Research	Yes
	Incident Areas by Turn Around Time to Customer	Ranks incident types by time from outage of service to when service restored	Performance indicator with attention on time of service outage for the customer by incident type.	Incident/Major Incident Manager/Users	Requires Research	Yes
	Trending Analysis	Utilization of current and past occurrencs to determine future probabilities	Forecasting tool to help identify potential problem areas and for training or staffing requirements.	Incident/Major Incident Manager/Process Owner	Incapable	Yes
	Multiple Incidents Escalated to Problem	Reports those incidents that are escalated to Problem Management for resolution	Performance indicator and touchpoint to Problem Management	Incident/Major Incident Manager/Problem Manager	Capable	Yes
	Ratio of Incidents by Customer Type	Comparison of volumes by 2-digit code derived by BCR type.	Identifies large and small volume by customer.	Incident/Major Incident Manager/Users	Capable (requires research of Customer Type)	No
	Ratio of Incidents by Type (call, email, walk-up, system generated)	Compares volumes by entry method for evaluation.	Comparison of reporting mediums for over/under utilization.	Incident/Major Incident Manager	Capable	No
	Ratio of Incidents Handled First-Time Final by Category.	Compares First-Time Final volumes by total incidents to assess efficiency. Goal is to see FTF percentages to increase over time. On the Peregrine tool, this includes items categorized as Calls and Incidents. Calls are classified as First-Time Final items.	Measures effectiveness of first time final and can be used for trending.	Incident/Major Incident Manager/Specialty Groups/ Process Owner	Capable	No
	Ratio of Incidents by Disbursement Code	Comparison of volumes by user who reported the incident. This needs to be further assessed as there are questions concerning how used and reported.	Identifies large and small volume by disbursement code.	Incident/Major Incident Manager/Users	Capable	No
	Ratio of Incidents Handled within SLAs	This would involve the capability of measuring overall, by group and by priority.	Looks at how effective we are in meeting SLAs.	Incident/Major Incident Manager/Users	Capable	No

	Cost of Service Provision/Failure	Business costs associated with incident types	Assigns a cost to incident types in order to assess priorities and value of service provided.	Incident/Major Incident Manager/Users	Incapable	Yes
Incident (Note most metrics for Incident are captured under Service Desk)	Elapsed Time of Resolution by Impact Code	Measures the length of time to resolve incidents by severity to assess performance	Performance Indicator	Incident/Major Incident Manager/Users/Process Owner	Capable	Yes
	First Time Finals	Indicates the number of incidents that are resolved at time of initial contact	First Time Final measurements should be used as a time-line indicator similar to a 2 year stock history. FTF should demonstrate highs and lows with a reference point indicating why the lows. A healthy process should trend upwards.	Incident/Major Incident Manager/Specialty Group/Process Owner	Capable	Yes
	Ratio of Incidents by Priority	Comparison of volumes by according to the assigned level of importance.	Notes trends regarding priority.	Incident/Major Incident Manager/Specialty Groups/ Process Owner	Capable	No
	Ratio of Incidents by Owning Group	Comparison of volumes by group creating the incident ticket.	Identifies large and small volume initiators.	Incident/Major Incident Manager/Specialty Groups/ Process Owner	Capable	No
	Ratio of Incidents by Responsible Group	Comparison of volumes by group in possession of the ticket when the SLA becomes measurable.	Used for capacity analysis of resources.	Incident/Major Incident Manager/Specialty Groups/ Process Owner	Capable	No
	Number of Incidents Related to Implementation of a Change	Related to root cause identification and used to identify issues with Change Process.	Used in root cause analysis and for correlation analysis to measure effectiveness of Change Management.	Incident/Major Incident Manager/Specialty Groups/ Process Owner/Change Manager	Incapable	No
	Number of Incidents not documented in Peregrine.	Need to determine a way to monitor incidents that were not documented in Peregrine but still worked.	Tracks items not documented in Peregrine, therefore, outside the Incident Management Process.	Incident/Major Incident Manager/Users/Process Owner	Incapable	No
	Elapsed Time of Phase Duration in Incident Management Process.	Elapsed time (minutes) of phases in the Incident Management Process at the Initiators, Owning/Responsible Groups, and Priority levels as well as compared to the SLAs (if any).	Establishes values for component evaluations for effectiveness measurement.	Incident/Major Incident Manager/Process Owner	Requires Research	No
	Variances Between Elapsed Times Between Measuring Points	Differences in time (hours or days) between phases in the Incident Management Process at the Initiators, Owning/Responsible Groups, and Priority levels as well as compared to the SLAs (if any).	Used to determine whether the variances in the durations of the components are within tolerances or if action might be needed to identify why out of tolerance.	Incident/Major Incident Manager/Process Owner	Incapable	No
	Ratio of Service Requests vs. Other Tools	Used to determine impact on current priorities and understand volume of service requests.	Comparison allows for the acknowledgement of other tools and the degree that Peregrine meets the needs of the process or when it no longer accommodates those needs.	Incident/Major Incident Manager/Process Owner	Incapable	No
	Ratio of Service Requests vs. Incidents	Compares volumes between SRs and Incidents to evaluate knowledge transfers vs. actual issues.	Evaluates effectiveness of knowledge transfer and classification of incoming calls.	Incident/Major Incident Manager/Process Owner	Requires Service Request Tracking	No
	Volume/Percentages of Incidents Resolved Remotely	Incidents resolved without having to visit the physical location	Performance Indicator	Incident/Major Incident Manager	Capable	Yes

	Volume/Percentages of Incidents Resolved Remotely	Incidents resolved without having to visit the physical location	Performance Indicator	Incident/Major Incident Manager	Capable	Yes
Problem	Trends on Post-Change Occurrence of Particular Problem Types	Validates that the Change implemented to resolve a Problem actually works	Trends on post-Change occurrence of particular Problem types evaluates success of Change. Touchpoint to Change Management	Problem Manager/Change Manager/Process Owner	Incapable	Yes
	Number and Impact of RFCs on availibility and reliability of service	Volume and impact description by Problem type	Grouping problems by type, this is an indicator to demonstrate areas of focus. Touchpoint to Availibility Management.	Problem Management Team/Process Owner/Availibility Manager	Incapable	Yes
	Amount of time worked on investigations and diagnoses per organizational unit split by Problem type	Length of time required to formulate solution to problem by Problem type	Useful for workforce analysis and for determining job costs.	Problem Management Team/Process Owner/Availibility Manager	Capable	Yes
	Number and impact of Incidents occurring before the root Problem is closed or a Known Error is confirmed	Evaluation of the extent of incidents arising from a Problem before the root cause is determined.	Measures the reaction time from both the Incident and Problem Management areas in determining root cause.	Problem Management Team/Process Owner/Incident Manager	Capable	Yes
	Ratio of Immediate (reactive) support effort to planned support effort in Problem Management	Evaluation of time spent conducting 'damage control' versus time spent on planned Changes	Determines how proactive the company is regarding the mitigation of Problems versus 'putting out fires'.	Problem Manager/Change Manager/Process Owner	Capable	Yes
	Elapsed Time to Close a Problem	Time measurement from the point a Problem is opened to the point where it is closed. Since this includes the execution of the solution, this would also include Change and Release Management elapsed time regarding the build and implementation of the solution.	Performance Indicator - This is a Touchpoint with Change and Release Management.	Problem Management Team/Process Owner	Capable	Yes
	Elapsed Time to Date on Outstanding Problems	A daily report designed to track outstanding problems and how they are progressing.		Problem Management Team	Capable	Yes
	Expected Resolution Time on Outstanding Problems	Expresses the anticipated resolution time for an outstanding Problem.	This is a speculative measuremena which may help regarding down time estimation or resource planning. It may point to a particular Problem that needs increased attention but is should not be considered as a trending indicator.	Problem Management Team	Requires Research	Yes
	Mean/Maximum Elapsed Time to close Problems	Compares averages and maximum times for trending purposes. Can also be used for variance analysis.	Performance Indicator - Establishes averages for comparisons in order to gauge the process efficiency.	Problem Manager/Change Manager/Process Owner	Requires Research	Yes
Change	Impact of Change (degree of Service increase)	Positive impact of Change on Service (Availibility)	Performance Indicator - Touchpoint to Availibility and Problem Management.	Change Manager/CAB/Process Owner	Incapable	Yes
	Decrease in service disruption over time resulting from Change	Validation that the Change being implemented is positively affecting Service by reducing or eliminating disruptions	Performance Indicator	Change Manager/CAB/Process Owner	Requires Research	Yes
	Number of Changes Implemented in the Period by CI, Configuration Type, Service	Volume count for a particular period viewed from several categories to evaluate process efficiency.	Performance Indicator	Change Manager/CAB/Process Owner	Capable	Yes
	Breakdown by Reason for Change	Assesses the volume counts by Reason for Change to note any trends or problem areas that may require further research.	Performance Indicator	Change Manager/CAB/Process Owner	Capable	Yes
	Number of Successful Changes	Measures the success of the process components such as RFC submission, Build and Testing phases by looking at the success of the implementation.	Performance Indicator	Change Manager/CAB/ITEC/Process Owner	Capable	Yes

Name	Description	Type/Purpose	Owner	Capability	
Number of Changes Backed Out and Reasons	Examines the volume of items implemented then backed out for one reason or another. Goal is to have few of these. Reasons help to identify causes for future elimination.	Performance Indicator	Change Manager/CAB/Process Owner	Capable	Yes
Number of Incidents Traced to Changes	Measure of Change efficiency in regards to communication, training and impact analysis. To be used for risk elimination in future.	Touchpoint to Incident Management.	Change Manager/CAB/Process Owner/Incident Manager	Incapable	Yes
Trending of RFCs by Type	Analysis of trends based upon past and current data by type to forecast future events to be used to address perceived issues.	Proactive analysis that identifies potential issues or ares of focus or investigation.	Change Manager/CAB/ITEC/Process Owner	Incapable	Yes
High Incident of RFCs to Particular CIs and Reasons	Identifies areas of risk by association of volume counts to particular CIs.	Proactive analysis that identifies risk and allows for appropriate action to be taken to midigate risk.	Change Manager/CAB	Capable	Yes
Previous Period Comparisons	Compare/contrast current to previous periods to gauge process performance.	Performance Indicator	Change Manager/CAB/ITEC/Process Owner	Capable	Yes
Number of RFCs Rejected and Why	Provides volumes and reasons for RFCs being rejected for action. Allows analysis of to prevent abuse or to highlight training requirements.	Performance Indicator	Change Manager/CAB	Requires Research	Yes
Proportion of Implemented Changes Unsuccessful (in total and by CI)	Analysis of authorized changes that were implemented but proved unsuccessful. By categorizing these numbers, focus may be placed on individual areas requiring adjustment in activities.	This metric identifies areas where training or execution may be lacking in the correct identification of requirements to provide successful Change implementations or Problem resolutions.	Change Manager/CAB/ITEC/Process Owner	Capable	Yes
Change Backlogs by CI and Stage	Measures Changes that are taking longer than average or estimated.	This identifies possible workload issues or procedural issues that may be the cause of the backlogs.	Change Manager/CAB	Requires Research	Yes
Ratio of Change Types	Comparison of Change Types to understand the workloads, the reasons for change and the exposure of the CABs/Change Managers.	Performance Indicator	Change Manager/CAB	Capable	Yes
Ratio of Standard:Minor:Significant:Major Changes	Comparison of volumes by category.	Performance Indicator - Notes trends regarding category.	Change Manager/CAB/Process Owner	Capable	No
Ratio of Submitted Changes by CAB	Comparison of volumes by CAB.	Performance Indicator - Compares efficiency by CAB.	Change Manager/CAB/Process Owner	Capable	No
Ratio of Authorized/Rejected/Pended Changes by CAB	Comparison based upon the CAB review of the RFCs.	Performance Indicator - Comparison of responsiveness by CAB.	Change Manager/CAB/Process Owner	Requires Research	No
Ratio of Successful vs. Unsuccessful Changes by CAB, Application & Technology Area	Comparison of the outcomes of the implementation of RFCs.	Performance Indicator - Quick comparison of the effectiveness of submitted changes.	Change Manager/CAB/Process Owner	Capable	No
Number of Incomplete Change Requests	Number of RFCs submitted that were incomplete for consideration by CAB. Requires a further breakdown of the rejection code to identify why rejected (new requirement).	Used to indicate possible training needs. Evaluates the efficiency of training for tool users.	Change Manager	Incapable	No
Variances Between Elapsed Times Between Measuring Points	Differences in time (hours or days) between phases in the Change Management Process at the Business Sponsor, CAB, and Priority levels as well as compared to the SLAs (if any).	Performance Indicator - Used to analyze differences in elapsed times to identify issues. Would require the development of averages and/or SLAs.	Change Manager/Process Owner	Requires Research	No
Aging by Status	Measurement of elapsed time in each status of the Change Process (Submitted/Authorized/Pended/Build/Test).	Prevents RFC's from 'falling between the cracks' and being forgotten.	Change Manager/CAB/Process Owner	Requires Research	No

Average Time to Create an RFC	Average time it takes to enter an RFC from the moment the screen is opened to the point that the submission is complete.	Evaluates the user interface to determine how fast and easy it is to use. Measures the effectiveness of the user interface.	Change Manager/Process Owner	Incapable	No
Correlation of Incidents to Change	Measures the number of incidents that arise related to a change. This could be done by comparing volume reports for each to see if spikes occur in incidents immediately after a change takes place.	An increase in Incidents as a result of a Change may point to a lapse or defect in the Change process. Measures the effectiveness of the Change Process via comparison to fallout on the Incident Process.	Change Manager/Process Owner/Incident Manager	Incapable	No

A6.14 Incident Metrics Report

Company ITSM Metrics Reporting - Incident Management

<#> Quarter <year>

Groups Reporting	Total <mm/dd/yy> Total # of incidents	Total # Never Transferred	Total <mm/dd/yy> Total # of incidents	Total # Never Transferred	Total <mm/dd/yy> Total # of incidents	Total # Never Transferred	Quarter Results Total # of incidents	Total # Never Transferred
Group 1 Total							This is the sum of the next 5 rows, ie. CA Total	
Severity 0								
Severity 1								
Severity 2								
Severity 3								
Severity 4								
Group 2 Total							This is the sum of the next 5 rows, ie. NF Total	
Severity 0								
Severity 1								
Severity 2								
Severity 3								
Severity 4								
Group 3 Total							This is the sum of the next 5 rows, ie. NI Total	
Severity 0								
Severity 1								
Severity 2								
Severity 3								
Severity 4								
Group 4 Total							This is the sum of the next 5 rows, ie. NSC Total	
Severity 0								
Severity 1								
Severity 2								
Severity 3								
Severity 4								
Total Company							This is the sum of the totals for each LOB	
Miscellaneous								

A6.15 Support Center Scorecard - Daily

ServiceDesk **Scorecard** for 5/4/2004
Data from ServiceCenter

**ASA(YTD) does not reflect waived months.
*WSL = % Within Service Level (AOA+ = 20sec, Other = 60sec)

Group	Volume	Answered	%Aband	Flow Out	Avg Talk Time	# of VM	ASA	MTD ASA	YTD** ASA	MTD WSL*	WSL	YTD** WSL
Agency	1647	1416	11.84	36	8:10	32	2:36	2:22	2:13	36.09	45.32	57.7
Agency - Apps	878	716	15.26	28	8:23		3:27	2:54	2:26	22.35	37.71	52.5
Agency - ESM	16	16	0	0	8:25		1:21	1:02	0:41	43.75	54.17	80.49
Agency - Password	176	163	7.39	0	6:44		0:58	1:09	1:32	65.03	65.96	74.33
Agency - PCG/Email	526	474	8.75	6	8:39		1:59	2:05	2:19	44.09	47.79	56.69
Agency - Status	51	47	3.92	2	4:32		1:53	1:24	1:02	61.7	67.86	76.3
AOA+	32	30	6.25	0	9:07		0:45	0:29	0:15	66.67	76.92	92.79
Claims	447	386	9.62	18	11:19	18	1:57	9:28	1:00	69.17	43.17	84.95
NF	237	214	5.91	9	4:52	7	0:46	0:56	0:50	80.84	76.59	80.52
NI	247	239	2.83	1	6:45	2	0:26	0:26	0:33	89.54	63.51	88.85
NSC	201	194	2.99	1	5:28	1	0:18	3:44	0:37	92.78	70.95	88.74
T-Comm	25	22	4	2	3:05	2	0:22	0:29	0:29	86.36	86	88.44
Total	2836	2501	9.45	67	7:59	62	1:55	3:27	1:40	55.34	52.37	68.32
OTHER GROUPS:												
Specialty Calls	67	51	13.43	7	1:03	7	1:05	1:25	0:27	76.47	64.58	78.53

Special CMS Data - Max Delay Times

Group	Max Delay Time	Skill	Occurrence
Agency	00:17:49	ITSD Agy McAfee 356	5/4/2004 10:00 - 10:30AM
Claims	00:17:58	ITSD Cl Business 93	5/4/2004 9:00 - 9:30AM
NF	00:12:45	ITSD NF Conctvty 113	5/4/2004 5:30 - 6:00PM
NI	00:05:48	ITSD NI Conctvty 282	5/4/2004 9:00 - 9:30AM
NSC	00:04:56	ITSD NSC Cnctvty 272	5/4/2004 9:30 - 10:00AM
Specialty Calls	00:11:01	ITSD SvcMgt Spec 77	5/4/2004 7:30 - 8:00AM
T-Comm	00:02:16	ITSD TCOM Brk_Fix 96	5/4/2004 12:30 - 1:00PM

General Ticket Data

Business Unit	FTF Tickets	FTF Eligible	FTF %	Total Tickets	Attached Tickets
Agency	1089	1295	84.09	1306	16
Claims	204	259	78.76	259	0
Customer Type 99	142	209	67.94	209	1
NF	77	168	45.83	169	4
NI	152	247	61.54	247	1
NSC & Corp Offices	33	83	39.76	84	5
Total	1697	2261	75.06	2274	27

Customer Convenience Tools

	IVR Status Tool					Ticket Tracker Tool					
Group	Calls To	Success	% Success	ITSD	Aborted	Total	Success	% Success	Sensitive	Blocked	Mismatch
AGENCY	83	12	14.5%	50	20	52	28	53.85%	4	0	20
CLAIMS	37	4	10.8%	30	3	8	7	87.50%	0	0	1
NF	32	7	21.9%	20	5	4	4	100.00%	0	0	0
NI	32	4	12.5%	22	6	24	20	83.33%	0	0	4
NSC	24	1	4.2%	17	6	4	3	75.00%	0	0	1
MISC	0	0	0.0%	0	0	41	21	51.22%	4	0	16
OTHER TOOLS:											
RAP	83	55	66.3%								

Non-Closed Incident Summary

Assignee	# Tickets	Oldest Date	Over 7 Days	Over 14 Days	Over 21 Days
NSC-ITSD-AGENCY-AUTO	2	5/3/2004 4:43:22 PM	0	0	0
NSC-ITSD-AGENCY-ESM	2	5/3/2004 10:19:22 AM	0	0	0
NSC-ITSD-AGENCY-HARDWARE	6	4/29/2004 8:57:51 AM	0	0	0
NSC-ITSD-MISROUTES	6	4/28/2004 1:11:48 PM	0	0	0
NSC-ITSD-AGENCY-AOAPLUS-ESCALATIONS	18	4/28/2004 1:02:48 PM	0	0	0
NSC-ITSD-AGENCY-CLIENT-MGMT-BUSINESS	5	4/26/2004 4:02:43 PM	1	0	0
NSC-ITSD-AGENCY-FIRE	3	5/3/2004 4:29:00 PM	0	0	0
NSC-ITSD-INTERNAL-SUPPORT	1	5/4/2004 1:49:57 PM	0	0	0
NSC-ITSD-NF	1	4/22/2004 8:53:53 AM	1	0	0

Generated by vaxxxm, 5/5/2004 2:47:06 PM

A6.16 Support Center Scorecard - Monthly

Year to Date	ITSD Total
Calls Offered	178723
Incident Tickets plus FTF Call Tickets	142843
Attaches to Incident Tickets	4490
Abandon	17496
ASA	00:01:08
FTF	80,12%
Customer Satisfaction [1]	90,40%
Utilization of Self Help	
RAP	5313
Ticket Tracker	3441
IVR	1151

Month to Date	ITSD Total
Calls Offered	60354
Incident Tickets plus FTF Call Tickets	50595
Attaches to Incident Tickets	1457
Abandon	4624
ASA	00:01:22
FTF	80,49%
Customer Satisfaction [1]	94,06%
Utilization of Self Help	
RAP	1456
Ticket Tracker	1202
IVR	317

[1] **Non-FTF Customer Satisfaction available upon request**

Bibliography

Interviews:
Collins, Mary Leigh (2004) US Army Information Technology Agency, The Pentagon. [Interview] May 4.

12 Conley, Janna (2004). Nationwide Process Management Specialist. [Interview] April 20.

5 Deacon, Leslie (2004). Bank One Infrastructure and Operations Senior Manager. [Interview] April 19.

15 Heere, Craig (2004). Nationwide IT Project Management Sr. Consultant. [Interview] April 26.

10 Koon, Scott (2004). Mayo Clinic Help Desk Director. [Interview] May 6.

8 Mahan, Suzanne (2004). Nationwide Program Support Lead for Continuous Process Improvements, Metrics and Training & Communication. [Interview] May 6.

13 McLaughlin, Kevin (2004). Procter & Gamble Service Manager. [Interview] May 6.

McTigrit, Fran (2004). Katy (Texas) Independent School District Director of Technology Customer [Interview] May 5.

19 Meeks, Christina (2004). Nationwide Process Management Specialist. [Interview] April 20.

18 Metcalf, Maureen (2004). Metcalf Associates President and Forman, John (2004) Integral Development Associates Managing Partner. [Interview] May 17.

20 Milligan, Jim (2004). JW&M Consulting Group Principal Consultant. [Interview] April 19.

9 Peterson, Paula (2004). Remedy Customer Support Manager [Interview] April 30.

4 Pierce, MaryLynn (2004). Nationwide Service Desk Director. [Interview] April 19.

7 Probst, Jack (2004). Nationwide Enterprise IT Process Integration IT Process Officer. [Interview] May 6.

11 Rozdeba, Stan (2004). Accenture Operations Consultant.
[Interview] April 20.

6 Shinault, Merle (2004). Process Management Specialist.
[Interview] April 20.

16 Snider, William (2004). Nationwide Systems Analysis Lead.
[Interview] April 20.

17 Stahl, Ron (2004). Nationwide IT Project Management Consultant.
[Interview] April 22.

14 Storts, Scott (2004). Nationwide IT Process Management Specialist.
[Interview] May 18.

Books:
Office of Government Commerce Staff 2000, *Best Practice for Service Support,*
The Stationery Office United Kingdom.

Pink Elephant 2003, *Establishing a Service Desk According to ITIL Best Practices,*
Ontario, Canada

1 Pink Elephant 2003, *ITIL IT Service Management Essentials Course Workbook,*
Ontario, Canada

Pultorak, Dave and Quagliariello, Pete, February 2003, *Microsoft Operations Framework,*
Van Haren Publishing, info@vanharen.net.

Document:
Pink Elephant 2004, *Critical Success Factors (CSF) and Key Performance Indicators (KPI).*
Ontario, Canada

Chapter 7:
Problem Management

7.1 Overview

7.1.1 Description

A problem may be the result of one or more incidents; the Problem Management process seeks to identify the root cause of those problems. The goals of the process are to minimize severity and any adverse impacts caused by problems and ultimately to eliminate them where it makes business sense to do so.

7.1.2 Relationships to other processes

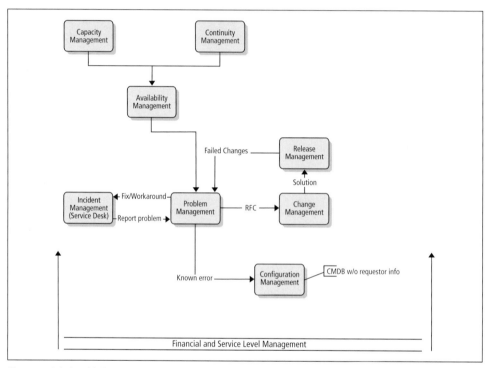

Figure 7.1 Relationship between processes

Each ITIL process relates with the others to some degree. Some of the processes are completely dependent on one another; this is the case with Problem and Incident Management. It is sometimes difficult to differentiate between these two processes. While the role of Incident Management is to find a quick resolution or a 'fix' so that the customer can get back to work as quickly as possible, Problem Management's purpose is to identify the root cause and eliminate it. When the symptoms are addressed and not the problem itself, the problem will almost certainly reappear.

The escalation of an issue from problem to a Request For Change (RFC) securely links the processes of Change and Problem Management as well. Knowing that a 'problem' can be the result of one or more incidents, these relationships can be illustrated as shown in Figure 7.2 below.

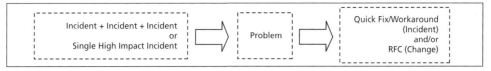

Figure 7.2 Relationship between incidents and problems

While Change and Incident Management are the two processes that most directly affect or are affected by Problem Management, other relationships can have an impact as well. The failure of any of the other ITIL processes can cause an incident and/ or a problem. For example, poor planning for load volume (Capacity Management) or lack of redundancy in critical systems (Continuity Management) can affect the availability of hardware, software, data or the network (Availability Management). It is easy to see the potential for these situations either to be, or to become, a problem for an organization. Similarly, a failed change that has been deployed (Release Management) can also generate a problem for the support team and core business users.

7.1.3 Key inputs and outputs to the process

Problem Management can be broken down into two components, reactive and proactive. In reactive mode, Problem Management is 'fire-fighting', similar to the mode that Incident Management typically engages in. All service events, whatever the cause, are (or should be) logged through the Support Center. Incident Management is a key source of information in isolating and identifying the fact that a problem exists. When Incident Management recognizes the possibility that an incident or group of incidents may be a problem, it then becomes Problem Management's responsibility to find the cause and eliminate it. Through this cycle disruptions for the customer are reduced by providing a workaround, or by solving the problem entirely.

These temporary fixes or permanent solutions are recorded in Configuration Management and become part of the knowledgebase. By reducing the number of issues that need to be escalated to second or third level support staff, the first level resolution rate will increase.

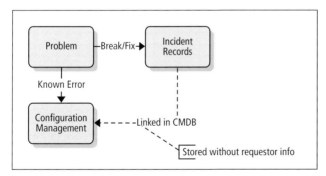

Figure 7.3 Problem tracking

Additionally, Problem Management has responsibilities that are proactive in nature. Most significant of these are root cause and trend analysis. In these, it becomes apparent why the data collected in Incident Management is so important. The quality of information gathered in trouble tickets directly affects the simplicity with which root cause and trend analysis can be performed.

Sometimes the Incident Management data that Problem Management relies is not 'clean'. For example, when tickets are not routinely reviewed to verify accurate classification (e.g. categorized in the system as activity directory issues when it has been determined that they are really DNS issues), analysis and reporting will be inaccurate as well. At other times, usability is an issue because data that would be useful to report on is not easily accessible. This typically occurs when the data is stored in free text fields in tickets. The data is there but not accessible for reporting purposes without an inordinate amount of manual labor and manipulation.

When the data is not accurate and/or usable, it is very difficult (if not impossible) to perform proactive Problem Management and accurately identify root causes, forecast trends or eliminate potential issues before they surface. Someone must tend to this data and prune it regularly to ensure its continued integrity. Otherwise, staff members tend to lose trust in the systems and develop their own ways of tracking problems on the side. Erroneous decisions can be made based on faulty data and management reports are either not run, or not used, because the integrity of the data is in question. Bad data is an internal process problem that should be addressed not only with data 'clean up' but with staff training as well.

Inputs	Source	Importance
Incident details	Incident Management	High
Configuration details	Configuration Management	High
Downtime details	Availability Management	High
Failed Change details	Release Management	High
Defined Workarounds	Incident Management	Medium
Potential problem reported	Incident Management	Medium
	Capacity Management Availability Management	
Trend reported	Incident Management	Medium
Event Survey results	Support Center	Medium
Annual Survey results	Customer Service Management	Low
Anecdotal evidence	All	Low
Outputs	**Source**	**Importance**
Known Error	Problem Management	High
Fix/Workaround	Problem Management	High
Management/Metric Reporting	Problem Management	High
Major problem review	Problem Management	Medium
Request for Change	Problem Management	Medium
Updated and closed Problem and Known Error records	Problem Management	Medium
Suggested improvements for procedures, documentation, training needs	Problem Management	Medium
Anecdotal evidence	Problem Management	Low

7.1.4 Possible problems and issues

Not separating Incident Management from Problem Management: these processes are closely related but distinct in their goals. The two processes have clearly different definitions and a built in conflict between their focuses. Organizations are often tempted to combine these two and this is often the case in smaller IT departments where resources are scarce. The firefighting inherent to Incident Management, and the need to get the customers up and running as quickly as possible often does not leave time to perform Problem Management and examine issues for root causes. On the other hand, time spent on more in-depth investigation of problems takes away from the quick resolution of incidents that customers want and need. Even where resources are not scarce, the same individual or group should not manage both processes unless the conflicts are acknowledged and time can be set aside to work exclusively on one process versus another. This is very difficult to balance and is not recommended.

No shared understanding of what a problem is: ITIL provides the definition of a problem as the unknown, underlying cause of multiple incidents or a single significant incident. Yet in some organizations this has either not been accepted or it is not internalized and understood by staff. Handing out guidebooks is not enough! Everyone in the Support Center should be speaking the same language and the distinction between an incident and a problem must be made clear to all. The processes surrounding them must also be clearly defined, documented and understood.

Lack of recognition of conflicting goals of Incident and Problem Management: it makes sense that a reduction in problems should result in a reduction of incidents and an increase in the Support Center's first level resolution rate at first. As the Support Center becomes more proactive, it will start solving problems before incidents can occur. Eliminating and preventing problems will then decrease the number of calls received and reduce the number of 'easy' tickets. This in turn makes the overall closure rates at first level decrease. This is one of the inherent conflicts between Problem and Incident Management that sometimes puts the processes at cross-purposes. The targets for first level resolution should be adjusted and measured accordingly.

Problem Management as a discipline: Problem Management should be adopted as more than just another mechanistic process. Common techniques must exist and be understood (e.g. how to perform root cause analysis in your organization). Managers must look for and reward the desired behaviors and react accordingly to unwanted outcomes with training and coaching where necessary. For Problem Management to become a discipline, it must become part of the culture. Team members should be clear about their responsibilities, know how to accomplish them and know what to expect if they do not.

Problem Management without a distinct process owner: Problem Management often fails at this level because either no one group or no one individual has been assigned ownership of the overall process. Without central responsibility for monitoring all existing problems, their status, business impact and resolutions, the speed and quality with which problems are resolved is extremely inconsistent. Some problems may be forgotten and never solved at all.

Problem Management seen as bureaucracy: when staff members see Problem Management as additional layers of regulations that keep them from getting the job done, they will resist it. They may also see Problem Management as a process designed to apportion blame. It is imperative that everyone understands the process is not about finding fault; it is about finding the answer to a problem and resolving it so that it does not occur again.

No Problem Management: often Incident Management is implemented without its complementary support process of Problem Management. While Incident Management is not enough, it is preferable to the customer than waiting until a permanent solution is found. But if Incident Management staff starts to focus on resolving problems instead of getting the customer up and running, customer satisfaction will suffer. Ultimately the customer wants both; to get back to work (Incident Management) and to never experience the problem again (Problem Management).

Problem Management versus the 'hero complex': incidents that are easy to resolve with quick fixes or workarounds provide constant positive rewards for a technician. By staying reactive, they can provide quick action on these issues, allowing them to 'rescue' customers and get them back to work. When staff members are rewarded for fixing rather than preventing, they have no incentive to proactively seek the elimination of recurring incidents. Establishing Problem Management can help break this cycle by rewarding people for preventing incidents.

7.2 Implementation

7.2.1 The implementation process
Begin by assigning functional and process ownership to a designated Problem Manager with the reputation, respect and resources to get the job done. It is most effective when the same person(s) does not handle Incident and Problem Management. Instead these responsibilities should be clearly delineated to avoid conflicts with competing objectives.

Separation of these functions provides balance of effort to both processes. While the Incident Management team, or Support Center, focuses on getting the user back to work (either through a temporary fix or a workaround procedure) the Problem Management team begins to work on a permanent solution. As the Single Point of Contact (SPOC) for the IT department, however, the Support Center and its Manager cannot abdicate responsibility for participating in the implementation of Problem Management in the organization. Incident Management will often be the first to realize the need for a Problem Management process and begin the drive for its implementation within the organization.

7.2.2 Support Center Manager's role
Responsibilities and activities
Because Problem Management cannot succeed without a firmly established Incident Management process, the Support Center Manager's key focus needs to be on the development and optimization of Incident Management. During implementation of Problem Management, the Support Center Manager should be working closely with the designated Problem Manager or Management team to design how the processes will work together. Notification, escalation and feedback loops should be of primary concern.

In a smaller organization, where responsibility for the Incident and Problem Management processes resides with the Support Center Manager, concentration should be on defining how much time can be spent exclusively on each. A lot of thought needs to be given to how to keep proactive Problem Management activities from being neglected during periods where there are high volumes of incidents or whether the organization should implement proactive activities at all. When responsibility resides within the same group, a lead should be assigned to each process to ensure coverage.

In an organization attempting to implement both components of Problem Management at the same time, or where resources are limited, Problem Management may have to be limited initially to reactive problem and error control. After enough historical data has been accumulated to be useful, the focus can increase to include proactive activities: root cause analysis, trend identification, problem prevention, instigation of RFCs, and providing management information. In any case, it is important to review time and resources periodically for both reactive and proactive processes to ensure balance.

Deliverables
- Notification Process Flowcharts
- Escalation Process Flowcharts
- Feedback Process Flowcharts
- Population of Knowledgebase: Process and Procedure

Competencies
People skills
- Business knowledge
- Technical knowledge
- Management skills (including measurement, metrics, reporting and analysis)
- Conflict resolution skills
- Root cause analysis skills
- Facility with Problem Management techniques, such as Root Cause Analysis
- Sound knowledge of the Incident Management process and Support Center function
- Understanding of Knowledge Management and learning organization concepts (especially as they pertain to problems, known errors, and workarounds)

Key performance indicators (KPIs)
- Percentage increase in first level resolution
- Percentage increase in knowledgebase entries
- Percentage decrease in escalations to second and third level support

7.2.3 Support Center Function's role

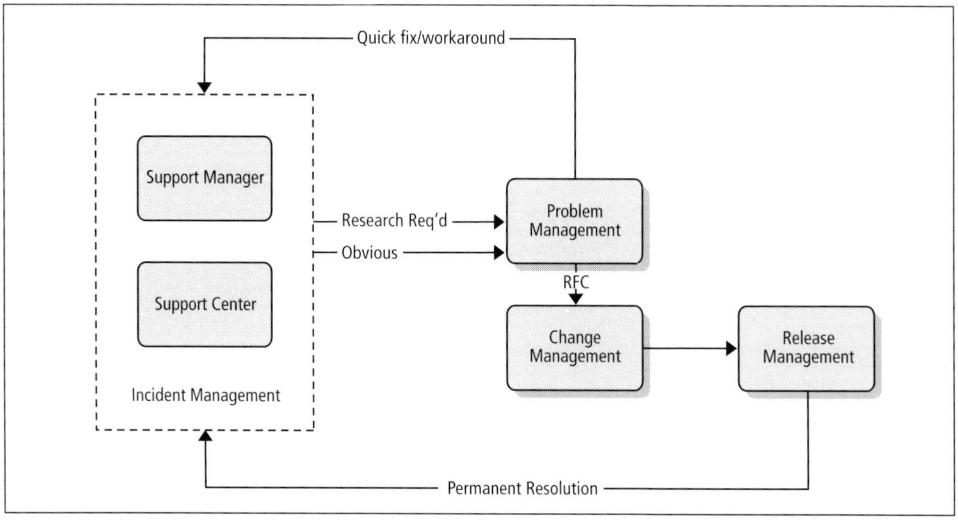

Figure 7.4 Support Center relationship to Problem Management

Responsibilities and activities
- Reviewing resolved incidents and identifying potential problems from incident records
- Associating incidents with existing problem records or creating new problem records if necessary
- Ensuring problems are dealt with according to agreed timescales and priorities
- Ensuring that accurate and complete information is entered in all problem records
- Ensuring that problems are assigned to the appropriate groups for investigation
- Ensuring that resolutions and workarounds to problems are verified
- Deciding whether Known Error records should be created and whether, if a permanent resolution has been found but not yet implemented, investigation work should continue in order to produce a workaround
- Assessing Known Errors to determine whether the permanent resolutions could or should be applied
- Closing problem records and Known Error records when appropriate and informing Incident Management so that resolutions or workarounds can be applied to associated incidents

Problem Management should be separated from Incident Management if at all possible. The Support Center staff should work with their manager to enable the Problem Management team to get their process started. As the SPOC to the customer, the Support Center is in a position to offer a great deal of input regarding the problems experienced and how they affect the business customers. They are also more familiar than anyone else in the department with the data accumulated within the trouble ticket application because they receive and record all calls and deal directly with users on a regular basis.

In a small IT department, where Incident and Problem Management cannot be separated, a

Support Center Manager might identify separate individuals in the Support Center to act as leads for the reactive and proactive aspects of Problem Management as a 'specialty'. Alternatively, staff could perform multi-week rotations on some periodic basis to focus on Problem Management, analyze data and initiate RFCs. It is important to periodically review the time and resources spent on each to ensure that enough attention is being given to both. It is especially important to pay attention to the proactive activities, as these quickly may be ignored when incident levels are high.

7.2.4 Planning for implementation

Steps to take

Step 1:

Establish a formal Incident Management system.

There should be some level of Incident Management already in place such as formal problem categorizations, descriptions, prioritizations, impact assessments, duration estimations and resolution processes. It is best practice, and wise planning, to segregate Problem Management responsibility from Incident Management. An individual or group must be made accountable and responsible for the Problem Management process in your organization. This need not be a full time role.

Step 2:

Use Incident Management data and information to drive the Problem Management system.

Assuming that the Incident Management process is well enough established to capture reliable and compliant data, begin to focus on using that data within Problem Management. If an effective process is not yet in place, the ticket tracking system is unlikely to be fully utilized to record it. Adjust existing methods or create new ways to capture the information needed to perform good, detailed analysis.

Step 3:

Define a process for gathering issues to review for further analysis.

The Problem Manager, or Problem Management team, will define a process for gathering issues from many sources (including incident records, faulty changes, discussions with Service Level Management regarding services and customer perceptions, client satisfaction surveys and industry benchmarking) to review for further analysis. They should plan two-way communication paths so that everyone in the department knows and understands the process.

Step 4: Provide sufficient resources to staff the Problem Management system.

The Problem Manager does not need to have the technical experience to resolve the problem hinself/herself. However, there should be someone in the team with the technical expertise to help guide Problem Management in your organization. They will be able to help pinpoint possible causes and suggest potential solutions and the correct people to implement them. If you cannot have a group dedicated to Problem Management, the Problem Manager should have access to the technical resources necessary to assist them in the analysis and resolution.

Step 5: Track the problems from identification to resolution.

Determine the method to employ for tracking problems. Choose or develop tools that will allow you to record problems through the entire life cycle, including its resolution. If your ticket tracking tool supports mapping incidents to a 'master ticket' or 'case' (or better still to a problem ticket) consider using this functionality to track problems and to associate related incident tickets to problem tickets (either manually or automatically).

Groups to contact
Customers - conduct focus groups, workshops or surveys to determine the areas of most concern to the customer base.

Incident Management - the front line support staff is the best source for reporting potential problems to Problem Management. Processes for ongoing communication need to be established between the two groups. This starts with mapping incidents within the ticket-tracking tool to problems, if your tool supports that functionality. At a minimum, the Support Center Manager must analyze tickets and produce reports to share with the Problem Manager as a basis for isolating potential or active problems based on ticket trends.

Service Level Management - understanding the core business and what is most important to your customers will have already been identified and documented in the Service Level Agreements established by this group. This is an invaluable source of information to Problem Management in identifying priorities in problem resolution.

Change Management - once the resolution to a problem is identified, an RFC may be required to implement the solution. Consult with Change Management to establish processes for submitting the RFCs, and a feedback loop for monitoring the results of the proposed resolution once implemented. Some ticket tracking tools have integrated change management systems. If yours does not, the ticket-tracking tool should be interfaced with your Change Management system. For example, in break/fix situations, when it is not a case of swapping like for like, an incident ticket should be generated and linked to a change ticket; this ensures a complete picture of 'what changed?' on the Change Management side.

Configuration Management - when the root cause of a problem has been identified and a workaround has been developed, the problem is then defined as a Known Error. Known error data should be stored in the Configuration Management database (CMDB), so a process needs to be developed for providing this information. (Note that the CMDB is a logical database that could be in multiple physical locations, so a 'bug tracking' knowledgebase containing problem, known error, and workaround information that stands separate from the incident system is within best practice). Not all Known Errors will be pursued to a complete resolution so other ways need to be found for tracking that information.

Necessary information and data
Ticket tracking - including solid descriptions of the issue and work done (and by whom) to assist in researching problems, trend analysis and root cause analysis. Good documentation in the trouble tickets cannot be stressed enough.

Change tracking - data should include the source of the RFC, when the change was implemented and whether the problem was resolved.

Configuration Database - tracking of the Known Errors in a knowledgebase that is a logical part of the CMDB is done here, in addition to all the hardware, software, and license information which can be invaluable in researching a problem.

Measurements that should be in place
- Number of tickets per week/month/quarter
- Percentage First Call Resolution
- Top Ten Issues/Incidents Reported
- Number of tickets due to failed Release Management
- Number of Requests for Change due to failed Release Management
- Number of repeat incidents/problems
- Average problem diagnosis and resolve time
- Number backlogged of 'open' problems and errors
- Number of proactive changes raised by Problem Management, particularly from major incident and problem reviews

7.2.5 Implementing key process activities: hints and tips
What to implement first
Incident Management: you will need access to reliable and compliant data for root cause analysis and trend analysis. Robust Incident Management will ensure a good starting point for you to collect, review and analyze this information.

Things that always work
The Pareto Principle : if you examine the top 80% of your tickets, you will probably find that they cover about 20% of the top issues in your department. You may want to investigate and consider purchasing a software application that can automatically apply this principle to your data for you.

Little things that deliver big returns
If the tickets have been entered and categorized correctly you will be able to look for tickets recorded on similar issues. A good ticket tracking system will allow you to 'relate' your tickets to make this even easier.

Little things that always get forgotten
Your customer: do not forget to verify the priority and business impact to your customer. It makes no sense to spend resources (time, people or money) working on problems that are not important to your customer.

7.2.6 Key process activities
Implement Incident Management: if the Incident Management process is not in place in your organization this will need to be implemented before implementing Problem Management or, less preferably, in tandem. Problem Management depends on Incident Management to identify issues that may be problems, and also on the data collected through Incident Management to perform root cause analysis.

Identify resources: determine whether you will be able to segregate Incident and Problem Management. Identify who will have overall responsibility for the Problem Management process. Establish a multifunctional support system for Problem Management, especially the process for obtaining technical resources when it becomes necessary.

Define roles and responsibilities: everyone involved with Problem Management needs to be clear about their roles and responsibilities. There should be no doubt on how to interact with one another, or how Problem Management interfaces with the other ITIL processes.

Meet with appropriate groups: in the implementation of Problem Management you will need to meet with the groups previously outlined. The most important of these are Incident Management and your customers. The relationship with Incident Management will be ongoing, and communication paths should be established as early as possible. While information obtained from Service Level Management may provide insight and input into the customers' perspective, you should not limit Problem Management by not connecting with your customers directly.

Review the Incident Management Tool: verify that the tool is capturing all the data that you need. Determine how you will be able to obtain data from the tool and how you will be able to produce reports.

Develop a method to track problems through resolution: if your ticket tracking application can be adapted, plan and design the changes that need to be made. Simple spreadsheets can be used for tracking temporarily, or may work adequately for your purposes. A sample is included in Annex A7.6.

Establish a notification process: it is best practice for potential problems to be passed to Problem Management through only one source, Incident Management. This provides consistency in categorization and understanding of the business impacts. A process for raising issues to Incident Management needs to be developed as well as how Incident Management will notify Problem Management.

Establish a submission/identification process: pursuing problems or Known Errors may or may not be required. Assess each to determine whether the time, cost or impact is justified. Is it more important to investigate a large number of insignificant issues or a smaller number of issues that have a high business impact?

Establish the prioritization process: define criteria for assessing a problem's priority such as business impact, business urgency and/or technical severity. Those with the highest priority should be resolved first.

Establish a feedback process: the status of problems and Known Errors should be continually communicated to Incident Management, which is responsible for following up with the affected customers. Determine the method and frequency for providing this feedback.

Establish an escalation process: establish a process for escalating those problems that will be tracked through resolution to the appropriate technical resources.

Define a method for performing root cause analysis: it is estimated that there are over 40 investigation methods. Select a method that makes sense for your organization and adopt it as a standard process. Provide training if necessary so that everyone can understand and follow the logic of the chosen method. A training guide is provided in Annex A7.7.

Define a method for processing Known Errors: once a problem has been identified and a fix has been determined, two primary processes need to happen. The fix needs to be communicated to Incident Management and the Known Error needs to be reported to Configuration Management to update the CMDB.

Define Resolution Process: Proposed permanent resolutions for problems or known errors will work their way through the Change Management and Release Management processes. Problem Management is responsible for tracking them through these phases until they are resolved. Your plan should define Problem Management's involvement in the other processes and how information will be passed between them. Additionally, the resolution process should include a plan for communicating the status to Incident and Configuration Management. Results of the attempted solutions should be monitored to verify that the problem has been permanently resolved.

7.2.7 Methods and techniques

Root cause analysis: the root cause of a problem can be found by examining all the data you can possibly gather surrounding an issue. You might start by mining the data in your ticket tracking system. Examine the data from multiple perspectives:
- who are the most frequent callers to your Support Center?
- which departments have the most problems?
- what are the most common issues being reported?

Popular techniques cited in ITIL that can be used in Problem Management include:
- Kepner and Tregoe Root Cause Analysis - for determining the root cause of a problem while it is active
- Ishikawa (cause-effect) diagrams and brainstorming - also useful for tracing root cause while a problem is active
- Service Outage Analysis - for determining, during post-implementation review of an event, factors contributing to the outage so proactive measures can be taken to prevent such failures in the future
- Failure Mode Effects Analysis and Fault Tree Analysis - for proactively identifying the causes of and downstream effects of failure to take measures to pre-empt such failures.

The most important thing about techniques is to ensure they are shared within your organization.

7.3 Ongoing operation

7.3.1 The ongoing process

Problem Management can be described in its most fundamental way as call avoidance. While Problem Management has a reactive component, it can and should be more focused on proactive activities. Removing root causes, preventing the occurrence (or recurrence) of Incidents and minimizing the consequences of those that cannot be prevented are the key activities involved. When your systems are stable, and your service processes are well defined and working as designed, incidents and problems become easier to manage.

The scope of this process is to count recurring tickets, analyze trends and identify problems. Incident Management can exist without Problem Management and it is far easier to manage each Incident as it arises than to invest the time necessary to perform root cause analysis. But by itself, Incident Management is ineffective. Many problems can have the same root cause but display different symptoms. This can make it difficult to recognize a problem or even to realize that a series of incidents may be related. Similarly, the organization could be experiencing a number of problems that share common symptoms but are not related at all.

7.3.2 Support Center Manager's role

Responsibilities and activities

The Support Center Manager should work very closely with the Problem Manager to ensure a continued feedback loop between Incident and Problem Management. The Support Center owns the Incident Management process, and functions as the SPOC, interfacing with customers. With the implementation of Problem Management, the Support Center will continue to be the main source of potential issues to be examined on the reactive side of Problem Management and instrumental in defining business impact. The Support Center will also act as the SPOC for Problem Management to receive requests to review incidents as potential problems. In this way, there can be consistency of definitions and interpretations.

On the proactive side, Problem Management will be investigating trends and root cause on data provided in trouble tickets by the Incident Management staff. There should be continuous dialog regarding the collection and categorization of this data and the Support Center Manager is ultimately responsible for the quality of this data. Ideally, Problem Management could automate parameter triggers to flag a specific set of conditions as needing Root Cause analysis.

As problems are categorized as Known Errors, Problem Management should be providing the workarounds back to the Service Manager and Incident Management team. For permanent solutions, it is expected that the Support Center Manager is actively participating in the Change Management process and therefore aware of the resolution before it is implemented and fully aware of Release Management's implementation schedule. It is the Support Center Manager's responsibility to keep the Support Center aware of information about the changes coming out of the Release and Change Management processes so that they will be informed and prepared when these changes occur.

In the case of a small center where the Support Center Manager is overseeing both Incident and Problem Management, it is important that the appropriate staffing is identified and kept informed as if they were separate groups. It is a good idea to have a proactive problem specialist on this team to participate with the Support Center Manager in the Change Advisory Board so neither process gets overlooked.

Deliverables
- Management reports, and associated analysis, required for the management of the Problem Management process
- Communication to other processes and functional managers, as well as to suppliers, users and customers
- A 'top 10' list of problems, including what has been done so far to deal with them, and what will be done next, is highly recommended

7.3.3 Support Center Function's role
Responsibilities and activities
Participating in the Problem Management process, staff should be seeking feedback regarding the potential problems they have reported. Either it is not a problem, or there should be some kind of workaround provided. The Support Center by nature is extremely reactive and will not necessarily have time to constantly ask for this information. However if these reports are not being provided, it is their responsibility to report that to their Manager to follow up. The Manager should ensure that the Support Center obtains the information that it needs to provide effective service and provide status updates to the customers. Other responsibilities would include analyzing data, investigating problems, submitting RFCs, monitoring Known Errors and monitoring the status of problem resolutions.

In a small center, the proactive Problem lead would be responsible for providing this information to the Manager and the rest of their team. This lead person should also attend Change Advisory Board meetings and work with the Support Center Manager to understand and communicate the impacts from the Problem Management perspective.

In either case, producing a daily report of the top ten most common issues each day is an effective way to provide a minimum level of ongoing reactive Problem Management. Workarounds or permanent solutions should be added to the knowledgebase and Support Center staff should be allocating the time needed to maintain this database regularly. The top ten lists can also be used proactively to monitor what the problems are, track what has been done to resolve them and plan what will be done next.

Deliverables
- Daily Top Ten Report of Problems

KPIs
- Percentage reduction in resolution time
- Percentage reduction in time to implement workarounds
- Percentage reduction of problem diagnosis time
- Percentage reduction of average number of undiagnosed problems

- Percentage reduction in repeat incidents/problems
- Percentage reduction in average time to diagnose and resolve problems
- Percentage reduction of the time to implement fixes to Known Errors
- Percentage reduction of the average backlog of 'open' problems and errors
- Percentage increase of proactive RFCs raised by Problem Management, particularly from major incident and problem reviews

7.4 Optimization

7.4.1 The optimization process

The more control over incidents an IT department has, the better availability and reliability it can provide to its customers. As more and more problems are eliminated from the environment, the Support Center can begin to focus on improvements in efficiency; isolating application errors, developing training plans and providing better service. With proper communication and management reporting, the benefits will be clearly visible and IT will be better positioned with the core business.

7.4.2 Support Center Manager's role
Responsibilities and activities

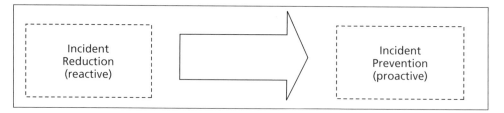

Figure 7.5: Optimization

Incident reduction leads to Incident prevention. To optimize the process, the Support Center Manager can now begin focusing on improving efficiencies internally. Working with the Service Level Manager, efforts to redesign Operational Level Agreements (OLAs), the internal 'service level agreements' between the Support Center and the second and third level support teams, can yield better turnaround time for ticket resolution. Review of historical data may reveal areas within the customer SLAs that should be revised as well. Developing training plans that involve the Support Center staff's interaction with the other teams provide value at the Support Center and open new career path opportunities. Successful companies train their staff to anticipate customer needs and to solve Problems before the customer even knows they exist.

Deliverables
- Updated OLA (internal)
- Updated SLA (external)
- Processes
- Training plans

KPIs
- Increase in proactive changes implemented as a result of Problem Management
- Number of service disruptions caused by incidents or problems
- Percentage of reduction in recurring incidents or problems
- Percentage of reduction in Known Errors
- Decrease in First Level Resolution rate
- Decrease in problems as result of failed Change/Release Management

7.4.3 Support Center Function's role
Responsibilities and activities
Good Problem Management will lower the number of tickets that are easily resolved. As problems and some of the routine incidents disappear, Support Center staff can begin to focus on the proactive goals of the Support Center. This includes more time to spend on difficult issues and in follow-up with customers. A Support Center that used to be too busy handling password resets can now find out why some tickets are still unresolved at second level. They can identify areas where training would be appropriate in giving them the skills they need to resolve more of the complex issues.

7.4.4 Future impact of this process on the Support Center
Proactive problem solving guarantees that your problems will stay fixed. The Support Center will be able to demonstrate savings to the organization and embark on a continuing program of process and service improvement. Above all, the purpose of implementing Problem Management is to improve service and provide quality support to your customers.

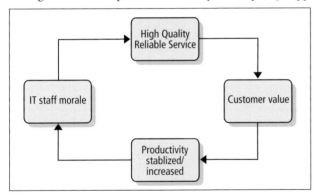

Figure 7.6 IT Service Quality Cycle

7.5 Measurement, costing and management reporting

7.5.1 Implementing
Benefits and costs
Most of your customers are not concerned about why a problem occurred, nor do they want to spend time on resolving it. They just want their computer system to work!

The cost of problems is proportional to the volume of incidents and number of customers that are affected by them. Duration of an incident and the resources needed to resolve them also accumulate costs to the business due to lost productivity. Implementation of Problem

Management will help offset these costs, reducing the Incidents that interfere with the ability of the organization to conduct its business. Ultimately, this will provide better system availability and reliability and a better overall customer experience.

Cost elements for implementation

Typically there are no costs for tools required to implement Problem Management because the tools should already be in place for other processes (i.e. ticket tracking for Incident Management). If you are not staffed to handle Problem Management, you may consider acquiring additional staff. In most cases, the roles and responsibilities for this process are distributed among existing employees.

Making the business case to implement Problem Management

If you have previously made the business case for the implementation of ITIL in your organization, Problem Management will already make sense. Discuss the drawbacks of remaining reactive as an IT organization. You should be able to articulate how recurring tickets affect productivity. A key point to make to customers is that a problem resolved through Problem Management stays resolved. You will be able to promise better availability and reliability of systems and improved service quality. But be careful to set your customers' expectations so that they expect continuous ongoing improvement rather than immediate results.

Management reporting

Top Ten reporting of incidents, broken out by individual and by department give a useful perspective of the issues facing the organization and allows the IT department to demonstrate its commitment to eliminating problems.

Management reports should explain how metrics and key performance indicators relate to the strategic objectives of the organization. For instance, if a strategic goal of IT is to provide systems and tools that maximize staff productivity, make sure that management reports show actual data and also compare that data to organizational goals. For example: in support of the goal to maximize productivity, the overall system availability goal is set at 98.5% during 24 hours of operation. The management reports should show the availability of individual systems and the overall average. Any major deviations from the goal should be explained along with a statement about what needs to be or is being done to address the cause(s). If the deviation was a one-time situation and is not expected to recur, your report should include a statement to that effect.

7.5.2 Ongoing operations

Cost elements for ongoing operations

To move beyond reactive Problem Management, it may be necessary to look at staffing levels. If feasible and justifiable in your organization, consider acquiring additional staff. If you have been managing Incident and Problem Management through one individual or group, now may be the time to consider breaking these processes out. Promoting one of your specialists to focus on Problem Management may be in order at this time.

If you do not have good reporting tools in place, it may also be the time to consider purchasing some. These products vary in price and functionality. Look for one that will interface easily with your ticket tracking system.

Metrics and Key Performance Indicators
- Number of RFCs generated through Problem Management
- Amount of time spent on problems (broken out by problem type)
- Comparison of number of tickets received for a specific problem before and after root cause and/or known error is established
- Comparison of reactive vs. proactive problem responses
- Problem's impact on availability

Management reporting
Because so much time is spent investigating incidents, finding workarounds, diagnosing root causes, and in the identification and implementation of problem resolutions, reports to management should reflect the time and effort spent on each. To give that information context, this should be measured against the impact of the problem to see the value in the resource expenditure.

7.5.3 Optimization
Benefits and costs
Ineffectiveness has a high cost for the organization in downtime and in employee turnover. If employees do not have adequate tools, they cannot work effectively (loss of productivity = cost to organization) and they may become dissatisfied (potential for increase in turnover).

Metrics and Key Performance Indicators
- Increase in proactive changes implemented as a result of Problem Management
- Decrease in number of service disruptions caused by incidents or problems
- Percentage reduction in recurring incidents or problems
- Percentage reduction in known errors
- Decrease in First Level Resolution rate

Management reporting
Problem Management reports should be geared towards monitoring the quality of the process.

7.5.4 Tools
Implementation
- Ticket tracking
- Change tracking

Ongoing operations
- Configuration Management Database (CMDB)
- Knowledgebase
- 'Canned' knowledge for common problems
- Report writing tool that interfaces with your ticket tracking application
- Word processing
- Spreadsheet with statistical 'plug-in'

Optimizing
- Automating aspects of the Problem Management process (event correlation to auto-problem ticketing, etc.)
- Driving shared techniques down to the organization (e.g. Kepner-Tregoe problem analysis) and continuously improving the use of these techniques
- Implementing problem management tools to support techniques (software that supports Failure Mode Effects Analysis or group brainstorming)
- Implementing continuous improvement of Problem Management though review and audit
- Launching improvement programs to improve the alignment of Problem Management with the business and its drivers

Annex A7.1 Problem Management Implementation Checklist

- Implement Incident Management
- Identify resources
- Define roles and responsibilities
- Meet with appropriate groups
- Identify and acquire tools
- Develop method to track problems through resolution
- Establish a notification process
- Define problem submission/identification process
- Establish a feedback process
- Establish an escalation process
- Develop a problem classification scheme
- Get training on and adopt shared problem management techniques, e.g., Kepner and Tregoe problem analysis, Ishikawa (fishbone) diagrams, brainstorming and flowcharting techniques, trend analysis
- Adopt a method for performing root cause analysis
- Develop a method for processing known errors
- Define a resolution process
- Establish a shared practice for problem post-implementation reviews
- Determine problem management metrics
- Establish content, target audience, and frequency of reports, review and audit procedures
- Define integration of problem management with incident management, change management, configuration management, availability and capacity management
- Define interface between problem management and application and infrastructure capability development, especially with regard to the transfer of bug tracking information to problem management during production acceptance

Annex A7.2 Problem Management Ongoing Process Checklist

- Identify problem
- Record problem
- Determine root cause
- Record known errors in CMDB
- Evaluate justification for resolution
- Pass resolutions to Change Management
- Pass known error, problem, and workaround information to incident management
- Conduct post-implementation reviews where appropriate

Annex A7.3 Problem Management Optimization Checklist

- Work with Service Level Management to redesign SLAs and OLAs
- Work with Availability and Capacity Management on availability and performance issues
- Identify process issues surrounding turnaround time
- Identify potential training issues
- Identify potential technology issues
- Adjust measurements and reports
- Continuous process improvement
- Continuous service improvement

Annex A7.4 Sample Problem Management Process Workflow

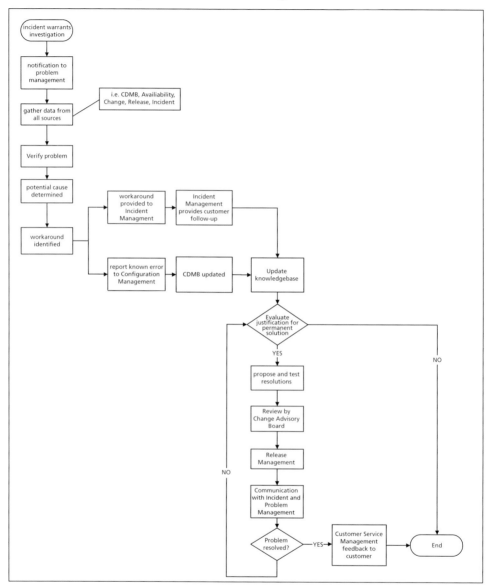

Figure 7.1 Sample Problem Management Process Workflow

Annex A7.5 Problem Evaluation Checklist

Questions to ask in determining justification for problem resolution.

☐ What is the impact of the incident(s) reported?
☐ What services are affected?
☐ What customers are affected?
☐ Is it a "problem"?
☐ Is there a quick fix?
☐ How will work be done?
☐ Who will do the work?
☐ What is the priority for resolving it?
☐ Does it require more technical expertise to resolve?
☐ How long will it take?
☐ How much will it cost to implement a fix?
☐ How much will the fix cost on an ongoing basis?
☐ How does the cost of the fix compare to the cost of doing nothing?
☐ Is the workaround an adequate solution?

Annex A7.6 Sample Problem Tracking Spreadsheet

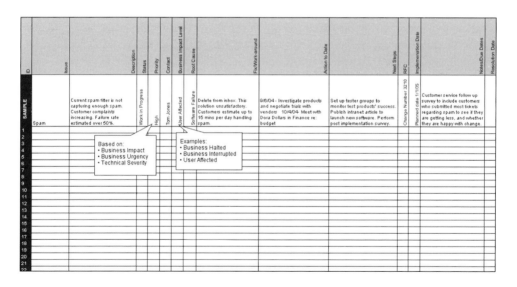

Annex A7.7 Teaching Guide for Statistical Process Control Using Colored Candies

Summary
As discussed in the chapter, a key element to providing effective root cause analysis in Problem Management is to have a "shared" method for performing the process in your organization. This teaching guide was developed by Bill McNeese of Business Process Improvement (BPI). The guide includes an overview of how to introduce statistical process control (SPC) tools to your staff, general construction steps and how to use bags of multicolored candy to practice use of the tools. This model is reproduced in this Annex by special permission to HDI. Further reproduction is prohibited without permission.

Examples of each SPC tool are included. The introduction to the SPC tool should only take 10 to 15 minutes. The rest of the time is spent applying the tools using any brand of candy that comes in a variety of colors. The colors in these bags may include red, yellow, brown, orange, blue, and green so these are the colors we will use throughout the teaching guide. You may, of course, change them to accommodate the colors in the type of candy you ultimately choose to use for the exercise. The training process is described below as if you were teaching a workshop.

Training process
Associates are taught the concept of variation before the SPC tools are introduced. Before starting, you need to have the candy available. You will need a bag for each person, one for each team and a couple for yourself (in case you get hungry).

The following is covered for each SPC tool:
- what the SPC tool is and looks like
- when to use it
- what you can learn with this tool
- how to use it.

The first SPC tool introduced is the **process flow diagram (PFD)**. The following points are made about the process flow diagram.

What is a PFD?	A PFD is a detailed picture of a process. It represents the logical flow of activities from the beginning of the process to the end of the process.
When do you use a PFD?	You use a PFD when you want to improve the process. This is the usually the first step in process improvement. PFDs are also useful for training.
What can you learn from using a PFD?	You gain agreement from everyone on what the steps in the process are. You also can identify potential areas for improvement and measurement.
How do you use a PFD?	You make a PFD using sticky notes following the steps in Figure 1.
Where have we used a PFD?	Entering an order; picking a line item in the warehouse, changing a work procedure, handling a customer complaint

You are now ready to distribute the bags of candy. Tell the class we are going to learn about the candy through the use of our SPC tools. Ask the class the following questions:
- Have you ever had trouble opening a bag of candy?
- Have you ever tried to open one end, could not and turned the bag around to try the other end?
- Have you ever ripped the bag open only to see the candy go everywhere, ending up on the floor?
- What is your horror story about opening a bag of candy?

It is evident that the people who make the candy need our help in developing the process for opening the bag. What SPC tool can you use to describe the process of opening a bag of the candy?

The answer to the last question, of course, is the PFD. Then:
- Divide the class into teams of 4 - 5 people to make a process flow diagram on how to open a bag of the candy using the PFD in Figure 7.2.
- Use the same teams throughout the SPC exercises.
- Give each team one bag to look at, but tell them not to open the bag.
- As a class, determine the starting and ending steps for the PFD.
- Each team constructs a process flow diagram using flip chart paper on the wall with sticky notes.
- Remind the teams that it is not a very good PFD without a decision box in it.
- When all teams are finished, have the teams move to the PFD to their left.
- Using that PFD, see if the team can open the bag of the candy.
- Then have the participants return to their seats and debrief the exercise.

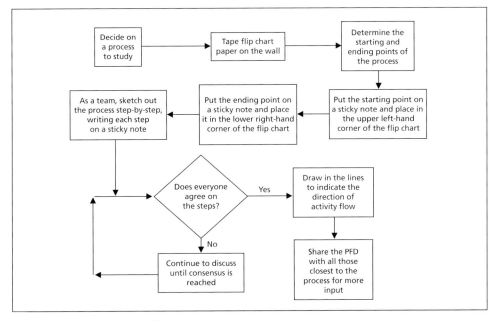

Figure 7.1 Steps in Constructing a PFD

When debriefing the PFD, ask the class the following questions:
- How many teams could open the bag of candy based on the PFD?
- Did the PFD you used agree with the one your team developed?
- Why are there differences in the PFDs?
- What insights into PFDs did this exercise give you?

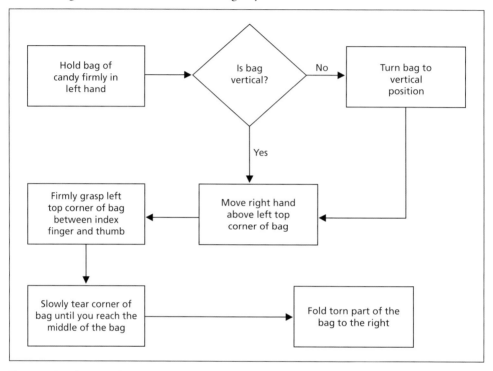

Figure 7.2 Sample Process Flow Diagram for Opening the Candy Bag

The next SPC tool introduced is the **Pareto diagram**. The following points are highlighted about the Pareto diagram.

What is a Pareto diagram?	The Pareto diagram is a special type of bar chart used to determine which problem to work on first to improve a process. It is based on the 80/20 rule (80% of our problems are due to only 20% of the possible causes).
When do you use a Pareto diagram?	You use a Pareto diagram to determine what problem to work on first.
What can you learn from using a Pareto diagram?	You can learn what the "vital few" problems or causes of a problem are. This allows you to focus your time and attention where you will get the most return.
How do you use a Pareto diagram?	You make a Pareto diagram using the steps in constructing a Pareto diagram shown in Figure 7.3.
Where have we used a Pareto diagram?	Reasons for credits, reasons for customer complaints, supplier errors by supplier, reasons for computer downtime.

Now return to the candy. Ask the class the following questions:
• What are the colors in the bag of candy?
• What color occurs most frequently?
• How many pieces of candy are there in one bag?
• How much variation is there in the number of pieces in one bag?
• What do we need to do to answer these questions?

The answer to the last question is data.

Then tell the class we are going to find out the answers to these questions by collecting data.

Hand out one bag of candy to each participant. Tell them not to eat the candy until you have said it is OK to do so.

Tell the class to open the bags and record the number of different colors they have.

Then have the class return to their teams and construct one Pareto diagram for the combined results of their team. This is done by totaling the number of each color for a team. The teams should use the steps in constructing a Pareto diagram shown in Figure 7.3. You should provide each team a blank Pareto diagram with the y-axis filled in.

When each team is done, have the participants return to their seats and debrief the exercise. Tell them they can now eat the candy.

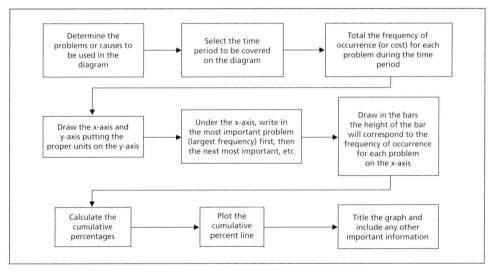

Figure 7.3 Steps in Constructing a Pareto Diagram

When debriefing the Pareto diagram, ask the class the following questions:
• What did you learn from your Pareto diagram?
• Which color appeared most frequently? Least frequently?
• Why don't all the Pareto diagrams look the same?

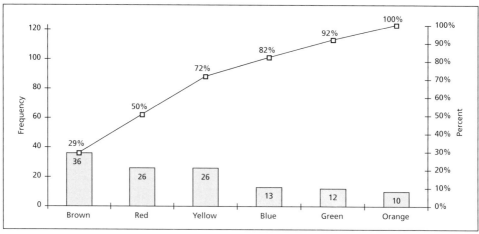

Figure 7.4 Sample Pareto Diagram for Colors Contained in Candy Bags

As the teams are making the Pareto diagram, take a data collection sheet and go around to each team and record the number of each color in each bag. This is the data you need to complete the rest of the SPC training. There should be one line completed on the data collection sheet for each person in the class. An example of the data collection form is shown in Figure 7.5. This type of sheet is easily setup in a spreadsheet program. Make copies of the completed data collection sheet for everyone in the class.

Bag Number	Number of Red	Number of Green	Number of Yellow	Number of Brown	Number of Blue	Number of Orange	Total Number
1							
2							
3							
4							
5							
6							
7							
8							
9							
10							
11							
12							
13							
14							
15							
16							
17							
18							
19							
20							
21							
22							
23							
24							
25							
26							
27							
28							
29							
30							

Figure 7.5 Data Collection Sheet Design

The next SPC tool introduced is the **histogram**. The following points are made about the histogram.

What is a histogram?	Histograms present a picture of how the process "stacks up" over time. Histograms illustrate how many times a certain data value or range of data values occurred in a given time frame.
When do you use a histogram?	You use a histogram to examine the variation in a process.
What can you learn from histogram?	You learn four things from a histogram: how much using a variation there is in the process, what the mode is, what the shape of the distribution is and the relationship of the specifications to the data.
How do you use a histogram?	You make a histogram using the steps in constructing a histogram shown in Figure 7.6.
Where have we used histogram?	Freight charges, time to close a customer complaint, lines a picked per hour, number of credits per week.

Now return to the candy. Ask the class the following questions:
- How many pieces of candy did you have in your bag?
- Did everybody on your team have the same number of pieces of candy in his or her bag?
- Why do you think there is not the same number each time?
- What would happen to the maker of the candy if there was too much variation in the number of pieces of candy in a bag (e.g., from 2 to 40)?

There appears to be valid reasons for the makers of the candy to control this variation. What SPC tool can you use to determine the amount of variation present in the number of pieces of candy in a bag as well as determining which value occurs most frequently and the shape of the variation?

The answer to the last question is, of course, the histogram.

Then pass out a copy of the data collection sheet.

Divide the class back up into their teams to do a histogram on the total number of pieces of candy in a bag (the total is on the data collection sheet). Have a blank histogram chart ready to hand out with the x-axis and y-axis already filled in. Ask the class simply to count how many times each number occurred and plot that as a bar on the chart.
When the histograms are complete, bring the class back together and debrief.

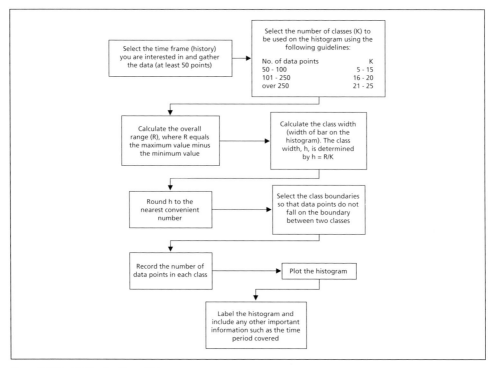

Figure 7.6 Steps in Constructing a Histogram

When debriefing the histogram, ask the class the following questions:
• What is the maximum number in a bag? The minimum?
• What is the mode (the most common value)?
• What does the shape of the distribution look like?
• What are the advantages to the manufacturer in keeping the variation in the histogram at a minimum?

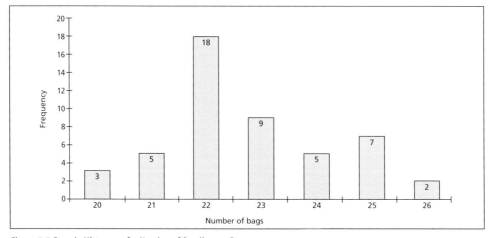

Figure 7.7 Sample Histogram for Number of Candies per Bag

The next SPC is the **cause and effect (fishbone) diagram**. The following points are made about the cause and effect diagram.

What is a fishbone diagram?	A fishbone diagram is a tool that shows the relationship between a quality characteristic (effect) and possible sources of variation for this quality characteristic (causes).
When do you use a fishbone a diagram?	You use a fishbone to determine the causes of a problem.
What can you learn from using a fishbone diagram?	The fishbone diagram helps organize the results of a brainstorming session on causes of the problem. It helps you identify the possible causes, discuss the causes and determine the most likely cause.
How do you use a fishbone diagram?	You make a fishbone diagram using the steps in constructing a fishbone diagram shown in Figure 7.8.
Where have we used a fishbone?	To find causes for late deliveries to customers, for uncollected freight, for picking errors, and for credits.

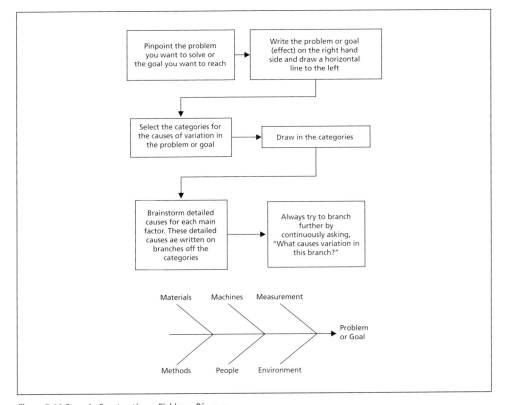

Figure 7.88 Steps in Constructing a Fishbone Diagram

Now return to the candy. The class is going to develop a fishbone diagram on possible causes of variation in the number of pieces of candy in a bag. Now ask the class the following questions:
- Did you think that there are ever any problems with the making the candy?
- What SPC tool can be used to determine the causes of a problem

The answer to the last question is the fishbone diagram.

Then divide the class back up into their teams to do a fishbone on the reasons for varying numbers of pieces of candy in a bag.

Debrief by going around the room for each team to highlight a few of their answers.

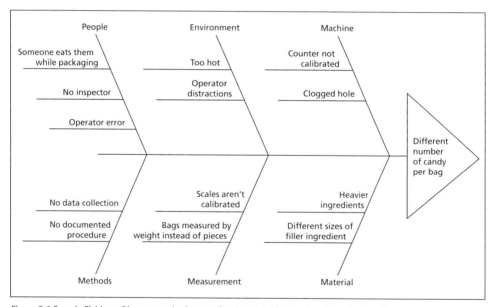

Figure 7.9 Sample Fishbone Diagram on the Causes of Variation in the Number of Candies in a Bag

The next SPC tool is the **control chart**. The following points are made about control charts.

What is a control chart?	A control chart is a picture of the variation in your process over time.
When do you use a control chart?	You use a control chart to monitor the key variables in any process.
What can you learn from using a control chart?	You can learn if the process is in statistical control - whether there are just common causes of variation present or if you have special causes present also.
How do you use a control chart?	There are five basic steps in developing a control chart: Gather data. Plot the data. Calculate the average. Calculate the control limits. Interpret the chart.
Where have we used a control chart?	Picking accuracy, service level, customer complaints, and average time for delivery.

The details of how to construct a control chart are not covered in this introduction. The focus is on interpreting the control charts. The following tests are taught to the class:
• points beyond the control limits
• seven points in a row above or the below the average
• seven points in a row trending upward or downward.

Time is spent examining control charts to determine if the chart is in or out of statistical control. The p, c and individuals control chart are covered.

Now, return to the candy.

For the entire class, determine the percentage of different colors in an "average" bag of candy (add up all of one color and divide by the total number of pieces of candy). The percentages from a sample class are shown below.

% Red	17%
% Yellow	25%
% Brown	20%
% Orange	6%
% Blue	19%
% Green	14%

Ask the class:

• How do you think this compares to what the manufacturer says is in an average bag of their candy?
• Can we predict, based on our sample, what a bag of candy may contain?
• If yes, what kind of SPC tool will tell us if a process is consistent and predictable?

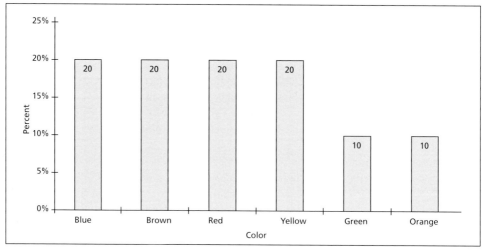

Figure 7.10 Color Percentages According to the Manufacturer

The answer to the last question, of course, is a control chart.

Then divide the class back up into their teams.

Ask each team to pick a color and use this SPC tool to determine the amount of variation present in a bag of candy for that color. A blank control chart form is used for this. The average and control limits (based on the average subgroup size) have been calculated previously using the data collection sheet contained in your spreadsheet.

When the exercise is done, tell the class to return to their seats and debrief the exercise.

When debriefing the control charts, ask the class the following questions:
• How did the averages on the control charts compare to what the manufacturer says should be in a bag of their candy?
• How much variation can you expect within a bag?
• Are there any special causes of variation?

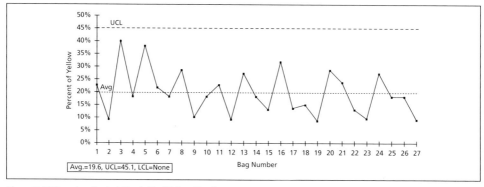

Figure 7.11 Sample p Control Chart: % of Yellow Candies

Scatter diagrams are not covered in this overview to SPC. However, it would be easy to include scatter diagrams and plot the number of one color against the number of another color.

Conclusions
This session has discussed how to use candy to introduce the concept of SPC to your organization. After using this approach at many companies, the feedback has been excellent. Participants are able to take the concepts back to the workplace, and more importantly, use them.

About the author
Bill McNeese is a partner in Business Process Improvement (BPI), a training and consulting firm that helps organizations build and implement world-class processes into their culture (www.bpiconsulting.com). McNeese has been a business process improvement consultant and trainer since 1989. He holds a Ph.D. in Chemical Engineering and holds several patents. His articles are published regularly in the industry, and he is the co-author of the book Statistical Methods for the Process Industries (1991, Quality Press). McNeese is an expert in the use of statistical process control (SPC) and has developed SPC software that runs as an add-in to Microsoft Excel® (www.spcforexcel.com) as well as numerous Microsoft PowerPoint® SPC training modules.

Bibliography
A Structured Approach to Service Level Management. http://www.csi.co.uk/papers/service.htm August 5, 2003.

Best Practice for Service Support. OGC ITIL. Crown Copyright 2000. Pages 95-175.

Best Practice for Service Delivery. OGC ITIL. Crown Copyright 2000. Pages 110-115.

Fox IT, Fox PRISM version 2.0c. *Problem Management Activities and Responsibilities.*

Gartner Consulting. *Key Ingredients of the IT Service Desk.* September 2001. Page 6.

LaBounty, Char. *Root Cause Analysis.* HDI Focus.

Lloyd, Vernon. *Planning to Implement Service Management.* OGC ITIL. Appendix G.

McKennan, Jim. *Using Root Cause Analysis to Reduce Support Cost and Increase Internal Customer Productivity.* STI Knowledge Mail, February 2003. http://www.stiknowledge.com/emails/kmail02_03/mckennan.html.

Pink Elephant. *The Benefits of ITIL.* White Paper. Pages 10-12.

Straker, Steve. *What's Up Doc?* Service Talk: Issue 63, October 2003.

Turner, Jason. *Root Cause Analysis: A Problem Management Best Practice.* Slide presentation, Connecticut HDI Chapter, February 2002. http://www.thinkhdi.com/chapters/connecticut/meetings/root%20cause%20analysis1_files/frame.htm

Chapter 8:
Service Level Management

8.1 Overview

8.1.1 Description

Service Level Management is the strategy of defining, achieving and maintaining required levels of IT service to the business user population within the organization. Service Level Management is effective because it focuses on the needs of the business user as the primary driver for the development of the IT infrastructure. Rather than arbitrarily deploying computers and networks of various capabilities and capacities, an effective Service Level Management strategy takes into consideration the needs of the user population for any given application area when designing and implementing that portion of the IT infrastructure. The by-products of this activity are threefold:

- a higher return on investment in IT expenditures. By using the needs of the IT customer to specify the capabilities and behavior of the IT infrastructure, costs are understood early in the cycle. Excess capacities can be avoided; proper on-going management activities are understood, can be planned for and staffed. Capital and personnel costs can be better understood and controlled.
- fewer failures through proper expectation setting. By working with the business user during requirements and planning activities, their needs are known and IT analysts can help them understand if their expectations can be met within the fiscal constraints of the IT department. They also feel their input was considered from the beginning and they are 'part of the solution', rather than 'part of the problem'.
- Service Level Management can be used when initially developing a distributed IT infrastructure, it can be used to gain control over resources that may have been deployed in a more 'ad hoc' manner. However, in both cases, Service Level Management should be adopted as a key strategy to be applied rigorously within the IT organization.

Service Level Management (SLM) is not new. The concept of setting a customer's expectations up front, then measuring performance to make sure the expectations are met is a necessary insurance policy in an industry where the stakes are often the continuation of internal business or outsourced to an outside vendor. However, SLM is not something that can be developed on paper. It has to be carried out with every customer of IT, both internal and external, through every support interaction, between all parties involved in meeting a customer's needs. IT departments are increasingly looked upon as strategic partners in achieving an organization's overall success. This trend is driving IT to measure its responsiveness, system availability and performance in terms of the business' objectives. While IT has long provided service-level agreements (SLAs), these agreements have traditionally been defined, managed and reported solely within the IT organization, with visibility to component/element/system performance, not to service performance. Terms typically found in objective statements in this area include 'timely', 'consistent', 'quality', 'productivity' and 'value'. Service Level Management is a concept that is of great importance to CIOs, CFOs, and Strategic Planners within the organization.

Service Level Agreements (SLAs) are the driving force behind Service Level Management (SLM). Operational Level Agreements (OLAs) are written agreements between the different support groups within the IT department; Underpinning Contracts (UCs) are written contracts with external vendors and supplier that support both OLAs and SLAs. SLAs are written agreements between the entire support department and the customer base. They should clearly define service goals, and prerequisites required to meet those goals. OLAs/SLAs should be flexible and fluid, to adjust for a rapidly changing technology environment and the changing needs of the customer.

Service Level Management (SLM) is the planning, coordinating, drafting, agreeing, monitoring and reporting on OLAs/SLAs. It is also concerned with the ongoing review of service achievements. This ensures that the customers' needs and requirements are fulfilled at a cost acceptable to both the customer and the IT department and that the required service quality is maintained and gradually improved. SLM involves both the customer and the IT service provider(s). Together they define, negotiate, agree and monitor service levels. This continuous communication provides a stronger relationship between IT Service Management and its customers. SLM communication focuses on continuous improvement and reaching agreement - not by holding one side or the other ransom. When done successfully, mutual relationships of respect are a by-product of SLM.

A critical requirement for SLM is for IT to establish Service Level Agreements (SLAs). Service Level Agreements are flexible, adaptable measurements that are directly aligned with business goals. Without SLAs in place, you are effectively telling your customers that you will provide support to them any time, under any conditions, without any limitations to the systems and services they have.

Service Level Agreements, and the processes associated with them, provide a methodology for introducing and implementing reasonable expectations between you and the customers you support. They establish a two-way accountability for service, which is negotiated and mutually agreed upon. SLAs can go far toward building credibility for your service organization, because they show how serious you are about providing support. SLAs can be the basis for evaluation and improving service levels on an on-going basis, and they become the standard for communicating service expectations throughout your organization.

Service Level Agreements are not enough to ensure the timely delivery of service as needed by the business. Operational Level Agreements (OLAs) need to be put in place between all IT groups to unify service delivery throughout IT before executing customer SLAs.

Operational Level Agreements establish specific technical, informational, and timeframe requirements needed for each IT group to provide the services that will be delivered to the customer. For example, the security administrator might require specific information, as well as a 48-hour span of time to create access to a specific service for a new employee. This needs to be documented and agreed between IT groups before the Support Center establishes an SLA with the customer.

Without OLAs in place, Service Level Agreements will frequently promise services that are impractical at best or impossible at worst. Clearly defined OLAs will prevent unmet promises to customers. Additionally, OLAs will present (and even create) a more united IT department to the customer. Ultimately, OLAs will hold each group accountable for their service, and also build understanding of each group's contribution to the overall delivery of service.

Key performance objectives and internal incentives need to be associated with OLA compliance throughout the entire IT department. Since the goal of IT is to service the business, well-defined OLAs should provide a template of objectives that show managers those activities that are most appropriate to monitor, report and reward. Lastly, OLAs need to serve as a benchmark whenever Service Level Agreements need to change to meet business requirements. If a specific service is required faster or differently by a business unit, the OLAs will show exactly which groups need to be consulted, and which services provided by those groups will ultimately affect the delivery of the desired service. If the providing group can agree to change how their service is delivered, then the SLA can be changed and the OLA will be altered accordingly.

Effective SLM has three continuous aims
Reducing service disruptions
Improving the quality of service especially responsiveness, resolution time, availability and reliability
Understanding the true cost of doing business

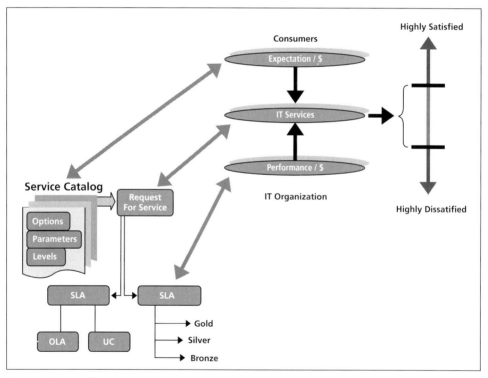

Figure 8.1 Overview of Service Level Management

8.1.2 Relationships to other processes

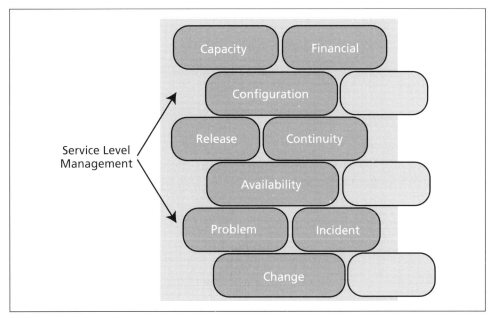

Figure 8.2 Relationship with other processes

When SLM is working efficiently (and in a fully integrated way with other processes such as Incident, Problem, Configuration and Change Management) end-user and customer satisfaction ratings increase significantly. Workflow disruptions decrease as a result for change process, recurring incidents decrease through Problem Management and IT customers have a clear understanding of how the Support Center will meet their needs through Service Level Agreements.

Relationship with the Support Center
The Support Center is the initial point of contact for users. Through Incident Management it aims to provide recovery to the agreed upon service levels for responsiveness and resolution or route work to the most appropriate internal support group as soon as possible in the event of an error.

Relationship with Availability Management
Availability Management is responsible for realizing and optimizing the accessibility of the services. SLM provides Availability Management with input about the required availability and accessibility of the IT services, whereas Availability Management provides information about the actual availability of the services being provided to Service Level Management.

Relationship with Capacity Management
Capacity Management supports SLM by providing information about the impact of a new service or extension of an existing service on the overall capacity. SLM provides information to Capacity Management about the expected current and future use of those services.

Relationship with Incident Management and Problem Management
Incident Management and Problem Management are good indicators of the effectiveness in implementing the OLA/SLA agreements.

Resolving incidents and problems is essential to providing a high quality service. SLM uses information from SLM compliance reports provided by these processes when reporting to the customer.

Relationship with Change Management
The SLA can define the changes that can be requested by the customer organization, and the agreements for responding to these changes (whom to address the changes to, cycle time, costs, informing the organization etc.). A change may also affect the service levels that have been agreed. Any changes to a service and the associated SLA are controlled by Change Management.

Relationship with Release Management
Release Management monitors the agreements made by SLM regarding the provision of hardware and software and general production releases. SLM reports on the quality of the IT service on the basis of information from Release Management reports.

Relationship with IT Service Continuity Management
IT Service Continuity Management is concerned with the rapid recovery of IT services in the event of a disruption to service, and monitors the appropriate measures and procedures. Agreements about the nature of service continuity with the customer are made in the SLM process. The measures and costs are then included in the SLA. It may be agreed that in the event of a disaster, certain service levels no longer apply or are temporarily reduced/suspended.

Relationship with Security Management
The security measures associated with the IT service can also be essential to effective Service Level Management. Both the IT organization and the customer will have certain security requirements. The corresponding responsibilities and agreements are defined in the SLA. Security Management ensures that the agreed security measures are implemented, monitored, and reported to Service Level Management.

Relationship with Configuration Management
Configuration Management is responsible for entering details of the components (Configuration Items - CIs) and documentation (OLA/SLA) related to a service in the Configuration Management Database (CMDB), and providing information from this database. Hence, the creation or modification of a service or OLA/SLA will affect the CMDB. The Support Center uses the CMDB to determine the impact of an error on the services, and to check the agreements about the response and solution times. The CMDB is also used to report about the quality of the CIs, so as to enable SLM to report about the quality of the service provided.

Relationship with Financial Management

Cost incurred by IT is the provision of services (as defined in the SLA) that may be charged to customers as stipulated in the SLA. These may be one-time charges, or charges for special or additional services. Financial Management provides SLM with information about the costs associated with providing a service. It also provides information about charging methods and the rate to be charged to cover the costs of a service.

8.1.3 Key inputs and outputs to the process

INPUTS:	
Incident	When an incident is submitted to Level 1, or when it is operationally escalated to a Level 2 or Tier 3 support group
System Faults / System Monitoring	With the use of system monitoring tools to help conduct on-going system health check and in the event a check should fail - auto open a ticket in the incident management system.
Provision Request - IMAC	Adds, moves, changes
SLA	Service Level Agreements with customers
OLA	Operating Level Agreements with internal Service Partners
UC - Underpinning Contracts	Underpinning Contracts with third party service providers
Service Catalog	Products and Services Provided

OUTPUTS:	
SLM Compliance Reporting	This is the assembly of all SLM inputs into meaningful real-time, static and decision support management reports. These reports validate the success or failure of the SLM process.
Customer Satisfaction Survey	Management & Feedback Reports
Incident Response (Acknowledgement) Time	When an incident is submitted to Level 1, or when it is operationally escalated to a Level 2 or Tier 3 support group, this is the time from the incident submission to contacting the customer in response to an incident, is the acknowledgement time.
Incident Resolution Time	Resolution time is the lapsed time from initial submission of the incident by the customer to Level 1, to the final resolution of the problem or request. The provider will resolve problems within a predefined time frame based on the priority level (P1, P2, P3, P4) of reporting. Samples SLA Expiration Service Hours Target Response Times Exceptions P1 12/31/07 Mon-Sat 6:30-23:00

OUTPUTS:	
	90%
	Open -> Acknowledge
	Open -> Work in Progress
	Open -> Closed
	00:15:00
	00:30:00
	02:00:00
	Pending Customer
	Pending Vendor
	Pending Other
	P2
	12/31/07
	Mon-Sat
	6:30-23:00
	90%
	Open -> Acknowledge
	Open -> Work in Progress
	Open -> Closed
	00:30:00
	02:00:00
	04:00:00
	Pending Customer
	Pending Vendor
	Pending Other
	P3
	12/31/07
	Mon-Sat
	6:30-23:00
	90%
	Open -> Acknowledge
	Open -> Work in Progress
	Open -> Closed
	01:00:00
	06:00:00
	08:00:00
	Pending Customer
	Pending Vendor
	Pending Other
	P4
	12/31/07
	Mon-Sat
	6:30-23:00
	90%
	Open -> Acknowledge

OUTPUTS:	
	Open -> Work in Progress
	Open -> Closed
	01:00:00
	1 00:00:00
	3 00:00:00
	Pending Customer
	Pending Vendor
	Pending Other
	A1 Default (Used if no department is present)
	12/31/07
	Mon-Sat
	8:00-17:00
	90%
	Open -> Acknowledge
	Open -> Work in Progress
	Open -> Closed
	00:15:00
	00:30:00
	02:00:00
	Pending Customer
	Pending Vendor
	Pending Other
Network Based Metrics	What percentage of the time will services be available?
	The number of users that can be served simultaneously.
	Specific performance benchmark to which actual performance will be periodically compared.
	The schedule for notification in advance of network changes that may affect users.
	Help desk response time for various classes of problems.
	Dial-in access availability.
	Usage statistics that will be provided.
System/Service Performance	Performance metrics are generally characterized in terms of response time and throughput.
Service/System Response time	Response time. This metric defines the maximum time for a service to respond to user requests.
Throughput	Throughput. This metric defines the rate at which data is delivered to the customer.
Utilization	This metric defines the maximum usage of a service during which the service will perform within guaranteed response times and throughput. For example, this metric could specify the maximum number of simultaneous users: The system will support 100 simultaneous users during the peak hours, where peak hours are between 8 a.m. and 3 p.m.
Reliability	Reliability metrics consist of availability guarantees over a period of time. For example: Unscheduled network downtime will not exceed one hour over the course of a year; The Web server will be available 90 percent of the time it is accessed over a period of a year.
Charge Back	If desired – SLM provides a definitive cost per service

Elements of Operational Level Agreements and Service Level Agreements
Definition of products/services covered
Definition of responsibilities for products/services
Time commitments on Service Level Events
Severity classifications for break/fix and for requests
Defined, measurable events, tracked through automation, with notification to responsible parties
SLA compliance tied to performance measurement

Components of Service Level Management
Responsiveness by severity code
Resolution by severity code
Availability
Transaction response time
Measurement/reporting
Escalation procedures
Penalties
Duration
Roles and responsibilities
Performance
Security
Defined Service Support procedures
Operational Level Agreements
Service Level Agreements
Service rates

Guidelines for the components of SLM
Must be challenging but attainable with clear statement of the end result expected
Must be cost effective
Must meet business needs
Must be supported by negotiated OLAs/SLAs
Must be measurable/reportable - with those responsible for the performance, involved in the development of the metric
Must be monitored continuously
Must be agreed by all parties

Possible positive outcomes from SLM	
IT Services are designed to meet Service Level requirements	Both parties to the agreement have a mutually agreed set of roles and responsibilities - thus preventing potential misunderstandings. In addition, SLM establishes - and keeps open - regular lines of communication between IT and its customers.
Monitoring specific targets	It is important to set specific targets to measure, monitor and report service quality. IT and customers need to have a clear and consistent expectation of the level of service. In addition, service monitoring allows weak areas to be identified, so that remedial action can be taken, improving future service quality. Sample: *Target WAN Data and Telecommunications Parameters* *Item* *Value* *Percentage uptime* *99.98%* *Schedule Outage* *Less than 30 min/month - Occur only from midnight to 5:00 a.m. client time* *Avg Response* *To Service Call* *< 15 Minutes* *Avg MTR* *< 30 Minutes* *Fail over/redundancy Occurs* *Immediately*
Service improvements	As a true partnership develops with the customer, problem identification and problem resolution becomes easier and increasingly productive. When issues arise during service delivery, the problems are solved as a partnership, thus creating a positive work environment for everyone
SLA can be used as basis for sharing cost	Improvements in service quality and the reduction in service disruption achieved through effective SLM can ultimately lead to significant financial savings.

8.1.4 Possible problems and issues

Possible problems and issues from SLM	
OLAs/SLAs too lengthy and intricate	IT organizations tend to want to use OLAs/SLAs as a defensive strategy; hence, they tend to include information that is not necessary to a functional OLA/SLA. Specific components that are essential to a good SLA include service descriptions, service standards, SLA duration, roles and responsibilities and evaluation criteria. However, including the right elements is only the first step. When drafting the SLA, it is easy to think of it as a contract rather than what it really is - an agreement. It may be simple to stipulate the terms of the service and to specify the exclusions and other specifics. But if the SLA is difficult to read or contains too much legal jargon, both parties will be hard pressed to follow or understand the terms. If an SLA becomes too long and complex, representatives will be less likely to refer to it - much less follow the terms specified. Critical elements for OLA/SLA Service Descriptions: define the exact service the Service Provider will deliver. Service Standards: define when the service will be available; include scheduled outages and response times. Service Rates: setup fees, where applicable. Monthly minimums and service rates. Escalations Procedure: who to call when a service fails during normal business hours and after hours. Penalties: credits received if the vendor does not provide services as promised. Duration: how long the SLA terms apply to you and the vendor. Roles and responsibilities Customer representative: who represents your organization in negotiations and implementation coordination. Service Level Manager: who ensures that your organization receives the level of service it has been promised. Service representative: who to call with questions about your account, for answers to service concerns, or unresolved issues. Contact information: how to contact representatives for each organization. Evaluation criteria: the metrics that your organization will track to ensure it receives the quality or service it has been promised.

Ineffective technology	Tools and technology cannot track and report timed service events, baseline system or networks performance, or monitor established service metrics
IT staff are over committed to other priorities	IT staff are too busy focusing on other efforts to give the SLM program the time needed to change organizational culture and buy-in.
Inadequate staffing	Senior management frequently believes SLM can be done in the margins of time. In order for SLM to be successful, it must have dedicated resources appropriate for the size of the organization, reporting to senior management, providing an objective view of service delivery throughout IT.
Not all levels of IT management have bought in to SLM	Not all levels of IT management have bought in to the SLM program, and therefore are not managing staff consistently.
Goals are too aggressive	This happens when there is no baseline period. It can have negative consequences to staff morale if they are not meeting the target goals.
Implementing customer SLAs before establishing internal	If SLAs are executed first without first going through the OLA process, service levels could be inadvertently promised to customers that your IT group will never be able to meet.
Monitoring actual achievements	This is a difficult problem. It must be addressed first as it affects the next three points. The following are important considerations in ensuring that targets are achievable before agreement: • ensure that targets are achievable before committing to them • verify the targets before agreement • base SLAs on achievable targets rather than what the customer wants.
Insufficient supporting agreements	SLAs may not be supported by adequate OLAs or underpinning agreements. When a service is defined within the SLA that is supported by another group, work with them to create an OLA and roll it into the SLA.
IT based rather than business aligned	SLAs might be IT based rather than business aligned; or may be lengthy, inconsistent and, not focused. In addition, SLM in commercial organizations is usually not a chargeable service, but an overhead; it can be viewed as a burden.
OLAs/SLAs not adequately communicated	Responsibilities of each party are not completely defined, creating a danger that some processes will become the responsibility of neither or the blame of both.

8.2 Implementation

8.2.1 The implementation process

Service Level Management requires a commitment at the highest levels of management. Service levels, acceptable outage periods, committed thresholds, and corresponding penalties should all be clearly stated in measurable terms. If it cannot be measured, you cannot enforce it, so be sure metrics are easily identified and tracked. At the start of the SLM process, these metrics should be reviewed on a daily basis among the service delivery team and weekly with the customer. When a successful pattern has been established and everyone is happy with the progress of SLM, then it can be reviewed on a monthly basis. Call vendors with questions when they arise, rather than waiting long periods to address them. Respond quickly to service providers' questions, to ensure that they receive the data and information they require to make rapid adjustments and correct failures.

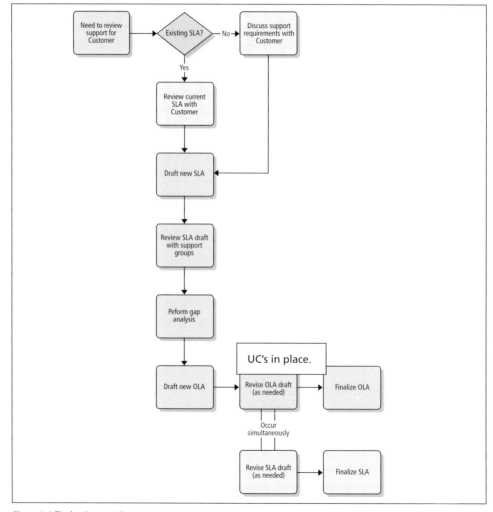

Figure 8.3 The implementation process

Without OLAs in place, IT departments are working as individual providers directly with the customer - typically working in 'silos'.

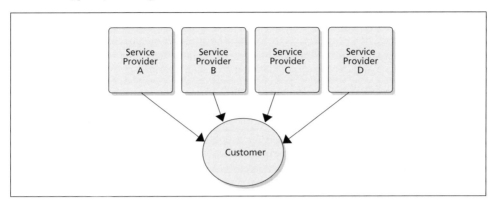

Figure 8.4 No OLAs in place

With OLAs in place, IT departments are better equipped to work together as a team with the customer through an SPOC, which ultimately provides

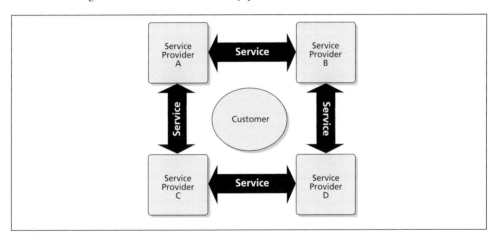

Figure 8.5 OLAs in place

Responsibilities and activities

The SLM process must be 'owned' in order to be effective and achieve successfully the benefits of implementation. Ideally it is a dedicated function that provides an objective assessment and observation of Service Level Management throughout the organization. It should report directly to the CIO or CTO of an organization. Like any set of key management processes, successful Service Level Management requires a commitment at the highest levels of management in order to reach its full potential.

Deliverables
- Creates and maintains a catalog of existing services offered by the IT department
- Formulates, agrees and maintains an appropriate SLM structure for the organization, to include
- Operational Level Agreements (OLAs) within the IT provider organization
- Service Level Agreement (SLA) structure (e.g. service based, customer based or multi-level)
- Third Party Supplier/Contract Management relationships to the SLM process
- Accommodates any existing Service Improvement Plans/Programs within the SLM process
- Negotiates, agrees and maintains the Service Level Agreements with the customer
- Negotiates, agrees and maintains the Operational Level Agreements with the IT provider
- Negotiates and agrees with both the customer and IT provider any Service Level Requirements for any proposed new/developing services
- Analyzes and reviews service performance against the SLA and OLA
- Produces regular compliance reports on service performance and achievement to the customer as well as the IT support groups at an appropriate level

Organizes and maintains the regular Service Level review process with both the IT customer and IT provider that covers:
- reviewing outstanding actions from previous reviews
- current performance
- reviewing Service Levels and targets (where necessary)
- reviewing underpinning agreements and OLAs as necessary
- agreeing appropriate actions to maintain/improve service levels
- initiating any actions required to maintain or improve service levels
- conducting annual (as appropriate) reviews of the entire Service Level Management process and negotiates, agrees and controls any amendments necessary
- acting as co-ordination point for any temporary changes to service levels required (e.g. extra support hours required by the customer, reduced levels of service over a period of maintenance required by the IT provider etc.).

Competencies/key skills
The Service Level Manager must have strong relationship management skills, which include:
- a good understanding of the IT providers' services and qualifying factors in order to understand how customer requirements will affect delivery
- understanding of the customer's business and how IT contributes to the delivery of that product or service
- excellent communication and negotiation skills
- patience, tolerance and resilience
- knowledge and experience of contract and/or supplier management roles
- good people management and administrative skills
- good understanding of statistical and analytical principles and processes
- good presentational skills
- reasonable numeric skills
- ability to interact successfully with all levels of the customer and IT provider organizations
- reasonable technical understanding and an ability to translate technical requirements and specifications into easily understood business concepts and vice versa

- innovative in respect of service quality and ways in which it can be improved within the bounds of the organization's limits (resource, budgetary, legal etc.)
- good listener with the ability to apply the knowledge gained effectively
- even-handed and fair in dealings with other parties.

Key performance indicators (KPIs)

- Number or percentage of services that are covered by SLAs
- Percentage of Underpinning Contracts and OLAs in place for all SLAs
- OLAs/SLAs monitored continuously and regular SLM reports are produced in a timely manner
- Daily SLM review meetings being conducted on time and action items documented for follow-up
- The currency of SLAs, OLAs and UCs and percentage that are in need of review and update
- SLM compliance of defined service targets and the number and severity of service breaches by severity classification

Effective follow-up of all service breaches

- Evidence that service level achievements are continuously improving
- Evidence that customer satisfaction statistics are improving
- Evidence that IT costs are decreasing for services with stable service level achievements

SLM activities include (but are not limited to):
forming clear alignment within the IT organization via OLAs
understanding where organization currently is
understanding what the organization aspires to be
dealing with challenges
capitalizing on opportunities
aligning with and influencing the thinking of senior management
establishing function to support the SLM activities
implementing the SLM process
managing the ongoing SLM process
conducting periodic reviews with all stakeholders

Implementing SLM should follow a cycle of defining, confirming, agreeing, monitoring, reporting and reviewing. Consider the following checklist/processes when getting started.

SLA/OLA negotiations:
Before entering into negotiations or making commitments to providers, customers should conduct a service assessment. This assessment entails gathering information from as many service recipients as feasible and as many sources of service data as possible, so as to answer such questions as: what services are you currently receiving? what aspects of these services are confusing or unclear? what services are you not currently receiving that would be beneficial? in what ways has service delivery been measured? in what ways has it fallen short? what aspects of the service need improvement? what changes in service delivery would be desirable? Confirm that you are comparing like-to-like. Insist on quantifiable and verifiable performance metrics. Determine how downtime credit will be calculated and paid.
The information gleaned from this assessment helps customers enter the SLA effort knowledgeably and better prepared.

Service Catalog	
Service Portfolio	A Service Portfolio should be a marketing document outlining at the highest level the services on offer of services. It does not need to focus on the detail of metrics and costs.
Service Catalog	A Service Catalog should be a more detailed breakdown of the services provided and often will include the infrastructure, the software and even the people that deliver the service. A Service Catalog could be defined as a list of services, applications, process, and hardware and support groups / people that will support the services provided.

Once the Service Catalog is defined, the pilot area should be interviewed, workshops/meetings conducted, and other discovery exercises (such as incident and change request reports) to learn which services are being consumed. Record only relevant information related to each service. This record of services should help provide a baseline to build on.

Information that will be valuable may include:
- priority of tasks
- systems used
- Hardware Inventory (servers, desktops etc.)
- effect on employees
- number of users
- service components used in the delivery of the service
- any third-party supplier or support contracts.

The information recorded in the service catalog can then be used as a reference in the implementation of the other processes for Service Level Management. This record is essential to the other processes because it documents the services that will be managed by the providers of the Service Level Agreement.

Implementing key process activities

Establish a customer service culture
Gain executive support
Obtain adequate staffing
Build appropriate mission and vision statements
vision
purpose
objectives
Clearly define Service Catalogs
Identify key stakeholders
Develop OLAs with internal support groups and UCs
Develop workflows and processes
Implement enabling technologies
Define reporting requirements
Define SLA/OLA/UC review/update process
Establish an internal baseline period for all OLAs
Develop Service Level Agreements (SLAs) with customer organizations

What should the SLA cover?
Introduction and purpose
Service to be delivered
Performance, tracking and reporting
Problem management
Fees and expenses
Customer duties and responsibilities

8.2.2 Planning for implementation

Steps to take

Step 1: Form clear alignment within the IT organization via OLAs.

Step 2: Understand where the organization is currently and understand where it aspires to be.

Step 3: Align with and influence the thinking of senior management.

Step 4: Establish a function to support the SLM activities.

Step 5: Implement the SLM process.

Step 6: Manage the ongoing SLM process.

Step 7: Support groups draft an OLA.

Step 8: Review, modify and finalize the OLA.

Step 9: Ensure workflow, processes, reporting and technology are all in place.

Step 10: Conduct a baseline of internal IT performance to develop an understanding of current run rate of service levels.

- Consult with the customer to understand and address all aspects of service delivery
- Review, modify and finalize the SLA.
- Conduct periodic reviews with all stakeholders.

Groups to contact
- Service Partner Organizations - OLAs: (to name a few)
- Support Center
- Network Management
- Systems Development
- Desktop Support
- Computer Operations
- Vendor Support
- Finance or Purchasing
- Customer - SLAs

Necessary resources and relationships
Successful SLM requires that the organization is properly structured to support it. Workflows and procedures must be clearly defined and documented that identify how the entire organization will work together. There must also be SLM compliance reporting and technology in place before rollout.

OLA/SLA elements
- Overview
- Scope
- Involved parties
- Environment
- Key contacts
- Terms and conditions
- Agreement period
- Review
- Hours of coverage
- Service goals, based on severity
- Response and resolution times
- Escalation frequency
- Supported services and charges
- Services provided
- Hardware and software supported
- Charges

Cost elements for implementation
The costs associated with implementing and executing SLM include:
- staff costs (salaries, training, recruitment costs, consultancy - if needed), both initial and ongoing
- development time to assemble Service Catalog
- development time to assemble workflows, business rules and processes
- support tools (monitoring and reporting, plus some element of integrated Service Level Management tools)
- hardware on which to run these tools
- marketing costs e.g. communication strategies and production of Service Catalog.

These costs should be seen as an investment and added value rather than a cost.

8.2.3 Hints and tips

What to implement first

Operational Level Agreements (OLAs) and Underpinning Contracts (UCs) should be developed, in parallel with customer SLA discussions. This gives IT and SLM Management a clear understanding of the IT department's capabilities while negotiating SLAs with customers.

During this process, the SLM team should clearly define the levels of service that can be achieved by the various IT support groups and third party vendors. They should also know which teams support or enable each service definition, and their capabilities for delivering those services.

Elements of Operational Level Agreements
- Definition of products/services covered
- Definition of responsibilities for products/services
- Time commitments on incidents by severity for responsiveness and resolution
- Severity classifications for break/fix and non-development work requests
- Defined, measurable events, tracked through automation, with notification to responsible parties
- OLA compliance linked to performance measurement

Things that always work
- Obtain senior management buy-in; this guarantees success for your SLM initiative.
- Review the SLM process and demonstrate how the SLM measurements are monitored and reported from beginning to end. Then show how the process is aligned with the business goals and the value IT is providing to the company.

Little things that deliver big returns
- Definition of the product and services to be provided (Service Catalog)
- Establishing quality standards to be achieved and clearly communicate them to all service partners
- Establishing measurement criteria and performance standards. These metrics should cover everything from availability (when the service is to be operational), reliability (Service Uptime) and responsiveness and resolution times.
- Establishing effective reporting criteria. As part of the effort to ensure quantifiable, verifiable performance metrics are tracked, the SLA should also state the reports (and their frequency) that the service provider will provide, the specific elements the reports will include and track, and when those reports will be provided to the customer.
- Negotiating and determining the cost of delivery per service
- Communicate, communicate, communicate!
- Candidly discuss the questions and myths about service level management (see below)

Questions and myths about Service Level Management	
Question/Myths	Response/Reality
OLAs have no value	An OLA is the contract that seals a service partnership within the IT department. It unifies the organization to provide a coordinated service delivery model.
SLAs have no value	An SLA is the contract that seals a customer's partnership with IT. It is the document that records the obligations of all parties involved to set realistic expectations for service.
SLAs merely outline services provided	While services provided are an important aspect of an SLA, the comprehensive contract also includes performance levels and legal aspects. Information that should be contained in an SLA includes the purpose of the SLA, description of service, duration of service, installation timetable, payment terms, termination conditions, and legal issues such as warranties, indemnities, and limitation of liability,
Business goals should not be included in an SLA	Writing the customer's business goals into an SLA provides the vendor with a greater understanding of the customer's priorities, which can prove invaluable in a time of technical crisis.
The services determine pricing	The single greatest factor in price determination, as specified in an SLA, is performance level. Customers pay the vendor according to predetermined performance criteria such as availability and response time. An SLA should also include specifications regarding financial penalties, in the event that the vendor is unable to meet the performance levels indicated in the SLA.
The vendor's standard SLA cannot be customized	Many vendors provide a standard SLA, and some even market their services based on the strength of their SLA. But almost all vendors will customize their services and their SLAs to satisfy customers' requirements.
The vendor will monitor performance	Vendors generally do not monitor their own performance, although an increasing number of software vendors are producing tools that monitor service provider performance on behalf of their clients.
An SLA only applies to the vendor that signs it	While this reasoning appears logical, service providers often participate in an entire network of service providers. This network can include IT functions that they outsource, as well as extended partnerships, which allow other organizations to cover their service responsibilities. To minimize third-party performance risks, customers should insert a clause stipulating that the primary vendor remains accountable for any damages caused by third-party partnerships.
If it's in the SLA, it's guaranteed	In the excitement of the sale, vendors sometime promise services that they cannot provide. For this reason, customers should be wary of exacting demands that the vendor is hesitant to meet. Customers should also remember that an SLA is only a contract that represents a partnership; they must continue to manage the vendor for the duration of the relationship.
Remediation of a failed SLA - or partnership - is impossible	Many consulting firms offer mediation services that help customers and service providers to renegotiate the SLA and the partnership. In fact, as outsourcing becomes more popular, consulting firms are doing more and more mediation work. And, if all else fails, there is always legal recourse.

What is the most common mistake you have seen in establishing SLAs?	A common mistake is for people to create a statement of services and mistakenly think they have created a service level agreement. While these service statements are useful, they are not SLAs. In particular, they lack information concerning the terms and conditions of service delivery, and often fail to describe how the SLA will be managed; that is, how compliance with the agreement will be tracked, reported, and reviewed, and how changes to the SLA will be handled.
I've heard people say that an SLM should include a glossary? Is that really necessary?	One of the biggest sources of misunderstanding between providers and customers is that they define key terminology differently, which leads to conflicts in service delivery. It is not at all unusual for the two parties to have different things in mind when they use such terms as availability, reliability, acknowledgment, response, uptime, access, and problem resolution—to name a few. Even members of the same team often interpret these terms differently. Because of the high potential for misinterpretation, the process of developing a glossary is an immensely valuable effort
What should customers keep in mind in preparing to negotiate an SLA?	Before entering into negotiations or making commitments to providers, customers should conduct a service assessment. This assessment entails gathering information from as many service recipients as feasible and as many sources of service data as possible, so as to answer such questions as: • what services are you currently receiving? • what aspects of these services are confusing or unclear? • what services are you not currently receiving that would be beneficial? • in what ways has service delivery been on target? • in what ways has it fallen short? • what aspects of the service need improvement? • what changes in service delivery would be desirable? • The information gleaned from this assessment helps customers enter the SLA effort knowledgeably and better prepared.
How often is it necessary to hold service review meetings?	Important problems, issues and concerns invariably surface during periodic service reviews, even when service delivery has been on target during the review period. Regular service reviews, with both provider and customer representatives participating, are essential to SLM success. The intention to conduct these reviews should be documented in the OLA/SLA. A formal review meeting should be held at least weekly, when the SLA is new, when service delivery has been below acceptable levels, or when the service environment is complex or undergoing significant change. When service has been stable and at acceptable levels, monthly reviews may be sufficient; then move to quarterly review meetings.

What can I do if my management doesn't want to create SLAs?	Start by trying to determine management's reasoning. An understanding of their perspective will help you build a case that is targeted to their specific concerns. In doing so, watch for problems that might not have occurred if SLAs had been in operation, such as customer confusion about service availability or conflicts between providers and customers about service quality. Point out to management the cost of lost productivity while dealing with these situations. Many of the steps involved in creating an SLA can be carried out without a formal SLA effort. For example, one of the biggest tasks in establishing an SLA is creating a service description or service catalog to clarify service offerings. Another task is defining and communicating service standards that document the time frames and conditions of service delivery. A third task is gathering customer feedback to service as a baseline for assessing service effectiveness. If management supports these and the other individual steps involved in implementing an SLA, you may be able to achieve the benefits of an SLA without ever formally defining it as an SLA.
What kinds of circumstances warrant making changes to an OLA/SLA?	Although everything in an OLA/SLA is eligible for change, changes should not be made lightly. Typically, it is best to limit changes to significant circumstances such that those arising from changing business or service needs, significant variations from agreed-upon service standards and unanticipated events. Whatever conditions are determined to warrant making adjustments to the OLA/SLA should be articulated in both the OLA/SLA.

8.3 Optimization

8.3.1 The optimization process

Support Center Manager's role, responsibilities and activities

The Support Center/Helpdesk Managers have the most important role in motivating staff. Managers' attitudes and actions set the tone for the entire staff. They should not think of themselves as managers; instead, they should consider themselves as team leaders. The Manager sets the tone and leads by example on a daily basis; he/she needs to spend time in front of and with the team. It is the Manager's job to establish the expectations and demonstrate the enthusiasm needed to meet and exceed them. They must do this every day to establish the culture.

If your organization is going through changes, such as implementing new Problem Management processes and implementing new tools, the Manager's participation is even more important. Your staff needs your support through times of change. They need to understand your vision and see your confidence and enthusiasm. This is your opportunity to turn vision into culture.

Measurement, costing and management reporting

Organizations are finding it difficult to collect, store and collate the metrics required to measure their OLA/SLA performance. In most cases this process requires extensive manual data collection and manipulation. It is often difficult or impossible for organizations to judge their SLA performance on an ongoing basis, due to the time consuming process of collecting and storing metric data. The situation is further complicated by the complex calculations required in generating these reports.

The next challenge lies in evaluating and meeting SLA performance. In the absence of automated tools, organizations are forced to rely on difficult, time-consuming, and error-prone manual processes to collect store and analyze the data required to measure OLA/SLA performance.

One metric that is almost universal is availability. It is important to remember that availability must reflect the complete service covered by the SLA and not individual components. Availability may be expressed in terms of percentage availability, minutes of downtime, number of outages, mean time between failures (MTBF), etc.

Another important area for SLA metrics is performance. However, there is a difference between what is being used (reported) and what should be used. An example is the average responsiveness and resolution time of an incident, broken down from the time the customer places the initial call until the ticket is closed. A key requirement is that the metrics must be meaningful to the customer or support group receiving the compliance reports. Another requirement is that the metrics reflect the customer experience. Both of these requirements are frequently violated.

Metrics are the key to success. Establish measurable goals and objectives for the organization. Break high-level organizational goals and objectives into smaller team-level goals and objectives. Your organization achieves its goals based on the contribution of your teams, so define what teams are to accomplish. Most importantly, make sure the goals/objectives are measurable.

You may be faced with some difficult decisions on setting targets. You are implementing new processes, so you may not have historical data to base your targets on. At this point, you should have defined what it means to be successful. Many organizations do this based on what their peers are doing. For example, suppose your peer Support Centers resolve 85 percent of their incidents during the initial contact. Set that as a target. Start measuring immediately, and after one or two quarters, review your goals and make realistic adjustments to the targets. You can still use first-level resolution as a metric to foster competition between first-level teams. Gather the data and publish it. You may need to adjust your processes if you find that, after measuring for the first two quarters, you are far from the goal. Meet with your team and share this information with them, both in the beginning and during the reviews. Make sure the team knows that the first set of targets is a starting point and that once metrics are gathered, better targets will be established. This is critical in the beginning.

Measure	Example
Responsiveness / acknowledgment time	When an incident is submitted to Level 1 or when it is operationally escalated to a Level 2 or Level 3 support group, the time from the incident submission to contacting the customer by telephone/voicemail/email, or arrive at the desk side in response to an incident is the acknowledgement time.
Resolution time	The time from submission of the incident by the customer to the Support Center to the final resolution of the incident or request. You must ensure that the Incident Management records are updated promptly in order to report on resolution time accurately. If technicians resolve issues but do not update the Incident Management record promptly, the incident will be out of compliance.
Availability	Days and hours the service is available or a percentage figure based on this.
Responsiveness and performance	Speed and volume (throughput or workload measures) of service, time to acquire data, speed of data transfer and response time, and technical and human speed of response.
Integrity and accuracy	The data in the service is doing what it is meant to do
Security	The security of the service.
Customer satisfaction	A formalized measurement of customers' perceptions of service delivery.

It is very common for IT departments to create OLA/SLA reports that only contain technical data. Examples of these metrics include: packet loss, latency, jitter, paging swapping, allocation failures, etc. Most end users will not understand this type of data or be able to relate it to their overall experience. The most commonly used metrics are not necessarily the best metrics to use; the choice of metrics depends upon the nature of the service and the technical sophistication of the user.

8.3.2 Tools

Organizations must define their objectives for service management first, then evaluate technology solutions to properly align current technology. Having the right information to monitor service level compliance is the biggest step toward successful Service Level Management. However, without the right support tools to help in the management task, Service Level Management can prove to be a daunting activity.

When reviewing SLM tools, it is important for the IT department to be able to align with the business units it supports. The tool must be able to provide the framework for establishing and monitoring service requirements and automating the tracking and reporting of critical metrics.

Most infrastructure management tools initially were developed to allow for generating alerts to managers letting them know a service was out of tolerance. Technology is also available for the logging and access of key management metrics for both reporting and troubleshooting purposes across multiple platforms, with more platforms on the way.

With proper planning and attention paid to establishing key service levels and the service objectives put in place to support them, Service Level Management can be achieved with today's tool offerings and the benefits of Service Level Management can be achieved that much sooner. Surprisingly enough, if the early phases of Service Level Management implementation are treated with rigor and properly applied, the implementation of the actual monitoring and reporting on established services levels becomes fairly easy.

Other important features include the provision of diagnostic tools, automated alerts, and automated recovery tools. The impact of changes upon the quality of service and how it affects the OLAs/SLAs also need to be considered. It is essential that incident and problem handling targets included in OLAs/SLAs are the same as those included in Support Center tool(s) and used for escalation and monitoring purposes. Organizations that have failed to do this end up monitoring something different from that which has been agreed in OLA/SLAs and as a result are unable to know whether OLA/SLA targets have been met not to mention the wasted effort. SLM cannot work in isolation; it relies heavily on the existence and effectiveness of all the other processes. Best practice states that nothing should be included in an SLA unless it can be effectively monitored and measured at commonly agreed points in time.

Measuring and reporting IT results

According to ITIL, Service Level Management aims at controlling the service delivered by the IT department to the business users. Although multiple factors relating to the IT service are relevant for improving the contribution to the business, two of them are the best known: performance and availability of the business applications. Whenever IT fails to deliver adequate performance and availability of key applications, business processes are halted immediately, affecting financial results and customer satisfaction negatively.

- A business customer only wants to know what the IT department delivers as a whole, not how the technical components and elements are performing.
- Provide fact based information on the delivered service by the IT department, providers and subcontractors
- Compare actual service delivered with the agreed service levels (OLA/SLA)
- Improve the relationship between the business management, IT management and IT providers/departments by separating facts from subjective opinions
- Set future service targets and responsibilities
- Reduce operating costs by avoiding unnecessary IT investments due to sub optimizing.

Some of the most common used metrics might include:	
Incident response (acknowledgement) time	When an incident is submitted to Level 1or when it is operationally escalated to a Level 2 or Level 3 support group, the time from the incident submission to contacting the customer by telephone/voicemail/email, or arriving at the desk side in response to an incident is the acknowledgement time.
Incident resolution time	The time from submission of the incident by the customer to the Support Center, to the final resolution of the incident or request.
Network based metrics	The percentage of the time that services will be available The number of users that can be served simultaneously Specific performance benchmark to which actual performance will be periodically compared The schedule for notification in advance of network changes that may affect users Help desk response time for various classes of problems Dial-in access availability Usage statistics that will be provided
Performance	Performance metrics are generally characterized in terms of response time and throughput.
Service/system response time	This metric defines the maximum time for a service to respond to user requests.
Throughput	This metric defines the rate at which data is delivered to the customer.
Customer support	These include typical help desk problem reporting and problem resolution guarantees. For example: the provider will deliver 24x7 supports; the provider will assign a single point of contact to the customer; the provider will resolve problems within a predefined time frame based on the priority level (P1, P2, P3, P4) of reporting.
Utilization	This metric defines the maximum usage of a service during which the service will perform within guaranteed response times and throughput. For example, this metric could specify the maximum number of simultaneous users: The system will support 100 simultaneous users during peak hours, where peak hours are between 8 a.m. and 3 p.m.
Reliability	Reliability metrics consist of availability guarantees over a period of time. For example: unscheduled network downtime will not exceed one hour over the course of a year; the Web server will be available 90 percent of the time it is accessed over a period of a year.
Business continuity and disaster recovery	This guarantees that steps have been taken to include specification of a recovery plan in the event of a disaster, such as facilities redundancy, distributed backups and storage plans. In addition to reliability and support metrics, service performance metrics are important for business-critical applications.

Sample Service Level Agreement Metrics				
	S1	S2	S3	S4
Acknowledge Problem 15 Min	30 Min	60 Min	60 Min	
Tech on-site 15 Min	2 Hrs	6 Hrs	48 Hrs	
Resolution Time	2 Hrs	4 Hrs	8 Hrs	72 Hrs
Target Goal	90%	90%	90%	90%
Q1 Target	70%	70%	70%	80%
Q2 Target	75%	75%	75%	85%
Q3 Target	80%	80%	80%	90%
Q4 Target	90%	90%	90%	90%
Answer Rate	90% of all calls answered within 60 seconds			
Abandoned Rate	< 10% abandoned calls			
Customer Satisfaction	90% satisfied or better from customer satisfaction surveys (ie on a scale of 1-5)			

Install/Move/Add/Change (IMAC) Service Targets:	
Standard Desktop - Forecasted	85% Within 10 Business Days
Standard Desktop - Non-Forecasted	85% Within 15 Business Days
Standard Laptop - Forecasted	85% Within 15 Business Days
Standard Laptop - Non-Forecasted	85% Within 20 Business Days
De-Install	Logins within 24 hours
Data Restores	90% Within 48 hours

8.4 Summary

SLM should focus on the customer's underlying interest in SLAs: they are trying to quantify a minimum performance threshold for the offering. By addressing the SLA question holistically in terms of both technical and business general SLAs, the IT department can provide an improved context for service delivery. Successful Service Level Management requires a commitment at the highest levels of management.

The evaluation process is very important. Without evaluation criteria; there is no objective means of determining how well your service provider is performing. The Customer Representative should select metrics with assistance of the Service Level Manager. Metrics should be meaningful and geared toward IT service delivery. Percentage of infrastructure availability, minutes lapsed until performance issues are corrected, average peak bandwidth and connectivity availability, average peak bandwidth capacity, and acceptable outage windows for maintenance should be specified. Ensure that your IT department has the tools in place to track the metrics requested before agreeing to the metrics.

Service Level Management has proven its worth in IT environments and data centers around the world. It has an even greater potential for key benefits for the distributed enterprise by strategically focusing on business users as the IT driver. Service Level Management can be used to help control rapidly increasing costs created by uncoordinated acquisitions of IT materials to support the distributed enterprise by focusing on providing required levels of service, rather than building infrastructure.

Bibliography

Implementing Service Level Management -Practical Guidelines for the IT Support Organization white paper, Char LaBounty, HDI website, October 2003

Service Level Management: An Overview white paper, Char LaBounty, HDI website, September 2001

Efficiency Tool Kit, Network World, Tom Duffy, November 5, 2001.

IT Best Practices, Network World Management Strategies Newsletter. Melissa Shaw, November 11, 2001

Practice Questions, Computerworld, Frank Hayes, October 7, 2002

Service Support. Norwich: The Stationery Office, 2000

Service Delivery. Norwich: The Stationery Office, 2001

Service Level Management at Zurich Life, USTechnology Asset Manager, Ecpweb.com, Mark Bradley February 2004. Web

http://www.ecpweb.com/images/ECP_TAM_Feb_04_Zurich_Life_prg_.pdf

State of the Support Industry: Visioning Your Support Organization Help Desk Institute, April, 2003.

Understanding and Improving: The Business Perspective On Your IT Infrastructure. Norwich: The Stationery Office, 1996

Chapter 9:

Capacity and Workforce Management

9.1 Overview

9.1.1 Description
Capacity Management is concerned with two main factors:
- the overall capacity and performance levels required to meet the current agreed service levels
- the ability to meet future workloads without reducing the service levels.

Capacity is mainly concerned with staffing levels and technology levels. An example would be a new system going live which would create more calls than the Service Desk can handle - so more staff are required. At the same time the Service Desk server will have to be changed or upgraded because it cannot handle any more workstations. Performance, on the other hand, is well known because all Service Desks are concerned with metrics such as 'time to answer,' 'call duration,' and 'first level resolution' rates.

To practice Capacity Management three questions must be continuously asked and answered:
- what is the current capacity?
- what is coming up (trends, changes and new services)?
- will it fit?

Workforce Management (or Workforce Planning), within the Support Center industry, refers to effective staff scheduling and staffing requirements planning and forecasting - i.e., scheduling 'the right people, in the right places, at the right times.' While ITIL essentially regards Workforce Management as a Service Desk line management responsibility (and not as a specific subset of Capacity Management) it uses many of the same processes and techniques and is therefore included in this section.

9.1.2 Relationships to other processes
Workforce Management does not have many relationships with the other processes because it is generally a standalone process. However, Capacity Management has relationships with most of the other processes as shown in Figure 9.1.

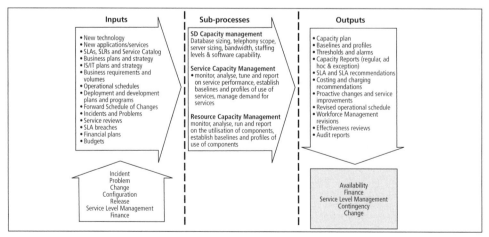

Figure 9.1 The Capacity Management process

The *input* processes supply data to show current volumes and provide data to calculate growth trends, whereas the *output* processes will be changed or upgraded as a result of capacity changes. Note that these can be capacity reductions as well as increases.

Figure 9.1 shows the inputs that are required to calculate Service Desk Capacity. As these are collated, the Capacity sub-processes can calculate their impact on capacity to produce the plans and recommendations shown in the outputs segment.

9.1.3 Key inputs and outputs to the process

The additional key inputs and outputs specific to Workforce Management are simply a human resources-focused subset of the inputs and outputs to the Capacity Management process:

Description	Source	Importance
INPUTS		
Telephony technology	Service Desk	High
Forecast incident volumes, by channel (telephone, e-mail, etc.)	Incident Management	High
Current operational schedules	Service Desk	High
General schedule exceptions (e.g., holidays)	HR	High
Specific schedule exceptions (e.g., vacations, sick days, planned meetings, off-phone activities)	Service Desk	High
Special events predicted to have an effect on incident volume (e.g., changes, deployment plans)	Service Desk	Medium
Personnel skill levels and training plans	Service Desk Manager	Medium
Staffing budget	Service Desk Manager, General Management	High
Changes (planned or actual) to Configuration Items in the CMDB	Varies	Varies
OUTPUTS		
Personnel schedule	Service Desk	High
Updated volume forecast	Service Level Management	High
Updated training plans	Service Desk	Medium
Staffing change recommendations	Service Desk	High
Capacity plans and recommendations	Service Desk	High

9.1.4 Possible problems and issues

There are several major problems and issues that make Capacity and Workforce Management difficult. These are outlined below.

Lack of basic data: this often occurs because Service Desk logging is based around performance rather than planning. Accurate data is required to reflect the workload of your Service Desk Agents: time spent on incidents (calls) plus time spent on any other activities.

You must not work on averages; therefore, you need to have categories for your incidents so that you can match like with like. For example, say an Agent has nine password incidents at one minute each and then has one 'just-in-time' question taking 11 minutes. The total time is 20 minutes divided by 10 incidents, which equals two minutes per incident. This is obviously flawed data to work from, especially if the next new application is complex to use and will not involve password-related incidents. Make sure that all the data is gathered and that incident averages by categories are calculated.

Lack of time: this is an issue that all Service Desk Managers need to address. Service Desk Managers must make time for planning or the Service Desk will always be fighting fires, rather than preventing them. Contrary to widespread practice, this approach should not be considered acceptable, much less a best practice.

Lack of involvement in purchase/development cycle of new systems/applications: lack of data can come from new systems and applications if the Service Desk is not involved in the purchase or development cycle until the last minute. How can the impact of a new system or application on your Service Desk be calculated? First, develop a set of questions to ensure that the correct data is gathered for new applications and new systems, and then get involved in all new projects from their start-up so that the data can be gathered before it is too late. See Annex A9.14, Service Desk Requirements for New Applications/Systems, with a ready-made list of questions and data to collect.

Lack of tools: true Workforce Management can be difficult to implement without using software designed for that purpose. Much of the information here assumes that the SCM is, or plans to be, making use of such software. While a Support Center may not be of an appropriate size to take best advantage of the large-scale, feature-rich tools available, the number of low-cost, minimum-feature tools available is greater today than ten years ago. The complexity of balancing multiple employees with varying skill sets across multiple sites and channels means manual scheduling and forecasting is a daunting task and is no longer cost-effective. However, there are some tools that can make the process easier; see the Tools section of this chapter for details.

Lack of buy-in: another, more insidious, problem that can arise when beginning to use Workforce Management is that of poor employee reaction. Employees often look with resentment on the prospect of Workforce Management software, and fear increased regimentation and 'Big Brother'-type managerial oversight. Communication with employees is critical, and must include details of the benefits they will receive when the software is implemented:
• improved schedule availability
• more employee impact on the scheduling process
• improved ability to manage schedule swapping
• improved ability to handle schedule preferences
• better off-phone scheduling (including breaks and training)
• ability to monitor and thus affect schedule adherence
• fairly and consistently applied rules across the employee population.

Quality issues
As far as Workforce Management is concerned, quality problems can occur when too much emphasis is placed on the numbers of staff members required as opposed to their skill sets. Filling a schedule gap with a new employee or one who does not possess the requisite skills can sometimes be worse, in terms of customer satisfaction, than leaving the gap unfilled and accepting the resulting impact on hold times and resolution times. To deal with this potential issue, make sure that forecasts are tied to employee training plans, and that employees have incentives to become skilled in as many areas of the Service Catalog as possible. New employees should not be formally placed on the schedule until they have completed enough training and have been certified to ensure that they can participate effectively.

The lack of Capacity Management is a quality issue in its own right. How can a Service Desk supply the best levels of support and service to the customer if it is not planning for the future? Mistakes will be made initially when planning capacity, but eventually good capacity planning will considerably improve IT quality and service.

Security issues
When planning capacity security, it must always be remembered that you should calculate Service Desk capacity volumes for those staff members who are authorized to use the services.

9.2 Implementation

9.2.1 The implementation process
Implementing Capacity Management requires careful planning and patience. Figure 9.2 shows a simple overview of the steps that need to be taken to implement Capacity Management.

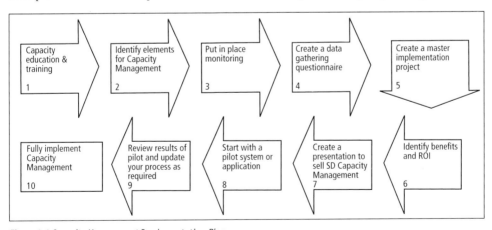

Figure 9.2 Capacity Management Implementation Plan

In this simplified implementation process there are ten steps that flow in a simple and logical order. The ten steps in Figure 9.2 are reviewed below.

9.2.2 Steps to take

Step 1: Capacity education and training - training in both Capacity Management and ITIL is critical. Start by reading the ITIL manuals or going to an ITIL course; remember to concentrate on the Capacity process; also try to get some training in Capacity Management principles. If this is not possible, try to find someone in the IT department who is responsible for capacity and learn all you can from them.

Step 2: Identify elements for Capacity Management - the two most important elements in Capacity Management are to ensure that the correct current and future staffing levels are in place and that the Service Desk technologies have sufficient capacities in which to perform. Identify the key elements of people, tools and technologies.

Step 3: Put monitoring in place - ensure that the required information capacities can be made for capacity calculations. Identify the monitoring sources and then make sure that they are recording the correct information to allow for calculation of capacity levels.

Step 4: Create a data-gathering questionnaire - create a list of questions to obtain the necessary data so that calculations of the capacity required for new systems/applications or significant changes can be made. There is a list of questions in Annex A9.11.

Step 5: Create an implementation project plan - create a master project plan listing all the tasks that will ensure that you calculate your capacity levels correctly.

Step 6: Identify benefits and ROI - identify the benefits and Return On Investment for Service Desk Capacity Management.

Step 7: Create a presentation to 'sell' Service Desk Capacity Management - although managing Capacity is the responsibility of the Service Desk, it cannot be achieved without input from other IT departments and support groups. Now is the time to make a business case. Prepare a presentation, or write a report, to make the case based upon all findings and actions so far.

Step 8: Start with a pilot system or application -link the master project and questionnaires with a pilot project. Pick a pilot that could affect Service Desk capacity. Throughout the pilot, adopt a continuous improvement mindset and adapt the overall project and questionnaire as you progress.

Step 9: Review results of pilot and update the process as required - at the end of the pilot, perform an in-depth review of successes and failures. Then make any necessary changes to the project and questionnaire.

Step 10: Fully implement Capacity Management - take the updated master project and questionnaire and fully implement Capacity Management.

9.2.3 Support Center Manager's role

Responsibilities and activities

Capacity Management is not an activity that can be delegated. It is possible to delegate the actions associated with Service Desk Capacity Management but the decisions made as a result of Capacity Management must always rest with the Service Desk Manager. A full list of the tasks required to be performed by the Service Desk Manager can be found in Annex A9.12 - Support Center Manager's Role for Service Desk Capacity Management.

The Support Center Manager should drive the process of implementing Workforce Management, as it is the Manager who is most concerned with the smooth day-to-day operation of the Support Center. The list of specific responsibilities may be found in Annex A9.13.

Deliverables
For Workforce Management, the deliverables are similar to those for Capacity Management in general; the differences merely involve the specific nature of Workforce Management. For example, the structure of the process needs to be developed and monitors need to be identified, but these will focus solely upon employee management.

One major difference involves defining the skills of each team member. The Support Center Manager must create a skills map that shows the skills needed to provide effective support for each item in the Service Catalogue and indicates the skill level of each employee. The skills map will then be used to help determine any coverage gaps. It can also be used as a software configuration aid.

When Workforce Management-specific software is being implemented as part of the process, the deliverables also include:
• the software budget
• the process by which the software was selected
• the list of software requirements
• an analysis of the vendor and/or in-house offerings that were evaluated
• a software implementation plan *(Annex A9.5)*.

Most of the above can also relate to Capacity Management but there are a few extra deliverables that apply specifically to Capacity Management:
• Service Desk Capacity plan
• recommendations to Senior Management for Service Desk investment
• improved staff skills and training
• planned buying, rather than panic buying, for Service Desk resources
• smoother implementation of new systems and services
• managed headcount on the Service Desk.

Key performance indicators (KPIs)
There are not many KPIs for Capacity Management, but not having enough capacity to manage the incidents within the terms of SLAs is the key KPI. Others may include:
• not enough staff to meet Workforce Management requirements
• under-performing Service Desk software
• not enough voice technology capacity
• reduction in ASA
• reduction in response time
• increased First-Call Resolution.

9.2.4 Support Center Function's role
Responsibilities and activities
Workforce Management is a process contained completely within the Support Center, so the Support Center function itself does not have a 'role' in the sense that other ITIL processes do. Members of the Support Center, however, have a responsibility to participate in the skills mapping process and training, and to ensure that data about their schedule adherence is captured.

9.2.5 Other groups' responsibilities and activities
The group responsible for Telecommunications, particularly ACD support, is usually very involved in implementing Workforce Management. When Workforce Management software is used, the ACD is generally integrated with it in some way. Even without special software, additional telecommunications reports are usually necessary for monitoring purposes, as are changes to the way calls are distributed.

The Human Resources group may also become involved. The creation of a skills map and the formalizing of the skills required for effective support often leads to a change in the way employees are evaluated and incentivised. New roles and career paths may also be developed. Human Resources can help to develop job descriptions and determine appropriate types of incentives.

If new software is being installed as part of the implementation, Change Management procedures should be followed. Depending on the Information Technology Department's organization, developers, database administrators, and other technical resources, as well as the Change Advisory Board, may also assist in implementing Workforce Management.

9.2.6 Planning for implementation
Some of the preparatory steps for implementing Workforce Management are described above; a checklist can be found in Annex 9.5.

Planning to implement Capacity Management for the Service Desk is not like many of the other processes because planning and implementing Capacity Management never completely stops. Capacity Management is a continuous cycle of learning how to manage capacity and implementing techniques to improve the process. The implementation of Capacity Management is a complex and dynamic process that depends on circumstances -that is, it is based on your current weaknesses. A typical plan may have the following steps.

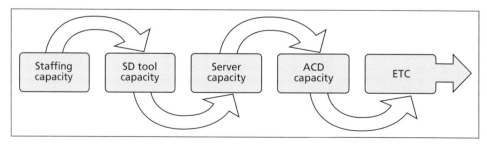

Figure 9.3 The implementation flow

Figure 9.3 shows a typical flow to implement Service Desk Capacity Management. Start with one Service Desk component and fully implement Capacity Management for it before moving to the next component. Capacity Management cannot be done by half measures. The details of Figure 9.3 are presented below.

Staffing capacity - this is the typical starting point for most Service Desks because staffing levels are a constant struggle of calculation, explanation, and justification. No organization likes to increase its headcount; in fact, it is often the opposite and demands for reduced headcounts are common. Figure 9.1 shows the inputs, sub-processes and outputs. You will need to put in place the monitoring to measure the current Service Desk staffing capacity levels. You would then need to set-up the processes to gather the data that could change the levels of staffing for the Service Desk; typically significant changes, significant releases and new services, systems, applications or technologies. With this data you can then calculate the potential staffing levels required to handle the extra volume that they may create. Take this data and add it to your current staffing capacity loadings to see the overall effect on our staffing levels. Finally, produce a capacity plan showing the impact and potential courses of action.

Service Desk tool capacity - Service Desk Agents must be able to record incidents as quickly and accurately as possible. If the Service Desk tool is slow or cannot cope with the current and future levels of staff the tool will need to be upgraded or replaced. The same pattern for staffing levels can be repeated here; gather current capacity and performance data, identify future data, and then produce a capacity plan.

Server capacity - if the Service Desk tool is slow or cannot cope with the current and future levels of staff, the need to upgrade or replace the tool may become unavoidable. It may be that the tool is adequate but the server cannot cope. Again the same pattern for staffing levels can be repeated here; gather current capacity and performance data and identify future data then produce a capacity plan.

ACD capacity - customers want to be able to get their calls answered as soon as possible and not have busy lines or have to abandon calls, so careful attention needs to be given to ACD capacity. The same pattern for staffing levels can be repeated here; gather current capacity and performance data, identify future data, and then produce a capacity plan. Several ACD simulation tools can be purchased for this task as well as numerous Erlang calculators that can be accessed via the Internet (see the Tools Implementation section for more details).

Etc. - extra Capacity Management will depend upon the services the Service Desk provides, but typically email and knowledge tools will also need a Capacity Management review.

Groups to contact
All IT groups should be contacted because all of them, at some time, use or support the Service Desk so all are potential sources for capacity growth. The Service Desk Manager should stay in constant contact with all IT groups. Some of the groups may be performing monitoring that is required by the Service Desk for capacity calculations, such as server usage for the server on which the Service Desk tools reside or network performance as it relates to

Service Desk response timings. The Service Desk should ensure that all relevant groups are measuring the correct components and forwarding that data to the Service Desk.

Necessary information and data
For Workforce Management, the required data includes:
- incident volumes by channel
- staff roles and skill levels
- staff schedules, schedule preferences, and schedule exceptions
- off-phone time requirements
- the budget allotted for Workforce Management process deployment
- staffing forecasts
- customer Service Level Agreements.

Measurements that should be in place
Besides the kinds of measurements needed to produce the necessary data, above (Incidents by channel, etc.), you will need to have an accurate percentage of what the Service Desk staff's schedule adherence has been over time. This will tell you how often the staff are performing assigned duties at assigned times and where discrepancies are likely to be found.

Some measurements required to manage Service Desk capacity are:
- Service Desk processor/server performance utilization
- Service Desk processor/server memory utilization
- percentage of incidents per incident category
- rates of incidents handled per Service Desk agent
- time to answer/respond, wait times and abandoned rates
- quality and number of incidents recorded (logged)
- volume of incidents reflecting peak and valleys during Service Desk availability
- incident duration timings by category.

9.2.7 Implementing key process activities: hints and tips
Capacity Management is an ongoing process that should be recalculated on a monthly, quarterly and as-necessary basis. Time to perform and analyze these calculations should be a routine item on every Service Desk Manager's 'to-do' list. The Service Desk Manager needs the tools and procedures that will be predicting, far in advance, when the Service Desk will have a staffing capacity problem.

Workforce Management is a complex activity, and it is best to start small. Begin by using a Workforce Management system to schedule (and ensure) adherence to breaks and lunches. Almost immediately there will be improved coverage and more satisfied employees, since they won't have to skip, delay, or abbreviate their breaks.

What to implement first
This depends upon the areas where the Service Desk has the fewest capacity measures, but Figure 9.3 shows the most logical order.

Little things that deliver big returns
The key to success and bigger returns lies with managed staffing levels. It is not always about headcount reduction. For example, your target could be to take on 25% more systems with the same headcount.

How can this be achieved? Reducing the number of incidents is a great source for big returns. Capacity Management is not only about increasing capacity; it is also about Demand Management, which includes reducing traffic, and whenever possible, incident levels. The Service Desk should regularly review its incidents and submit 'Requests For Change' where they can see an opportunity to reduce the number of incidents. This concept is covered in greater detail in the chapter on Problem Management.

As far as Workforce Management is concerned, many Support Center Managers avoid scheduling shifts outside of the regular eight hours. However, you can almost always provide better coverage at less cost by incorporating shifts of different lengths into your schedule.

9.2.8 Audits for effectiveness
Thoroughly investigate any capacity failures or issues and make sure that they do not occur again.

9.3 Ongoing operation

9.3.1 The ongoing process
The ongoing process for Service Desk Capacity Management is regular monitoring, looking for impact on current capacity and creating options to solve potential capacity problems. Figure 9.4 below highlights the main stages required for ongoing Service Desk Capacity Management:

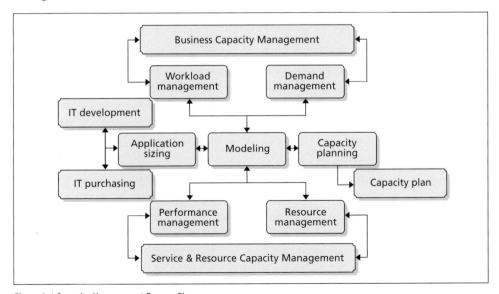

Figure 9.4 Capacity Management Process Flow

Given the complexity of the entire process, it should be examined in smaller components starting with Business Capacity Management.

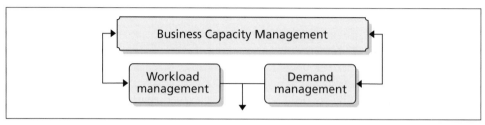

Figure 9.5 Business Capacity Management

There are three components for monitoring and understanding Business Capacity:
- Business Capacity Management is concerned with understanding the current and future needs of the business community in regard to the Service Desk. This will require regular meetings with all business units to determine their future growth or possible shrinkage. An example may be a department about to increase its headcount; another example may be extending some existing IT services within the organization or even for a marketing campaign. Hold regular meetings with one focus: 'Will our Incident (or contact) volume rise or decrease?' The Service Desk Manager will have to spend considerable time emphasizing the importance and the potential for seemingly innocent actions triggering an increase in contact volume. The results should be carefully documented and reviewed with management on a monthly and quarterly basis.

- Demand Management looks at the ebb and flow of incidents and at utilization and schedules. Most Service Desks have daily peaks and off-peak times in their incident volumes: typically 8-10 am is busy and has high volumes of incidents; 3-5 pm is also busy; other periods have lower volumes of incidents. Sometimes demand can be affected by policy. For example, calls are cheaper off-peak than during peak periods; here it is hoped that the peaks would be reduced for monetary advantage. To manage demand, peak and off-peak times must be carefully monitored on a daily basis and, where possible, the demand should be 'flattened' to even-out the incident flow. Also ensure that SLAs state that performance (i.e. time to answer) will be longer in peak times.

- Workload Management focuses on resource usage. For example, many Service Desks used to escalate incidents via phone calls to second level. This was usually time-consuming. Today, most Service Desks use their Service Desk tool to escalate incidents electronically to a second level support group. This results in more time available for the Service Desk: better managing the workload can increase available capacity. Another example is reducing the time to handle all incidents by 30 seconds (for example). Again, the same result - extra staff capacity is created. Regular reviews of how you manage your workload will enable you to find ways to handle the workload more efficiently. It also requires an explicit description of the roles and responsibilities of each support group. The hand-off of Incidents from one group to another must be uncomplicated and executed one time and only one time.

In summary: trend, forecast, model, prototype, size, and document future business requirements, because they will affect the service the customers need and the daily operations of the Service Desk.

Service and Resource Capacity Management is concerned with any future changes that may affect the service requirements or the resources used by the Service Desk. Some questions to ask are:
- what can affect the services?
- are there any changes to the Service Level Agreements, Operational Level Agreements or the Underpinning Contracts that the Support Center Manager has not been informed of?
- have any Service Level Requests (SLRs) been submitted by the customers?
- if so, what effect will they have on the Service Desk?

In any event, the Service Desk must stay in constant contact with Service Level Management and evaluate the effect of changes in service on the Service Desk.

There may have to be changes to the resources used by the Service Desk. For example, a change to the server where the Service Desk software and databases reside could result in an impact on capacity. The Service Desk must be fully involved in Change Management so that they can identify any potential effects on their resources.

Resource Management covers all the resources required by a fully operational Service Desk. This includes staff, servers, telecommunications, ACD, Service Desk software and any other resources. This is primarily a monitoring function: the future capacity of all resources is measured and then compared with the amount of available capacity. For example: an agent can handle 30 incidents in a day, but currently there are 22 incidents per day per agent; therefore, there are still 8 incidents per day per agent available. You should also set safety thresholds; e.g., you may set the level for agents at 25 incidents because this gives you a buffer to make capacity calculations and decisions rather than work to 30 where capacity cannot be expanded any further. By using your current capacity levels and the information from Service and Resource Capacity Management, you can determine when you will have capacity issues on a resource. Monitor, generate reports, analyze, and brief senior management on the utilization of components. Establish baselines and profiles of component usage.

Performance Management is similar to Resource Management but focuses on the performance of all of the resources required to run a Service Desk. Often slow performance can indicate low levels of capacity. The longer Service Desk staff members are confined to their desks without breaks or training, the more tired they will become, with a resulting drop in performance.

It is imperative that the Service Desk Manager monitors, analyzes, tunes and reports on service performance, establishes baselines and profiles of use of services and manages demand for services.

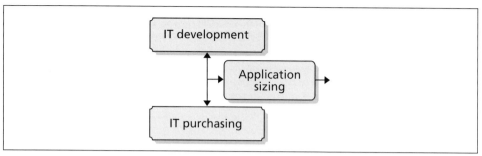

Figure 9.6 Relationship to purchasing

This section is about building relationships and getting involved in IT development and purchasing policies to get an early warning for potential capacity issues:

• IT Development is primarily about new applications and systems developed in-house. Any activity that affects any customer will, sooner or later, affect the Service Desk. The Service Desk Manager must be involved in all new projects to determine whether these projects will have an effect on Service Desk capacity. The sooner the Service Desk Manager knows if capacity will be affected, the longer the Service Desk Manager will have to explore alternatives and solutions. Annex 14 contains a list of questions for project leaders to help determine the capacity needs of new applications or systems. For each new application or system a calculation will have to be made about the extra capacity required by the Service Desk resource to support the new application or system.

• IT Purchasing is similar to IT Development, except that it concentrates on technology purchasing. This includes both IT hardware and IT software.

• Application Sizing is normally performed by the project team. The objective is to size all of the resource requirements and budget for the resources required for those resources. The Service Desk Manager must be involved in this step and make sure that all of the Service Desk resource requirements are included. Use the information that was collected from IT Development and IT Purchasing to justify the case. The Service Desk Manager must have a close relationship with purchasing, contract management, Change Management, Release Management, and Service Level Management so that the Service Desk is never surprised by new purchases, services, initiatives, etc.

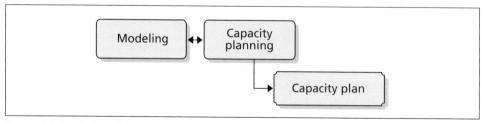

Figure 9.7 Putting it all together

Modeling is all about 'what if' scenarios. Here, all of the measurements, projects and findings from everything that has been discussed so far are brought together. Whenever areas are found that do not have enough capacity, then all potential solutions must be explored. At the end of Modeling, all of the potential capacity shortfalls and potential courses of action should be identified, documented and resolved.

Capacity Planning identifies the shortfalls, potential solutions and the recommendations to management showing how capacity failures can be avoided.

Capacity Plan - see Annex A9.15 for a list of the contents of a Capacity Plan. Distribute the plan to all IT Managers and selected Business Managers. Do not just issue the Capacity Plan: make sure that actions are taken to avoid capacity failures on the Service Desk.

9.3.2 Support Center Manager's role
Responsibilities and activities
The Support Center Manager's activities in the ongoing operation of Workforce Management are listed in Annex A9.8.

Deliverables
New forecasts and schedules

Training plans
Recruiting plans and budgets

KPIs
First call resolution and incident handling time: by implementing Workforce Management, incidents should be much more likely to be delivered to people with the right skill set to handle them. As a result, first call resolution rates should go up and incident handling times go down.

Hold times, abandoned call rates and average speed of answer (ASA): with better schedules in place, hold times and abandon rates should go down and average speed of answer improve.

Payroll costs: payroll costs for Incident handling should go down over time and the need for overtime should decrease, based on the fact that incidents will be more likely to be routed to the person best suited to handle them. There will be fewer re-assignments of Incidents and they will be handled more quickly in general.

Capacity Management KPIs include the number of issues, incidents or problems due to Service Desk capacity failures and the number of SLA failures due to Service Desk capacity issues.

Increase in IT Employee Satisfaction survey ratings.

9.3.3 Support Center Function's role
Responsibilities and activities
Support Center employees must monitor their compliance with the Support Center schedules; they must also ensure that the training system is up-to-date with newly-acquired skills, schedule preferences and exceptions.

9.3.4 Other key roles and functions in the ongoing operation process
The Support Center Manager may be responsible for handling reporting and Workforce Management system administration. However, most Support Centers will have a person specifically assigned to administer the system and perform forecasting and scheduling. This person will be responsible for:
• ensuring the workforce/scheduling system is updated with call volume and employee schedule and skills information
• producing new forecasts and schedules
• handling intra-day changes (either by direct management, or by reporting to the Support Center Manager)
• producing reports as required by management.

9.4 Optimization

9.4.1 The optimization process: Support Center Manager's role
Responsibilities and activities
The optimization activities for Workforce Management are the same as those for ongoing operations, and are listed in Annex A9.6.

Deliverables
• Adjusted forecasts and schedules
• Training plans
• Recruiting plans and budgets

KPIs
The KPIs for Workforce Management are the same as those listed in the Ongoing Operation section: as Workforce Management is optimized, you should see an improvement in those KPIs.

9.4.2 Other key roles and functions in the optimization process
The Workforce Management system administrator will play a role in optimization, as may IT and Telecommunications resources.

9.4.3 Steps and tips for optimizing this process
See the Annex for ideas on how to optimize Workforce Management *(Annex A9.7)*.

9.4.4 Future impact of this process on the Support Center
Workforce Management results in more cost-effective Incident handling in the Support Center and improves staff job satisfaction.

9.5 Measurement, costing and management reporting

9.5.1 Implementing: benefits and costs
Why implement this process and what can be gained
There are many benefits that accrue from implementing Workforce Management. They can be broken into five categories:
- improved staffing efficiencies
- employee satisfaction
- customer satisfaction
- reduction in management workload
- cost savings.

Improved staffing efficiencies: forecasting tools can examine a Service Desk's call history and predict the expected call volume over the course of the day. By feeding this information into a scheduling module, an optimum schedule based on previous call histories can be developed. This schedule can take 'shrinkage' (the time agents are on break, at lunch, absent, etc.), agents' preferences and skills and all sites into account. Besides making better use of staff, this 'schedule smoothing' effect means that the Service Desk will be able to provide more consistent levels of support to your customers.

It can also help determine the optimum schedules for each customer contact channel. Some packages can manage chat and web-based channels as well as phone queues. Response-style work, such as responding to emails and faxes, can be difficult to schedule. The right kinds of software tools can help identify the best times to handle response work while still taking your SLAs for emails and faxes into account. In a similar way, workforce-planning software can automatically schedule staff members' breaks and lunches while still ensuring that the maximum coverage is in place, and it can suggest the best times to hold meetings and training sessions.

Workforce management tools help you predict and plan for 'shrinkage' - that is, the percent of staff likely to be sick, out, on a break or occupied with other tasks. Every support manager has wondered how 40 people can be scheduled, but no one is logged into the phone system, while monitoring the email and IRC (Internet Relay Chat) queues. Forecasting can also help predict seasonal peaks and valleys; 'what-if' analysis allows you to see the effects a new rollout or special promotion might have on call volume and provide the opportunity to proactively schedule for it.

Intra-day forecasting helps a manager to respond to shifts in customer calling patterns 'on the fly.' Workforce planning tools with intra-day functionality allow a manager to see if the volume is higher or lower than predicted, and help to adjust staffing levels accordingly.

Increased employee satisfaction: employee satisfaction is a particular benefit to come from the use of workforce planning software. A workforce planning system usually results in a somewhat more regimented workplace. Employees have specific duties built into their schedules, shifts may be assigned by the system, and adherence reporting gives management a view into exactly what they're doing at any particular time. This 'Big Brother' aspect of workforce planning is why many employees look with alarm on the prospect of having it implemented at their company.

After implementation, though, it is another story. The newer, robust, scheduling packages can allow staff members to 'bid' for preferred schedules, input requests for days off, state their preferences around scheduling and handle shift swapping with other employees. The systems can be set up with rules around seniority and skill sets. The net effect is that employees understand how the system applies scheduling rules, and know that the system is being consistent, objective and fair when assigning shifts and days off.

Schedule availability also has an impact on satisfaction levels. When staff schedules are produced by hand, they are likely to be posted no more than a week in advance. Scheduling software allows schedules to be posted as far in advance as is practical for a Service Desk. Depending on the features of the system, employees can also access their schedule over the Web, or, in some cases, by telephone - they will no longer need to come in to pick up the schedule, or call to see if they need to work on a certain day. Between the ability to affect the schedule through preferences and the potential to access it at any time, employees feel as though they have more control over, and impact on, the scheduling process.

Service Desks without some type of automated scheduling or forecasting system usually cannot effectively schedule training time, meetings or other off-phone work. They might try to schedule it; however, without a way to plan peak call times or shrinkage, training and meetings are scheduled, but may be postponed. The same thing can happen with breaks and lunches - how many times have staff members worked through their breaks or eaten lunches at their desks? Forecasting and scheduling systems help plan for the best times for off-phone activities, and thus help keep employees from burning out.

Schedule adherence reporting is probably the biggest reason for employee concern when a system is first implemented, since it can indicate performance problems with individual employees. However, it also allows for fair, objective metrics for employee performance evaluation, and it gives employees the ability to monitor, and thus affect, their adherence. Morale often improves as a result of the increased control that staff members have over their performance evaluation.

Increased customer satisfaction: the improvement in customer satisfaction levels seen after implementing a workforce management system is a side effect of two of the other benefits listed above: improved staffing efficiencies and increased employee satisfaction. That customer satisfaction will increase when there is a better match between staffing levels and workload should come as no surprise. What customer would not be pleased to have their call answered more quickly, and by the person best suited to handle it?

The relationship between customer satisfaction and employee satisfaction may be a little less obvious. However, repeated studies have shown that there is a link. Employee satisfaction is directly proportional to customer satisfaction.

Sears, the retail chain, did a study that quantified the impact of employee satisfaction on customer satisfaction and increased revenue: every 5% improvement in employee satisfaction led to a 1.3% improvement in customer satisfaction, which translated into a 0.5% increase in store revenues. IBM, MBNA, Nortel, and dozens of other companies and research firms have come to similar conclusions with their own studies. All help desks appreciate improvements in their customer satisfaction levels! Technical support operations, in particular, may be able to quantify the impact of their improvement efforts on revenue.

Reduction in management workload: scheduling software, once it has been set up, automates the production of the support operation's schedule week. Even the most basic scheduling program can turn a several-hour-job into a task that takes minutes. By being able to view holidays, vacations and other planned 'time off' requests into the future, it is possible to identify scheduling problems and plan for them well in advance.

Those are only some of the advantages that come with the ability to automate your schedule. More advanced workforce planning tools help free up time in other ways. Budget time can be a weeks-long effort of putting together the numbers to justify staffing projections for the upcoming year. A forecasting package can help demonstrate the impact that staffing requests will have on service levels, and, perhaps more importantly, what happens if changes are not made. Add sophisticated what-if analysis capabilities into the mix and the validation of budget proposals will be more efficient and effective. In addition, day-to-day time tracking and payroll activities become easier when a workforce planning system is tied to payroll. Schedule adherence features can eliminate time sheets and clock punching, and move to time reporting based on actual activity. Adherence reporting also allows documenting specific areas of excellence or improvement for each agent, so that preparing for performance reviews is easier and demonstrably objective.

A subtler plus that comes with the use of scheduling and forecasting software is improved regularity in performing various workforce management tasks. According to a survey by Professional Planning Forum, Ltd., companies using workforce management systems were more likely to produce variance reports, monitor adherence, re-forecast based on a day's activity; they are even more likely to schedule breaks and lunches! While performing these administrative tasks can add to the manager's workload, the regular examination of staff members' performance and work volume can produce a more smoothly running Service Desk. By performing them regularly, the tasks are easier to accomplish.

Cost savings: the cost savings inherent in workforce planning software flow from all the other benefits listed above. There are a few particular points worth highlighting.

By using software that can forecast and schedule for technicians with multiple skills, a better fit between the caller and your available agents is achieved. The Help Desk Institute has shown that increasing first call resolution provides an opportunity for cost reduction. Besides saving employees' time by not escalating calls, there is also a savings on telephony costs - both by avoiding callbacks, and by merely shortening your customers' wait in the queue.

Some Service Desks prefer to use full-time, rather than part-time, agents - in part because of the increased complexity of scheduling them. A good scheduling package can help identify the areas where the Service Desk can be better served by less expensive part-time resources.

Employee retention is increased, thus saving on the costs associated with recruiting and training new staff.

Purdue University's call center benchmarking studies have found that the average call center (including Support Centers) budgets somewhere between 10% and 15% for employee overtime. By optimizing scheduling, the Service Desk may be able to spend less of the budget on overtime.

Workforce management software allows organizations to 'do more with less'. Using software to help optimize schedules and future planning will facilitate the goal of better service with fewer people…and fewer headaches.

Cost elements for implementation
Cost elements for implementing Workforce Management include:
- software (and hardware) costs. If you are implementing new software, these costs are likely to be the largest component. These can vary widely, depending on the software selected. When calculating costs, do not forget to include associated hardware; maintenance and support; integration and customization; project management; and specialized software training for the software administrator
- administrative costs. Someone's time is going to be spent administering the system. Large Support Centers will require at least one full-time person dedicated to administration and reporting, while smaller Centers may be able to handle it by using part of an existing resource's time
- staff training and communication costs. Staff training should be fairly minimal. Depending on the software used, employees may need to be trained to access the system to input schedule preferences, check schedules, etc. If specialized software is not being used, the training may be limited to ensuring employees understand the importance of keeping to their written schedules, especially for breaks and lunches. In either case, time will need to be dedicated towards staff meetings to communicate the changes resulting from the implementation of Workforce Management.

Making the business case to implement Workforce Management
When should Workforce Management software be implemented? The size of your Support Center is the primary factor to consider. There are workforce-planning packages that are suitable for Support Centers ranging in size from 30 employees up to the tens of thousands. However, there are other factors that can have an effect on the decision to whether or not special software is necessary.

Fluctuating volumes: a Service Desk with a rigidly repeating contact volume pattern doesn't need software to help predict the workload. However, if the volume is very different from one day to the next, or if there are frequent 'special events' that have an effect on volume, an analysis of history may help the support operation prepare more effectively.

Multiple skills: scheduling multi-skilled technicians 'by hand' can result in inefficiencies and over-staffing and affect the quality of customer support.

Multiple channels: multiple channels - phone, email, chat, etc. - can also complicate workforce planning.

Multiple sites: consistency in scheduling across multiple support centers can is critical, especially when tasks are shared, or overflows are routed between the centers. Use of a single scheduling package by the managers of multiple sites can allow for synergy in scheduling.

SLAs: complicated SLAs are much easier to manage and report on with Workforce Management software, thanks to the software's ability to track what each staff member is doing and when they are doing it.

Off-phone time: Support Centers with aggressive training programs and different types of off-phone or response-style work, may find such software to be advantageous. Training, professional development time, team meetings, departmental meetings and customer account responsibilities all need to be scheduled and can affect a Support Center's 'shrink factor.' A workforce-planning tool can efficiently turn these scheduling tasks into a routine exercise.

A mix of inbound and outbound work: some workforce planning tools have outbound modules that help forecast and schedule the most effective times for outbound operations. If your center performs any sales- or marketing-related calling activities, software can help maximize results.

Problems with scheduling: an unusually volatile schedule can be time-consuming to manage and lead to frustration on everyone's part. The defined scheduling rules and objectivity of a software package can keep staff members happy and free up some of the Support Center Manager's time.

Return on Investment
There are some items that should be understood when preparing to calculate the return on investment (ROI) for Workforce Management software.

ROI is a measurement of the value - usually in the sense of cost savings, cost avoidance, or profit - that will result by proceeding with the action under consideration. In this case, acquisition of a workforce planning system. It also looks at the rate of payback: How long will it take before the new system has paid for itself via cost savings, profit, etc.?

ROI is not just about hard numbers. Hard numbers will be needed to justify the project. But do not neglect intangible benefits when putting together ROI documentation.
Some examples of quantifiable factors to look at include:
• management time savings in developing schedules and budgets
• new staff cost avoidance. Make sure you include the cost of recruiting, training, benefits, and infrastructure/equipment cost.
• potential reduction in staff size. Thanks to greater efficiencies, you may be able to release poorer performers

- telephony cost savings. Include the reduction in the number of abandoned calls - which increase the number of customer callbacks - as well as the reduction of hold times
- increase in first-call resolution rates. While this affects your staffing costs, it also affects the overall activities of your organization. Callers' questions are answered more quickly, allowing them to return to productive activities.

Intangible factors generally involve employee and customer satisfaction. Document what goes into the soft ROI factors that are presented: assumptions, examples and time estimates should be completely described for management. Current measurements around both hard and soft factors need to be accurate and documented. For example, if a workforce planning system will save some amount of time each week in scheduling-related tasks, it will be necessary to know the average amount of time it takes to prepare the schedule, as well as the amount of time spent on schedule adjustments. While the process is time consuming, it can ensure that the right decisions and measurements can be used as input to the project scope and objectives when the time comes to implement the software.

Several workforce planning software vendors maintain ROI calculators on their sites. Please note: every Support Center is unique, and these calculators may not adequately model your situation - but they can be a good starting place.

Workforce management software is not beyond the reach of the smaller support operation. Many vendors have responded with smaller-scale offerings and hosted solutions, where it is possible to 'rent' the software on a per-user, per-month basis. This low initial investment can put workforce-planning tools within the reach of most Support Centers.

Even if these types of solutions will still break your budget, there are options. Very inexpensive, even free, Erlang calculators and scheduling software packages are available on the Internet. The sorts of efficiencies and time savings that can be garnered by using even the simplest of tools makes workforce planning software a sensible investment for any support operation regardless of its size.

9.5.2 Ongoing operations
Cost elements for ongoing operations
Ongoing operational costs for Workforce Management include:
- Workforce Management system administration
- system costs (maintenance and support).

Management reporting
Incident volume statistics: the numbers of Incidents presented for specific time periods (hourly, daily, weekly, etc.)

Incident handling statistics: average hold times, average speed of answer, abandon rates, talk times, and after-call work for specific time periods (this information is generally collected through the Workforce Management system's interface with the ACD, but may be taken directly from the ACD)

Support Center staff statistics: schedule adherence

Forecast vs. actual reporting: actual Incident volume and staff schedule adherence as compared to forecasted volumes and schedules

9.5.3 Optimization: benefits and costs
Why optimize this process and what can be gained
The benefits of optimizing Workforce Management are the same as those of implementing it: by optimizing your schedules and forecasts you achieve better Incident handling, resulting in more effective operations.

9.5.4 Tools
Implementation
For large and/or complex Support Centers, Workforce Management software is essential for implementing the process of Workforce Management. There are many packages available on the market. For smaller Support Centers, other tools may be used to implement the process:
- 'Rules-of-thumb,' or forecasting by hand. All Support Center Managers make use of rules-of-thumb, or rough models based on experience: for example, the oft-quoted 'one technician for every one hundred customers.' However, every such model must be tailored to the customer base, employee skill sets and SLAs for the Support Center. It is possible to enhance these rough models by using historical data; a description is attached that explains the methods used. *(Annex A9.9)*

- Free or inexpensive tools: there are several resources available to help with forecasting. Most of these resources make use of the formula known as Erlang-C, which uses the average call length, average call volume and desired hold time to calculate the number of agents needed. Erlang-C contains some embedded assumptions, however, that make it less than perfect. It assumes that the arrival of calls is random - that there are no peaks and valleys - and that there are no abandoned calls. As a result, the number of required agents is generally overstated. Many free Erlang-C tools can be found by searching the Internet for 'Erlang calculator'.

- There are also shift-scheduling resources available on the web, including web-based software and Microsoft Office templates. A template is included in the chapter Annex. *(Annex A9.8)*

Finally, ACD and unified messaging software are invaluable when implementing Workforce Management. Project management software is also helpful during the implementation.

Reporting
Most Workforce Management-specific software comes with a range of useful reports and can be used with third-party reporting packages. Data can also be exported to spreadsheets and databases.

Annexes

Annex A9.1 Workforce Management Implementation Responsibility Checklist: Support Center Manager

☐ Software implementation project management

☐ Staff communication

☐ Staff training

☐ Put monitoring functions/activities in place

☐ Data analysis

Annex A9.2 Skill Definitions

Demonstrated Behaviors: Core Competencies	1 Basic Skills Definition	2 Full Skills Definition	3 Expert Skills Definition
Verbal Communication Skills	• Mature phone skills • Able to give and take concise directions • Able to describe technical issues to a non-technical audience • Mature listening	• Demonstrated interpretive skills • Translate non-technical issues into technical direction	• Mentor of…
Written Communication Skills	• Good grammar and spelling • Able to be concise or detailed based on the event. • Discreet and business-focused • Sensitivity to recipient(s)	• Mentor of…	• Evaluation of…
Customer Relationships	• Achieve and maintain high customer satisfaction • Understand key customers	• Understand cultural impact	• Demonstrate ability to raise customer relationship levels across all IT services
Problem Solving	• Identify basic/routine problems • Effective troubleshooting • Ability to present solutions • Ability to escalate	• Identify root-cause problems and solution recommendation • Identify workarounds • Ability to manage and resolve escalations	• Alternative thinking • Ability to include other groups/resources in solution
Technology Orientation	• Basic aptitude for technology learning • Monitor and maintain competency in industry standards, customer-specific technologies, trends, and issues	• Mastery of a group of products from a single vendor or similar functionality • Mastery of a single service line	• Mastery and/or certification across multiple products and functionality • Mastery of multiple service lines • Facilitate learning with peers and reports • Identify changes in direction for learning requirements

Demonstrated Behaviors: Technical	1 Basic Skills Definition	2 Full Skills Definition	3 Expert Skills Definition
Shrink-Wrap App Support	• Familiar with desktop products at average user-level • Resolve 90% of functional (how-to) issues within baseline applications • Resolve 50% of functional (how-to) issues with extended applications	• Familiar with desktop products at advanced user-level • Resolve functional escalations of applications in designated areas of expertise • Able to resolve 90% of technical (break/fix) issues within applications	• Research solutions for application • Resolve escalated issues
Proprietary App Support	• Understanding of business impact of application • Understanding of application configuration • Diagnosis, triage and documentation of issues	• Primary escalation point • Liaison with appropriate application development group	• Participate in change control process as appropriate
Operating Systems Hardware Support (desktop/laptop)	• Standard knowledge of Microsoft operating systems • Knowledge of standard operating equipment list • Knowledge of standard configuration installation • Diagnosis, triage and documentation of issues	• Advanced knowledge of Microsoft operating systems • Familiarity with Sun/HP UNIX • Evaluate hardware requests • Repair • Installations • Special configurations • Component support • O/S interactions • BIOS • Drivers • Application interactions	• Escalation point for... • Approval for upgrades • New equipment testing • Liaison with third-party vendor
User Administration	• Password resets • Lockouts • Account enable/disable • Diagnosis, triage and documentation	• Escalate to third-party vendor as appropriate • Account creation • Group requests • Permission requests • Respond to escalations as appropriate	• Administer changes to Active Directory Services

Demonstrated Behaviors: Hard Skills	1 Basic Skills Definition	2 Full Skills Definition	3 Expert Skills Definition
Corporate Proficiency	• Understand corporate culture • Understand customer's lines of business • Understand key members of customer's organization	• Understand business function • Develop business relationships	• Navigating corporate infrastructure for enhanced customer advocacy • Deliver value to all levels of corporate structure
Ticket Handling	• Categorization • Issue documentation • Timely routing/escalation • Documentation of basic-level resolution • Customer follow-up	• Resolution responsibility for escalated calls • Documentation of full-level resolution	• Review of… • Mentor of…
Ownership	• Demonstrated ability to own issues to resolution within stated SOPs • Customer advocacy	• Leverage resources for issue resolution • Ability to seek/develop solutions	• Ability to authorize and implement solutions
Escalations/Service Provider Relationships	• Understand and follow escalation process	• Document escalation process • Build relationships with service teams • Identify service gaps and recommend changes	• Negotiate and gain buy-in • Implementing recommended changes
Knowledgebase	• Use knowledgebase	• Contribute solutions to knowledgebase	• Validate solutions
Scheduling and Allocation	• Understand coverage strategies • Adhere to schedule • Follow process for planned and unplanned time off	• Recommend changes to process • Develop schedules • Allocate people to projects • Resolve scheduling conflicts	• Indicate new people /allocation requirements

Annex A9.3 Role/Skill Mapping Table

Once you've identified the skills your Support Center requires, map the skill levels to your Support Center's roles. Then evaluate each employee in light of the skills necessary to perform his or her role. Finally, within your Workforce Management system, ACD, and other routing tools, make sure that Incidents are routed to the people best able to resolve them.

	Support Center Level 1	Deskside Technician	Support Center Level 2	Team Lead	Supervisor
Demonstrated Behaviors: Core Competencies					
Verbal Communication Skills	Basic	Basic	Full	Expert	Expert
Written Communication Skills	Basic	Basic	Basic	Full	Expert
Customer Relationships	Full	Full	Full	Expert	Expert
Problem Solving	Basic	Full	Full	Expert	Expert
Technology Orientation	Basic	Basic	Full	Full	Expert
Demonstrated Behaviors: Technical					
Shrink-Wrap App Support	Basic	Full	Full	Expert	Expert
Proprietary App Support	Basic	Full	Full	Expert	Expert
Operating Systems	Full	Full	Expert	Expert	Expert
Hardware Support (Desktop/laptop)	Basic	Full	Full	Expert	Expert
User Administration	Basic	Full	Expert	Expert	Expert
Demonstrated Behaviors: Hard Skills					
Corporate Proficiency	Basic	Basic	Basic	Full	Expert
Ticket Handling	Basic	Full	Full	Expert	Expert
Ownership	Full	Full	Full	Expert	Expert
Escalations / Service Provider Relationships	Basic	Basic	Full	Expert	Expert
Knowledgebase	Full	Full	Expert	Expert	Expert
Scheduling and Allocation	Basic	Basic	Basic	Full	Expert

Annex A9.4 Software Selection Template Instructions

The Software Selection Template has two functions: it is used to collect, categorize, and prioritize your requirements; and it is used to evaluate vendor responses. It is designed for use by large organizations that have multiple groups and/or individuals creating and prioritizing many requirements that can be grouped into multiple categories. However, smaller groups can also use it by removing some of the columns and using simple ranking systems instead of more complex priority weighting schemes.

The template has three worksheets: Functionality, Vendor, and Technology.
All three worksheets are organized in the same way: requirements are listed and organized into categories. There are some sample requirements and categories listed in each of the worksheets. These are very general, and are meant to help jump-start your thinking - while some may be applicable to your business and the type of workforce planning system you are preparing to select, you should prepare requirements that are specific to your situation.

Empty rows for additional requirements have been left as "reminders" that you may have hundreds of requirements, if you're seeking a complex, feature-rich workforce planning/routing/analysis system. But even if you're looking for a bare-bones tool to help streamline your management tasks, you'll still have more requirements than the few listed here! There are four priority columns for various stakeholder groups or individuals participating in requirements development (columns can be added or removed, depending on the number of stakeholder groups/participating individuals in your organization). Each stakeholder group should evaluate any listed requirements, add new requirements, and prioritize each of them by noting a priority or rank in the appropriate "Stakeholder Group Priority" column.

The priority or rank can be simple (low, medium, and high), or more complex. For example, the following numerical codes or similar ones could be used:
• Unnecessary - the stakeholder group has no need for this requirement and would prefer it not be included
• Indifferent - the stakeholder group doesn't care whether this feature is included or not
• Helpful - while not truly required by the stakeholder group, it may be helpful
• Useful - the stakeholder group believes that this requirement makes a difference in terms of system usability/functionality
• Required - the stakeholder group believes that this requirement has a significant impact on system usability/functionality
• Showstopper - the stakeholder group will not accept a system that does not have this functionality.

If a numerical ranking scheme is employed, the "Average/Weighted Priority" column may be used to calculate the average priority across all stakeholder groups, as in the table below:

Category/Description	Support Center	Payroll	Telecom	Average/ Weighted Priority
Scheduling				
Multi-skill scheduling	5	1	3	3
Schedule adherence	3	5	1	3
Shift swapping	4	2	2	2.6

The "Average/Weighted Priority" column can also be used to determine a weighted priority in the event that stakeholder groups' priorities are not given equal weight. For example, a Support Center that is actually going to be using the tool may use a multiplier on its priorities, while a payroll group that will be viewing reports may not, as shown below (the multiplier used to weight the priorities appears at the top of each group's column):

Category/Description	Support Center (*3)	Payroll (*1)	Telecom (*2)	Average/ Weighted Priority
Scheduling				
Multi-skill scheduling	5	1	3	22
Schedule adherence	3	5	1	16
Shift swapping	4	2	2	18

As you can see, weighting can make a difference in how requirements are prioritized.

The "Phase" column can be used to indicate whether a requirement can be postponed to a later phase of implementation.

The "Notes" column is for any explanatory text associated with the requirements.

The next three groups of columns are for evaluating different systems. (If more than three systems are evaluated, the columns can be copied.) Within each group are fields for "Performance" and "Method of Performance."

The "Performance" field can be used as a Yes/No field, or with a numerical ranking, such as:
• Cannot perform this function
• Performs the function poorly
• Performs the function
• Performs the function well
• The "Method of Performance" is used with a numerical ranking. For example:
• Not applicable (used when the requirement cannot be met)
• Requires extensive custom coding
• Requires minimal custom coding
• Requires integration with a 3rd-party package
• Can be accomplished via workaround
• Requires configuration
• Out-of-the-box.

Alternatively, the two fields can be combined for a simpler system. Any columns that use a numerical ranking can then be summed to calculate an overall "score" for each system being evaluated.

The "Comments" column is used for any explanatory text associated with the product's ability to meet the requirement.

Finally, the "Demonstration Notes" column is used to capture each software selection team member's notes during vendor demos. Again, some type of numerical system can be used, or the column can be used for comments.

Annex A9.5 Workforce Management Implementation Planning Checklist: Support Center Manager

☐ Review of existing data sources (ACD, call volume history, etc.)

☐ Budget development and ROI calculation

☐ Skills map development

☐ Software requirements gathering

☐ Software package analysis and selection

☐ Software implementation plan development

☐ Identify Workforce Management-related roles (such as administration)

☐ Identify required reporting

☐ Staff communication

Annex A9.6 Workforce Management Operation Responsibility Checklist: Support Center Manager

☐ Management (or performance) of Workforce Management software administration

☐ Analysis of forecasts and schedules

☐ Attention to the monitors that have been put in place - is the right information still being captured effectively?

☐ Development of Support Center staff training plans

☐ General Support Center staff management

Annex A9.7 Optimizing Workforce Management

Forecast Incident volumes over shorter periods of time. You probably began forecasting using one-hour increments; change to half-hour or 15-minute blocks. Your forecasts and schedules will become more accurate as a result.

As noted in the Implementation section, experiment with different-length shifts.

Look at scheduling part-time staff to handle peaks in Incident volume. You may also have staff members willing to work split shifts, especially those who are attending classes or who have a second job.

Schedule Support Center staff members for longer shifts. Try a four-day week, with 10-hour per day shifts, or a three-and-a-half-day week with three12-hour shifts and one 4-hour shift. You might schedule some staff members for longer shifts on your peak days, then shorten shifts over the rest of the week - for example, if Monday is a peak day, schedule a 10-hour shift that day, then use 8-hour shifts on Tuesday, Wednesday, and Thursday, and end with a 6-hour shift on Friday.

Adjust your policies to ensure fairness in scheduling: require all staff members to work weekends and holidays according to set rules (depending on the size of your staff, you might try one weekend per month, or one weekend day per week; two holidays per year; etc.). You might also want to consider rotating schedules.

Allow staff members to "bid" on different shifts. Some Workforce Management tools allow this as a matter of course and will even take seniority into account.

Make schedules available earlier, even as much as a month in advance.

Push schedule exception approval to lower management levels. In some Support Centers, the Support Center Manager must approve all schedule exceptions. With Workforce Management in place, supervisors, team leads, or the Workforce Management system administrator can see the effect of a change and take steps to ensure that it will not affect service. Some systems can allow staff members to handle shift-swapping via business rules - for example, a system will let two staff members swap days if both have the skill sets required for those days - so no management involvement is required (beyond setting up the original business rules).

Make sure performance reviews include schedule adherence as a component, and allow staff members to monitor their ongoing adherence. Staff members will be able to see adherence and take their own steps to improve it.

Annex A9.8 Schedule Template

Schedule Date:

Employee Name	12	1	2	3	4	5	6	7	8	9	10	11	12	1	2	3	4	5	6	7	8	9	10	11
Employee 1																								
Employee 2									C	C	C	C	L	E	C	C								
Employee 3											C	C	C	C	L	C	C	C	C					
Employee 4								C	E	C	C	L	C	C	C	C					E			
Employee 5	C	L	C	C	C																C	C	C	C
Employee 6									C	C	E	C	C	L	C	C	C							
Employee 7								E	C	C	C	C	L	C	C	C	C							
Employee 8								C	C	C	L	C	C	C	C	E	C							
Employee 9											C	E	C	C	L	C	C	C	C					
Employee 10										C	C	C	C	C	L	E	C	C						
Total Phone Count:	1	0	1	1	1	1	1	2	2	5	6	6	6	7	5	6	5	4	3	2	2	2	1	1
Total E-mail Count:	0	0	0	0	0	0	0	0	1	1	1	0	1	1	1	1	0	0	0	0	1	0	0	0

Legend:
- C = Calls
- E = E-mail response
- L = Lunch
- T = Training
- M = Meeting
- O = Off

The schedule can be expanded to half-hour or 15-minute intervals and additional activity types added, if desired.

Annex A9.9 Forecasting techniques

In order to look at your future staffing needs, you must be familiar with your past. A ratio, based on your Support Center's history, can be a good, rule-of-thumb way to plan for future staffing requirements.

The ratios most Support Centers use are staff-per-customer and staff-per-incident. In order to determine your current ratio, review your problem tracking system or ACD reports to find today's staff-per-customer or staff-per-incident. Then start moving back in time: was the ratio the same prior to your last change in staff numbers? Before your company expanded? What about during the big rollout? In this way, you can see what your ratio has been over time and use it to predict upcoming needs.

Are there industry-standard staff ratios that you can use? Not really. While you can find recommendations for "standard" staff-to-customer and staff-to-incident ratios, there are many factors that affect them. For example:

Your customers' current technology. A Support Center supporting a mix of proprietary applications and older platforms will need more resources than one supporting stable, standard technologies.

The presence or absence of company hardware/software standards. Closely linked to the factor listed above, the presence of company standards can limit the different types of platforms and tools you need to support and thus decrease the number of required personnel.

Your customers' locations. Mobile employees generally require that you have additional resources to support them effectively.

Your customers' level of technical sophistication. Customers with knowledge of their technical tools will not generate as many calls as customers who are new to the technology.

Support Center tools. Many of the tools on the market today, particularly knowledge bases and remote diagnostic tools, can decrease your staffing requirements.

Your company's "appetite" for software/hardware change. A company that is frequently rolling out new applications to its employees will require more support resources.

All of these factors can have an impact on the number of staff you need. You are much better off examining your history and using it as a predictor of future requirements than using an anonymous average as your guide. One potential alternative approach might be to talk with other Support Centers that are very, very similar to your own. As a group, you can perform benchmarking analyses to determine "the best" staffing ratio values to use.

Regardless of the method you use to develop your ratio, continue to test it over time. New software deployments to your customers, additional training for your staff, and new Support Center technologies can result in modifications that must be taken into account.

Other methods of determining staffing needs involve digging into your history a little more deeply in order to build a model. Begin by figuring out your staff members' availability to answer calls. This is not just the amount of time they're supposed to be at work, but the amount of time they're actually taking calls: breaks, lunches, and other scheduled off-phone activities should be excluded. Next, estimate your shrinkage rate (the amount or percentage of time your employees are vacationing, sick, etc.). Many people use 15% as an average, but you may be able to determine it directly from your Support Center's historical data.

You will also need to figure out your utilization rate, or the time your agents spend actually delivering service to your customers as opposed to doing after-call work or waiting for the next Incident to arrive. And you need to know how many incidents you receive in a given time period (per day, per hour - however you'd like to calculate it), and how long the average handle time is for each incident, including after-call work.

Now you have enough information to establish the number of staff members you'll need. The formula is:

$$\text{Required staff} = \frac{(\text{Number of incidents})(\text{Time per incident})}{(1 - \text{Shrinkage \%})(\text{Utilization rate})(\text{Agent available time})}$$

You'll need to do the same calculation for each channel of customer communication you manage, since the utilization rates, number of incidents, and so on will be different for each one. Note that this includes different ACD queues: while you can lump every call together, you'll get a more accurate forecast of requirements per queue if you calculate them separately.

You can also look at your per-hour, or per-half-hour, statistics from your ACD. By graphing the results over several weeks, you'll see the average daily pattern. Any unusual spikes or drops in call volume should be investigated. Once you have a feel for the "real" average, you can estimate staffing needs by interval. If you don't have an ACD, you can attempt to forecast using your problem tracking system's data. However, you should remember that there is almost certainly some number of calls that don't get logged, and that call handle time is not usually calculable from these systems.

Another way to forecast your staffing requirements is to use a service/task-based model. With this method, you look at the activities of your Support Center, and estimate the skill set or type of employee needed to perform the task, the amount of time each instance of the task will take (including after-call work, if appropriate), and the number of instances of the task within a given time period, as shown in the chart below:

Service	Employee Type	Time (minutes)	Quantity (per day)	Total Time (minutes)
MS Office calls	1st level	7	75	525
Connectivity calls	1st level	15	15	225
Proprietary Application #1 calls	1st level	20	40	800
E-mail responses	1st level	5	80	400
Sum:				1950
Divide by the number of minutes your agents will provide these services per day*				390
1st Level Agents Needed:				5
Proprietary App #2 calls	2nd level	10	5	50
etc.				

* For example, if your agents have two fifteen-minute breaks, one half-hour lunch, and one one-hour training session, meeting, or other activity each day, an agent is available to provide services for 390 minutes out of each eight-and-a-half hour day.

The advantage to this model is that you estimate the time taken for all tasks, including off-phone work, and you can drill into the differences in the time it take to provide various services. However, it requires you to collect historical data on a more granular level than the other methods (particularly if you go to the per-hour level, rather than the per-day level in the example shown above).

What happens if you don't have any history? Say, for example, you're setting up a brand-new Support Center - how do you forecast your requirements? You can use the same sort of model given above, but each of the values will need to be an estimate, rather than based on actual history. (And you'll probably want to make sure you have a little padding, or a contingency plan to call in additional workers, in case you've underestimated.) Once you begin operations, you can re-visit your estimates and continue to fine-tune your forecasting.

Regardless of how you develop your forecast - even, or perhaps especially, if you use a software package - review it with an eye to upcoming special events, technologies, vacation periods, etc., that will have an impact on it. While your history can predict your future needs, there's no guarantee that the prediction will always be correct. Your own judgment should be the final arbiter.

Annex A9.10 Workforce Management Step-by-Step Implementation Guide and Checklist

Review your existing data and systems. You are almost certainly performing forecasting in some way, even if it's unsophisticated. Identify:
• who is handling schedule creation
• how schedules are set (i.e., what forecasting data feeds into the schedules)
• how schedule exceptions are handled
• current staff roles and skills.

You also need to be aware of your staffing budget, and you need to understand your management's commitment to implementing Workforce Management.

Determine the organizational structure you'll need. Someone will need to administer your Workforce Management system, whether you use software specifically designed for the purpose or use your historical data for forecasting.

Determine your budget for the implementation. Include software, staff, consulting, and implementation costs.

Determine the skills your staff members need in order to provide effective support, and associate skill levels with staff roles. Skills definition and roles/skills mapping templates can be found in the Annex *(Annexes A9.2 and A9.3)*.

Prepare your staff communications. You should explain why you're implementing Workforce Management and how it will affect them.

Identify your Workforce Management system requirements. A requirements template and instructions for using it can be found in the Annex *(Annexes A9.4 and A9.5)*.

If you will be buying Workforce Management software, research software vendors and submit your requirements (in RFP form) to those who look like good fits.

Review the responses to your RFP and select the top two or three vendors to provide you with onsite demonstrations and vendor references.

Prepare a guide, or script, for the vendors. Standard demonstrations may place too much emphasis on features you don't need, or may skip something particularly important to you. Provide your guide to the vendors.

Prepare a vendor reference questionnaire in advance *(Annex A9.12)* and interview each reference. Document your discussions.

Invite stakeholders to attend the vendor demonstrations. Stakeholders may include supervisors; team leads; staff representatives; Human Resources, Telecommunications, and IT Department representatives; and your upper management. The resource you identified as your system administrator should definitely attend. However, the overall group should be fairly small so as to ensure meaningful discussion and decision-making.

Prepare a demo score sheet, so that as you watch each vendor demonstration, you can capture your notes. You'll find that, after viewing multiple demos, details will become confused - your notes will help you remember each software package's features.

Attend the demos.

With your team, discuss the demos and reference information. If no clear-cut winner is identified, you may want to conduct a reference site visit, and visit the vendor's own site to meet the implementation and support teams. (It's a good idea to do this even if you have selected the finalist.)

Prepare a software implementation plan. Your vendor will have a standard plan, but you should adapt that for your specific needs. *(See Annex A9.6)*

Execute your implementation plan.

If you'll be implementing Workforce Management without special software, determine how you'll meet your requirements: will you need additional ACD information? How can you best track staff schedule adherence? Identify all the monitoring points you'll need, and the data you'll need to collect from each.

Prepare your forecasting system (this could be a spreadsheet or database designed to hold historical data) and set up a scheme to populate it, perhaps by importing ACD data on a weekly basis. *(See Annex A9.11)*

Design the reports you'll need to get from your system.
Prepare your schedule template. *(See Annex A9.10)*

Annex A9.11 Reference Question List

The list of questions below is designed to help you interview vendor reference customers. It's a "starter set" of questions: they are very general and can be used regardless of what features you're looking for in a workforce planning product. You will be able to think of other questions that are more specific to your business and the nature of the product you're selecting. For example, if one of your "showstopper" requirements involves the vacation request approval process, make a point of asking whether the reference makes use of that functionality, and whether they've experienced any problems with it.

- How long have you been using (the product), and do you plan to continue using it?
- What areas or modules of (the product) are you using?
- How many users are using (the product)? How many agents are (scheduled/forecasted)?
- What kind of volume do you put through (the product)?
- What sort of response time do you get (include discussion of platforms)?
- What are the best features of (the product)?
- What are the biggest problems you have with (the product)?
- What additional features would you like to see in (the product)?
- How have your systems and processes changed since (the product) was installed?

Implementation:
- how long did it take?
- what resources were required from your organization?
- did you receive satisfactory support and project management from (the vendor)?

Integration:
- have you integrated the product with any other systems or databases?
- how difficult was the process of integration?
- how has the integration impacted performance and data integrity?

Customization
- have you customized (the product)?
- how easy was it to make the changes?
- how have upgrades been handled with regard to the customizations?

Support and Administration
- how easy has it been to support (the product)?
- how many instances of downtime have you had?
- how many administrators do you have?
- when you've contacted (the vendor) for support, have you been satisfied with the quality and timeliness of the response?
- would you select (the product) again?
- what other products did you evaluate before selecting (the product)?
- what was the reason that you selected (the product)?

Annex A9.12 Support Center Manager's Role for Service Desk Capacity Management

The Service Desk Manager should either perform the following Capacity Management tasks, or ensure that appropriately skilled members of staff are delegated perform the following tasks:

- ensure that appropriate levels of monitoring of incidents, resources and system performance are set, and that the information recorded in a Capacity Data Base (CDB) is kept up-to-date and used by all parts of the Service Desk function
- produce Capacity Plans in line with the organisation's business planning cycle, identifying Service Desk Capacity requirements early enough to take account of procurement lead times and staffing recruitment
- document the need for any increase or reduction in Service Desk hardware based on the changing volume of incidents, Service Level Requests and cost constraints
- produce regular management reports which include current usage of Service Desk resources, trends and forecasts. This should include not just the volume of incidents but also any other tasks performed by the Service Desk Agents.
- calculate the impact and volume of all incidents for all proposed new systems to be supported by the Service Desk to determine the staffing, computer and network resources required to perform to service levels and within cost implications
- assess new technology and its impact on the Service Desk in terms of new incidents, performance and cost
- assess new hardware and software products for use by the Service Desk that might improve the efficiency and effectiveness of the process
- review performance testing of new systems for potential new incidents and their impact on the Service Desk
- report if that performance does not meet targets contained in SLAs
- maintain a knowledge of future demand for IT Service Desk services and predict the effect of demand on staff and performance service levels
- determine performance service levels that are maintainable and cost justified
- recommend tuning of Service Desk systems on the design and use of those systems to help ensure optimum use of all SD hardware and SD software resources
- recommend resolutions to performance-related Incidents and Problems
- recommend to IT management when to employ Demand Management, to dampen Customer demands on the Service Desk
- carry out ad-hoc performance and Capacity studies on the Service Desk
- ensure SD requirements for reliability and Availability are taken into account in all Capacity planning and sizing activity
- ensure that the Service Desk is represented on the CAB, assessing and authorising Changes
- ensure that regular and ad hoc audits are carried out on SD the Service Desk Capacity Management process.

Inspired by a list in the ITIL publication 'Service Delivery' (ISBN 0 11 330017 4).

Annex A9.13 Service Desk requirements for new applications/systems

A9.14.1 Service Desk requirements

System description
- Does a full description of the business functionality for this new application exist, if so please supply a copy?
- Have we documented the potential business risks to our existing system/s?
- Is there documentation for all the business processes and procedures?
- Do we have a description of the system processes?

Technology details
- Do we know how this application is going to interface with our other current systems and applications?
- Is there any software that has to be installed or upgraded to support the new application?
- Is there any hardware that has to be installed or upgraded to support the new application?
- Is there any telecommunications technology that has to be installed or upgraded to support the new application?
- Will this application require proactive support?
- Do we need to make any changes to the standard user workstation configuration?
- What will be the platform and operating system?

Supplier details
- What level of support will the supplier provide?
- Is it possible for us to visit other sites where this application has already been installed?

New application functionality
- Does a description of the transaction types exist?
- Are there examples of the user screen layouts?
- Description of how to use the new application
- Is there any information available on potential problems?
- Are there any documented resolutions to anticipated problems?
- Does a complete list of system messages exist, if so please supply the list?

Incident management system new fields
- What is the expected percentage of incidents that should be solved at first level support?
- Can we create any scripts or workflows to enhance incident solving?

Customer community details
- What is the number of users by department/division/location that will have access to this new application?
- Do we have the names and contact details for the user communities' contact staff?
- Have we identified the potential user community growth for this application?
- Will users have dial-in access, wireless access or PDA access etc. and if so how will these function in the application?
- What Service Desk contact methods will be used by the Users?

- What is the knowledge and skill levels of the users?

Support Group details
- Has it clearly been determined who will form the second level support staff?
- What is the availability support personnel?
- What is the procedure for contacting support staff out of regular business hours?
- Do we have all the names and contact details for the second level support staff?
- What access will be provided to support staff (e.g., dial-in access, wireless access ,or PDA access, etc.)?
- What are contact methods are going to be used?

External support services
- What are the names of external support services?
- Provide complete contact details for external support services
- Do we have maintenance contracts in place for hardware and software?

Incident details
- Are there any Known Errors/Problems, including workaround data?
- What categories will be required to log/record Incidents?
- Is there a clear indication of priorities?
- Do we have documented escalation procedures?
- Is there a clear indication of feedback criteria?
- How serious does a problem need to be before higher levels of management are notified?
- How long should each support person/team look at the problem before getting additional help?
- When do support personnel get involved or are notified when incidents occur?

Reporting requirements
- What are the report layouts and information required by the customer?
- What is the reporting frequency required by the customer?
- What is the method to be used to send customer reports?
- What are the report layouts and information required by IT Groups?
- What is the reporting frequency required by IT Groups?
- What is the method to be used to send IT Group reports?

Service Level requirements
- What processing service levels have been promised to the customer?
- What are the Service Desk hours of coverage required by the customer?
- What is the maximum call waiting required by the customer?
- What is an acceptable call duration for the customer?
- When does the customer require communication on open incidents?
- What is the expected response timings for outside support services?
- Have Service Level Agreements been produced,?
- Have Operational Level Agreements been produced?
- Have Underpinning Contracts been produced?

Help Desk security specifications
- What security access levels will be authorized for Service Desk personnel?
- Which customers are authorised to use the new application/system?
- Who is responsible for customer security?

Additional ITIL data
- What are the rollout plans for the new application/system?
- Will any other software need to be changed to support the new application/system; if so, what software and what are the new release details?
- Will the Configuration Management Data Base need new Configuration Items; if so, what are the CIs?
- Will any existing CIs need to be changed; if so, what are the changes?
- Will any changes be required to implement the new application/system; if so, which changes and what are the RFC details?
- What levels of availability will be required from the Service Desk?
- Will the new application/system need a contingency plan?
- What role will the Service Desk play in the contingency plan?

Annex A9.14 Contents of a Capacity Plan

- Introduction
- Scope of the plan
- Methods used
- Assumptions made
- Management summary
- Business scenarios
- Service summary
- Current and recent service provision
- Service forecasts
- Resource summary
- Current and recent resource usage
- Resource forecasts
- Options for service improvement
- Cost model
- Recommendations

Bibliography

Office of Government Commerce, *ITIL Service Delivery*, The Stationery Office, London, 2001.

The Diagonal Group, *Workforce Planning Guide*, Help Desk Institute, 2002.

Chapter 10:
Availability Management

10.1 Overview

10.1.1 Description

Availability Management is the control (and continuous improvement) of the availability and reliability of IT services and the supporting IT infrastructure and organization. Availability Management ensures that the requirements of the business are met.

Availability Management entails systematically undertaking preventative and corrective maintenance of IT services, within justifiable cost. Technical, organizational, procedural, security and contractual aspects have an important role in this process.

This chapter examines Availability Management from the perspective of the Support Center. It is not a guide to traditional Availability Management; nor is it definitive in scope (as an example, none of the statistical analyses that are essential to Availability Management are discussed or included).

Availability Management is a complex, technology-led process that underpins much of IT Service Management. This chapter focuses on the issues that should be known to the Support Center and discusses interfaces that the Support Center could be integral to facilitating.

10.1.2 Relationships with other processes

The responsibility for ensuring that the data required within an IT service is available to end-users is that of the process Availability Management. The organizational function that actually carries out the tasks involved can vary from a representative of end-users to the Operations unit.

10.1.3 Key inputs and outputs to the process

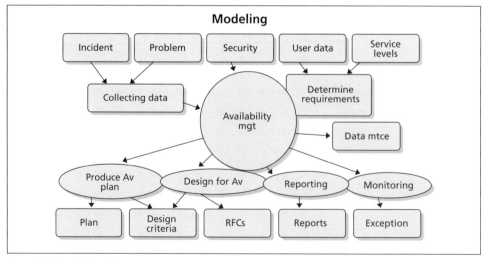

Figure 10.1 Key relationships

Availability Management is at the center of a spider's web of activities, as described below.

Configuration Management
- Manages the Configuration Management Database where information on Configuration Item failures are stored
- Obtains and provides information on the current IT infrastructure Configuration Items and mean-time between failures

Network Services Management
- Records incidents against Configuration Items

Computer Operations Management
- Records incidents against Configuration Items
- Issues requests for preventative maintenance

Support Center
- Records user-reported Configuration Item failures
- Records incidents against Configuration Items
- Provides information on incidents, problems and Configuration Items, which are the root cause of the failure
- Provides information on end-user complaints of IT service and non-availability
- Restores data as a measure to bring the IT service back after failure
- Obtains information on Configuration Items and mean time between failures
- Issues request to restore data as a measure to bring the IT service back after failure

Problem Management
- Identifies which Configuration Item is the root cause of the incident.
- Provides information on IT service downtime.
- Obtains information on Configuration Items and mean time between failures.
- Communicates the need for change, or for preventative maintenance, as a pro-active measure
- Provides information on incidents, problems and Configuration Items, which are the root cause of the failure
- Issues request to restore data as a measure to bring the IT service back after failure

Procurement
- Identifies when service contracts are not being met

Change Management
- Issues a request for change to satisfy recommendations for improvements in IT service availability
- Processes Request For Change
- Evaluates proposed changes

Capacity Management
- Ensures that the availability plan takes into account trends in system usage
- Ensures that the system monitors record Configuration Item failures automatically

Finance
- Provides financial authorization
- Provides charging information

IT Contingency Planning (and /or Business Continuity Management)
- Ensures continued availability or at least insure minimized interruption and proper restoration of IT services (either on or off site) in the case of an extended outage or disaster.

Operations
- Covers all relevant procedures including backup, restoration and security

Development
- Ensures that IT service availability is an issue considered within the development lifecycle

Testing
- Ensures that software Availability Management requirements are being met

Security
- Establishes and maintains physical and logical security

Description	Source	Importance
SUMMARY OF KEY INPUTS		
Business requirements	Customer	High
Impact assessment of requirements	Availability Mgt	Medium
IT requirements (e.g. reliability, maintainability)	Various	High
Incident, problem, change and config. data	Various	High
Monitoring event data	Systems	Medium
SLA	SLM	High
SUMMARY OF KEY OUTPUTS		
Design criteria for recovery	SCM	High
Availability Management techniques	Availability Mgt	High
Availability Management targets	Availability Mgt	High
Monitoring requirements	Availability Mgt	High
Availability Management plan	Availability Mgt	High

10.1.4 Availability Manager

The Availability Manager calculates the actual IT service availability (using service targets), correlates system-detected errors and errors reported through incident records, and validates IT service availability depending on which data source provided the availability information.

The Availability Manager's responsibilities are to:
- plan customer awareness campaign for Availability Management
- define and obtain agreement on the scope and objectives of the Availability Management function within IT, and its integration and interface with business and technical groups
- define and obtain agreement on the interface between Availability Management and other

processes e.g. Change Management, Problem Management, security, Service Level Management etc
- propose, introduce and oversee standards and procedures to meet availability requirements
- create availability plan
- decide on availability monitoring and reporting structure
- set up communication structure for availability reviews
- conduct post-implementation reviews of Availability Management implementation.

Role implementation
The Availability Manager role can be taken by a single individual, or by a team of individuals, not necessarily organizationally collected into one unit.

It is possible to combine the roles of Availability Manager (AM) and Service Level Manager (SLM), but the roles of (proactive) Problem Manager and Availability Manager should not be merged. Note that the above does not describe the role of the Support Center Manager (SCM), but it is included to clarify that the SCM role and AM role should be properly delineated.

10.1.5 Possible problems and issues
Possible problems
Commitment: it is rare to find that Availability Management goals are shared and conflicting priorities do occur. Senior management commitment should be sought at an early stage.
Tools: specific tools are hard to find and not always as described. Research the tools market carefully to ensure that the range of tools needed to support the function and to interface with other disciplines is available and cost effective.

Supplier dependency: serviceability requirements may not have been defined because of the reluctance of suppliers' commitment to provide data. Make sure all new contracts include serviceability in the requirements specification.

Quick wins
Try to establish Availability Management through evidence of rapid improvement. Problem Management and other similar roles will be the best source of such data.

Quality issues
Availability Management is a process that underpins good quality provision of IT services. By its very nature, analysis of points of vulnerability, risk assessment and building-in of redundancy, Availability Management ensures that customers are provided with first-rate service.

Security issues
Confidentiality, Integrity and Availability (CIA) are the fundamental building blocks of IT security. IT security was defined by OGC as 'balanced security in depth'; justifiable countermeasures are in place to ensure continued IT service within secure parameters. The Availability Management function has a closer relationship than most with the IT security management function.

The major security issues of Availability Management are:
- products, data and services only available to authorized personnel
- products, data and services must be recoverable within acceptable (and secure) parameters following failure
- service contracts must adhere to security policy
- countermeasures must be available to meet identified risks.

10.2 Implementation

10.2.1 The implementation process

The major support function to Availability Management arises in the activities of the Support Center (SC) team. The SCM has a more limited role.

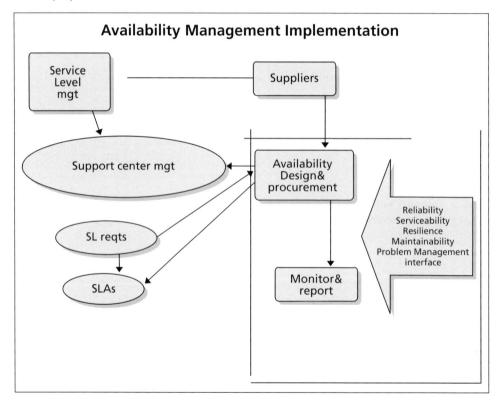

Figure 10.2 Availability Management implementation

In Figure 10.2 it is assumed that the SCM and team are peripheral to both Availability Management and SLM, and are coordinating activities.

10.2.2 Support Center Manager's role
Responsibilities and activities
Unless the SCM also fills the Availability Management role, their contribution is restricted to defining appropriate SLA and SLR criteria with the customer community and creating a monitoring function to ensure compliance to agreed targets of availability. The SCM should ensure that Incident Management processes are followed to contribute ticket data effectively to Availability Management.

A role to assist with design of policy and procedures and to contribute to ARCI/RACI matrices is recommended.

Deliverables
- SLA(s)
- SLRs
- Service plans for the education of the Availability Management function

Competencies
The SCM does not require specific competencies in order to liaise with the Availability Management function.

Key Performance Indicators (KPIs)
- Compliance with SLA targets
- Compliance with SLR criteria
- Positive customer feedback

10.2.3 Support Center Function's role
Responsibilities and activities
Availability Management covers the entire lifecycle of IT service components, from initial design to decommissioning, and meets the availability requirements stipulated by the business.

Support Center activities to be carried out in support of Availability Management include:
- establishing the availability ranges of which the IT infrastructure is technically capable (and hence scoping the service level management negotiations with the end-user representative / customer)
- planning for IT service availability
- monitoring and reporting on IT service availability
- monitoring adherence to contracts by suppliers and maintainers.

Availability of an IT service could be monitored up to 24 hours per day, seven days per week or according to Availability Management and Service Level requirements in place. From a security perspective, it is important that the IT service is only available according to required specifications to the end-users specified in agreements between IT and the business (and to those involved in the Availability Management process and software development process), and to representatives of the end-users.

Deliverables

The information that has been collected by Availability Management is now examined and evaluated to identify ways in which availability can be improved (for example weak Configuration Items identified, changes to procurement policy or the IT infrastructure initiated etc.).

A well-documented Availability Management plan is a key deliverable

Competencies required

The SC does not require specific competencies in order to liaise with the Availability Management function.

KPIs

- Compliance with SLA targets
- Compliance with SLR criteria
- Positive customer feedback

10.2.4 Other key roles and functions in the implementation process

A detailed list of the functions (and therefore the roles) having major impact on Availability Management was included under 'inputs and outputs', together with information about activities and deliverables. Note that with regard to Availability Management, the SCM role is one of coordination rather than a specific task.

10.2.5 Planning for implementation

Steps to take

Step 1: Obtain management commitment. Before anything else, ensure that senior management is committed to the project. Availability Management is neither cheap nor quick to get underway.

Step 2: Develop an Implementation Plan. As with any IT Infrastructure Library discipline, planning for implementation of Availability Management is vital. It is recommended that you use a recognized method such as PRINCE2 or PMI. The principal tasks are: project design, project plan, resource allocation, development of cost models, monitoring and plans for future review.

Step 3: Determine the Availability Management requirements. These are derived from business requirements. Processes and procedures must be in place to obtain all relevant requirements of all the IT services required. These requirements must be agreed before full scale planning takes place.

Step 4: Design for Availability Management. The primary task is to ensure that availability of IT services does not fall below the management requirements, as Availability Management is integral to the change process and to the IT development processes.

Step 5: Design for security. As mentioned earlier, see CIA.

Step 6: Produce Availability Management plan. The plan should be produced and updated periodically and should focus on changes in Availability Management requirements, IT architecture, technology and demand.

Groups to contact
If the SCM is coordinating the Availability Management implementation, the following groups must be contacted:
• Configuration Management
• Network Services Management to record incidents against Configuration Items
• Computer Operations Management
• Support Center
• Problem Management
• Procurement
• Change Management
• Capacity Management
• IT Finance
• Development
• Security
• IT Contingency Planning (and /or Business Continuity Management)
• Operations
• Testing.

10.2.6 Support Center Manager's role
A liaison role is the only requirement if SCM is not coordinating activities.

Necessary resources and relationships
• See above.

Necessary information and data
• Monitor IT service availability
• Monitor supplier compliance to serviceability requirements
• Assess reliability and maintainability of components produced or maintained by IT services
• Assess the effects of changes on the IT infrastructure
• Compare planned availability with actual results
• Downtime data for any item with distinct contractual conditions

Measurements that should be in place
• The key inputs and outputs to the process along with the necessary information and data elements above should form part of the measurement system.
• The SLA(s) will provide the architecture for a full and comprehensive list.

10.2.7 Implementing key process activities: hints and tips
What to implement first
To implement an Availability Management function successfully, there are two main elements that should be developed concurrently:
• procedures, because the majority of the work is to be performed regularly
• support tools to support the function.

A number of process/procedural components must be in place (covered in Annex A10.1 in more detail):

- record Configuration Item failures: this process records Configuration Item failures in order to identify unreliable components
- monitor availability: this process monitors the actual availability of IT services provided to end-users
- analyze service availability: this process analyzes the registered availability and failure rates on Configuration Items to identify where improvements can be made in IT system availability
- monitor contracted service support: this process monitors the performance of suppliers who have an IT service contract, to ensure that they are meeting their contractual obligations
- manage availability: this process initiates changes that are intended to improve the availability of an IT service
- forecast service availability: this process examines Configuration Item availability (reliability) and the relationship with IT services to determine the ranges of availability possible. This can be used by Service Level Management to negotiate service level agreements; it forms the basis of an availability plan wherein actions to ensure future improvements in availability are described
- improve IT system resilience: this process examines the current IT infrastructure to identify cost-justified changes that would improve the availability of IT services through improving the IT infrastructure resilience
- manage data backup and recovery: this process manages the back-up and recovery logistics of corporate data to ensure business continuity in the event an IT contingency is required
- maintain security: security consists of three major aspects: availability, integrity and confidentiality. The purpose of this process is to maintain the security of the IT services and infrastructure in order to ensure the availability of the IT services.

Things that always work

If senior management is committed, then implementation will be (relatively) simple. Keep everyone involved but keep the decision-making apparatus simple. Work assiduously to persuade your critics and your managers that 'staying the course' is the only way that the project will be successful. Do not underestimate the tendency of one or more participants to find the process complex and time consuming.

If you do only one thing 'by-the-book' make sure it is project management.

Little things that deliver big returns

Train everyone involved. It is often overlooked! Be sure to keep management informed, especially when things are going well; even bad news, so long as it is advance knowledge and not a surprise, can work to your advantage if delivered in the right way.

Little things that always get forgotten

Make sure you have enough time to carry out the activities. Even in a small organization, Availability Management data will have similar volume and complexity to Configuration Management data. Determination of business requirements alone can take many weeks.

10.2.8 Methods and techniques

Other than the tried and tested methods of managing projects, communicating and obtaining commitment, the rest is down to skill, or luck. Availability Management is often under-resourced and underrated; successful implementations cost a lot of time and money. If you can find a friendly organization that will offer a site visit, you can achieve much by taking along your executive sponsors to find out the benefits first hand.

10.2.9 Audits for effectiveness

Availability Management is unusual in that three types of audit are necessary:
• for efficiency and effectiveness of IT Availability processes
• for compliance of IT Availability Management processes with procedures
• to ensure compliance with security policy.

A project evaluation review should be carried out once Availability Management has been implemented to determine if budgets/timescales were adhered to - then prepare a more formal post implementation report (PIR).

The PIR should represent the final phase of the project and cover whether the objectives were achieved as well as lessons learned.

Reviewers should check that the following indicators of an effective Availability Management function have been met:
• reports on deviation from agreed contractual terms regarding serviceability are correct and on time
• RFCs are promptly and correctly assessed for Availability Management impact
• SLAs regarding availability are met
• forecasts on Availability Management are correct
• Availability Management compliance to procedures
• the Availability Management plan is published and appropriate
• actual Availability Management data is collected and recorded according to procedures
• interfaces to other functions are effective
• Availability Management reports are timely
• compliance with security policy.

Other items to be included are more general and include the number of service failures resulting in downtime, quality of products and services from external suppliers, as well as customer and management satisfaction, all of which are indicators of project success---or otherwise.

10.3 Ongoing operations

10.3.1 The ongoing process

The SCM and team are at the center of activities in the Availability Management process as described in this chapter. They are not actively involved in Availability Management, unless the Availability Management role has been assigned to them.

10.3.2 Support Center Manager's role
Responsibilities and activities
Unless the SCM is coordinating Availability Management activities, the role is restricted to managing the SCM team and liaising with the Availability Manager to ensure service levels are maintained.

Deliverables
None.

Competencies required
None, other than the generally expected management competencies.

KPIs
Compliance with agreed service levels.

10.3.3 Support Center Function's role
Responsibilities and activities
Depending on where the Availability Management role is located (inside or outside SCM), the responsibilities and activities to be carried out by the appropriate person are:
- calculate the actual IT service availability using service targets
- correlate system-detected errors and errors reported through incident records
- validate IT service availability depending on which data source provided the availability information
- note that the KPI here is to analyze the registered availability and failure rates on Configuration Items to identify where improvements can be made in IT system availability
- examine the IT service and item (Configuration Item) availability data and identify weak Configuration Items, and trends in IT service availability
- identify measures which can be taken to improve IT service availability
- review information from support groups such as Operations, Network Management, Support Center and Problem Management on the actual performance of the contracted external organization and compare it to the contract with that organization
- calculate the probable mean time between failures of each of the IT services, based on the service's dependency on resources and Configuration Items, and the reliability of those Configuration Items
- use data on expected ' failure to restore' times (i.e. maintainability), along with information on alternative resource, to calculate the expected availability. Maintainability covers automated failure detection, call-handling procedures, diagnostic scripts and recovery procedures to reduce restoration time. Serviceability is also relevant, e.g. an engineer from a vendor or supplier is contracted to be on site within a certain time period to begin diagnosis of a failure
- use cost / benefit analysis to evaluate various scenarios of IT infrastructure configuration, procedure changes and supplier contracts for benefit to Availability Management
- publish chosen proposals as an availability plan
- examine the current IT infrastructure using information on incidents and problems that are affecting the business, in order to identify potential changes in the IT infrastructure configuration (e.g. disk mirroring, duplexing communication lines) which would improve the resilience of the IT infrastructure to failure

- make a case for an investment in and/or change to the IT infrastructure
- forward a Request For Change to Change Management for evaluation and authorization before implementation
- establish data backup requirements for services for which he or she is accountable as part of security maintenance
- arrange for the backup data to be restored periodically, in a test of contingency procedures
- as part of the Problem Management process, in the event of a service becoming unavailable or otherwise impaired, the Support Center Manager assists with direction of data recovery actions
- interface with software and system development (generally via operability standards) to ensure that when new Configuration Items are handed over into the live environment, they have been designed and tested to meet the availability criteria required as described in the plan
- evaluate changes planned for the live environment with a view to availability of IT services
- maintain records covering which user has what level of access to which services. Procedures for this task cover authorization and creation of new user IDs, blocking user IDs for which security violations have occurred and deleting user IDs that are no longer required according to established security procedures
- pass user information to Cost Management for charging purposes, and to Capacity Management for identifying usage trends
- establish and maintain the logical security within the IT infrastructure (network access, modem dial-back, application access, terminal/PC access, and logical security levels / structures within applications) by liaising with technical domains (e.g. technical specialists, software designers, external suppliers, end-users and appropriate Technical Support Partners (TSPs).

Deliverables
Management reports and updates, documentation, and a continually updated database (or databases) are the deliverables of these activities.

Competencies required
- Statistical analysis
- Communication skills
- IT expertise (the Availability Management role is suited to a person with deep technical understanding of hardware)
- Some understanding of contractual issues is desirable and an understanding of how IT and business are aligned; business understanding can be the liaison role offered by the SCM and team.

KPIs
- Compliance with agreed SLAs

Steps and tips for maintaining this process
Step 1: Establish a Configuration Management Database. Detailed knowledge of the IT infrastructure is the most important maintenance tip; ensure a Configuration Management Database is in place. If not, take stock of all Configuration Items (CIs), determine the relationships between them and record all information about component availability.
Step 2: Determine a process for registering incidents. The processing paths, the connections between CIs that make for understanding how a single failure can create a 'domino' effect need

to be determined. Registration of incidents and problems must then be set up and documented. **Step 3**: Regular management updates. Positive results following introduction of Availability Management often take time to reflect; therefore keep management apprised of any improvements through regular reporting.

10.4 Optimization

10.4.1 The optimization process

Optimization (CMM level five) of processes will occur only when all the ITIL disciplines are being practiced to a level of integration at least to CMM level four. Some experts argue that optimization can never be achieved because best practices are themselves continually updated and improved. A good example is the gradual 'standardization' of the ITIL best practices into the BS 15000 organizational standard. As the ITIL changes, so will BS 15000, though clearly over a different timescale; either way, organizations will find that they are constantly updating their own best practices and such updating will be easier if all processes are under control (CMM level three).

Full integration of the ITIL processes is time consuming, expensive and often difficult to cost-justify. You must think hard about the value of the investment if the desire is to go beyond full control into integration and optimization.[1]

10.4.2 Support Center Manager's role

The demarcation lines between SCM and Availability Management must be clear; then the appropriate person can be assigned to one or more, (or all) of the following tasks:
- maintain availability plan: review, assess and revise
- provide input to the design and development of new IT services to ensure availability requirements are met
- provide input to the Change Management process to ensure that proposed changes to IT infrastructure and procedures are not detrimental to IT service availability
- provide input to maintenance of security policy and procedures
- establish what range of availability is available at what cost (e.g. Help Desk can open at a time between 06:30 and 09:00, and can close at a time between 17:00 and 24:00) and provide this information to the Service Level Management process for negotiation with the customer
- monitor compliance to the availability requirements as expressed in service level agreements (e.g. data from Help Desk and system monitors)
- monitor vendor compliance to serviceability criteria in (underpinning) contracts
- collect data from Configuration Management on Configuration Item reliability and from Problem Management on downtime for analysis, possibly leading to the generation of a change request for the IT infrastructure.

---

1. *To explain the difference between 'full control' and 'integration' of ITIL:*
When organizations measure against a CMM model, they generally wish to be in control of their processes and therefore target compliance with certain control criteria. At the next level (integration), the CMM criteria becomes much harder to achieve and demonstrate, and becomes more costly as well. Thus, the investment decision needs to be taken in context of cost and benefit of each level of compliance. Will spending (much) more on integration bring more business benefit than remaining at the control level?

All of the above must be planned tasks; to achieve optimization, nothing should be reactive to events. Whether the tasks are carried out by the SCM or by the team is immaterial so long as overall accountability and responsibilities are clear.

All contracts must be robust in terms of serviceability, reliability and maintainability clauses. The tools infrastructure must be unimpeachable in its ability to monitor and flag issues in advance of problems. It is likely to be the integration of the tools architecture—particularly for global organizations - that will hinder full optimization, because of the cost and because of the sheer scale of change needed.

10.4.3 Other key roles and functions in the optimization process
It is impossible to achieve optimization without involving every one of the other ITIL roles/managers in the work. Optimization of Availability Management in particular of the ITIL disciplines is beyond the scope of any organization unless every other process is perfectly harmonized and managed.

10.4.4 Future impact of this process on the Support Center
A successful implementation will cause the business community to align more closely with IT because they will depend on the high availability achieved. The SC will find that high availability will be a double-edged sword of opportunity, where ever-higher availability levels will be sought yet the business will not expect to pay more for the privilege.

10.5 Measurement, costing and management reporting

10.5.1 Implementing: benefits and costs
Why implement this process and what can be gained
Without Availability Management, it is unlikely that IT services with a required level of availability will be delivered and managed to meet the target. Availability Management helps to deliver IT services, at a known and justified cost, to a predetermined level of quality and security that is in-line with business requirements.

Without Availability Management, it is nearly impossible to underpin SLAs that are measurable, comprehensible and relevant. Contractual serviceability conditions will not be monitored unless Availability Management is in place.
There are gains in:
- service quality
- cost effectiveness
- manageability
- security
- overall planning for the IT infrastructure.

Cost elements for implementation
Besides the usual people cost, the principal costs arise in selecting and installing the spectrum of software tools needed to support the function; as mentioned throughout, a single tool is not yet available and custom solutions are generally required.

You may need to produce a detailed cost plan (and it is strongly recommended that you do this so that everyone is aware in advance of the investment required). Consult the cost manager (or financial manager if there is no IT cost manager), for advice about how to go about preparing cost data, to ensure that Availability Management financial plans follow the same standards, depreciation criteria and same terms as other organization financial plans. The cost manager may have templates, or perhaps may have collected data that will support Availability Management planning or reduce the overhead of collecting information again.

Costs will break down into the usual categories of material, labor and overhead. Make sure that the labor cost covers all of the time needed by all of the people needed throughout the planning and implementation phases and that the operations phase is properly costed to illustrate ongoing cost. The materials should cover equipment (hardware) and software and overheads should at least cover accommodation and costs that can be transferred (i.e. goods or services that can be attributed and transferred from one functional group or department to another). It is another strong recommendation that the cost of project management is clearly and unambiguously defined, and where possible, the labor costs are clearly defined by phase and milestone.

Making the business case to implement
Availability Management is no different from any of the ITIL processes. Hard data on cost and cost benefit is lacking. In the case of Availability Management, evidence is possibly even harder to find than it is for other processes such as service desk implementations, or Problem Management. This is because service delivery processes generally are 'second wave'; most organizations begin with Service Support processes and the available evidence is based on those early implementations.

The business case should focus on what Availability Management can do to support the business; lack of availability will cost money, it will cost customers, it will ultimately lead to the business challenging the ability of the IT department to deliver.

Metrics and Key Performance Indicators
The measurements and KPIs put in place should be relevant beyond implementation, throughout ongoing operations. Depending on your organization you may want to combine component availability metrics with customer metrics.

For example, percentage measures of availability (or unavailability) are commonly used; '99.8%' available ----or '0.2%' unavailable, being the opposite side of the coin. The percentages can be converted into actual time. However, the true impact of unavailability may not be obvious. The customer type metrics would typically include the frequency and impact of failures (hence a measure of reliability), duration of downtime and impact and the scope of the downtime. A failure that inconvenienced one customer for six hours may actually be worse than one that the entire organization suffered for six minutes.

Some organizations require an analysis of impact on business transactions that could not be processed, or overtime that had to be worked in order to 'catch up'. Make sure the business requirements have been met when deciding what to measure.

Management reporting
The quality and effectiveness of the Availability Management function depends on the reports produced. Typically, reports include information to illustrate non-contractual causes of unavailability, compliance with SLAs and compliance of suppliers to serviceability criteria especially regarding their contribution to downtime.

Regular reporting should be incorporated in service level reporting (possibly via the SCM); an exception reporting procedure should be agreed with customers, the purpose of which is to inform them of substantial deviations from the agreed requirements.

The Availability Management plan should be reviewed annually. Also consider the frequency of reporting; it may be useful to have weekly, monthly and perhaps quarterly reports that summarize things in different ways for different audiences.

It is advisable to limit the recipients in order to be able to establish the need for detailed reports and to guarantee the quality of reports.

10.5.2 Ongoing operations
Cost elements for ongoing operations
Other than the points that the cost of managing the project and any capital investment no longer apply, the advice provided earlier applies. See the section on implementation.

Metrics and Key Performance Indicators
See the section on implementation. However, keep in mind that improvements should be seen over time.

Management reporting
See the section on implementation. However, keep in mind that improvements should be seen over time.

10.5.3 Optimization: benefits and costs
The benefit of full optimization is an IT infrastructure that runs forever, never breaks down and has no outages---scheduled or otherwise—that affect customers. It is also likely to be very costly and complex. Continuous improvement using British Standard 15000 as the underpinning model is a more modest and achievable goal and a more pragmatic target.

Cost elements for optimization
It is beyond the scope of an overview of Availability Management to collect together all of the elements (and issues) that would need to be discussed.

Making the business case to optimize
Optimization of a single process is not possible because of the inter-dependent nature of all support processes. Lack of availability of an IT service may be related to loss of revenue and/or lost productivity, and both may result in increased costs to the organization. The cost required to optimize must be weighed against the benefits it will provide to the organization.

Consideration must be given to how optimizing this area meets (or does not meet) strategic business objectives.

10.5.4 Tools

Tools for Availability Management are not generally available as unique, standalone items. For the most part, organizations use a combination of performance management software used in capacity planning, data collection, performance tracking and simulation software, resource accounting and utilization software, Service Level Management/monitoring software and reporting software.

The performance software is interfaced to event automation tools that automate system response to non-scheduled system and application events. These include event-action engines, global event management applications and console automation products.

It is not uncommon to find tailored combinations of software that, for example, combine a suite of automated software applications that allow reporting to be carried out on the Availability Management of individual systems, to a monitor program. That program may be configured to categorize and analyze system crashes, sending the data to a central system; the central system then accumulates the data, processes it graphically and in text format and presents it for management consumption.

Annex A10.1 Availability Management sub-processes checklist

Use these annex materials to determine what needs to be in place for each of the Availability Management sub-processes and what data should be collected by the toolset.

A10.1.1 Record Configuration Item failures

*Objective: To record Configuration Item failures in order to identify unreliable components

Associated sub-processes
- Collect Details. The purpose of this process is to collect details of an incident, not of a Configuration Item failure for the purpose of an availability analysis.
- Plan Resolution. This process does not formally record Configuration Item failures, but data collated is theoretically sufficient for Availability Management purposes.

Data stores
- Configuration Management Records
- Configuration Item Availability
- Known Error Records

Tool specification implications
- System management: automatic failure detection and alerts.
- Ability to extract information on Configuration Items from Configuration Management Database / incident log / problem log / known error log:

- failure time, restoration time.
- number of failures in a time period.
- A link to service catalogue is both possible and desirable.

Management information
- Knowledge of the dependency of the IT service on the operational status of its components (service catalogue linked to Configuration Management Database).
- Downtime data on individual components: time of component failure; time of component restoration.
- Number of failures per component in a given time period.

A10.1.2 Monitor availability
Objective: This process monitors the actual availability of IT services provided to end-users.

Associated sub-processes
- Collect Availability Data
- Analyze Data and issue report

Data Stores
- Service Catalog
- Service Target
- Service Availability Report
- Problem Management Records
- Availability (Performance) Database

Tool specification implications
Specific Availability Management software is not always what it appears to be. Availability Management needs can generally be met using a combination of tools for other process domains (e.g. Problem Management) and in-house developments based on proprietary software and obtaining availability data from systems monitors.

Management information
Service availability report: actual service availability against target.

Analyze service availability
Objective: To analyze the registered availability and failure rates on Configuration Items to identify where improvements can be made in IT system availability.

Associated sub-processes
Reliability: the capability of an IT component to perform a required function under stated conditions for a stated period of time.
Maintainability: the capability of an IT component or IT service to be retained in, or restored to, a state in which it can perform its required functions.
Serviceability: a contractual term used to define the availability of IT components as agreed with external organizations supplying and maintaining these components.
Security: providing access to IT components or IT services under secure conditions.

Data Stores
- CMDB or purpose built availability database.
- Service Availability Report
- Service Level Agreement
- Configuration Management Records
- Item Availability - Configuration Item Failure Rate

Tool Specification Implications
See ' Monitor Availability' above

Management information
- Technical evaluation of failing Configuration Items.
- Evaluation of impact of preventative measures.
- Technical and procedural recommendations for improvements in IT service availability.

A10.1.4   Monitor contracted service support
Objective: This process monitors the performance of suppliers who have an IT service contract to ensure that they are meeting their contractual obligations.

Associated Sub Processes
- Manage Network Vendors
- Manage Suppliers
- Manage Underpinning Contracts

Data Stores
- Call details
- Help Desk Procedures
- Vendor Contract
- Reports
- Configuration Management Records - IT infrastructure maintenance records
- Problem Management Records - incident data relevant to service contract
- Serviceability Contracts

Tool Specification Implications
No specific requirements.

Management information
For Configuration Items serviced by external suppliers:
- call-out time
- time of component restoration
- contractual information e.g. time of arrival of engineer
- call out frequency
- maintenance schedules.

A10.1.5 Manage Availability

Objective: This process initiates changes that are intended to improve the availability of an IT service.

Associated sub-processes

See ' Analyze Service Availability'

Data Stores

- CMDB (RFCs)

Required Data Stores

- Service Availability Report
- Computer Schedule

Tool specification implications

No specific requirements.

Management information

- Number and type of change requests issued.
- Details of preventative maintenance.

A10.1.6 Forecast service availability

Objective: This process examines Configuration Item availability (reliability) and the relationship with IT services to determine the ranges of availability possible, which can be used by service level Management to negotiate service level agreements, and which form the basis of an availability plan wherein actions to ensure future improvements in availability are described.

Associated sub-processes

- Performance management

Data Stores

- Service Availability Report
- Service / Configuration Item Relationship

Tool specification implications

- Performance monitoring tools are necessary..

Management information

- Probable mean time between failures for critical components.
- Probable availability per IT service.
- Availability plan.

A10.1.7 Improve IT system resilience

Objective: This process examines the current IT infrastructure to identify cost-justified changes, which would improve the availability of IT services through improving the IT infrastructure resilience.

Associated sub-processes
• Provide IT System Resilience

Data Stores
• Infrastructure Data
• Technical Infrastructure

Tool specification implications
• Performance monitoring tools are necessary.

Management information
• Proposed changes to the IT infrastructure.
• Cost-benefit justification for the proposed changes.

A10.1.8 Manage data backup and recovery

Objective: This process manages the backing up and recovery of corporate data to ensure business continuity in the event of an IT contingency.

Associated sub-processes
• Back Up Data
• Recover Data

Data Stores
• Server File store
• Data Vault
• Mainframe File store
• Computer Schedule

Tool specification implications
No specific requirements.

Management information
• Reports on (the success of) back-up schedules.
• Reports on (the success of) test restore schedules.
• Requests for data restore following contingency.
• Reference to incident / problem.
• Configuration Item details of associated system.
• Details of (success of) restoration.
• Number of requests per time period.

A10.1.9 Maintain security

Objective: Security is comprised of three major aspects: availability, integrity and confidentiality. The purpose of this process is to maintain the security of the IT services and infrastructure in order to ensure the availability of the IT services.

Associated sub-processes
- Provide Physical Security
- Provide Logical Security

Data Stores
- Security Policy
- Critical Data Register
- Service Priority Register

Tool specification implications
- Authorization control.
- Authentication control
- Control /audit logging of access to security information.
- Control /audit logging of access to directories and information databases.
- Control setting of threshold levels and accounting tables.
- Prioritized access to requested network resources.
- Event logging.
- Monitoring usage and users of security related resources.
- Control of distribution of information.
- Control of printing of classified information (application level security?).
- Maintaining user profiles, usage profiles for specific resources.
- Reporting security violations.
- Virus detection.
- Modeling tools, ability to judge impact of new development / system on current availability levels.

Management information
- Number of security breaches (physical, logical) in a specified period.
- Report on all changes (are tested and verified against availability criteria) before being introduced into live environment.

Bibliography

Availability Management, Brian Johnson, HMSO ISBN 0-11-330551-6

In times of radical change, Brian Johnson, John Stewart and Rene van't Veen, The Stationery Office, ISBN 0-11-330687-3

Service Delivery, Various authors, The Stationery Office, ISBN 0-11-33017-4

Chapter 11:
IT Service Continuity Management

11.1 Overview

11.1.1 Description

The purpose of the IT Service Continuity Management (ITSCM) process is to ensure that the IT organization can continue to provide services in the event of an unlikely or unexpected disruption to the IT infrastructure. This process should be seen as being a fundamental part of an overall Business Continuity Management process, which considers all the elements required to operate a business function, including the IT infrastructure.

In the event of a major disruption, it will be necessary for the Support Center to continue to provide support for the IT services which will continue to operate, though IT operations may possibly be at a reduced level. It is essential that the continued operations of the Support Center are included in any plans for the continuity of IT services.

11.1.2 Relationships to other processes

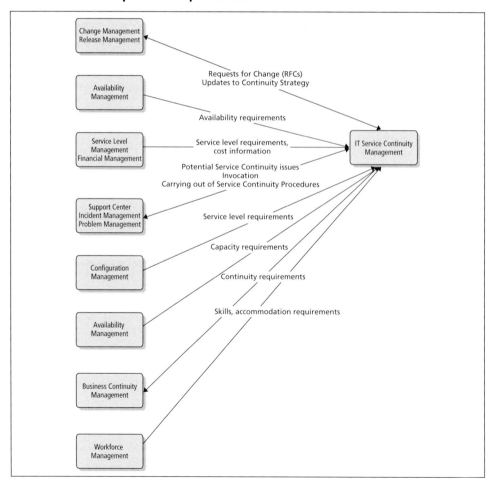

Figure 11.1 Relationships to other processes

Ensuring the continuity of IT services in the event of a disruption requires a thorough understanding of IT services provided and how they operate under normal circumstances. The ITSCM process must be aware of and take account of any factors that affect the operation of IT services, including all processes used to manage IT services. The following processes have particularly strong relationships with ITSCM.

Support Center, Incident Management and Problem Management: these operational procedures must continue to function effectively throughout any disruptions; the ability to resolve incidents will be even more important since users will probably have reduced levels of service. The Support Center will have a key role during any transition to a failover site, keeping users informed of progress.

Change Management and Release Management: it is vitally important to ensure that any changes made to an IT service are considered for their impact on the service's continuity arrangements.

Configuration Management: understanding the infrastructure components which make up an IT service enables effective risk analysis and provides details of what components need to be considered for a failover site.

Service Level Management and Financial Management: users' requirements for IT service levels must be understood to determine an acceptable level of contingency at an acceptable cost.

Capacity Management: the capacity and performance requirements of a service in a disrupted state must be considered when planning the capacity of the service.
Several processes outside IT Service Management also have an influence on ITSCM, including:

Business Continuity Management: this process identifies critical business functions and the impact of their unavailability

Workforce Management: plans for continuity of key skills must be in place as well as plans for transportation, lodging and meals for staff working at a remote failover location.

11.1.3 Key inputs and outputs to the process

Inputs	Source	Importance
Service Catalog. This document, produced by the Service Level Management process, details all the services delivered by the IT department.	Service Level Management	High
Service Level Requirements. Also a product of the Service Level Management process, these detail service levels that users require under normal circumstances and in a disaster situation.	Service Level Management	High
Business Impact Analysis. Produced as part of Business Continuity Management, this establishes the impact to the organization of the disruption or loss of each IT service provided.	Business Continuity Management	High
Comprehensive configuration details of each service. Provided by the Configuration Management process and ideally held in a Configuration Management Database (CMDB), this will be used in the analysis of risks to the infrastructure and to design contingency solutions.	Configuration Management	High

Outputs	Source	Importance
A risk analysis for each IT service, identifying risks, vulnerabilities and proposed risk reduction methods, recovery options and mitigations.	IT Service Continuity Management	High
A strategy report identifying the approach toward continuity, business-critical services, priorities, costs, and timescales.	IT Service Continuity Management	High
A contingency plan with details of precisely how the contingency solutions will operate, from invocation of the plan through transition to the failover solution, operation of the solution, and reversion back to normal operations. This plan should be thoroughly tested; the results of those tests, including timings, problems encountered, and suggestions for improvements should be attached to the plan.	IT Service Continuity Management	High
A risk analysis for each IT service, identifying risks, vulnerabilities and proposed risk reduction methods, recovery options and mitigations.	IT Service Continuity Management	High
A strategy report identifying the approach toward continuity, business-critical services, priorities, costs, and timescales.	IT Service Continuity Management	High

11.1.4 Possible problems and issues

Lack of management commitment and funding: IT Service Continuity Management is like an insurance policy - you pay the premiums, but hope that you never have to make a claim. The problem is that providing continuity solutions for IT services can be expensive and it can be difficult to secure funding for something that might never be used. Determining the cost-effectiveness of continuity measures requires two important steps:

• establish the impact of the unavailability of a business function
• determine the IT services that support that function.

Keeping the contingency plan up to date: as noted earlier, it is critical to ensure that any alteration in the way a service is delivered is reflected in the contingency plan for that service. Changes not reflected could cause problems if the contingency plan is ever invoked.

11.2 Implementation

11.2.1 The implementation process

The ITSCM lifecycle is summarized in Figure 11.2 below. Each stage is described in more detail later in this chapter.

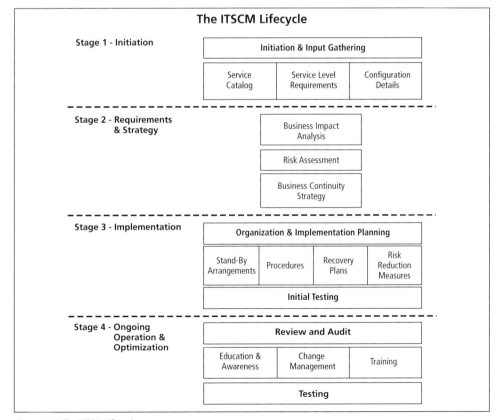

Figure 11.2 The ITSCM Lifecycle

11.2.2 Support Center Manager's role

The Support Center Manager (SCM) has a key role in the implementation of an organization-wide ITSCM plan. Because support is a key element of service, this area is critical in a disaster situation. The SCM works with the ITSCM Manager in each stage to ensure the role of the Support Center is understood and achievable in the recovery process of all services as well as the recovery of the Support Center itself.

The SCM has input into the Business Impact Analysis and works with specialists to perform a Risk Analysis of the Support Center itself. In addition, the SCM agrees and approves the strategy for risk reduction and disaster recovery. The SCM also produces the elements of the overall recovery plan for the Support Center and is responsible for initial and subsequent testing of the Support Center recovery plan. The SCM chairs a post-test review meeting to ensure any lessons learned are incorporated into the plan.

Deliverables
- Sign-off of the Business Impact Analysis
- Sign-off of the strategy
- Sign-off of the recovery plan to meet all the requirements of the Support Center

11.2.3 Support Center Function's role

All Support Center staff must be fully aware of their role in any planned recovery procedures. Fundamentally, they must be aware of the location of the Support Center following a disaster and the procedures that will be followed. Staff members will also play a key role in all tests related to the recovery plan. Staff should be rotated through the testing processes to enable as many people as possible to become familiar with the recovery procedures.

11.2.4 Planning for implementation

Before embarking on an ITSCM implementation project, it is essential to obtain the support and sponsorship of senior management. This level of support is critical to a successful implementation and must include adequate financial backing.

Once support is obtained, a team should be assembled and a project initiated to implement the ITSCM plan. If possible, this team should include be the same people who will have ongoing responsibilities for ITSCM, though temporary external specialists may be used during the implementation phase.

Groups to contact
Disaster Recovery suppliers who may be required to supply some of the external contingency:
- offsite storage suppliers
- real estate agents for possible accommodation provisions
- fire protection services
- disposal
- insurance
- security systems
- uninterruptible power supply system providers
- external specialists.

Necessary resources and relationships
In addition to expert specialists and ITSCM software tools, it is wise to involve experienced project management personnel and robust tools in the implementation. Strong relationships with Business Continuity specialists, Risk Management personnel, security staff and relevant external suppliers are very important to building a successful plan.

Necessary information and data
The BIA and Risk Analysis will produce all information required to proceed with implementation of the ITSCM process.

Measurements that should be in place
- All services covered by the Business Impact Analysis
- All locations covered by the Risk Analysis
- Recovery procedures written
- ITSCM plan produced and initial test conducted

11.2.5 Implementing key process activities: hints and tips
Things that always work
It is very important to make the test of the ITSCM contingency plan as realistic as possible. For example, banning all access to the data center and staff by the test team will most closely mimic an actual disaster scenario.

Little things that always get forgotten
When conducting a Business impact Analysis (BIA), do not forget the application that started on someone's PC and has now developed into a business critical application.

When conducting a BIA, do not just speak to managers and do not just consider financial impact. Think of all the possible impacts including impact to company reputation and impact to customer relationships.

When conducting a Risk Analysis, identify single points of failure in the staff as well as in the hardware and network configuration

All changes must be assessed for their impact on the ITSC plans, so do not forget to make sure the change process is updated during the ITSCM implementation phase.

11.2.6 Key process activities
This section contains details of the key activities to implement ITSCM. These are:
- acquire the Service Catalog
- acquire the Service Level Requirements
- conduct a Business Impact Analysis
- conduct a Risk Analysis and Risk Management
- produce a strategy including the appropriate continuity solutions
- produce an integrated IT Service Continuity Plan
- test the plan
- maintain the plan.

In addition to the activities above, you should conduct an awareness briefing for senior management with a presentation of the findings resulting from the business impact and risk analysis. This can take the form of a workshop during which the various options could be discussed.

Acquire the Service Catalog
The IT organization must define and document the services it provides. The mechanism for this, the Service Catalog, should contain basic details about the services such as hours of operation and hours of support. This document is produced and maintained by the Service Level Management team.

Acquire the Service Level Requirements
Before finalizing Service Level Agreements (SLAs) and Operating Level Agreements (OLAs), the SLM team will need to understand business requirements as well as the ability to deliver against the requirements. A key aspect of an SLA is the content on continuity covering basic details about the planned recovery time following a major disaster. Developing this content will involve ITSCM staff as well as the SLM staff; Support Center requirements will be of paramount importance as the ability to recover the Support Center it self will be vital following a disaster.

Business Impact Analysis
A Business Impact Analysis (BIA) is part of the business continuity function. This analysis will assess the criticality of each service in order to ascertain its relative business priority, and therefore the recovery order and level of recovery required. For example analysis may indicate that a reduced level of service at the Support Center may be acceptable for a defined period of time while full recovery is in operation.

Input for the business impact analysis will be obtained through a series of structured interviews with business representatives. Interview data presents a clear picture of the nature and timing of any required continuity measures to meet business needs. This involves:
- assessing the potential impact of loss of services to employees and clients
- determining key deliverables from each service and essential timings
- identifying any legal, political, moral or business obligations
- determining the extent and nature of any manual backup procedures
- assessing the impact of loss of services (impact could be financial, legal, moral, political etc.)
- interviews should also be performed with Support Center and IT staff to ensure a full appreciation of the impact following loss of service. The findings from the analysis should be documented in a report and updated regularly.

The BIA exercise has other benefits to IT and to the business areas:
- it helps improve communications between the business areas and the IT department. The BIA provides tangible evidence that the management of IT Services is aligned
- it facilitates any future introduction or review of agreements over the levels of service to be provided to business areas
- it assists in the planning and design of the IT service infrastructure that underpins the various business processes

- it provides an understanding of the impact and risks involved when making changes to the IT infrastructure
- it assists in prioritizing the resolution of the underlying problems that may jeopardise the ability to meet service levels
- it surfaces any communication gaps such as having access to toolkits and alternate contact numbers, as well as any access gaps such as physical access to required premises.

Risk analysis

The goal of risk analysis is to reduce the possibility and impact of a disaster and to ensure a speedy recovery is possible should one actually occur. A risk analysis identifies possible threats and ascertains vulnerabilities. Business case cost justifiable countermeasures to the identified threats should be documented in the report in the areas of hardware, physical layout of equipment, backups, software, security, documentation, skill levels, and network infrastructure.

Specific areas that need to be addressed in the Support Center will be:
- people - the most important part of the Support Center will be the front line staff who take the calls. The risk analysis needs to assess skill levels and dependency on individuals as well the whole team
- technology - the system being used for call taking as well as the actual data will need recovery so backup strategy (including off-site storage) must be assessed
- telephony - resilience to failure of the telephony will need to be assessed
- operating procedures
- logistics, including getting to the backup sites, interstate accessibility, and airport dependencies.

Production of strategy including the appropriate continuity solutions

The output of business impact analysis and risk analysis should form the overall continuity strategy. This is likely to be a combination of risk reduction measures as well as recovery options or continuity solutions. Once the risk analysis has been carried out, and the results correlated with the business impact information, the most suitable option for system recovery will have to be identified. This must take into account the suitability of any available internal facilities and the identification of suitable external providers. There are various options available as follows:
- manual workarounds and backup: this may be an effective interim measure, but most services cannot be provided this way. Paper backups work for a limited period in the Support Center, providing telephone and staff availability
- reciprocal arrangements : this is where resources are shared with another organization. This is a possibility for Support Centers, but not a practical long-term solution
- gradual recovery (also known as Cold standby): this provides accommodation with environmental infrastructure but no computer equipment. This can be internal, third party fixed or third party mobile and would provide accommodation for the Support Center staff
- intermediate recovery (also known Warm standby): this provides replacement-computing equipment ready to use in a suitable environment on which services can be recovered relatively quickly. This can be internal, third party fixed or third party mobile portable where the computer equipment is contained in a trailer and transported to the site by truck

- immediate recovery (also known as Hot standby): this means dedicated computer equipment mirroring critical business systems is ready to take over live running immediately with no loss of data (continuous availability in Availability Management terms).

Production of an integrated IT Service Continuity Plan

The purpose of the IT Service Continuity Plan is to provide complete documentation for the continuous availability of critical IT services identified during the BIA. It is essential that this plan is incorporated into the overall Business Continuity Plans. In accordance with industry best practice, the continuity plan should encompass:

- business requirements for disaster recovery
- essential services covered by the plan with recovery priority ratings
- business continuity team members and their duties
- names (individuals and organizations), telephone numbers and addresses of all relevant contacts
- a description for disaster detection and impact assessment up to the point of invoking the plan
- a description of the disaster recovery procedures
- guidelines on salvaging equipment from the disaster site and arranging cleaning and repair as necessary with details of possible contacts
- all relevant insurance details
- procedures following failure of air conditioning or power
- procedures invoked when changes are implemented that affect the contingency plan.

The plan should interface with the recovery procedures for the systems and applications.

The organization-wide Business Continuity Plans and IT Service Continuity Plans will cover the recovery of the organization as a whole. The Support Center is often not integrated into this process as well as it should be. The services provided by the Support Center are clearly vitally important to all organizations and should be integrated into the overall recovery process.

Testing the plan

It is important that the plan is tested as soon as possible after it is produced. Clear Terms Of Reference (TOR) should be produced for the test including definition of acceptance criteria and identification of who needs to be involved during the test.

During the test, it is recommended that an independent observer documents any deviation from the plan and milestones achieved.

Following the test, a short report should be produced that defines deviations from the plan, performance against recovery criteria, and recommended changes to the plan. This report should be presented as part of a post test review.

Ongoing maintenance of the plan

The plan must be maintained to ensure it is current and up to date; further details of this are included later in the chapter. It is imperative that the plan is considered as a Configuration Item (CI) in its own right and that all changes are reviewed for their potential impact on the plan.

11.2.7 Methods and techniques

Figure 11.3 illustrates the Business Impact Analysis Method. Business impact analysis (BIA) focuses on the business needs of IT services. Being without any IT service will have a detrimental affect on the business but the severity of the impact will vary with time and also be affected by its point in the processing cycle. The impact of the loss of a real time service, such as trading in the money market, will be felt immediately while the business may cope for some time without other services. As well as establishing the urgency of each service, the BIA identifies the minimum requirements of each service to meet the critical business needs. In conducting a BIA, it is best to begin with a message to participants outlining the purpose and process for the BIA. This message should include a questionnaire to aid interviewee preparation *(see Annex A11.1 for a sample)*

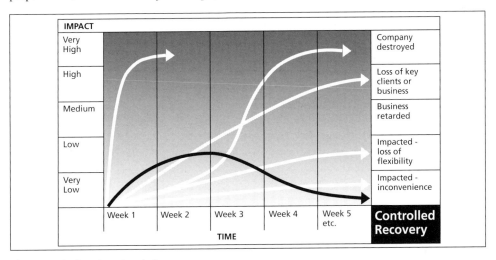

Figure 11.3 Business impact analysis

Risk Analysis - Figure 11.4 below illustrates the risk analysis and risk management activity.

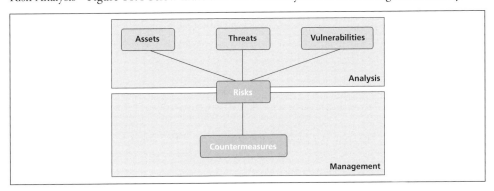

Figure 11.4 Risk analysis

Risk analysis begins with the identification of assets that includes anything required to run the services (a Configuration Management Database will hold this information). This includes hardware, software, people, documentation, network equipment, telephony equipment, buildings and so on. Threats need to be associated with each asset type and these will differ depending on the asset. For example, potential threats to hardware include hardware failure, fire, flood and theft whereas potential threats to people include sabotage, absenteeism and lack of knowledge. The next stage is to analyze the likelihood of realization of the identified threat and the potential impact if it does happen. With this information cost-justifiable countermeasures can be taken from mirroring the whole installation to backing up data and skills transfer. There are specialist tools available to assist with conducting a risk analysis review. These tools normally contain a large database of possible countermeasures.

Production of the continuity plan - the actual plan is normally a simple word-processed document outlining actions to be taken and by whom in the event of a disaster occurring. Again, there are specialist tools available that assist with the production and maintenance of a plan.

Testing the plan - during testing of the plan, it is recommended that an independent observer documents any deviation from the plan and milestones achieved.

Following the test a short report should be produced, which defines:
• deviations from the plan
• performance against recovery criteria
• recommended changes to the plan.

This report will be presented as part of a post test review.

It is recommended that tests should simulate real life as much as possible. For example, ensure that data is only used from the offsite backup store and ensure that no one calls the live Support Center to request passwords, as the live Support Center may not be in place after invocation.

The Support Center will need to be sure that it can recover its services if a disaster occurs. The center may also have a role to perform during the recovery of other areas, perhaps undertaking the role of independent observer.

11.2.8 Audits for effectiveness

The following checklist lists items to audit to ensure the process has been implemented fully.

Activity/Item	Confirmed date
Aware of services provided and key customers	
Business Impact Analysis conducted, results analysed and reports produced	
Risk Analysis performed and prioritized risk reduction measures implemented	
Overall strategy recommendation produced and signed off by senior management	
Risk Management activities performed to mitigate against the possibility of disasters affecting service operation	
Service Continuity plan produced including full details of locations for recovery and details of transportation and accommodation, if working away from normal place of work	
Initial test conducted to include location facilities, telephony equipment, PCs and servers, network connectivity, access to users and customers	
Test report produced	
Test post-mortem meeting conducted, actions agreed and plans in place to update the plan	
Service Continuity plan is integrated into the overall Change Management process	

11.3 Ongoing operation

11.3.1 The ongoing process

After initial implementation, IT Service Continuity Management is concerned with the maintenance and testing of the continuity plans. It ensures that staff is aware of the plans and properly trained, auditing compliance with related procedures and coordinating any invocations of the plans.

It is critical that once developed, the IT Service Continuity strategy, plans and procedures are maintained and updated when necessary - not placed on a shelf and forgotten. There must be a good interface with Change Management to ensure that all significant changes are assessed for impact on service continuity. Where a proposed change will degrade the level of continuity currently present, this risk needs to be assessed as part of the overall change assessment. The change request could be rejected, the additional risk formally accepted or resource allocated to update the continuity strategy and plans to address the change. In other cases where the change necessitates a minor update to continuity plans or preparations, this needs to be identified, recorded and tracked to completion.

Major projects (e.g., a change in Support Center locations, a major change in Support Center technology, the introduction of additional services for Support Center customers) should all trigger a review of Service Continuity strategy and plans. Depending on the size and nature of the change, this may require Business Impact Analysis to be revisited and almost certainly will require further Risk Analysis to be conducted. It is important to foster strong communication within the organization, with partners and with customers so that any business plans or proposed projects that will affect the Support Center are identified as early as possible so that planning can take place.

Continuity plans should be tested on a regular basis, at least annually but preferably every six months. A testing program should include a range of test exercises. These could include:
- a tabletop 'walk-through' of the plan with key Support Center staff
- a detailed technical test of one aspect of the Support Center's technology
- a more involved test involving relocating the Support Center operation to an alternate location and recovery of the necessary facilities at that location.

In many instances the recovery of the Support Center may only be one element of a much wider test of IT and Business Continuity plans. In planning each test, a realistic scenario presenting a slightly different challenge to previous exercises should be developed and documented. Each test exercise should seek to break some new ground, perhaps by testing an area which has not been tested before, an area where there has been significant change, or by taking the test further than previous exercises by involving customers, key partners and interfaces with other systems.

One key benefit of testing is in the training and experience it gives staff in performing critical recovery procedures and in operating in the recovered environment. As noted earlier, staff involved in testing should be rotated to ensure that knowledge and experience is spread as broadly as possible.

Testing must be planned carefully to ensure that functionality is tested as much as possible without causing unnecessary impact on the normal functioning on the Support Center. For complex testing situations where critical live operations could be jeopardized, planning the test should involve a risk analysis exercise aimed at identifying and managing the operational risks involved.

Objectives should be identified in advance for each test exercise. These objectives may include the recovery of specific Support Center facilities within a certain time period, the validation of a new recovery procedure, the training of staff in a particular aspect of the recovery operation, or the testing of corrective actions taken following a previous test.

During any testing exercise a log and timeline of actions, events, issues and decisions should be maintained. Following each exercise, a post test review should be carried out to discuss achievements and any issues encountered, to ensure that the lessons learned are not lost and to plan any corrective actions necessary.

Another ongoing activity is that of promoting awareness of the continuity plans and the role that staff would be expected to play in the event of an invocation. This information should be included as part of orientation training for new Support Center staff. Annex A11.2 contains example templates for the following documents used for testing the plan:
- IT Service Continuity Management Test Planning Form
- IT Service Continuity Management Testing Schedule
- Post Test Review Contents Page.

IT Service Continuity Management should seek to review and audit procedures such as those for making and verifying backups, updating continuity plans, and maintaining recovery facilities. This is aimed at ensuring compliance; where non-compliance is identified, corrective action should be instigated.

In the event that the Service Continuity plans are invoked, IT Service Continuity Management should ensure that the invocation is properly managed and that recovery and restoration actions are properly coordinated.

11.3.2 Support Center Manager's role
Responsibilities and activities in ongoing operation
The Support Center Manager works closely with both Business Continuity Management and ITSCM staff to ensure that measures exist to support continued operation of the Support Center according to agreed service levels during any interruption to normal operations. The Support Center Manager owns the part of the overall IT continuity plan which deals with continuity of the Support Center, and is responsible for ensuring that it is maintained and updated as continuity requirements change over time.

The SCM is involved in assessing change requests for impact on the Support Center, part of which involves considering whether the continuity strategy would be compromised or whether an update to plan will be required. The SCM should review the continuity plan at least annually to ensure that it still meets business requirements.

The SCM participates in determining the schedule and objectives for testing the parts of the plan involving the Support Center. The SCM also plays an active role in testing exercises to ensure familiarity with the plans. However, sometimes another staff member should perform the role to simulate a situation in which the Support Center Manager is unavailable. Following tests, the SCM provides input to post test review processes and where issues are identified, the SCM ensures that corrective actions are tracked and completed.

The SCM ensures that all Support Center staff are aware of the continuity plans and their roles in the event of an invocation and ensures that staff conform to the ITSCM process and procedures, including participation in audit activities, when appropriate.

Deliverables
- Sign off on testing schedule and objectives
- Input to post test review meeting and report
- Support Center continuity plan awareness materials
- Input to induction training materials
- Input to change request impact assessments

Competencies
- Knowledge of Support Center Service Level targets
- Good understanding of Support Center operations
- Familiarity with Support Center continuity plans
- Other normal competencies such as managerial skills, business awareness, negotiation skills, numeric skills etc

KPIs
- Frequency at which Support Center continuity plan exercises occur
- Post test reviews undertaken following tests
- Frequency at which Support Center continuity plan is reviewed
- Number of change requests assessed for impact on Support Center continuity

11.3.3 Support Center Function's role
Responsibilities and activities
Support Center staff is responsible for carrying out any routine procedures in their area that are required in order to support the continuity plans. This may include updating contact lists, ensuring that emergency backup telephones are charged, and maintaining a supply of paper based call-logging forms as part of manual backup procedures.

Where staff identify changes or issues that may affect Support Center continuity, they report these to the SCM. Support Center staff is also responsible for familiarizing themselves with continuity plans and take part in testing exercises in order to practice the procedures involved. In many instances the Support Center staff will be the first to become aware of a major Incident that necessitates the invocation of continuity plans. Depending on the Incident Management process, and more specifically the procedures for handling major Incidents, Support Center staff may play key roles in determining whether an invocation should be initiated.

During invocation, Support Center staff perform their roles as defined within the Support Center continuity plan which may involve traveling to an alternate location and working as members of a recovery team to restore service.
When continuity plans have to be invoked for other areas of the organization but the Support Center is not directly affected, staff will often still have to perform a role. They may need to provide communication and awareness about the event, updates on progress towards restoration and prioritization of support resources between 'business as usual' incidents and recovery operations.

Deliverables
- Updated contact details
- Updated procedural documentation

KPIs
- Percentage of staff with experience of testing Support Center continuity plans

11.3.4 IT Service Continuity Manager's role
Responsibilities and activities
The IT Service Continuity Manager is responsible for the ongoing maintenance and testing of the integrated overall IT Service Continuity strategy and plan. The IT Service Continuity Manager should work with the Support Center Manager to ensure that the continuity strategy and plan for the Support Center continues to meet the business needs and integrates smoothly with the overall continuity plan covering all service areas. This should include the provision of the necessary skills, tools and templates to support the ongoing maintenance of the continuity plan.

The IT Service Continuity Manager is responsible for maintaining a testing schedule and liaising with the Support Center Manager to determine scheduling, objectives and resources when tests will involve the Support Center.

Overall responsibility for promoting awareness of the continuity plans and ensuring that appropriate training is provided to recovery team members lies with the IT Service Continuity Manager. This individual should ensure that the IT Service Continuity Management process is complied with, by coordinating regular audit and review activities, so as to provide assurance to senior management as to the effectiveness of continuity provisions.

Deliverables
- Overall IT continuity strategy
- Integrated overall IT continuity plan
- Testing schedule
- Post test review reports
- Input to the impact assessment of proposed changes
- Updated business impact and risk analysis data due to changes
- Provision assurance to senior management

Competencies required
- Business Impact Analysis skills
- Risk Analysis skills
- Continuity Planning skills
- Project Management skills
- Normal competencies for any service management role such as good interpersonal skills, analytical skills etc

KPIs
- Number of tests carried out per quarter
- Number of tests occurring as scheduled
- Number of post test review reports produced
- Number of updates to business impact data
- Number of risk assessment carried out
- Number of instances of non-compliance to ITSCM policies

11.3.5 Steps and tips for ongoing operations
Ensure that there is a close interface with Change Management to make sure that proposed changes are assessed for potential impact on continuity plans. Have procedures to ensure that the plans are updated to reflect any changes that are implemented.

Keep plan documentation under change control and version control, with procedures to identify when, why and who has made changes to the plans. Use version control procedures to ensure that everyone is working from the same version of the continuity plan.

Build good communication channels with key business functions, partners and customers, to allow early identification of major projects that are going to impact the Support Center and require the continuity strategy and plans to be reviewed.

Review the Support Center continuity plan against business requirements and service level targets at least annually to ensure that it still meets those needs.

11.4 Optimization

11.4.1 The optimization process

Depending on the starting point, it may not be possible to immediately develop and implement all of the resilience desired to support continuity of the Support Center operation. Sometimes telephony or network changes will require that time is taken to build a business case, obtain funding, and initiate a project to plan, test, and implement. In some cases these changes will have to wait for larger plans for upgrading and improving the IT infrastructure. Similarly, changes to support contracts may have to wait until an appropriate point in the contract lifecycle at which time the contract can be renegotiated. Continuity planning cannot wait until all the ideal components are in place, so plans have to be made based on what is currently available and then updated and optimized as improvements are made to the infrastructure or new contracts are signed.

Regular testing of continuity plans is a major component of optimization. It allows issues to be identified and resolved, procedures to be adjusted, and staff to learn the process, all of which provide for improved recovery times. As noted earlier, staff participation in testing is very valuable because the experience that staff pick-up during testing helps instill a recovery mindset that improves their ability to respond and to recognize potential continuity issues in their normal work.

Audit and review activities also play a part in optimizing the process by identifying instances when plans have not been updated or when changes have occurred and their impact on the plans has not been initially appreciated. Recognizing these issues and taking steps to inform staff and improve procedures can improve the effectiveness of plan maintenance.

11.4.2 Support Center Manager's role
Responsibilities and activities

The SCM constantly seeks to maintain and improve both the Support Center's resilience and the efficiency of Continuity Plans. When involved in planning meetings, the SCM ensures that all risks to the operation of the Support Center are considered and that plans support improvements to continuity provisions. When audit and review activities identify areas where improvement to Support Center continuity plans and procedure are needed, the SCM owns and track these improvements to completion.

Deliverables
- Improved procedures and plans
- Corrective actions

KPIs
- Decrease in the number of non-compliances reported by audit
- Reduction in recovery time for services provided by the Support Center

• Reduction in the number and severity of risks

11.4.3 Support Center Function's role

Responsibilities and activities

As staff become more familiar with the continuity plans and recovery procedures they may often be able to identify potential improvements. These should be discussed during tests or in post test review meetings.

Deliverables

• Improvement suggestions from the Support Center staff

11.4.4 Steps and tips for optimizing this process

Always consider ways in which resilience measures or recovery procedures can be improved. Ensure full value is achieved from testing exercises by making sure that all the lessons learned are captured and action is actually taken to resolve issues and implement improvements. Do not forget that reviews should also be held following any live invocations as again issues and potential improvements will often have been identified.

Where possible, make sure that testing validates the ability of the Support Center Plan to work smoothly alongside plans for other functions and business areas.

11.4.5 Future impact of this process on the Support Center

In the case of ITSCM, it is worthwhile to consider the potential impact of not having this process. The Support Center is often the key contact point with customers during major incidents and disaster. The criticality of the Support Center operation must be recognized and its continuity assured.

ITSCM provides a structured mechanism for underpinning the Support Center operation with cost-justified resilience measures and 'tried and tested' recovery procedures, in order to make the future a little less uncertain.

11.5 Measurement, costing and management reporting

11.5.1 Implementing: benefits and costs

The costs of ITSCM are sometimes difficult to justify as the majority of the benefits will not be realized until a major incident or disaster occurs. There are costs associated with planning, implementation, and optimization activities; costs may include the involvement of external suppliers and experts.

As noted earlier, it is often helpful to examine benefits by highlighting the potential costs of doing nothing. Some disaster impacts may be easily quantified (e.g., lost sales) while some will be more difficult to measure (e.g., damage to reputation.) The fundamental benefit of a fully implemented and tested continuity plan is that business continuity can be guaranteed under all planned for circumstances.

Making the business case to implement

Again, an examination of the impacts of a disaster should be the foundation of business justification of ITSCM. BIA and Risk Analysis will help identify the impacts and risks associated with loss of key IT services; these impacts and risks will suggest the appropriate level of spending on ITSCM. As noted above, ITSCM is very much like an insurance policy and the business decision to be made is a matter of how much coverage is desired. Obviously, it is impossible to predict a disaster and therefore it is impossible to budget precisely for ITSCM.

11.5.2. Ongoing operations

Costs

There will be an ongoing cost for any external continuity options and external off site storage activities as well as costs associated with the test.

Metrics and Key Performance Indicators

The key performance indicator will be a continuously up to date and fully tested IT Service Continuity Plan that is integrated with the overall Business Continuity Plan.

Annexes

A11.1 Business Impact Analysis Questionnaire
Annex A11.2 Testing process documents

Annex A11.1   Business Impact Analysis Questionnaire

Name:		Telephone:	
Title:		Email :	
Department:	Section:		Location:

In the table below, list all of the IT applications or systems that your department accesses as part of their normal business processes. Include main business applications, corporate systems (e.g.: email), and any departmental databases that are used. Highlight any changes that are now needed to this information, including removing systems no longer used and / or adding any new systems.

System Name	Business Impact	Recovery Timescale	Minimum Access
Internet access			
Email / diary facilities			
Telephone system / Phone Link			
Faxes / modems			

Assign a 'Business Impact' to each system you have listed above, based on the options detailed below. The ratings should be based on the impact of loss of service to your department.

Business Impact	Description
MAJOR	Potentially serious impact to the organization (serious financial, public relations, health and safety, political or legal consequences)
SIGNIFICANT	Not 'major' for the organization in the overall scheme of things, but would prevent the department from performing its main business processes
DISRUPTIVE	Department could still function but with reduced throughput, staff disruption and a potential impact on service quality
MINOR	Could be worked around in the short term so would not prevent the department from functioning as normal
NONE	Little or no impact to the department's business

Assign a 'recovery timescale' to each system you have listed above, based on the options detailed below. The ratings should be based on the requirements of your department. Of course, nearly all service interruptions will result in staff disruption, so the aim would always be to recover systems as soon as possible. However, following a major incident some disruption is to be expected; so give thought to how a service interruption would affect your department, and what length of interruption could be recovered from.

Recovery Timescale	Description
1	The impact is such that expenditure is justified to allow recovery within 24 hours
2	An interruption of up to 2 days could be recovered from
3	An interruption of up to 3 days could be recovered from
4	An interruption of up to 1 week could be recovered from
5	An interruption of up to 2 weeks could be recovered from
6	Would be OK for up to 6 weeks as long as the system was eventually recovered
7	The system does not require recovery

Consider the minimum number of staff that would require access to each service during a major incident and document this figure in the 'Minimum Access' column.
Critical Periods – for some systems the Business Impact and Recovery Timescale may differ according to the time of year. In these cases, fill out the table below.

System Name	Critical Period	Business Impact During critical period	Recovery Timescale during critical period

Are there any paper records, manuals, invoices or documents stored in your area that the department would not be able to function without if based elsewhere during an emergency? What would be the impact if these documents were destroyed? Give details below.

Signed   Date

A11.1.1 Implementation

The following checklist lists items to audit to ensure the process has been implemented fully.

Activity/Item	Confirmed date
Aware of services provided and key customers	
Business Impact Analysis conducted, results analysed and reports produced	
Risk Analysis perform and prioritized risk reduction measures implemented	
Overall strategy recommendation produced and signed off by senior management	
Risk Management activities performed to mitigate against the possibility of disasters affecting service operation	
Service Continuity plan produced including full details of locations for recovery and details of transportation and accommodation if working away from normal place of work	
Initial test conducted to include, location facilities, telephony equipment, PCs and servers, network connectivity, access to users and customers	
Test report produced	
Test Post mortem meeting conducted, actions agreed and plans in place to update the plan	
Service Continuity plan is integrated into the overall Change Management process	

Annex A11.2 Testing process documents

A11.2.1 IT Service Continuity Management Test Planning Form

System / Services to be tested	
Date of test	
Staff performing test	
User contacts	
Location of test	
Equipment required	

Test Scenario: (type of failure, day of the week, time of day, any special runs)

Test Objectives:

A11.2.2 IT Service Continuity Management Testing Schedule

Last Updated Date:			Last Updated by:			

Server / System	Date of last test	Resultof last test	Planned dates	Personnel of days	Location & eqquipment	User contacts

A11.2.3 Post Test Review Contents Page

1 Introduction
2 Management Summary
3 Objectives of the Exercise
4 Scenario
5 Achievements Against Objectives
5.1 Recovery Within Target Timescale
5.2 Provide Recovery Experience For New Staff
5.3 Test Database Recovery Following Upgrade
5.4 Validate Updated Procedure For Filestore Recovery
6 Personnel Involved
7 Equipment Used
7.1 In House Items
7.2 Externally Supplied Items
8 Recovery Times
9 Events and Issues Encountered
9.1 Erroneous Tape Procedures
9.2 Connection Problems
9.3 Application Password Incorrect
9.4 Laptop Connection
9.5 User Permissions
9.6 Database Corruption
9.7 Inconsistencies Following Restore
9.8 Space Problems
9.9 Insufficient Skills

Bibliography

Beisse, Fred, *A Guide to Computer User Support for Help Desk & Specialist Specialists,* Boston: Course Technology, 2001

Blythe, Bruce T., Blindedsided: *A Manager's Guide to Catastrophic Incidents in the Workplace,* New York: Penguin, 2002

McBride, Dione., *A Guide to Help Desk Technology, Tools & Techniques,* Boston: Course Technology, 2000

Muns, Ron, *The Help Desk Handbook,* Colorado Springs: Help Desk Institute, 1993

Service and Support Handbook. Colorado Springs: The Help Desk Institute, 2002

The 9/11 Commission Report. New York: W.W. Norton & Company, 2004

Wooten, Bob. *Building & Managing a World Class IT Help Desk,* New York: Osborne/McGraw-Hill, 2001

Chapter 12:
Customer Satisfaction Measurement

12.1 Overview

12.1.1 Description

The goal of Customer Satisfaction Measurement (CSM) is to collect, process and analyze customer feedback. CSM is used to gather:
- incident-based measurements
- periodic measurements
- spontaneous feedback.

This chapter will discuss customer satisfaction measurement from an IT Service Management perspective, but all of the principles apply to a Support Center environment as well. Customer feedback is essential for the whole service and support management process. Customer satisfaction is the ultimate measurement of success in service. Users are typically captive, and therefore have no other service option. Without customer satisfaction measurement capabilities in place, it is impossible to know how the whole process is performing since defections do not occur.

In ITIL terminology, customers and users have different roles. While both represent customers, a customer is a person who negotiates the Service Level Agreement and a user is a person who actually uses the service. Both groups are important in the CSM process.
CSM can be best used to measure the whole process, not just some part of it. The Support Center plays a major role in overall service to the user. From the user point of view, it is difficult to separate the Support Center from the overall enterprise or IT organization. The Support Center is often the only human contact for the user and users tend to blame the desk for all IT errors.

While the CSM process is not measuring solely IT service or Incident Management, the Support Center is the single point of contact (SPOC) for the users, and it is clear that the Support Center Manager must be involved in the CSM process.
It is recommended that periodic surveys are used to measure overall satisfaction to IT Services and these periodic surveys can be a sub-process of Service Level Management. Incident based measurements are usually the best tool for measuring the Incident Management process and Support Center services. In some cases, it may be necessary to conduct periodic measurement on only the Support Center.

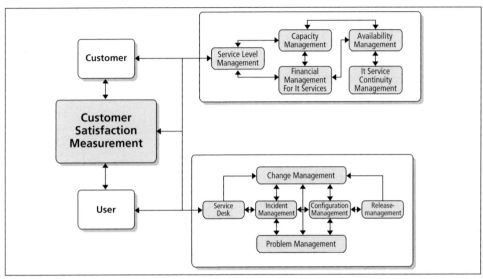

Figure 12.1 CSM process

12.1.2 Relationships to other processes

CSM is related to Service Level Management, Incident Management and the overall Service Desk/Support Center function.

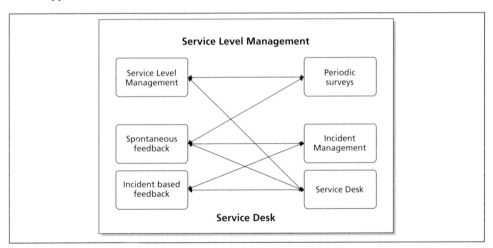

Figure 12.2 Relationship to other processes

12.1.3 Key inputs and outputs to the process

The following chart shows key inputs and outputs to the CSM process.

Description	Source	Importance
INPUTS		
Spontaneous feedback	User	Medium
Spontaneous feedback	Customer	High
Response to Incident Survey	User	Low
Response to Periodic Survey	User	Low
Response to Periodic Survey	Customer	Medium
OUTPUTS		
Spontaneous Feedback Reports	Support Center Manager	Medium
Spontaneous Feedback Reports	Service Level Management	High
Incident Survey Report	Support Center Manager	High
Periodic Survey Report	Support Center Manager	High
Action items	Support Center Manager	High

12.1.4 Possible problems and issues

Possible problems

Too many surveys: it is important that IT Service Management coordinates all surveys through the CSM process in order to avoid overloading the customers and users with surveys from potentially multiple service providers. The respondent can become confused about what service is being measured in the various surveys and 'survey burnout' can occur. Respondents may complete a survey only when they have a complaint.

Service not recognized: customers may have difficulties in recognizing an embedded service. IT service may be seen as an integrated component of an application or a network service. In such situations it is important to work in close cooperation with the other service providers to create a CSM process that provides useful information to all providers.

Quality issues

Low response rate: low response rate may indicate bad survey instrument design, low recognition, lack of interest, or survey burnout. It leads to low quality in reports because the statistical accuracy of the results is lower. The response rate should be at least 35% of the sample selected.

The reasons for a low response rate must be investigated.

Unreliable results: a poor instrument design may also lead to another type of error. If the question phrasing is poor, then the instrument may not measure what its creators intended it to measure. This is perhaps the most dangerous type of error since the survey manager may be blind to it. Thus, rigorous instrument design is essential.

Input error: statistical data is vulnerable to input errors. A typical case might be where a customer on a scale of 1-10 inputs 99 instead of 9. In a group of 100 answers this error increases the average with 0.9, which is a significant amount.

It is good practice to avoid scales with two digits and the input can be limited to allow only valid choices. In all cases you should check minimum and maximum values before reporting the results.

12.2 Implementation

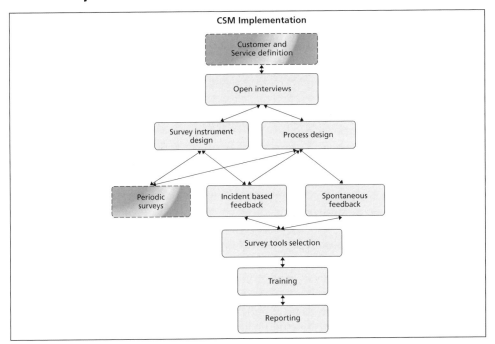

Figure 12.3 Implementation process

12.2.1 Support Center Manager's role
Responsibilities and activities

The Support Center Manager is responsible for incident based feedback and spontaneous feedback. Both processes are closely related to the Incident Management process.

The Support Center Manager can also be responsible for a part of the periodic survey process.

Deliverables
- Survey instrument design
- Sampling plans
- Spontaneous feedback management process
- Incident based feedback process
- Tool selection
- Training staff for handling spontaneous feedback
- Model reports

Competencies
- The ability to design survey instruments
- The ability to analyze results
- Good understanding of customers' business needs

Key performance indicators (KPIs)
- Response rate
- Comments on the instrument - independent of the survey or on the survey instrument if hardcopy
- Lack of errors
- Management feedback on reports

Other key roles and functions in the implementation process
- Customer satisfaction process owner

12.2.2 Planning for implementation

Steps to take
- Ensure executive management support
- Create project plan
- Define customers of interest for survey process
- Define services to be surveyed
- Design surveys instrument and interview questionnaire
- Design process
- Select survey administration tool
- Make a pilot survey
- Train appropriate staff on survey administration and response processing
- Define reports

Groups to contact
- Service management
- Service level management
- Customers
- Users

Necessary information and data
- Customer contracts
- Service level agreements
- Customer and user contact information

12.2.3 Implementing key process activities: hints and tips

What to implement first
It is best to start with interviews. These will be useful in identifying the questions to ask on the survey instrument and the interviews will generate useful, detailed information.

Things that always work
- Simple questions, open-ended questions
- Involve executive management. A message from the CEO or President will be given higher priority than a message from Department Manager

Little things that deliver big returns
First surveys usually identify some problems in the service delivery process. If these are promptly solved, customers will react very positively.

Little things that always get forgotten
It is easy to forget to inform the customer of the results, and subsequent action plans, which is critical to gaining credibility with the customer base for future surveys. It is also very easy to design a process that is too complex. Do not underestimate the amount of work to do a survey properly.

12.2.4 Key process activities
Step-by-step prescriptive implementation guidance for each activity
Step 1: Ensure executive management support: it is important that your executive management approves and supports this activity. Make sure that you have approval for the measurement process. A good indication is the permission to use the executives' name in the actual survey.

Step 2: Process design: the first part of implementation is the process design. A service matrix, based on the customer, needs to be defined first.

In the support environment, three types of customers can be recognized.

Customer	A person that buys (negotiates) the service
User	A person that uses the supported service
Caller	A person that has personally contacted the support group, by phone, e-mail or other media.

Callers are easy to find, but a user who is not a caller can be hard to contact.
One of the key problems in support services is that the customers and the users may have different views on the service. The customer who negotiates the service levels can be under cost pressure and want the lowest cost option. This may mean that the users will be very unsatisfied with the service they are getting.

Step 3: Determine type of service.
What exactly is the service? Support is definitely a service but it is also a part of the service it supports. In a normal Support Center desk environment, there are three levels in the service concept:

Concept	Example
The support service	One call or email to help desk
The supported service	E-mail service
The whole organization	IT-services

These levels are interrelated in many ways. The experience of one service call can ultimately affect the way we see the whole organization. The way the organization manages the service will affect the customer and may or may not cause him/her problems with the service.

There are cases where one has to accept that the customers are those who contact the support and the service is what they get through the contact. For example; if the users or business units are very independent and use whatever technology they want, it will be quite impossible to take responsibility for their technology choices.

The matrix below shows that there are nine different views to the question of who the customer is and what the service is. Each view is relevant and will provide different information.

Support	Service	Organization
Customer		
User		
Caller		

The actual process has three sub-processes of which the periodic survey process may be a SLM sub-process but it is described here as well. These sub-processes are listed below:
• periodic surveys
• Incident based surveys
• spontaneous feedback.

Step 4: Periodic surveys: these are frequently called 'relationship surveys' since they focus on the broad relationship between the respondent and the service organization.

Periodic surveys can be done one to four times a year. An annual survey can be enough if the environment is stable. Typically, an internal Support Center in a mature industry does not need more than one measurement per year. Consider doing multiple periodic surveys during a year with each survey focusing on different aspects of service.

Design simple and short surveys. Ten questions are easier to answer than a hundred questions.

Step 5: Incident based feedback: this is linked directly to one single incident and thus is an excellent tool for monitoring the quality of service. The user/customer is contacted soon after the incident and is asked how well this particular incident was handled. The survey administration activity is quite similar to the period survey. It is important to make sure that the same person does not receive too many surveys. A reasonable rule of thumb is to not survey one person more than once every quarter - but you can always ask customers how often they are willing to be surveyed.

The Support Center Manager or a third party can make the contact, which can be a call, a hardcopy mailing, or an email.

This can be a continuous process or a regular activity. The form used should be very simple with no more than three to five questions.

Step 6: Spontaneous feedback: this is one type of incident. In this case a user gives feedback related to some service. This feedback is not different from the feedback that might be received as a response to an open question in a survey. The major difference is that that this feedback is given unsolicited. A user might point out that the new system is quite difficult to use or that they got poor service in a recent service request. The actual incident could be a problem with the system or a user error. The feedback must be sent to appropriate person/unit for processing when applicable.

It is important to train Support Center staff to be receptive to spontaneous feedback. As a SPOC, the Support Center receives most of the spontaneous feedback and is able to produce reports on it.

Step 7: Select a survey tool: there is a wide selection of survey design tools on the market. It is quite possible that your organization already has a tool for market research or other purposes. The tool should be easy and intuitive to use.

Step 8: Make a pilot survey: this is a test of the actual survey. Select a group of people to answer it, do not use help desk staff. The pilot may be just a small sample of the actual population or, if you are unsure, just a group of friends and colleagues in other departments etc. It can be a good idea to actually observe the respondents while he or she is answering the survey. Any problems that come out during the pilot must be analyzed and solved.

Step 9: Train appropriate staff on survey administration and response processing.: training will depend upon the selected method of surveying.

Step 10: Define reports: these should be simple and easy to understand. Remember that the goal is not to show off your report generating skills but to give people useful information, which can help them to change their behavior or make better decisions.
Remember to use the actual scale in surveys (i.e if your actual scale was 1 to 5 use it in graphics. Excel may suggest something else; the scales tend to start from zero.
Use simple graphs. A horizontal bar is a good representation of a satisfaction scale

12.2.5 Methods and techniques
Methods of asking
The main methods are interviews and forms. Forms can be paper or electronic. Some general rules follow.

Ask one question at a time. Do not ask questions like this:
When you are analyzing the applicability of the concepts brought forward here in the context of your environment, how do you like the length, content and style of this book so far?

Keep it simple. Ask one simple question:
How do you like the content of this book?

Use open-ended questions. These are very useful. They are usually more valuable than the numbers. A typical pair of questions would be:
Is there anything that we could do better?
Is there anything we have done very well?

The response to the first question will give a lot of valuable information but the response to the second one is valuable too. Your team will enjoy the positive feedback and it will point out your strengths. However, too many open-ended questions increase the respondent burden and the analyst's burden. Use them judiciously.

Interviews

A face-to-face interview is expensive but sometimes it is the only way to understand what the customers think. A face-to-face interview should contain mainly open questions. This requires that the person doing the interview understands the issues and can make intelligent, clarifying questions. Face-to-face interviews are a good instrument for a small group to gain an understanding of the field of inquiry to allow for better survey instrument design. Interviews can be very effective for a select group of particular unhappy customers or a select group of key business clients.

Interviews do not generate data that allows for statistical analysis and general statements about the population of interest. Also, the interviewer has to know how to ask follow-up probing questions.

It is essential to ask open questions in a customer satisfaction interview. A possible structure is this:
1) What is important for you in this service?
2) How is the Support Center doing in the areas you mentioned?

Just two questions will give you a lot of information. Do not argue with your customer even if they have opinions that seem to conflict objective reality. You may ask clarifying questions.

Generally, it would be best if the person conducting the interviews were an outsider who understands the issues. In many cases, consultants are used. If this is impossible, the manager can make these interviews. In some cases, even the staff could do some interviews. Naturally, this affects the reliability and the objectivity of the data. On the other hand, it can be a valuable learning experience for the staff and will help them to a better understanding.

Telephone interviews might be the only method available when customers are geographically dispersed. A telephone interview should be short.

Forms

A questionnaire is a non-interactive method. Of course, it is possible to build some intelligence in an electronic form but that is not true interaction.

In the Support Center environment, email is a good choice. The most common method is to do a web-form and send a link to it in email. You can also use old-fashioned letters. All methods have their strengths and weaknesses. Do not send survey forms as email attachments due to the fear of viruses in attachments. You can conduct forms based surveys also as interviews, either face to face or on telephone. This is in most cases unnecessary and a waste of resources. Interviews should be used for in-depth discussions

Again, here are some basic rules:
• make the form simple and easy to understand (remember the Florida elections).
• do not use many different scales and do not crowd the questionnaire.

A simple example is shown below.

	Dissatisfied			very satisfied	
How satisfied you were with the service overall	1	2	3	4	5
How satisfied you were with the speed of our service	1	2	3	4	5
How satisfied you were with the friendliness of our service	1	2	3	4	5

Sampling
Sampling is a statistical method to estimate the characteristics of some populations. A representative random sample will give a good estimate and save a lot of work.

It is very important to understand the meaning of a representative random sample. It means that each unit in the population has an equal chance of becoming selected. A problem with simple random sample is that especially small groups can be over or under represented. In US political polls, the sample is carefully constructed to represent the whole USA. In the same way you can make sure that each department or site will have right representation.

Any non-random method of picking a sample can lead to bias. In the support world, one important source of bias is the customer/user attitude towards the Support Center. The customers have a choice and those who have called the Support Center have chosen it as their support channel. This means that all event-based surveys are biased and may give too positive results because of that.

Here is a simple method for choosing a random sample of 100 names from a population. Copy the names and addresses into an Excel sheet. Add important information like site or department names/numbers.

Calculate a random number for each name (Excel has a function, RAND, for doing this) Using the Paste Special function, copy the value of the numbers to another column called SELECT.

• Sort the names by SELECT.
• Pick the first 100 names.

In the example sheet below, the first three have been selected.

Name	SELECT
Graham Grey	0.075
Mary Brown	0.144
Barry White	0.173
John Doe	0.198
John Dark	0.208
Polly Pink	0.438
Francois Yellow	0.442
Tina Light	0.756
Stephen Mauve	0.761
Cilla Black	0.901

By this method, your sample will be truly random.

If you want to have the sample to represent many departments, repeat the process for each department or subgroup.

12.2.6 Audits for effectiveness

Return rate

Return rate means the percentage of those who completed a questionnaire compared to those asked to respond to the questionnaire. Internal customers should have a good rate; external customers usually have a lower rate. Satisfied, loyal customers tend to feel it is their duty to answer.

A bad rate might indicate bad survey instrument design or improper administration practices. Here are some rules:

- do not send survey requests just before or after holidays
- make sure that your instructions are clear and that questions are easy to answer
- make sure that the respondents know who is sending the mail; it must not look like SPAM or junk mail
- tell respondents how long it will take to fill out the survey (this can be estimated in the pilot survey).

Customer satisfaction

There should be a clear cycle of recognized and solved problems. It is not possible to have continuously improved results in customer satisfaction surveys but recognized problems should vanish.

12.3 Ongoing operation

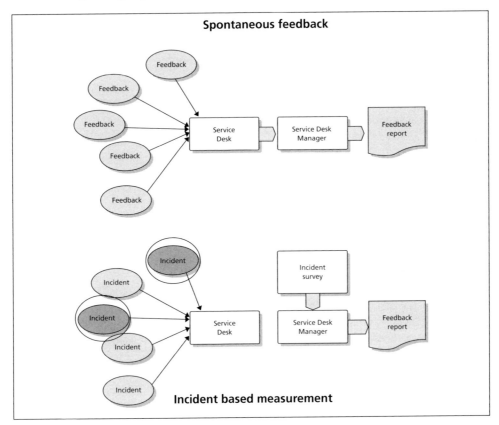

Figure 12.4 Ongoing process

12.3.1 Support Center Manager's role
Responsibilities and activities
The Support Center Manager is responsible for the collection of spontaneous feedback. This is an ongoing process where the staff need to be trained and monitored. Unusual findings and serious customer issues must be reported promptly to IT Service Management.

Incident based measurements are collected regularly according to process design. Usually this means that a survey questionnaire is sent to a sample of users who have reported incidents. The responses are analyzed and presented to management.

Deliverables
• Spontaneous feedback report
• Incident based measurement report

Competencies required
- The ability to analyze survey data
- Project management skills
- MS Excel

KPIs
- Response rate

12.3.2 Support Center Function's role
- *Responsibilities and activities*
- To register spontaneous feedback

Deliverables
- To deliver readable and concise reports of user feedback

Competencies required
- Listening skills
- Writing skills
- Ability to brief peers and managers

KPIs
- Amount of feedback reported

12.4 Optimization

12.4.1 The optimization process

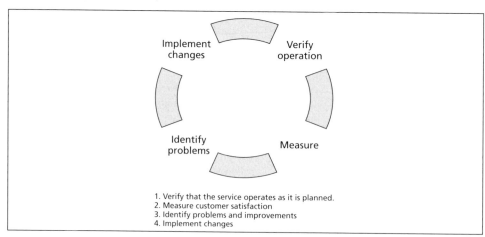

Figure 12.5 The optimization process

The customer satisfaction measurement process should lead to clear improvements. Reported problems should be corrected. As customer satisfaction is measured on a limited scale, it is not possible to have continuously improving results.

The process should be efficient and should not cause management overhead.

12.4.2 Support Center Manager's role
Responsibilities and activities

Monitor:
- the quality of written feedback reports
- response rates
- level of satisfaction
- repeating issues
- efficiency of process.

Deliverables
- Process design improvements
- Process management

KPIs
- Number of improvements which have resulted from CSM
- Cost of survey

12.4.3 Other key roles and functions in the optimization process
IT Service management must take an active role in CSM; reports must be taken seriously and resources must be allocated for fixing reported problems. If senior management is not interested in CSM results, there is very little need for the whole process.

12.4.4 Future impact of this process on the Support Center
A successful SLM process is essential for the future development for both the Support Center and overall IT Service Management. The Support Center Manager who speaks with the voice of the customer will be listened to more closely.

12.5 Measurement, costing and management reporting

12.5.1 Implementing: benefits and costs
Why implement this process and what can be gained

CSM is essential for successful ITSM. Without customer feedback, it is impossible to judge the overall quality of the process.

Cost elements for implementation

The design of the process is the major cost element. Professional help should be used. Also consider costs for tools for handling input, processing and reporting if necessary

Making the business case to implement
Costs should be justified. The process is easy to design and implement but tools and automation are necessary if the volume of feedback is high.

12.5.2 Ongoing operations
Cost elements for ongoing operations
Data collection; this includes:
- the cost of the software used
- mailing cost
- interview costs
- customer time.

It is important not to forget customer time. This can be calculated as shown below.

Formula for Annual Cost:
Number of users X number of surveys X (response rate X time to answer + (1-response rate) X time to discard survey) X cost per time unit

Here is an example:
20,000 employees receive quarterly an electronic survey form. 35 % answer and spend 5 minutes at it. 65% do not answer but spend 30 seconds discarding the survey. The cost of customer time would be $132.800 if one minute costs 80 cents:
Annual Cost= 4 * 20.000((35*5min + 65*0,5 min)/100) * $.80 = $132.800 $

12.5.3 Tools
Implementation
There exist tools for survey instrument design; these can be useful particularly in web-surveys.

Ongoing operations
There are a variety of tools and services available for web-surveys.

Reporting
Excel is adequate in most cases but if you have multiple levels (departments/services) a more advanced tool can be useful. The tool should have capabilities for statistical analysis and ad-hoc reporting.

Annex A12.1 Checklist of required activities for CSM

The following checklists can be used to ensure that all required activities have been undertaken for the implementation and ongoing Operations of CSM.

☐ Implementing
☐ Customer list
☐ current contact information
☐ correct addresses
☐ titles, job descriptions or roles
☐ services used
☐ Service descriptions
☐ Survey forms or emails
☐ Cover letter
☐ Preferably personalized letter with date
☐ introduction
☐ service description
☐ reason for survey
☐ how and when to reply
☐ what the customer will get
☐ thanks
☐ signature
☐ Survey questions
☐ Helpful for ongoing operations
☐ Schedule of future surveys
☐ trends analysis
☐ follow up of actions taken
☐ return rate

Bibliography

Customer Surveying: A Guide for Service Managers by Fred C. Van Bennekom, soft cover, 256 pages, 2002

About the authors
Glossary

About the authors

An international range of Support Center practitioner authors and subject matter experts provided the guidance in this book. The table below shows the authors and SMEs for each chapter. Brief biographies for each contributor are presented in alphabetical order after the table.

Chapter Author/Subject Matter Experts (SMEs)

1: Financial and Operational Management	*Authors/SMEs:* Mark Ellis Ron Muns *SMEs:* Glen Purdy
2: Knowledge management	*Authors:* Michael Devaney Brian Johnson *SMEs:* Greg Oxton Ron Muns
3: Configuration Management	*Authors:* David Chiu *SMEs:* Troy DuMoulin
4: Change Management	*Authors:* Peter Pace *SMEs:* Faye Rukstales
5: Release Management	*Authors:* Cheryl Simpson *SMEs:* Jayne Groll
6: Incident Management	*Authors:* Julie Quackenbush Michelle Ross-McMillan

	SMEs: Pat Albright
7: Problem Management	Pam Suekawa-Reynolds *Author:* Paula "Tess" DePalma *SME:* David Pultorak
8: Service Level Management	*Author:* Mark Bradley *SME:* Char LaBounty
9: Capacity and Workforce Management	*Author/* Chris Broome *SMEs* Malcolm Fry
10: Availability Management	*Author/SME* Brian Johnson
11: IT Service Continuity Management	*Author:* Vernon Lloyd *SME:* David Pultorak
12: Customer Satisfaction Measurement	Author: Aale Roos *SME:* Dr. Fred Van Bennekom

Author and SME biographies

Pat Albright - IT Support Consultants, Inc.

Pat Albright is president of IT Support Consultants, Inc. which she founded in 2000 in order to fully devote her efforts to the Help Desk and Support Center industry. She has previously held business and technology management positions in small business, non-profit and corporate environments and has been involved in the implementation and support of technology for more than 20 years. She has worked with a wide variety of clients - in manufacturing, health care, legal, retail, education, state government, insurance, real estate and other industries to implement or enhance both internal and external customer support organizations.

Mark Bradley - JP Morgan Chase

Mark Bradley is a Senior Application Development Analyst with JP Morgan Chase. He is responsible for production support for JP Morgan Chase's Peregrine suite of applications, and is a frequent speaker on service level management and service desk topics. With over 15 years of experience, Mark is accomplished in the information technology field. His career includes roles as Senior Network Engineer - Team Lead prior to being IT Service Center Manager for Zurich Life (Now Chase Life); he was instrumental in consolidating the company's help desk and implementing SLM within the business units. In addition, he has held IT positions within BankOne, Prudential Securities, Vector Securities, Sysco Food Service of Chicago, Inc., and United Stationers.

Mark has a BA in Computer Science & Speech Communication from Monmouth College & Masters of Science in Computer Information Systems from University of Phoenix. Mark has obtained certification in ITIL, MCSE+I, CNE, A+, MCP and is working towards CISSP.

Chris Broome - The Diagonal Group

Chris Broome has been involved in the technical support industry for twenty years, both as a practitioner and as a consultant. She is one of the four partners of The Diagonal Group, a consulting company that helps businesses in industries ranging from manufacturing and finance to government and education improve their customer service and support by providing insightful, objective and useful solutions. Her focus is on support tools and technology: she works with organizations to define requirements and workflow, and then aids them in selection of the appropriate software and hardware to accomplish their goals. Chris is an HDI Support Center Auditor and was on the committee that developed the standards for HDI's training classes. She is also a Project Management Institute-certified Project Management Professional (PMP). Chris, along with other Diagonal Group members, has authored HDI's Workforce Planning Guide, and has contributed to HDI's Service and Support Handbook.

David Chiu - BMO Financial Group

David Chiu is an ITIL Process Engineering Consultant at BMO Financial Group. He plays a key role in BMO Financial Group ITIL program as an internal ITIL Advisor and Process Manager. He is one of the process architects for many of the ITIL processes implemented in BMO over the last five years, including Release, Change, Configuration and Service Level Management. As a Process Engineering Consultant, he provides leadership and expertise on IT Service Management improvement initiatives for his organization. David has also been actively promoting ITIL best practices outside his company. He has been a speaker in many of the IT Service Management conferences presenting topics on Configuration Management, COBIT, Service Management Tool selection and ITIL Implementation. He won two awards (in year 2003 and 2004) for 'Best ITIL Case Study' in Pink's Elephant's 7th and 8th Annual IT Service Management Conferences.

David has been working in the IT industry for 15 years, with business experience in the manufacturing and financial sectors. In addition to his IT business process engineering and continuous process improvement experiences, he has managed many IT projects and he has technical expertise in systems design, systems management and integration.

David has a Bachelor of Applied Science degree from University of Waterloo. He has obtained certification in ITIL and is currently working towards his PMP designation.

Michael Devaney - Independent Consultant
Michael Devaney has over 20 years of experience in providing service and support to Fortune 500 corporations. After an undergraduate and graduate education at Southern Methodist University, Michael has held service, network support, and call center management positions with CompuShop, Bell Atlantic and CompuCom Systems. Michael has extensive experience in the design, development, implementation, and ongoing administration of telephony, problem management, workforce management, web-based support and knowledge management systems.

Paula 'Tess' DePalma - Nemours
Paula 'Tess' DePalma is the Director of Service Delivery in Information Systems at Nemours, one of the nation's largest pediatric subspecialty group practices (www.nemours.org). Since 1992, she has helped develop IT support at Nemours, by using her interest in computers to participate in a 'super user' program and later by becoming the HelpDesk Coordinator before landing in her current position as Director of Service Delivery. Tess became a certified Help Desk Analyst through HDI and simultaneously managed the Help Desk and Training Teams for four years. Tess received certification in IT Service Management from Loyalist College in 2003 and hopes to be certified in Service Management by the end of 2004. She is now working with Senior IT Management at Nemours to lead the IS Department in a major initiative to implement ITIL's set of best practices. Tess is the Vice President of Communications for the Orlando Chapter of the HDI. She is also a member of the IT Service Management Forum (itSMF) and Health Information and Management Systems Society (HIMSS).

Troy DuMoulin - Pink Elephant Inc.
Troy DuMoulin is an experienced Senior Consultant with a substantial background in business process re-engineering. Troy holds the Management Certificate in IT Service Management, the highest level of certification in the ITIL program. His main focus at Pink Elephant is to deliver effective consulting and educational services to clients, based upon a demonstrated in-depth knowledge and experience of IT Service Management best practices. Troy is a frequent speaker at ITSM events and is a contributing Author for the ITIL 'Planning to Implement IT Service Management' book.

Mark Ellis - Kronos Inc.
Mark Ellis is currently the Director of Emerging Technologies for Kronos Inc., with over 25 years experience in Operations Management and Customer Support. In addition to a strong background in Customer Service Management and Materials Distribution, Mark played a major role in the design, development and management of Digital Equipment Corporation's remote Customer Support Centers, a 'world class' provider of remote technical support. Mark has worked with over 400 different companies' Call Center - Remote Technical Support operations worldwide and is recognized as a leading results-oriented authority in Remote Support services and the operational aspects of technical support. Mark has been a Principal Consultant in The Bentley Company/Technology Solutions Company Help Desk practice for

four years. He is a past Director of Worldwide Service Operations at FutureTense/Open Market as well as VP of Worldwide Technical Support for Mediabridge Technologies focusing on e-business content management solutions.

Mark is a past Vice President of the New England Chapter of HDI and has spoken at numerous conferences sponsored by Gartner Group, Service News, DECUS and HDI, among others. Mark's presentation focus deals with the constantly evolving trends in Help Desk design and delivery, and operational service modeling designed to achieve balanced performance.

Malcolm Fry - Executive Remedy Partner

Malcolm Fry began his IT career in 1967, and in the following years took on development, operational and management roles. He has worked for retail, manufacturing, oil and pharmaceutical organizations. More recently Malcolm has entered the consulting field, and has received worldwide recognition as one of the foremost authorities in the areas of help desk and IT service management.

He is the author of four best-selling books on IT service and support, and has had many articles and papers published in multiple languages. Malcolm is innovative and informative, and has the unique ability to communicate his thoughts with audiences who have regularly voted him best speaker at many conferences around the world. He is also sought-after as a strategic consultant by many large organizations that see Malcolm as a catalyst to initiate improvements by reviewing their facilities and processes, and most importantly, preparing plans to allow them to meet their business and IT objectives.

Jayne Groll - ITSM Academy, Inc.

Jayne Groll is a founder and current president of ITSM Academy, Inc., a full service IT Service Management training and consulting organization based in Fort Lauderdale, FL. Jayne is a local instructor for the accredited ITIL® Foundation certification course and an IT Service Management advisor. For many years, Jayne has helped raise IT Service Management awareness in South Florida as a founding officer of the local IT Service Management Forum and the Help Desk Institute chapters. Jayne was one of the first practitioners to achieve Help Desk Manager and Help Desk Support Engineer certifications. Before founding ITSM Academy, Jayne spent over 20 years in senior IT Service Management roles spanning multiple industries and platforms.

Brian Johnson - Computer Associates

Brian Johnson is one of the original authors of the IT Infrastructure Library, writing five of the titles. He originated and authored 'The business perspective series' of the library and in 1998/9 designed the current version two of the library. He has worked variously for the UK government (most recently as Director of Knowledge Management for the OGC), and for Pink Elephant in the UK, Canada and the Netherlands. Brian joined Computer Associates in 2004 as Practice Leader for IT Service Management.

Together with a cartoonist colleague, Brian wrote the 'Not the IT Infrastructure Library' books published by Van Haren and the itSMF, best practice spoofs that received a 'High Tech humor' award from USA Today.

Char LaBounty - LaBounty & Associates, Inc.
Char LaBounty is founder and President of LaBounty & Associates, Inc., a service management consulting firm focused on the growing field of customer support services, dedicated to providing quality technology support practices that enhance client's business initiatives. Char is one of the pre-eminent experts on the development and deployment of Service Level Management throughout the IT Enterprise and writes and speaks extensively on the subject, throughout the world.

Before her current position, she was the Director of the Membership Services Division for the Help Desk Institute. Char joined the Institute from Disney Worldwide Services where she was head of the Business Services Division. As Vice President of the Customer Relations Group for Norwest Corporation, Char was responsible for establishing their two Support Center organizations, as well as managing all disciplines associated with customer training, implementation, marketing, support and corporate acquisitions.

Char has authored several books and published industry research on Outsourcing and has published many articles on the topics of technology service and support. She is a much sought after speaker at technology and service and support events around the world, and has dedicated her career to providing sound customer service practices. Char is the past chairperson to the HDI Strategic Advisory Board.

Vernon Lloyd - FoxIT
Vernon Lloyd is an internationally recognized ITIL expert. Throughout his career, spanning over 25 years Vernon has always led from the front in his contribution to the advancement of Best Practice within the IT Service Industry.

Vernon is a Lead Author for many of the ITIL Books and has developed many of the industry courses and associated qualifications. He is an active and valued contributor to the itSMF over its thirteen years; he is a member of the ISEB and OGC Management Boards and has been an ISEB examiner for over ten years.

Vernon is a Founder Member and Vice President of the Institute of Service Management. He is a keynote speaker at conferences worldwide, including USA, Sweden, the Netherlands, Denmark, Switzerland, Luxembourg and more recently India and Japan, where he is very much in demand. Vernon is currently Business Manager at Fox IT.

Ron Muns - HDI
Ron Muns, CEO and founder of HDI, is an international leader in IT service and support industry and is frequently quoted on key issues and concerns. He is credited with having a significant global impact on the professionalism of the IT service and support industry. Ron has more than 25 years of experience as the founder of HDI, creator of several successful commercial software products, consultant with an international accounting firm, and as an IT strategist. Ron is a Certified Public Accountant, Certified Information Systems Auditor, and holds several ITIL and HDI Certifications. He has a Bachelors Degree in Business Statistics from the University of Texas at Austin.

Greg Oxton - Consortium for Service Innovation

Greg Oxton is the Executive Director of the Consortium for Service Innovation. Greg has extensive experience in the support business and has held numerous management positions in his sixteen years at IBM and six years at Tandem Computers in operations, planning and support strategy development. Greg's specialty is customer service strategy and organizational development.

Through his work with the Consortium members in facilitating the process of collective thinking and collective experience Greg has developed insight into the KCS^{sm} principles and the process of adoption. Greg has coached companies such as Compaq, EMC, Ericsson, Hitachi Data Systems and StorageTek on developing adoption strategies for KCS. The Consortium for Service Innovation is partnering with HDI on bringing the KCS methodology to both internal and external support organizations. Greg is a member of the Strategic Advisory Board for the Help Desk Institute and participates with the HDI Executive Forum.

Glen Purdy - Fujitsu Consulting

Glen Purdy is a Management Consultant and Associate Director with Fujitsu Consulting. With over 20 years of experience as an Information Technology Service Management (ITSM) practitioner, in both insourced and outsourced environments, his experience in assessing, designing, and operating IT service organizations enables him to provide his clients with insightful guidance from a combined business, technology, and customer perspective.

As an early adopter of the IT Infrastructure Library (ITIL), Glen was certified at the 'Service Manager' level in IT Service Management in 1999, and has since assisted a number of clients improve the efficiency and effectiveness of their IT service delivery and support organizations utilizing the ITIL framework for industry best practices. (new paragraph) Glen has been an active member of HDI over 10 years, participating at the Local Chapter level and on the Member Advisory Board.

Peter Pace - United Airlines

Peter Pace, Manager of Integrated Production Services for United Airlines, is an experienced IT Service Management professional with expertise in change management, process reengineering and ITIL. Peter has successfully implemented change management best practices for MyPoints.com, UAL Loyalty Services, and United Airlines, as well as for companies in the services, distribution, and food services industries. In addition, he has also initiated and deployed a full breadth of IT Service Management processes in large corporate environments, increasing overall operational efficiency. His experience with process reengineering includes involvement in an ISO-9000 implementation and the deployment of an ERP product for a major enterprise.

Peter also has extensive business experience in product line development, national account management, and new business development, as well as e-commerce infrastructure deployment and e-commerce program management.

Peter is actively involved with industry organizations. He is a Certified Project Management

Professional (PMI) and is certified in ITIL. In addition, he is an active member of the Beta Gamma Sigma and Delta Mu Delta Business Administration Honor Societies and the Information Technology Service Management Forum. He has a Bachelor's degree in biology from Marquette University in Milwaukee, Wisconsin, and an MBA in marketing from De Paul University, Chicago.

David Pultorak - Fox IT

David Pultorak is president of Fox IT, a global IT service management consulting and training organization, and founder of Pultorak & Associates (www.pultorak.com), which specializes in agile business process improvement. A recognized authority in service management, David has devoted nineteen years to the IT industry helping IT organizations better manage IT for business value. Before his nine years in consulting, he spent ten years at Johnson & Johnson, where he managed client support and data center operations. David is regularly featured in leading IT magazines and websites, including BetterManagement.com, Data Center Management, Support World, and ITSMwatch.com. His most recent books are the popular MOF, A Pocket Guide (Van Haren Publishing 2003) which has been translated into six languages, The Definitive Guide to IT Service Management for the Adaptive Enterprise. (Realtime Publishers 2004) with Kevin Behr, and IT People: Doing More with Less (Prentice Hall 2004) with Harris Kern.

Julie Quackenbush - Nationwide

Julie Quackenbush is a project manager for the Technology Delivery department at Nationwide in Columbus, Ohio. She has the responsibility and privilege of leading a team performing IT Service Management process implementations based on ITIL.
Julie's professional insurance career has extended eight years. She has been in her current role for three years. Before joining Nationwide, Julie has had twenty years of sales and marketing experience in consumer products. She has worked for the Thomas J. Lipton [Tea] Company and the makers of Ovaltine.

She has been involved in community leadership activities throughout her career from currently serving on the Board of the itSMForum Central Ohio Local Interest Group, to a former role as the Communications VP & Board member of the Central Ohio Chapter of the Project Management Institute. She and a colleague teamed up to launch a research study on the State of Project Management in Ohio in 2004, and they plan to take that to a national level in 2005.

Julie has her PMP, holds a BS degree in Elementary Education from Miami University in Oxford, Ohio, and is certified as a Practitioner in Problem and Service Level Management.

Aale Roos - Quint Wellington Redwood

Aale Roos has more than 25 years' experience in the IT industry. He began his career at Finland's State Technical Research Centre with responsibility for statistical computing services. He was Head of Customer Service in the IT Service Division of Tietotehdas for six years, then joined TT-Innovation. Following an MBO, he became a consultant and partner at DPM Consulting Oy. Aale was Managing Director of the Help Desk Institute Nordic Oy within DPM and SQM Finland for twelve years before his current role as Managing Director of Quint Wellington Redwood Oy.

Aale has a Masters degree in Science from the University of Jyväskylä. He is a HDI Certified Auditor and holds a Managers Certificate in IT Service Management/Service Support and Service Delivery.

Michelle Ross-McMillan - Nationwide

Michelle Ross-McMillan has worked in multiple support capacities at Nationwide in Columbus, Ohio. Most recently, she led a Tier 3 technical support group responsible for incident management for multiple end-user applications. She also participated in initial Incident Management rollout activities at the company, and was a member of the team that provided requirements for the company's newest Incident Management tool.

Michelle has been with Nationwide since 1994. She began her career working as a licensed agency staff member in two Nationwide offices in West Virginia and later served as the state's Sr. Training and Development Instructor. Since then, she has held various positions in both Business and Systems support.

Michelle holds a Bachelor's degree in Journalism and Mass Communications from Marshall University and a Master's in Marketing and Communication from Franklin University. She has received certificates for the ITIL courses Foundation Certificate in IT Service Management and Establishing a Service Desk According to ITIL Best Practices.

Faye Rukstales - BMC

As Customer Advocacy Manager for BMC Software, Faye Rukstales has nearly two decades of IT experience. Faye has held positions in product management and strategic marketing, and currently manages the Remedy Customer Executive Advisory Council - a vital part of BMC Software's outreach for a true outside-in customer perspective. Using her practitioner experience and her strong background in frameworks, such as ITIL and ISO 9000, she regularly contributes to thought leadership and industry activities.

She has a Management degree from Lake Forrest, Illinois, and a traditional IT background. She worked as a programmer, systems analyst and principal analyst and was later promoted into a service management role, where she provided service support for a major division at a Fortune 50 pharmaceutical company. There she managed Incident, Problem and Change Management; Configuration Management, Release Management, Service Level Management, end-user training, IT procurement, and software license management. She also managed the Business Service Management Team for each of the division's lines of business, developed an internal mentoring program, and a managed highly regarded supplier diversity program.

Cheryl Simpson - BMO Financial Group

Cheryl Simpson is an internal process advisor and process manager at BMO Financial Group. She is a process architect for many of the ITIL processes implemented in the organization over the last five years, including Incident/Service Desk, Release, Problem, Change and Configuration Management. She provides leadership and expertise on IT Service Management process maturity, process and continuous improvement and governance in her organization.

In her 15 years of IT experience, half stems from the service/helpdesk. Her experience there ranges from technical support for both internal and external customers to leadership roles. Cheryl received her first ITIL certification in January 2000 and has since been awarded the Master's/Manager's Certificate in IT Service Management. Cheryl enjoys contributing to IT Service Management industry publications and speaking at conferences. Topics have included service/helpdesk, Configuration and Asset Management, CobiT and Governance, Successful Communication Strategies, Service Management Tool Selection, and ITIL Implementation.

Pam Suekawa-Reynolds - Remedy Corporation

Pamela Suekawa-Reynolds joined Remedy in 1997, which is now part of BMC and has worked in both the sales and services organizations. A subject matter expert for the Remedy technical applications team, she has received her ITIL Foundation Certification in October 2003 and currently an Enterprise Support Account Manager for Remedy's premier accounts. A strong customer advocate, she is very familiar with the incident life cycle management process from submission to resolution within the Remedy global call centers. As an Account Manager, she helps customers with strategic planning for managing costs and improving efficiencies of applications, specializing in the proactive assessment of Remedy application opportunities and risks, working with all levels to effectively resolve issues in an expedient manner.

Dr. Frederick Van Bennekom - Great Brook Consulting

Dr. Frederick Van Bennekom is Principal of Great Brook Consulting and teaches operations management and service management courses at Northeastern University and the Hult International Business School in the graduate and executive programs. Frederick's business practice examines the use of customer feedback for organizational improvement, with a special focus on the strategic linkage between customer support and product engineering.

Frederick's customer survey practice focuses on training people to conduct survey programs through his Survey Design Workshops, and has authored many surveys used by service organizations for service program development and quality control purposes. He recently authored Customer Surveying: A Guidebook for Service Manager and the Support Services Questionnaire Library, published by the Customer Service Press. Frederick has also co-authored a major research report on Problem Prevention Through Design for Supportability: Gaining Competitive Advantage from Customer Support, with Keith Goffin of the Cranfield School of Management in England.

Before his academic career, Frederick served ten years as an information systems consultant for Digital Equipment Corporation's Field Service organization, developing management reporting systems for field management. He received his A.B. from Bowdoin College and his masters and doctoral degrees from Boston University's School of Management. Frederick has published in both industry and academic journals and is a frequent speaker at industry conferences worldwide. He is president of the Boston chapters of AFSMI and the Association of Support Professionals and is a HDI member.

Glossary

The following terms have been defined in context in the chapters of this book. They supplement the ITIL glossary definitions.

ARCI Matrix (a.k.a. RACI Matrix) - a technique for identifying which stakeholders should be Accountable, Responsible, Consulted and Informed

Availability Management - Availability Management is responsible for realizing and optimizing the accessibility of the services. SLM provides Availability Management with input about the required availability and accessibility of the IT services, whereas Availability Management provides information about the actual availability of the services being provided to Service Level Management.

Balanced Scorecard - developed in the early 1990s by Drs. Robert Kaplan (Harvard Business School) and David Norton. They named this system the 'balanced scorecard'. The approach provides a clear prescription as to what companies should measure in order to 'balance' the financial perspective. The balanced scorecard is a management system (not only a measurement system) that enables organizations to clarify their vision and strategy and translate them into action. It provides feedback around both the internal business processes and external outcomes in order to continuously improve strategic performance and results. When fully deployed, the balanced scorecard transforms strategic planning from an academic exercise into the nerve center of an enterprise. The balanced scorecard suggests that we view the organization from four perspectives, and to develop metrics, collect data and analyze it relative to each of these perspectives:
- The Learning and Growth Perspective
- The Business Process Perspective
- The Customer Perspective
- The Financial Perspective

Business Impact Analysis (BIA) - the identification of critical business processes, and the potential damage or loss that may be caused to the organization resulting from a disruption to those processes.

Capability Maturity Model (CMM-I) - the Capability Maturity Model for Software (also known as the CMM and SW-CMM) has been a model used by many organizations to identify best practices useful in helping them increase the maturity of their processes. In 2000, the SW-CMM was upgraded to CMMI® (Capability Maturity Model Integration). The CMM-I frameworks help organizations increase the maturity of their processes to improve long-term business performance.

Capacity Management - managing the overall capacity and performance levels required to meet the current agreed-upon service levels and to meet future workloads without reducing the service levels.

Client - a.k.a. User - this is the end user who requests support

COBIT - issued by the IT Governance Institute and now in its third edition, COBIT is increasingly internationally accepted as good practice for control over information, IT and related risks. Its guidance enables an enterprise to implement effective governance over the IT that is pervasive and intrinsic throughout the enterprise. In particular, COBIT's Management Guidelines component contains a framework responding to management's need for control and measurability of IT by providing tools to assess and measure the enterprise's IT capability for the 34 COBIT IT processes.

Cold standby/gradual recovery - this is applicable to organizations that do not need immediate restoration of business processes and may include the provision of empty accommodation fully equipped with power, environmental controls and local network cabling infrastructure, telecommunications connections, and available in a disaster situation for an organization to install its own computer equipment.

Continuous availability - masking all component failure and planned downtime from Users (in ITSCM terms, immediate recovery) A combination of high availability (minimizing or masking component failures from users) and continuous operation (Minimizing or masking planned downtime from users).

Customer - the business that actually pays for the service

Customer Representative - the company or organization staff member that represents the company or organization in discussions and negotiations with the service provider and service provider's service representative.

Delphi Technique - developed by the RAND Corporation in the late 1960s as a forecasting methodology; later used as by the US Government as a group decision-making tool resulting in Project HINDSIGHT - which established a factual basis for the workability of Delphi. Overall this helps groups of experts come to some consensus of opinion when the all options are not knowledge-based but subjective. This opinion consensus can be converted once the data is more knowledge-based.

Demand Management - managing the demands placed on the Service Desk; related to Capacity Management in that the Service Desk's capacity must be at least equal to the demands placed on it.

Deming Cycle - continuous step by step improvement from the works of W. Edwards Deming (1900-1993)

Erlang C - a formula that uses the average call length, average call volume, and desired hold time to calculate the number of agents needed on the phones.

eTOM - eTOM describes the full scope of business processes required by a service provider and defines the key elements and how they interact, creating a guidebook that is fast becoming the common business language of the telecom industry. The eTOM Business Process Framework represents the whole of a service provider's enterprise environment. The

Business Process Framework begins at the Enterprise level and defines business processes in a series of groupings. The Framework is defined as generically as possible so that it is organization, technology and service independent and supports the global community. At the overall conceptual level, eTOM can be viewed as having the following three major process areas:
- Strategy, Infrastructure and Product covering planning and lifecycle management
- Operations covering the core of operational management
- Enterprise Management covering corporate or business support management

Framed Solution - solution placed in the context of the end-user's terms.

Force Field Analysis - a problem solving tool developed by social psychologist Kurt Lewin which uses a creative process to force agreement about all facets of a desired change.

Hot standby/immediate recovery - provides for the immediate restoration of services following any irrecoverable incident. This recovery option would typically be provided by replica systems running in parallel.

Incident Response/Acknowledge Time - when an incident is submitted to Level 1 or when it is operationally escalated to a Level 2 or Level 3 support group, the time from the incident submission to contacting the customer by telephone/voicemail/email, or arriving at the desk side in response to an incident is the acknowledgement time.

Ishakawa Diagramming (or fishbone diagram) - Kaoru Ishakawa was one of Japan's quality control pioneers, developing a cause and effect diagram in 1943. It is used to diagram process elements and analyze potential sources of variation or problems.

ISO 9000 - An international good quality management system that how you manage the processes of identifying exactly what it is you do, how you plan the requires resources (people, infrastructure, work environment, equipment, etc) how you monitor how well the processes are working, and how you improve the processes so as to meet the requirements and expectations of your Customers.

IT Service Continuity Management - the process of assessing and managing risks to IT services by examining Configuration Item (CI) values, threats and vulnerabilities, developing appropriate countermeasures, creating an IT Service Continuity plan, and managing any disaster situations that occur. (Compare to Business Continuity Management).

Knowledge management - managing information in context. The goal of Knowledge Management is to simplify the process of capturing the incident descriptions and associated contextual information the first time information is gathered. Another goal of Knowledge Management is to resolve incidents in such a way that information can be easily re-used and referenced in the future.

- **KCS**^{SM} - Knowledge Centered Support
Developed by the Consortium for Service Innovation, its objective is the collection, categorization, ongoing administration, dissemination and use/re-use of knowledge in the incident resolution process.

- Knowledge Developers:
  - **KCS I** (front line support analyst) - basic user of the knowledgebase, familiar with searching techniques, the basic concepts of Knowledge Centered Support (KCS), and able to frame questions/solutions. All initial framing work done by a KCS I will be reviewed by the KCS Coach before release for others to view.

  - **KCS II** (more experienced front line support analyst) - has sufficient experience in creating and modifying knowledge to enable the coach to review only part of his/her work before making the knowledge available to others. The proportion of review decreases as the analyst become more experienced and as the knowledge created improves.

  - **KCS Coach** - this role is likely to be a senior or lead analyst. In larger organizations this may be a dedicated position. The KCS coach reviews 100% of the work done by a KCS I and only part of the work done by a KCS II analyst.

  - **KCS Champion** - this role is responsible for monitoring and sampling of the knowledgebase. The KCS Champion looks after the health of the knowledgebase and usually focuses on a collection or domain of content. This role requires technical expertise in the domain and profound understanding of KCS processes. The KCS Champion has responsibility for recognizing those who contribute well to the knowledgebase and those who need further training. The KCS Champion is the quality monitor for knowledge. This may be a dedicated position in a large organization or it might be part of the responsibility for a support manager, supervisor or team leader.

  The KCS Champion should involve the entire organization from time to time in a continuous improvement process for Knowledge Management. The results of organizational involvement efforts lead to process improvements, creation of internal knowledge standards and development of reward and recognition programs.

Operational Level Agreement - an OLA is an agreement between the IT Support Groups within the IT department to unify internal service delivery.

Operating Level Objective - objectives within an operating level agreement that indicates the measures to be reported in the operational environment. The operating level objectives are aligned to the service level objectives.

PIR - Post Implementation Review

PMI - Project Management Institute

PRINCE 2 - PRojects In Controlled Environments, the OGC approved method of project management

Plan-Do-Check-Act - continuous step by step improvement, adapted from the works of W. Edwards Deming (1900-1993)

Quality of Service (QOS) - QOS commonly refers to response time, latency and effective throughput thresholds. QOS assumes application availability and then seeks additionally to define a minimum 'customer experience' standard by employing metrics that define 'time to response' from the customer's point of view.

Resolution Time - the time from submission of the incident by the customer to the Support Center to the final resolution of the incident or request.

Risk analysis - the identification and assessment of the level (measure) of the risks calculated from the assessed values of assets and the assessed levels of threats to, and vulnerabilities of, those assets.

Service - a business function deliverable by one or more IT service components (hardware, software, and facility) for business use.

Service Catalog - a service catalog, written in business (rather than technical) language, is a definitive guide to the services available to the business. It provides end-to-end descriptions of the service components used to deliver the services and the IT functionality used by the business. This information is then used to create and define OLAs/SLAs within each area, as OLAs/SLAs are developed according to the priority and business requirements of the service.

Service Components - the Configuration Items (CIs) relating to the delivery of the service. They can vary in complexity, size, and type.

Service Level - Service Level is a measurement that reflects the rate at which a Service Provider is performing compared to a specific level of performance outlined in an SLA. If a company is matching its committed service levels, it is performing at 100 percent. If the company is performing five percent below its committed Service Level, its Service Level is 95 percent.

Service Level Agreement - an SLA is an agreement between a Service Provider and a specific customer group or department within an organization. SLAs are an essential, beneficial, and often the most visible part of the Service Level Management. The SLAs are a mutually agreed upon and negotiated offering for both the IT department and the business unit.

Service Level Agreements (SLAs) - types of SLA
- **In-house SLA**
  There are three basic types of SLAs, and the most common of these is the in-house SLA. This is an agreement negotiated between the service provider, such as an IT department, and an in-house customer department.

- Because the nature of some companies' business requires significant levels of availability, they have in-house SLAs in place with their IT departments that require 100% availability. This level of service can be used as a selling point to external customers.

- **External SLAs**
  External SLAs are agreements that the organization must have in place if purchasing services

such as IT from an external provider such as an ASP or MSP. If the organization gets less-than-acceptable service from its ASP, for example, and does not have an SLA in place, it may not have many options to either force the ASP to address the problem or terminate their contract without penalties. Conversely, if the organization does negotiate an SLA with a service provider, an attorney should review the agreement before signing, since it is a legally binding contract.

- **Internal Operational Level Agreement (OLAs)**
  These types of OLAs are usually informal agreements within a department for achieving certain performance goals, with interdependent relationships, to distribute tasks and responsibilities in an effort to support a Service Level Agreement and Service Level Management, and for measuring progress in achieving those goals. They may not even be written as separate documents, but may be part of other plans such as individual achievement goals for the purpose of receiving bonuses.

Service Level Agreement Review - The service level agreement is formalized in a review process: the service level agreement review (SLA Review). The SLA Review is a two-way communication between the IT department and the organization, or Service Provider and the customers of a particular service. It ensures that the services are being delivered efficiently and are optimized to meet the organization's requirements.

Service Level Compliance Reporting - Service level compliance reports, used by both the business and the IT department, contain the monitoring data used to measure performance against objectives.

Service Level Monitoring - Services are monitored and measured according to the agreed-on SLA criteria in order to ensure compliance with the SLAs. Service level monitoring entails continual measurement of mutually agreed service-level thresholds and the initiation of corrective actions if the thresholds are breached.

Service Provider/Support Group - An organization, company, business or other entity that provides services.

Service Representative - the company or organization staff member who represents the Service Provider in discussions and negotiations with the customer or client's Customer Representative.

Service Threshold - Service Thresholds are minimum performance benchmarks defined in an SLA that a service provider commits to provide to a customer

Setup activities - setup activities are a series of appraisal steps that are carried out at the beginning of an SLM project. These preliminary steps help the business determine if there is a need for SLM and if it has the resources to implement it. As part of this process, the IT department establishes a baseline for the business by taking a snapshot of the existing services and management activities. The final step is to analyze the information collected in the previous steps and use the results to plan the implementation of SLM for maximum benefit to the business.

Six Sigma - a management methodology meant to drive process improvements in the manufacture of goods and services, Six Sigma has kept its edge while some other management approaches have not. The basic idea behind Six Sigma is to achieve product perfection by eliminating defects in the business processes that create the product. To reach Six Sigma, a process must yield no more than 3.4 errors per million chances at generating them. Near perfection is demanding, but not impossible. GE, for example, claims that it saved $8 billion in three years using this rigorous approach to quality control.

Standby arrangements - see cold, warm, and hot standby.

TORs - Terms of Reference

Underpinning Contract - a legally binding contract in place of or in addition to an SLA. This contract is with a third-party service provider on which service deliverables for the SLA have been built.

Warm standby/intermediate recovery - typically involves the re-establishment of the critical systems and services for organizations that need to recover IT facilities within a short predetermined time to prevent impacts to the business process.

Workforce Management - managing staff scheduling and staffing requirements planning and forecasting.